Enforcing the English Reformation in Ireland

This book explores the enforcement of the English Reformation in the heartland of English Ireland during the sixteenth century. Focusing on the diocese of Dublin – the central ecclesiastical unit of the Pale – James Murray explains why the various initiatives undertaken by the reforming archbishops of Dublin, and several of the Tudor viceroys, to secure the allegiance of the indigenous community to the established church ultimately failed. Led by its clergy, the Pale's loyal colonial community ultimately rejected the Reformation and Protestantism because it perceived them to be irreconcilable with its own traditional English culture and medieval Catholic identity. Dr Murray identifies the Marian period, and the opening decade of Elizabeth I's reign, as the crucial times during which this attachment to survivalist Catholicism solidified, and became a sufficiently powerful ideological force to stand against the theological and liturgical innovations advanced by the Protestant reformers.

DR JAMES MURRAY has published a number of articles on aspects of Ireland's sixteenth-century religious history. He is Director of Framework Implementation and Qualifications Recognition at the National Qualifications Authority of Ireland.

Cambridge Studies in Early Modern British History

Series editors

ANTHONY FLETCHER
Emeritus Professor of English Social History, University of London

JOHN MORRILL
*Professor of British and Irish History, University of Cambridge, and
Fellow of Selwyn College*

ETHAN SHAGAN
Associate Professor of History, University of California, Berkeley

ALEXANDRA WALSHAM
Professor of Reformation History, University of Exeter

This is a series of monographs and studies covering many aspects of the history of
the British Isles between the late fifteenth century and the early eighteenth century.
It includes the work of established scholars and pioneering work by a new
generation of scholars. It includes both reviews and revisions of major topics and
books which open up new historical terrain or which reveal startling new
perspectives on familiar subjects. All the volumes set detailed research into our
broader perspectives, and the books are intended for the use of students as well as
their teachers.

For a list of titles in the series, see end of book.

ENFORCING THE ENGLISH REFORMATION IN IRELAND

Clerical Resistance and Political Conflict
in the Diocese of Dublin, 1534–1590

JAMES MURRAY

CAMBRIDGE
UNIVERSITY PRESS

CAMBRIDGE UNIVERSITY PRESS
Cambridge, New York, Melbourne, Madrid, Cape Town, Singapore, São Paulo, Delhi

Cambridge University Press
The Edinburgh Building, Cambridge CB2 8RU, UK

Published in the United States of America by Cambridge University Press, New York

www.cambridge.org
Information on this title: www.cambridge.org/9780521770385

First published 2009

Printed in the United Kingdom at the University Press, Cambridge

A catalogue record for this publication is available from the British Library

Library of Congress Cataloguing in Publication data
Murray, James A., 1932–
Enforcing the English Reformation in Ireland : clerical resistance and political
conflict in the Diocese of Dublin, 1534–1590 / James Murray.
p.   cm. – (Cambridge studies in early modern British history)
Includes bibliographical references and index.
ISBN 978-0-521-77038-5 (hardback)
1. Reformation–Ireland.   2. Reformation–England.   3. Ireland–Church
history–16th century.   4. Church of Ireland. Diocese of
Dublin–History–16th century.   I. Title.   II. Series.
BR380.M87 2008
274.18′3506–dc22   2008043672

ISBN 978-0-521-77038-5 hardback

For Gaye and Alan

CONTENTS

TABLES

ACKNOWLEDGEMENTS

I owe a great debt of gratitude to many people, too numerous to mention by name, for their help in the preparation of this book. However, as someone who spent his formative years working as an archivist in the Public Record Office in London, I am acutely aware of the often unsung contribution that archivists and librarians make to the writing of history. At the outset, therefore, I would like to record my thanks to the many librarians and archivists I have dealt with during the period of research for this book. Their knowledge, patience and efficiency made the task a much more pleasant experience than it might otherwise have been. In particular, I would like to thank the staff of the following institutions: the Bodleian Library in Oxford; the British Library; Dublin Corporation Archives; Lambeth Palace Library, London; Marsh's Library, Dublin; the National Archives (formerly the Public Record Office); the National Archives of Ireland; the National Library of Ireland; the library of the Royal Irish Academy; the library of Trinity College Dublin; and the Representative Church Body Library, Dublin.

I am also greatly indebted to the many scholars I have encountered, both in person and in print, during the lengthy gestation of this book. The following historians merit particular thanks for keeping my interest in the subject alive at those times when it was in danger of flagging: Dr Amanda Beavan, Professor Brendan Bradshaw, Dr Trevor Chalmers, Professor Aidan Clarke, Professor Alan Ford, Dr Elizabeth Hallam Smith, Dr Helga Hammerstein-Robinson, Professor Richard Hoyle, Professor Colm Lennon and Dr Stephen O'Connor. Special thanks are also due to Dr Brian Jackson and Professor Mary O'Dowd for offering valuable advice and encouragement along the way and to Professor Steven Ellis, a fine teacher, who first stimulated my interest in the history of the Tudor dominions. In addition, I have also benefited greatly from personal encounters or engagement with the work of the following scholars: Professor Nicholas Canny, Professor Patrick Corish, Dr David Edwards, the late Professor Sir Geoffrey Elton, Professor Raymond Gillespie, Professor Christopher Haigh, Dr Henry

Jefferies, Dr John MacCafferty, Professor Diarmaid MacCulloch and Dr Hiram Morgan.

Apart from scholars and archivists, there are many others who contribute to the production of a history book. My colleagues at the National Qualifications Authority of Ireland have been very supportive during the latter stages of the book's preparation, and I would like to extend my thanks to them. I would also like to thank Mr Michael Watson and his colleagues at Cambridge University Press for their professional assistance and courtesy throughout the book production process.

Finally, three debts of gratitude require special mention. First, to Ciaran Brady who, from the time I started working with him as a doctoral student, through to the completion of this book, has been a valued friend and mentor. Much of what is best in this book is due to Ciaran. Second, to my parents and brothers and sisters for their constant love and support. Above all, to my wonderful wife Gaye, and son Alan. Their patience and love throughout this project, which has been above and beyond the call of duty, has helped me to see it through to completion.

ABBREVIATIONS

AC	J. and J. A. Venn, *Alumni Cantabrigiensis*
AH	*Archivium Hibernicum*
Alen's register	*Calendar of Archbishop Alen's register*, ed. C. MacNeill
Analecta	*Analecta Hibernica*
AO	J. Foster, *Alumni Oxoniensis*
APC 1554–6 (etc.)	*Acts of the privy council of England*, ed. J. R. Dasent
ARD	*Calendar of Ancient Records . . . Dublin*, ed. J. T. Gilbert and R. M. Gilbert
Berry, *Register of wills*	*Register of wills and inventories of the diocese of Dublin in the time of Archbishops Tregury and Walton*, ed. H. F. Berry
BL	British Library
BMD	Bibliothèque Municipale, Douai
Bodleian	Bodleian Library, Oxford
Brady, *Episcopal succession*	W. M. Brady, *The episcopal succession in England, Scotland and Ireland, 1400–1875*
Brady, *State papers*	*State papers concerning the Irish Church in the time of . . . Elizabeth*, ed. W. M. Brady
BRUO 1500	A. B. Emden, *A biographical register of the university of Oxford to A.D. 1500*
BRUO 1501–40	A. B. Emden, *A biographical register of the university of Oxford A.D. 1501 to 1540*
BSJ	*Butler Society Journal*
Campion, *History of Ireland*	E. Campion, *Two bokes of the histories of Ireland*, ed. A. F. Vossen
Carew MSS, 1515–74 (etc.)	*Calendar of the Carew Manuscripts . . . 1515–1624*, ed. J. S. Brewer and W. Bullen
CNWAHSJ	*Chester and North Wales Architectural and Historical Society Journal*

CCD	*Christ Church Deeds*, ed. M. J. McEnery and R. Refaussé
CPR, *papal letters*	*Calendar of papal registers, papal letters*, ed. W. H. Bliss *et al.*
'Cromer's register'	'Archbishop Cromer's register', ed. L. P. Murray (contd. by A. Gwynn) in *LASJ*
CS	*The Civil Survey*, A.D. 1654–56, ed. R. C. Simington
CSPD Edward VI	*Calendar of state papers, domestic series, Edward VI*, revised edn, ed. C. S. Knighton
CSP Ireland	*Calendar of state papers relating to Ireland, 1509–1603*, ed. H.C. Hamilton *et al.*
CSP Rome	*Calendar of ... state papers ... Rome...* ed. J. M. Rigg
CSP Spain	*Calendar of ... state papers ... Spain*, ed. G. A. Bergenroth *et al.*
CSP Venice	*Calendar of state papers ... Venice*, ed. R. Brown *et al.*
DCA	Dublin Corporation Archives
Dignitas decani	*'Dignitas decani' of St Patrick's Cathedral*, ed. N. B. White
DHR	*Dublin Historical Record*
DIAS	Dublin Institute for Advanced Studies
DNB	*Dictionary of National Biography*
'Dowdall's register'	'A calendar of the register of Primate George Dowdall', ed. L. P. Murray in *LASJ*
EHR	*English Historical Review*
ERP	*Epistolarum Reginaldi Poli*, ed. A. M. Quirini
Fiants, Henry VIII (etc.)	Calendar of Fiants, Henry VIII to Elizabeth in *Reports of the deputy keeper, PROI*
GASJ	*Galway Archaeological Society Journal*
Griffith, *Exchequer inquisitions*	*Calendar of inquisitions formerly in the office of the Chief Remembrancer of the Exchequer prepared from the MSS of the Irish Record Commission*, ed. M.C. Griffith
HMC	Historical Manuscripts Commission (now part of the National Archives of the United Kingdom)
IER	*Irish Ecclesiastical Record*
IG	*The Irish Genealogist*
IHS	*Irish Historical Studies*
IMC	Irish Manuscripts Commission
JBS	*Journal of British Studies*

JEH	*Journal of Ecclesiastical History*
JRSAI	*Journal of the Royal Society of Antiquaries of Ireland*
LASJ	*Louth Archaeological Society Journal*
Lambeth	Lambeth Palace Library
LM	*Liber Munerum Publicorum*
LP	*Letters and papers, foreign and domestic, of the reign of Henry VIII*, ed. J.S. Brewer *et al.*
Mason, *History of St Patrick's*	W. Monck Mason, *The history and antiquities of the collegiate and cathedral church of St Patrick near Dublin*
Morrin, *Patent rolls*	*Calendar of the patent and close rolls of chancery in Ireland of the reigns of Henry VIII, Edward VI, Mary and Elizabeth*, ed. J. Morrin
NAI	National Archives of Ireland (formerly Public Record Office of Ireland)
NHI	*New History of Ireland*
NLI	National Library of Ireland
NMAJ	*North Munster Antiquarian Journal*
Octavian's register	*Registrum Octaviani*, ed. M.A. Sughi
ODNB	*Oxford Dictionary of National Biography*, ed. Matthew and Harrison
Ormond deeds, 1509–47 (etc.)	*Calendar of Ormond deeds*, ed. E. Curtis
Patent rolls 1485–94 (etc.)	*Calendar of patent rolls preserved in the Public Record Office*
PBA	*Proceedings of the British Academy*
Pembroke deeds	*Calendar of ancient deeds and muniments preserved in the Pembroke Estate Office, Dublin*
PRIA	*Proceedings of the Royal Irish Academy*
PRO	Public Record Office, London (now part of the National Archives of the United Kingdom)
PRONI	Public Record Office of Northern Ireland
RCB	Representative Church Body Library, Dublin
RDD	'Registrum Diocesis Dublinensis'. A sixteenth century Dublin precedent book, ed. N. B. White
RIA	Royal Irish Academy
RSCHS	*Records of the Scottish Church History Society*
RN	*Reportorium Novum*

Refaussé with Lennon, *Registers of Christ Church*	*The registers of Christ Church Cathedral, Dublin*, ed. R. Refaussé with C. Lennon
Shirley, *Church in Ireland 1547–1567*	*Original letters and papers in illustration of the history of the Church of Ireland during the reigns of Edward VI, Mary and Elizabeth*, ed. E.P. Shirley
SP	*State papers, Henry VIII*
SR	*Statutes of the realm*
Statutes at large	*The statutes at large passed in the parliaments held in Ireland*
Statutes Ireland, Edward IV	*Statute rolls of the parliament of Ireland . . . reign of King Edward the Fourth*, ed. H. F. Berry
Statutes Ireland, Henry VI	*Statute rolls of the parliament of Ireland: . . . reign of King Henry the Sixth*, ed. H. F. Berry
Statutes Ireland, John to Henry V	*Statutes and . . .acts of the parliament of Ireland: King John to Henry V*, ed. H. F. Berry
Statutes Ireland, Richard III – Henry VIII	*Statute rolls of the Irish Parliament Richard III – Henry VIII*, ed. P. Connolly
TCD	Trinity College Dublin
TNA	The National Archives of the United Kingdom
TRHS	*Transactions of the Royal Historical Society*
White, *Monastic extents*	*Extents of Irish monastic possessions, 1540–1*, ed. N.B. White
Wood, *Liberty of St Sepulchre*	*Court book of the liberty of St Sepulchre*, ed. H. Wood
Zurich letters	*The Zurich letters, 1558–79*, ed. H. Robinson

NOTE ON CONVENTIONS

All spellings have been modernised. Dates are given in Old Style, but with the year beginning on 1 January, not 25 March. With regard to currency, the distinction is made in the text between pounds sterling (£) and pounds Irish (*IR£*). *IR£*1 was generally worth two-thirds (13*s*. 4*d*.) of one pound sterling.

Introduction

This book was prompted by an important, but inconclusive, historio-graphical debate on the failure of the Reformation in Ireland, which took place in the 1970s. Prior to that exchange, virtually all studies of the subject were hopelessly symmetrical. Characterised by *parti pris*, and afflicted by a deterministic vision, the majority of them contended that the Tudor state failed immediately and irreversibly to win the allegiance of the indigenous population to its religious dictates, mainly because of the inherently con-servative character of the island's inhabitants. The only significant differ-ences displayed by such studies were their use of opposing confessional models to interpret and explain the nature and significance of Ireland's religious conservatism. For Catholic writers, native conservatism repre-sented a deep-seated and laudable attachment to the ancestral faith of Ireland, which found expression in the people's valiant, and ultimately successful, struggle to preserve the faith in an unsullied form during the Reformation. Protestant writers, in contrast, saw it as a collective character defect, an unremitting force built upon an ingrained and wilful ignorance, which was impervious to the 'true' religion advanced by the 'godly' reformers of the sixteenth century.[1]

In the late 1960s and 1970s this cycle of crude deterministic writing was broken by Brendan Bradshaw, whose pioneering work applied what was, in Irish terms, a fresh series of intellectual templates for the exploration of the Reformation. Earlier attempts to do so, following the emergence of the modern 'scientific' school of historical writing, had been unsuccessful, because the perspectives adopted then were still heavily coloured by con-fessional concerns, or because the authors themselves – despite the new directions suggested by their own source-based researches – seemed unable to break free from the habits of thought associated with the older tradition. The classic examples of this were Robin Dudley Edwards's *Church and*

---

[1] J. Murray, 'The Church of Ireland: a critical bibliography, 1536–1992. Part I: 1536–1603', *IHS* 28 (1993), pp. 345–6; A. Ford, '"Standing one's ground": religion, polemic and Irish history since the Reformation', in A. Ford, J. McGuire and K. Milne (eds.), *As by law established: the Church of Ireland since the Reformation* (Dublin, 1995), pp. 1–10.

state in Tudor Ireland and Canon G. V. Jourdan's contributions on the Reformation in the three-volume *History of the Church of Ireland*.[2] Though Edwards's book was a considerable achievement, his concern to find a 'scientific' explanation for an already accepted fact – that the Irish people's struggle to preserve Catholicism in the sixteenth century contributed to the birth of the Irish national tradition – prevented him from exploring in a more nuanced fashion the complex responses of the Gaelic and English Irish to the Reformation, which his own investigations had begun to uncover. Indeed, it compelled him to employ an emotional rhetoric to explain away discoveries that conflicted with his general thesis: witness his implied criticism of the Palesmen for failing to support 'the scheme of a Catholic and independent Ireland' during the Nine Years War. Canon Jourdan also employed the 'scientific' historical method in writing his very thorough analytical narrative of the Reformation. Yet like Edwards, his work displayed strong links with earlier less scholarly writing. For Jourdan, the failure of the Reformation was due to the inability of the pre-existing, 'uncivilised' Irish culture to engage with Protestantism's more advanced tenets, the crucial factor being the 'general ignorance of the Irish'.[3]

Bradshaw, in contrast, removed the subject out of this insular, polemical and necessarily constrictive setting by treating the Reformation initiative seriously and by placing the movement firmly within its contemporary political and social contexts. Thus in studying the career of Dublin's first Reformation archbishop, George Browne (1536–54), he avoided the traditional stereotypes of the archbishop as an ogre to Catholics and a patriarch to Protestants, and produced the more realistic assessment that he was a desultory royal functionary.[4] By examining the Irish Reformation parliament of 1536–7 in the broader context of the major political concern of the day – the fallout from the failed Kildare rebellion – he uncovered the previously hidden secular motivation that underpinned the laity's opposition to the Henrician ecclesiastical legislation. His dispassionate treatment of the dissolution of the religious orders – as an administrative process with its own internal logic – enabled him to identify the spiritual ennui that affected many late medieval Irish religious houses and to conclude thus that the

[2] R. D. Edwards, *Church and state in Tudor Ireland: a history of the penal laws against Irish Catholics, 1534–1603* (Dublin, 1935); W. A. Phillips (ed.), *History of the Church of Ireland from the earliest times to the present day* (3 vols., Oxford, 1933–4), ii, pp. 169–524.

[3] J. Murray, 'Historical revisit: R. Dudley Edwards, *Church and state in Tudor Ireland* (1935)', *IHS* 30 (1996), pp. 233–41; Edwards, *Church and state*, pp. 301–2; Phillips (ed.), *Church of Ireland*, ii, pp. 244–5; Ford, 'Standing one's ground', p. 9.

[4] B. Bradshaw: 'George Browne, first Reformation Bishop of Dublin' (MA thesis, University College Dublin, 1966); 'George Browne, first Reformation Archbishop of Dublin, 1536–1554', *JEH* 21 (1970), pp. 301–26.

process was not without some external justification too.[5] Most novel of all, the Reformation in its entirety was examined not as a discrete, climactic spiritual conflict between incipient Catholic Irish and Protestant English nations, but, *à la* Geoffrey Elton, as an integrated element of a 'constitutional revolution' which the Tudor monarchy wished to impose in all its dominions, including not only Ireland, but also the outlying parts of England and the principality of Wales.[6]

The cumulative effect of this body of work was the development of a new conceptual framework and chronology for the failure of the Reformation in Ireland. The new chronology fell into two phases. In the first, which covered the reigns of Henry VIII and Edward VI, Bradshaw put forward the novel argument that the political community of English Ireland willingly accepted the main alterations made by the Tudors to their traditional religious culture – in particular, the introduction of the royal supremacy – although the advent of radical Protestantism under Edward VI was greeted with much less enthusiasm. The main reason the early Reformation received such a favourable welcome was because it was deliberately linked to the conciliatory programme of political reform, promoted by the crown during the viceroyalties of Sir Anthony St Leger. Indeed, this feature also ensured that the Reformation secured some support in Gaelic Ireland. Thus, as the reign of Edward VI came to a premature end, Bradshaw concluded that there was no definitive local response to the religious changes that he and his father had instituted in their Irish dominion.

The second phase of Bradshaw's new chronology, which began in the reign of Mary Tudor, was decisive for two reasons. In the first place, it witnessed the official restoration of Catholicism, which allowed the Counter-Reformation to gain an early foothold amongst the old colonial community in the crucial battleground of the English Pale and its satellite towns. By the 1580s, following a period of confessional struggle ushered in by the enactment of the act of uniformity in 1560, this nascent attachment

---

[5] B. Bradshaw: 'The opposition to the ecclesiastical legislation in the Irish Reformation parliament', *IHS* 16 (1969), pp. 285–303; *The dissolution of the religious orders in Ireland under Henry VIII* (Cambridge, 1974).

[6] B. Bradshaw: 'The beginnings of modern Ireland', in B. Farrell (ed.), *The Irish parliamentary tradition* (Dublin, 1973), pp. 68–97; 'The Edwardian Reformation in Ireland, 1547–53', *AH* 24 (1976–7) pp. 83–99; *The Irish constitutional revolution of the sixteenth century* (Cambridge, 1979). For more recent restatements of the theme see B. Bradshaw: 'The Reformation in the cities: Cork, Limerick and Galway, 1534–1603', in J. Bradley (ed.), *Settlement and society in medieval Ireland* (Kilkenny, 1988), pp. 445–76; 'The Tudor Reformation and revolution in Wales and Ireland: the origins of the British problem', in B. Bradshaw and J. Morrill (eds.), *The British problem, c. 1534–1707. State formation in the Atlantic archipelago* (Basingstoke and London, 1996), pp. 39–65; 'The English Reformation and identity formation in Wales and Ireland', in B. Bradshaw and P. Roberts (eds.), *British consciousness and identity. The making of Britain 1533–1707* (Cambridge, 1998), pp. 43–111.

had hardened into a thoroughgoing, ideologically driven recusancy. Secondly, it also coincided with the related political alienation of the colonial community, which was a consequence of the growing loss of office and influence experienced by the reform-minded Palesmen to hard-line English officials in the Dublin administration. The coercive political and religious policies advanced by the new generation of English officials were, according to Bradshaw, philosophically rooted in their pessimistic Calvinist faith, which contrasted sharply with the optimistic Erasmian humanism, and increasingly Catholic bent, of the native reformers. This intellectual split, he concluded, was also important in practical terms as it was responsible for creating a debilitating division over the strategy to be employed by church and state in their combined effort to promote the Reformation in Ireland.[7]

Bradshaw's revision of the traditional story of the Irish Reformation, a story hitherto told in terms of the movement's rapid and absolute failure, was immensely stimulating for Irish historians.[8] Yet it did not receive unqualified acceptance. His pronouncements on the later Reformation, in particular, lacking the same evidential basis as his views on the Henrician and Edwardian periods, were the subject of some trenchant criticism from Nicholas Canny in his essay 'Why the Reformation failed in Ireland: *une question mal posée*'. This critique of the Bradshaw *oeuvre* provided a useful corrective to some of the latter's more exaggerated claims. In particular, he challenged the ideas that the English Irish community and their leaders abandoned the state church in the years immediately following the passing of the act of uniformity, and that most English reformers in Ireland favoured compulsory rather than persuasive methods in promoting the established religion.[9] Yet Canny's essay contained its own distracting exaggeration – that the dating of the failure of the Reformation could be postponed indefinitely – a contention which was subsequently and decisively challenged by Karl Bottigheimer.[10]

Canny's most important contribution to the debate, however, was his identification of areas requiring further research, most notably, the Pale community's attachment to conservative religious practices. This was not, he argued, an attachment to Counter-Reformation norms, but the survival of traditional medieval Catholic forms practised within the established

---

[7] B. Bradshaw: 'Fr. Wolfe's Description of Limerick city, 1574', *NMAJ* 17 (1975), pp. 47–53; 'Sword, word and strategy in the Reformation in Ireland', *HJ* 21 (1978), pp. 475–502; 'English Reformation and identity formation in Wales and Ireland', pp. 48–54.

[8] K. S. Bottigheimer, 'The Reformation in Ireland Revisited', *JBS* 15 (1976), pp. 140–9; A. Clarke, 'Ireland, 1534–1660', in J. Lee (ed.), *Irish historiography 1970–79* (Cork, 1981), pp. 34–55.

[9] *JEH* 30 (1979), pp. 423–50.

[10] K. Bottigheimer, 'The failure of the Reformation in Ireland: *une question bien posée*', *JEH* 36 (1985), pp. 196–207.

church; an observation which enabled him to recast one of the key questions concerning the fate of the Reformation in Ireland. If, as was the case in England, survivalist Catholicism or 'church-papism' could be turned into an attachment to the state church just as easily as into a devoted loyalty to the Counter-Reformation, its durability in Ireland throughout most of Elizabeth's reign implied that the fate of the Reformation was far from settled as the sixteenth century drew to a close. The real question to be answered, therefore, was not why the Reformation failed in Ireland, but, as Canny put it, why the movement failed to 'strike deeper roots when the opportunity to do so still existed down to the 1590s'.[11]

Overall, then, the Bradshaw–Canny debate gave rise to a more intellectually mature version of Ireland's Reformation story. The sixteenth century is now generally recognised as a period of blurred and ambiguous religious allegiances on the island, until the beginning of Queen Mary's reign in Bradshaw's case, until the 1590s according to Canny. Yet in one important respect the impact of the debate has been equivocal. Because of its refreshing novelty, and the resultant tendency of historians to value it for its own sake, it failed, in general, to ignite the kind of sustained and systematic research needed to answer the particular questions which the debate itself raised, or to produce a new and authoritative synthesis on the Irish Reformation generally. Indeed, a number of historians would now argue – perhaps out of a sense of frustration at this paradoxically unproductive outcome – that the debate has led the subject into an intellectual cul-de-sac.

Where such criticism has found expression in print, it has tended to focus, either explicitly or implicitly, on what is perceived to be the unnecessarily narrow conceptual framework upon which the debate was originally conducted. Raymond Gillespie, in his study of the religious experiences and belief systems of the people of early modern Ireland, has been particularly critical of the 'top down', institutional framework favoured by Bradshaw and Canny, because it concentrated on the views of the political and clerical elites at the expense of the common religious ideas held by the majority of individuals.[12] A similar dissatisfaction has also been articulated by Karl Bottigheimer and Ute Lotz-Heumann, in their essay 'The Irish Reformation in European perspective'. Among other things, they take issue with the

---

[11] Canny, 'Why the Reformation failed', pp. 432–5. Bradshaw subsequently conceded that the mass non-conformity encountered by the ecclesiastical commissioners in the Pale in the mid-1560s may well be attributable to survivalism. However, drawing a distinction between religion as 'practice' or as a 'code of behaviour' (characteristic of survivalism) and religion as 'ideology', or 'confession', and 'subscribed to as a form of socio-political identity' (characteristic of the Counter-Reformation in Ireland), he argues that the English Irish community had adopted the latter as their definitive religious stance by the 1580s (Bradshaw, 'English Reformation and identity formation in Wales and Ireland', pp. 48–54).

[12] *Devoted people. Belief and religion in early modern Ireland* (Manchester, 1997).

commonly held view, often reiterated by Bradshaw, that Ireland's Reformation experience was unique and, by implication, can be studied in isolation without reference to the Reformation experiences of continental European polities.[13]

At the heart of both of these criticisms is a call for the application of a broader range of conceptual models to the study of religion in early modern Ireland than have been used hitherto. Gillespie, following continental early-modernists like Jean Delumeau and Carlo Ginzburg, advocates the use of sociological and anthropological ideas to describe the religious condition of Ireland from the sixteenth to the eighteenth centuries; while Bottigheimer and Lotz-Heumann argue strongly for the adoption of the German historiographical concept of 'Calvinist confessionalisation' or 'Second Reformation' to help us understand the Dublin government's efforts to impose the Elizabethan settlement after 1560. Yet, while in principle both of these approaches are to be welcomed, and may in time offer valuable new perspectives, their usefulness at this juncture is questionable. This is because the subject still lacks a critical mass of more basic research, with the result that the exploitation of these newly recommended models, in the same, sophisticated manner as they have been utilised elsewhere, is not yet possible.

Gillespie's analysis of popular religion in early modern Ireland, which suffers acutely from the deficit in the research base, is a case in point. Crucially, as he readily admits, it lacks definition in terms of the charting of chronological change and regional variation in religious ideas and practices,[14] a problem which would have been more readily overcome had he been able to draw upon a greater volume of antecedent studies.[15] The same gaps in our knowledge also raise concerns about the comparative approach employed by Bottigheimer and Lotz-Heumann. The continental analogues that they chose for the religious and ecclesiastical upheavals of sixteenth

---

[13] *Archiv für Reformationsgeschichte* 89 (1998), pp. 268–309. See also U. Lotz-Heumann, 'Confessionalisation in Ireland: periodisation and character, 1534–1649', in A. Ford and J. McCafferty (eds.), *The origins of sectarianism in Early Modern Ireland* (Cambridge, 2005), pp. 24–53.

[14] Gillespie, *Devoted people*, p. vii.

[15] A good start in remedying this deficiency has been made through projects like the publication of the Christ Church Cathedral documents series. These make more accessible a number of important texts on the history of the cathedral, and provide valuable information on a range of topics including religious practice in Dublin in the sixteenth century. The relevant texts are: R. Gillespie (ed.), *The proctor's accounts of Peter Lewis 1564–1565* (Dublin, 1996) and *The first chapter act book of Christ Church Cathedral Dublin, 1574–1634* (Dublin, 1997); R. Refaussé with C. Lennon, *The Registers of Christ Church Cathedral, Dublin* (Dublin, 1998); B. Boydell (ed.), *Music at Christ Church before 1800: documents and selected anthems* (Dublin, 1999). See also R. Gillespie and R. Refaussé (eds.), *The medieval manuscripts of Christ Church Cathedral, Dublin* (Dublin, 2006); and K. Milne (ed.), *Christ Church Cathedral, Dublin: a history* (Dublin, 2000).

and early seventeenth-century Ireland are drawn from mature and abundant historiographies, built upon a rich seam of documentary evidence. By comparison, the historiography of the Irish Reformation is much more modest, is constructed from a relatively meagre body of evidence and provides only a fragmentary and incomplete picture of the religious upheavals of the period. Thus it would be unwise to set too much store on the conclusions they draw from their comparisons until a more detailed view of the progress of the Reformation is built up within both the English and Gaelic areas of the island. When this is achieved, it should be possible to assess more accurately whether the opposition of the Old English community to the English crown's political and religious policies was genuinely akin to the opposition of the Brandenburg estates to the 'state-building' and 'confession-building' policies of their Electors; or whether the Catholic religious stance adopted by the patricians of Dublin city closely paralleled the Lutheran credal allegiance of the burghers of the town of Lemgo in Lippe in the German Empire.[16]

The original agenda set by the Bradshaw–Canny debate, then, remains valid and, in the intervening years, many historians have attempted to build upon their pioneering work. For convenience and ease of classification, it is possible to identify at least four coherent lines of enquiry or approaches that have emerged in the subsequent period, though the demarcation lines between them are not rigid or fixed, and particular works can easily fit into one or more category. The first of these lines of enquiry has concentrated upon the creation of an ideological attachment to the Counter-Reformation amongst the Englishry of Ireland. Following Bradshaw, most historians would accept that this was part of a wider process of alienation from the governing methods of the Tudor regime in Ireland, though disagreement persists about how the process occurred. Ciaran Brady's work on the government of Ireland in the period 1540–80 has cast into doubt Bradshaw's early dating of the Palesmen's alienation by moving forward in time the Tudor regime's adoption of an intrinsically violent and more expropriatory policy, and by questioning the whole notion of a preconceived policy of conquest. He has also put forward an alternative explanation of how their political alienation influenced their religious concerns. For him their disaffection stemmed not from the regime's abandonment of

---

[16] Bottigheimer and Lotz-Heumann, 'Irish Reformation in European perspective', pp. 293–305. Lotz-Heumann's ideas have been developed much more extensively in her book *Die doppelte Konfessionalisierung in Irland. Konflikt und Koexistenz im 16. und in der ersten Hälfte des 17. Jahrhunderts* (Tubingen, 2000). Notwithstanding this, the essential question about whether she is comparing like with like remains unanswered. For a valuable review of Lotz-Heumann's work see H. Robinson-Hammerstein 'Review article: the confessionalisation of Ireland? Assessment of a paradigm', *IHS* 32 (2001), pp. 567–78.

their favoured policy of assimilating the Gaelic Irish, but, paradoxically, from the great financial burden that this policy imposed upon their own community, as a result of the Elizabethan governors' efforts to implement it systematically. Yet their distaste for the English administration did not lead directly to their rejection of the state church in favour of the Counter-Reformation. While some border magnates like Viscount Baltinglass did reappraise Ireland's relationship with what they saw as an unacceptably aggressive and Protestant monarchy, and elected to rebel under the papal banner, it was the government's draconian reaction to the revolts, rather than any widespread sympathy for the rebels' treasonable actions, which pushed the Pale community into the arms of the Counter-Reformation.[17]

In broad terms, this analysis has been endorsed by Colm Lennon, whose original research has focused on the development of a post-Tridentine Catholic ideology amongst the 'socially ascendant patricians' of Dublin city and its environs.[18] Adopting a lengthy time-span that charts the transition from nominally conformist and Catholic survivalist religious positions to a fully articulated Counter-Reformation faith, his work on the city's mercantile elite and the gentry in the countryside portrays a social grouping whose general religious attitude was one of uncommitted or nominal conformity to the Church of Ireland until the late 1570s. Thereafter, in response to the actions of an increasingly unpopular government, which included the savage suppression of the Baltinglass and Nugent rebellions, and a new and concerted attack on the privileges and liberties of the city of Dublin, they defined their religious position with growing certitude. This process, which was part of a wider defence of the political and cultural traditions of their community, took place in two stages. First, the social elite assumed a recusant position during the 1580s and early 1590s. Then, during the later 1590s and the first decade of the seventeenth century, they adopted a 'more all-embracing Catholicism', which became evident in the very substantial support they provided for the establishment and

---

[17] C. Brady: 'Conservative subversives: the community of the Pale and the Dublin administration, 1556–86', in P. J. Corish (ed.), *Radicals, rebels and establishments: historical studies XV* (Belfast, 1985), pp. 11–32; 'Court, castle and country: the framework of government in Tudor Ireland', in C. Brady and R. Gillespie (eds.), *Natives and newcomers. The making of Irish colonial society 1534–1641* (Dublin, 1986), pp. 22–49; *The Chief Governors. The rise and fall of reform government in Tudor Ireland, 1536–1588* (Cambridge, 1994).

[18] C. Lennon: 'Recusancy and the Dublin Stanihursts', *AH* 33 (1975), pp. 101–10; *Richard Stanyhurst the Dubliner, 1547–1618* (Dublin, 1981); *The lords of Dublin in the age of Reformation* (Dublin, 1989); 'The chantries in the Irish Reformation: the case of St Anne's Guild, Dublin, 1550–1630', in R.V. Comerford, M. Cullen, J. R. Hill and C. Lennon (eds.), *Religion, conflict and coexistence in Ireland* (Dublin, 1991), pp. 8–25; 'Mass in the manor house: the Counter-Reformation in Dublin 1560–1630', in J. Kelly and D. Keogh (eds.), *History of the Catholic diocese of Dublin* (Dublin, 1999), pp. 112–26.

maintenance of a network of mass houses and Catholic clergy throughout the city and county.[19]

The second line of enquiry to emerge after the Bradshaw–Canny debate is concerned with the structural deficiencies of the Church of Ireland. In a closely crafted essay Aidan Clarke sought 'to recall attention to the existence of very practical reasons why the Church of Ireland should have evolved the way it did', all of which he showed were intimately connected with its 'prime dilemma': how best to proceed with making a Protestant church a social reality given the facts of its statutory inheritance of Catholic personnel, and of medieval institutional structures.[20] At the heart of Clarke's argument was his definition of these 'practical reasons' as insuperable problems of human and material resources, which prevented it from adopting what many contemporaries saw as the solution to its central dilemma: the creation of a learned, preaching ministry through the provision of adequately remunerative livings. For Clarke, this proved to be an impossibility because of the legacy of the Church of Ireland's medieval past. This legacy, an interlocking of its structures and property with the local community – in particular, the lay impropriation of parochial tithes and the accompanying right to select parochial curates – gave its Catholic enemies proprietary rights over its resources and control over its personnel. Evangelical failure, then, stemmed from the ecclesiastical establishment's inability to act independently of the local community.

Clarke's broad overview was supported by Steven Ellis's 'Economic problems of the church: why the Reformation failed in Ireland',[21] which provided a critical introduction to an important and hitherto neglected source: the Irish equivalent of the *valor ecclesiasticus*. Although Ellis's essay also ranged widely – it included an interesting, though excursive, discussion on the limitations of Tudor government in border societies and how they affected the progress of the Reformation – its main focus is on the Church of Ireland's resource problems. These are thrown into sharp relief by a very welcome statistical analysis of the clergy's finances, which is based on the Tudor *valor*, and on Jacobean certificates from the state papers that detail the contemporary wealth of many of the same benefices. It complemented Clarke's suggestion in its analysis of the state of those livings over which the Church of Ireland did maintain autonomy and control. His conclusion – based on a quantitative comparison of the values of Irish and Welsh

---

[19] The process is conveniently summarised in C. Lennon, 'The rise of recusancy among the Dublin patricians, 1580–1613', in W. J. Sheils and D. Wood (eds.), *The churches, Ireland and the Irish, studies in church history, xxv* (Oxford, 1989), pp. 123–32.

[20] A. Clarke, 'Varieties of uniformity: the first century of the Church of Ireland', in Sheils and Wood (eds.), *The churches, Ireland and the Irish*, pp. 105–22.

[21] *JEH* 41 (1990), pp. 239–65.

ecclesiastical livings, and the assumption that modern evaluations of the significance of Welsh clerical poverty are applicable to the Irish situation – is as dismal as Clarke's. For him, poverty of Irish parochial livings was the central impediment to the Reformation's progress, a view which has had a significant influence on a number of local studies undertaken at county and diocesan levels in the past decade.[22]

The third line of enquiry to appear in the wake of Bradshaw and Canny's early work explores the response of the Gaelic Irish to the Reformation. Subsumed generally under the broader discussion of the Gaelic reaction to the Tudor conquest and the related development of Irish nationality, the subject received considerable attention in the 1990s but, as yet, no interpretative consensus has emerged among those historians engaged in the field.[23] Samantha Meigs, for example, has argued in her book *The Reformations in Ireland. Tradition and confessionalism, 1400–1690*[24] that Catholicism endured in Gaelic Ireland because the medieval Irish religious tradition was inextricably linked with the social and mental structures of the traditional Gaelic world; and that its scholar elites played a very active role in transmitting religious beliefs and practices from one generation to another throughout the Reformation era. Yet while this idea is intriguing, it is not clear – given the very limited treatment afforded by Meigs to the implementation of official religious reform in Gaelic Ireland during the sixteenth century – whether the tradition survived by default, in the face of a weak campaign of enforcement on the part of the Dublin government; or because it was sufficiently strong to withstand the challenge mounted by English Protestantism until such time as it was bolstered by the Counter-Reformation.

Meigs dates the emergence of a Counter-Reformation culture in Gaelic Ireland to the early seventeenth century. Other historians, most notably Brendan Bradshaw,[25] Hiram Morgan[26] and Marc Caball,[27] firmly locate it in the latter half of the sixteenth century, and have identified a number of

---

[22] See, particularly, H. Jefferies, *Priests and prelates of Armagh in the age of reformations* (Dublin, 1997); M. A. Lyons, *Church and society in County Kildare, c. 1470–1547* (Dublin, 2000); B. Scott, *Religion and Reformation in the Tudor diocese of Meath* (Dublin, 2006).

[23] For a useful introduction to the historiography see S.G. Ellis, *Ireland in the age of the Tudors 1447–1603: English expansion and the end of Gaelic rule* (London and New York, 1998), pp. 243–65.

[24] Dublin, 1997.

[25] 'English Reformation and identity formation in Wales and Ireland', pp. 54–61.

[26] 'Hugh O'Neill and the Nine Years War in Tudor Ireland', *HJ* 36 (1993), pp. 1–17.

[27] 'Faith, culture and sovereignty: Irish nationality and its development, 1558–1625' in Bradshaw and Roberts (eds.), *British consciousness and identity*, pp. 112–39 and *Poets and politics. Reaction and continuity in Irish poetry, 1558–1625* (Cork, 1998); 'Religion, culture and the bardic elite in early modern Ireland', in Ford and McCafferty (eds.) *Sectarianism in Early Modern Ireland*, pp. 158–82.

factors which combined to give it its distinctive character: the missionary activities of the mendicant friars and papally appointed bishops and vicars apostolic; a growing identification of Catholicism with Gaelic cultural and political concerns, and Protestantism with the new expansionist, English colonial elite; and the creation and adoption of a new militant 'faith and fatherland' ideology by key political figures like James Fitzmaurice FitzGerald and Hugh O'Neill. They are also agreed that this culture provided, from the 1570s on, an ideological underpinning for the late sixteenth-century rebellions against Tudor rule in Ireland.[28] Nevertheless, there was nothing inevitable about Gaelic Ireland's adherence to the Counter-Reformation. As Bradshaw's work on the early Reformation has shown and, more recently, Mícheál MacCraith's analysis of the promotion of Protestantism in Gaelic Ireland under the auspices of influential figures in Scottish Gaeldom in the 1560s,[29] there were periods throughout the sixteenth century when the Reformation held a genuine appeal for certain Gaelic constituencies.

The fourth and final line of enquiry to have emerged after the Bradshaw–Canny debate has attempted to examine the Irish Reformation through the genre of 'British History' writing. The most significant contribution to have appeared so far is Felicity Heal's *Reformation in Britain and Ireland*, which is an ambitious attempt to construct a synthetic, analytical narrative of religious change in England, Wales, Ireland and Scotland during the course of the sixteenth century.[30] Although, necessarily, it draws heavily on existing literature, and does not seek to present new information on the individual religious histories of any of the three kingdoms, it says a number of important things that have long needed restating and which are particularly germane to the study of the Reformation in Ireland. In particular, on the back of her exhaustive narrative, Heal quite rightly concludes that the Tudor Reformation was an 'incontrovertibly political' phenomenon. She also argues that – notwithstanding the current interest of historians in exploring 'popular' religion and the forms of religious identity – an understanding of the nature of the Reformation in the Tudor dominions demands, first and foremost, a 'careful analysis' of the ecclesiastical proceedings of Henry VIII

---

[28] See also B. Ó Buachalla's essays: 'Poetry and politics in early modern Ireland' in *Eighteenth-century Ireland: Iris an dá chultúr*, vii, pp. 149–75 and 'The Gaelic response to conquest', in D. Ó Ceallaigh (ed.), *New perspectives on Ireland: colonialism and identity: selected papers from the Desmond Greaves summer school and related essays* (Dublin, 1998), pp. 52–97.

[29] 'The Gaelic reaction to the Reformation', in S. G. Ellis and S. Barber (eds.), *Conquest and union: fashioning a British state, 1485–1725* (London, 1995), pp. 139–61.

[30] Oxford, 2003. For other examples see W. I. P. Hazlett, *The Reformation in Britain and Ireland* (London, 2003); Bradshaw, 'English Reformation and identity formation in Wales and Ireland', pp. 48–54 and 'Tudor Reformation and revolution in Wales and Ireland', pp. 39–65.

and Elizabeth I. In this context, the history of the Tudor Reformation is primarily concerned with exploring the manner in which different elite groupings in English, Welsh and Irish society responded to the efforts of the crown to transform traditional religious and ecclesiastical politics. And she concludes that the extent to which the crown succeeded or failed was determined, in part, by the local cultural context but, more especially, by the attitudes of indigenous clerical elites.

In summary, then, the four fields of investigation undertaken in the wake of the Bradshaw–Canny debate have added considerably to our knowledge of the Reformation process. Yet they have not provided any definitive answers to the central questions posed by it. Although the work of Clarke and Ellis has drawn our attention to the fact that the Church of Ireland faced serious structural problems, which severely undermined its capacity to mount a proper campaign of evangelisation, the ultimate failure of the Reformation in Ireland cannot be attributed solely to these problems. Quite apart from the fact that research on the 'professionalisation' of the English clergy has shown that the provision of a well-educated, Protestant ministry was not dependent on the availability of well-endowed livings alone, but on the expansion of the universities and their ability to increase the supply of graduates coming on to the 'job' market;[31] their deterministic view of the fate of the Reformation precludes the possibility that the indigenous religious culture of the English Pale played any significant part in the process, especially during the quiescent phase of the Reformation identified by Nicholas Canny.

Similarly, while Lennon and Brady have shown that the Pale community's alienation from the Tudor regime, and its adoption of a fully fledged Counter-Reformation faith, did not occur until the end of the sixteenth and the beginning of the seventeenth centuries, the question of when, precisely, the Reformation can be said to have failed still remains open, largely because the nature and strength of Catholic survivalism in English Ireland in the early decades of Elizabeth's reign, and the manner in which it affected the progress of the Reformation, has received comparatively little attention. Indeed, the importance of this issue is now thrown into sharper relief by Felicity Heal's work, as it effectively challenges historians working in the field to explore the local cultural context and the attitudes of local clerical elites. The same may also be said of those studies recently undertaken on the Gaelic response to the Reformation, given that the militant 'faith and fatherland'

---

[31] On the crucial role that the provision of university education played in reforming the ministry in England see R. O'Day, *The English clergy. The emergence and consolidation of a profession 1558–1642* (Leicester, 1979) pp. 127–43 and 'The anatomy of a profession: the clergy of the Church of England' in W. Prest (ed.), *The professions in Early Modern England* (London, 1987), pp. 25–63.

ideology espoused by the leaders of the late sixteenth-century rebellions secured little support from the old colonial community in the English Pale.

It is with this fundamental question, then, the nature of the response of the English Irish community to the Reformation during the sixteenth century, that this book will be primarily concerned. When it was originally conceived, developments in the historiography of the English Reformation suggested that the most fruitful methodological approach for exploring the Englishry's response to the Reformation would be by means of a diocesan history. At the same time that Brendan Bradshaw was revitalising the study of the Irish Reformation, a new generation of English historians began to explore the practical implications of the movement at the grassroots level of English society. Conducted, generally, at diocesan or county level, and making use of previously ignored or underused records such as visitation act books, consistory cause papers, wills and churchwardens' accounts, these studies revealed that the rate of religious change in the localities, the speed with which the Reformation was enforced and accepted, varied considerably from region to region. The main result of all this was that the traditional view of the English Reformation as a process in which crown policy, and a developing reformist allegiance amongst the people – built upon the native Lollard heresy, an emerging Lutheran sect and popular anti-clericalism – combined to create a successful Protestant Reformation, was seriously undermined.[32] Although a number of historians have subsequently produced authoritative syntheses of the revisionist view of the English Reformation,[33] it seemed reasonable to assume that the adoption of the methodological approach which opened up the subject for them in the first

[32] The most scholarly exposition of the traditional view is A. G. Dickens, *The English Reformation* (London, 1964); its early development is surveyed by R. O'Day in *The debate on the English Reformation* (London, 1986). The development of the revisionist view of the English Reformation, and the part played in it by diocesan and local histories, is best approached through the series of essays edited by C. Haigh, *The English Reformation revised* (Cambridge, 1987); see also his article 'A. G. Dickens and the English Reformation', *Historical Research* 77 (2004), pp. 24–38. For some examples of these diocesan and local studies see R. B. Manning, *Religion and society in Elizabethan Sussex* (Leicester, 1969); C. Haigh, *Reformation and resistance in Tudor Lancashire* (Cambridge, 1975); R. A. Houlbrooke, *Church courts and the people during the English Reformation, 1520–70* (Oxford, 1979) [based on evidence from Winchester and Norwich dioceses]; M. Bowker, *The Henrician Reformation in the diocese of Lincoln under John Longland, 1521–47* (Cambridge, 1981); D. MacCulloch, *Suffolk and the Tudors* (Oxford, 1986); S. Brigden, *London and the Reformation* (Oxford, 1989); R. Whiting, *The blind devotion of the people: popular religion and the English Reformation* (Cambridge, 1989) [covers the south west of England].

[33] For some examples of these general revisionist studies see J. J. Scarisbrick, *The Reformation and the English people* (Oxford, 1984); E. Duffy, *The stripping of the altars. Traditional religion in England 1400–1580* (Yale, 1992); R. Rex, *Henry VIII and the English Reformation* (Basingstoke and London, 1993); C. Haigh, *English Reformations. Religion, politics, and society under the Tudors* (Oxford, 1993). The debate continues however: for a recent re-consideration of the debate and its significance see A. Pettegree, 'A. G. Dickens and

place – the particular, local study – would yield new and comparable insights into the problems and questions raised by Bradshaw and Canny vis-à-vis the English Pale. Proceeding on this basis, then, the diocese of Dublin, the region's central ecclesiastical unit, was selected as the most obvious candidate for such a study.

In practice, however, this methodological approach proved problematical. Although there are sufficient sources extant to reconstruct the basic structure and workings of the diocese of Dublin during the sixteenth century,[34] it soon became apparent that the documentation that was used by English historians to plot the rate of religious change in the localities was almost wholly lacking. The hugely important churchwardens' accounts, for example, exist for only one parish in the diocese – St Werburgh's in the city of Dublin – and even then the series is very incomplete. Crucially, there are no documents for the period of most intensive religious change, 1534–69, the period in which the surviving English churchwardens' accounts record the alterations that were made, or not made as the case may be, to the fabric, fittings and decoration of parish churches, consequent upon the introduction of the various Tudor religious settlements.[35]

The same is true of visitation records, documents produced by the church courts and testamentary material. Apart from one very unusual document from the episcopate of Archbishop Browne – a set of local visitation injunctions issued to the Irish clergy as a whole[36] – and some *acta* from an archiepiscopal visitation of St Patrick's Cathedral undertaken in 1569–70,[37] visitation records from the diocese are entirely lacking for the duration of the Tudor Reformation. Church court proceedings likewise are represented only by the surviving portion of a single act book from the archbishop's consistory, dating from the late 1590s, which reveals little about the

---

his critics: a new narrative of the English Reformation', *Historical Research* 77 (2004), pp. 39–58.

[34] Most of these are in print: *Alen's register*; Wood, *Liberty of St Sepulchre*; *Dignitas decani*; N. B. White (ed.), 'The Reportorium Viride of John Alen, archbishop of Dublin, 1533', *Analecta* 10 (1941), pp. 180–217; *RDD*; White, *Monastic extents*; Berry, *Register of wills*; *CCD*; Survey of the possessions of St Patrick's Cathedral, 1547, RCB, C2/1/27, no. 2 (printed in Mason, *History of St Patrick's*, pp. 28–99); Gillespie (ed.), *The proctor's accounts of Peter Lewis* and *First chapter act book of Christ Church*; J.C. Crosthwaite (ed.), *The book of obits and martyrology of the Cathedral Church of Holy Trinity* (Dublin, 1844) now reprinted in Refaussé with Lennon, *Registers of Christ Church*.

[35] RCB, P326/27/1/1–21 (Churchwardens' accounts of St Werburgh's, 1481–1627); J. Robinson, 'Churchwardens' accounts, 1484–1600, St Werburgh's Church, Dublin', *JRSAI*, 6th series, 4 (1914), pp. 132–42; R. Hutton, 'The local impact of the Tudor Reformations', in Haigh (ed.), *English Reformation revised*, pp. 114–38.

[36] J. Murray, 'Ecclesiastical justice and the enforcement of the Reformation: the case of Archbishop Browne and the clergy of Dublin', in Ford, McGuire and Milne (eds.), *As by law established*, pp. 40–1, 231–2 (nts. 33–8)

[37] See Chapter 8.

enforcement and progress of the Elizabethan Reformation, as the bulk of the cases recorded in it are party versus party actions.[38] Finally, although a late fifteenth-century register of wills from the diocese has survived to the present day, nothing comparable exists for the sixteenth century. Indeed, this absence is compounded by the fact that *c*.274 original diocesan wills, covering the period 1534 to 1605, as well as the contemporaneous testamentary material produced by the Prerogative Court of Faculties, were lost in the conflagration of the Irish Public Record Office in 1922.[39]

An absence of the requisite documentation, then, precludes the possibility of undertaking the kind of close regional analysis of the progress of the Reformation in Dublin as has been undertaken in England. Indeed, the limitations imposed by the sources are not restricted to Dublin. It is a problem which afflicts all Irish dioceses, as is evidenced by Henry Jefferies's study of the diocese of Armagh.[40] With its unique collection of late medieval registers, Armagh has the richest archival inheritance of any Irish see during the early Reformation period, and Jefferies has utilised this material effectively to produce a detailed institutional analysis of the diocese during the episcopates of Archbishops Cromer (1521–43) and Dowdall (1543–51, 1553–8). His study shows that Armagh was an effectively administered unit at this time, that the pastoral needs of the laity were met in most respects by the diocesan clergy, and the laity, in turn, reciprocated by displaying a pronounced commitment to traditional religion, evinced in the investments they made in their parish churches. Yet, while Jefferies's work has revised the traditional view that the late medieval church in Ireland was everywhere in decline, and now provides a context for analysing the impact of, and reaction to, religious change in the reigns of Henry VIII, Edward VI and Mary, it does not directly address the questions of why and when the Reformation failed, largely because the documentation which the author has exploited for the first half of the sixteenth century has not survived for the reign of Elizabeth. Instead, having concluded his study at the point where the registers cease – by coincidence the end of the Catholic Queen Mary's reign – he suggests that the popularity and resilience of late medieval Catholicism in Armagh, a popularity and resilience due in no small part to the pastoral activities of the local clergy, was a factor, though not

---

[38] Act book of the Dublin consistory court, Michaelmas 1596 to Michaelmas 1599 (Marsh's Library, MS Z4.2.19, pp. 1–126 *passim*).

[39] Berry, *Register of wills*, pp. vii–xliii; 'Index to the act or grant books, and to original wills, of the diocese of Dublin to the year 1800', *Appendix to the 26th report of the Deputy Keeper of the Public Records . . . Ireland* (Dublin, 1895), pp. 1–942 *passim*; H. Wood, *A guide to the records deposited in the Public Record Office of Ireland* (Dublin, 1919), pp. 222–5, 241–3.

[40] Jefferies, *Priests and prelates of Armagh*; see also Scott, *Tudor diocese of Meath*.

necessarily the only one, in Protestantism's failure to win the support of the local population.[41]

It is clear, then, that the effectiveness of the conventional diocesan history as a means of exploring the impact of the Reformation in the Irish localities is circumscribed by the paucity of the sources. Yet, paradoxically, this difficulty also suggests an alternative line of enquiry. Although the absence of the conventional ecclesiastical documentation is in part an historical accident,[42] the extraordinary poverty of such material as has survived is in itself symptomatic of a deeper problem. The very preservation of documentation in England attests very strongly to the fact that the enforcement of the Reformation, an administrative process engaged in jointly by the agencies of the church and state, was systematically undertaken, however uneven its results were at the outset. By the same token, the very pronounced absence of analogous documentation in Ireland suggests very strongly that that routine collaboration, which was necessary for the survival of such a continuous record, never occurred there.

This contention is borne out by other evidence. It has long been recognised that the indigenous clergy were reluctant to lend their support to the Reformation cause. Not only did they resist the imposition of the Reformation legislation in the Irish parliament of 1536–7, but thereafter they actively subverted the efforts of reformers like Archbishop Browne of Dublin to enforce the provisions of this legislation amongst the local community.[43] What has not been generally appreciated, however, is the extent and significance of this clerical opposition. In exploring the structures of the diocese of Dublin, a necessary preliminary to the original idea of investigating the enforcement of reform in the parishes, it became apparent that this clerical opposition was both powerful and highly motivated, because it controlled the institutional fabric of the local church and because it possessed its own unique ethos and identity, which was embodied by that fabric. The implications of this for the study of the Reformation in Ireland were striking. Because the Tudors chose to enforce their reformations through the preexisting ecclesiastical structures, through the bishops, their officials and the

---

[41] Jefferies has attempted to transcend the limitations of his sources in his essay, 'The early Tudor Reformations in the Irish Pale', *JEH* 52 (2001), pp. 34–62.

[42] The same historical accident has led to considerable variation – from diocese to diocese and from jurisdiction to jurisdiction – in the rate of survival of manuscripts in the English Church. On this point see R. O'Day and F. Heal (eds.), *Continuity and change. Personnel and administration of the church in England 1500–1642* (Leicester, 1976), pp. 17–18; D.M. Owen, *The records of the established church in England* (Cambridge, 1970) and 'Handlist of ecclesiastical records: a supplement to records of the established church', *Archives* 10 (1971–2), pp. 53–6.

[43] Edwards, *Church and state*, pp. 9–10, 47–64; Bradshaw, 'George Browne', p. 310; Jefferies, *Priests and prelates of Armagh*, pp. 133–73 *passim*.

traditional courts Christian – a feature which distinguished them markedly from their continental equivalents[44] – it was evident that the clerical opposition possessed a significant capacity to negate the best efforts of the reformers to secure indigenous allegiance to those reformations, as they controlled a substantial part of the administrative framework through which this process was supposed to be effected. This led to one other inescapable conclusion. The definitive nature of the English Irish community's response to the Reformation would not be found, as was originally supposed, by charting the impact of a reform-led diocesan administration's efforts to enforce the Reformation in the parishes of the diocese of Dublin. Rather, it would be found in the battle conducted within that administration itself, between reforming archbishops enjoined to use the conventional ecclesiastical structures for reformist purposes, and a conservative clerical elite which was equally determined to maintain its traditional stranglehold over those same structures and to use them for its own, essentially Catholic, ideological ends. It is this struggle for power and control over local church structures, a struggle that was played out during the decisive years of change between 1536 and 1569, that comprises the main theme of this book.

But the struggle for power was not only confined to the reforming archbishops and the conservative clergy. In researching the ecclesiastical politics of the Tudor diocese of Dublin, it also emerged that another distinct grouping was involved in the drama: the secular men of action or, more particularly, the Tudor viceroys. Although it has long been recognised that the viceroys were the principal agents of English policy in sixteenth-century Ireland, it has generally been presumed by historians that their standing obligation to oversee the enforcement of religious reform did not feature prominently among their day-to-day priorities for governing the country. However, a recent study of the Elizabethan viceroy, Sir Henry Sidney, and his attempts to institute national programmes of religious reform during his two viceroyalties (1566–71 and 1575–8), has challenged this supposition. Indeed, not only does the Sidney study demonstrate that it has little basis in fact, but it also suggests that the presumption itself represents a deeper historiographical problem: the persistence of a dichotomy in the manner in which political and religious historians view and treat sixteenth-century Irish history.[45] For the Tudor viceroys, unlike their historians, there was no

---

[44] O'Day and Heal (eds.), *Continuity and change*, p. 15; D. MacCulloch, *The later Reformation in England 1547–1603* (Basingstoke and London, 1990), pp. 32–3. On the construction of new institutional structures in the continental reformed churches during the sixteenth century see E. Cameron, *The European Reformation* (Oxford, 1991), pp. 257–61.

[45] C. Brady and J. Murray, 'Sir Henry Sidney and the Reformation in Ireland', in E. Boran and C. Gribben (eds.), *Enforcing Reformation in Ireland and Scotland, 1550–1700* (Aldershot, 2006), pp. 14–39.

underlying need or impulse to compartmentalise their political and religious responsibilities. From Lord Leonard Grey through to Sir John Perrott and beyond, they took their religious responsibilities, and the authority that went with them, very seriously indeed. More than that, they made many decisions and inaugurated numerous initiatives, which they considered would bring about the religious change that was demanded by their sovereigns at different points in the sixteenth century, and which interacted with, and impacted upon, the reforming initiatives overseen by the churchmen.

The continually optimistic nature of the viceroys' interventions in the enforcement of the Reformation during the sixteenth century, which is so much at odds with the traditional historiographical treatment of the subject – at no point, did they consider failure to be an inevitable outcome of their actions – demands to be taken seriously. However, it also presents the writer with a methodological problem, especially in a study that is centred on a delimited territorial unit like the diocese of Dublin, and which is concerned to a large degree with the internal administrative workings of that unit. Two particular aspects of the problem stand out. First, there is a need to capture and contextualise the viceroys' optimistic outlook on the prospects for reform at different points in the sixteenth century. Second, there is a need to identify those factors that advanced or obstructed their endeavours, and, indeed, those of the reforming archbishops, to effect religious change during the same periods of time. In seeking to address both aspects of the problem, one overriding feature of the viceroys' involvement in the enforcement of the Reformation continually presents itself: this was their uniquely national perspective on the affairs of sixteenth-century Ireland. Not only did they formulate and implement policy, including religious and ecclesiastical policy, from a broad national perspective, which inevitably went beyond and, by turns, was sometimes at odds with, the narrower concerns of the reforming archbishops of Dublin or the conservative clergy. But they were also, by their very nature, deeply embroiled in the complex sphere of contemporary Irish and English secular politics, and were thus vulnerable to a bewildering series of contingencies that frequently and abruptly impacted upon their religious responsibilities. The challenge for the diocesan historian in engaging with the viceroys, then, is not only to identify when and where their national activities – whether in the strictly religious or broader political arenas – intruded upon diocesan affairs and affected the course of the Reformation, but also to find a mode of expression for communicating what is, by definition, an exceedingly complex story.

The strategy employed in this book to address these methodological difficulties is deliberately old-fashioned. What follows is an attempt to recount in narrative form the history of the struggle for power within the local church in Dublin from the varying perspectives of the three men who served as its archbishop during the Reformation period – George Browne (1536–54), Hugh Curwen (1555–67) and Adam Loftus (1567–1605); of the indigenous clerical elite who served under them; and, where it is adjudged to be essential to the elaboration of this central narrative, of several of the Tudor viceroys. Further, in seeking to capture the nationally oriented vice-regal perspective, the narrative will, on occasion, extend to events and happenings that took place outside the diocese or, indeed, beyond the religious sphere altogether. It will also require at different points the inclusion of a minutely detailed description of particular political, admin-istrative and legal processes in order to demonstrate how these apparently unrelated events and happenings made such a big impact within the diocese and on the progress of religious change generally. Most importantly of all, in order to capture some sense of the way in which unexpected or abrupt political changes affected what many a reformer anticipated would be a positive outcome to their various reforming initiatives – whether these were led by the viceroys or the reforming archbishops – the thrust of the narrative is prospective rather than retrospective. Before proceeding with this central narrative, however, it is necessary to set the scene by examining in some detail the Tudor diocese of Dublin's medieval inheritance. As we shall see in the opening two chapters, this inheritance created the very unique set of circumstances in which local opposition to the Reformation would arise and from which it would draw its strength and effectiveness.

1

'Handmaid' of the English Church: the diocese of Dublin on the eve of the Reformation

The metropolitan see of Dublin was one of thirty-two territorial units through which the church in Ireland was administered during the sixteenth century.[1] Although Armagh had long maintained its title to the ecclesiastical primacy of all Ireland, Dublin was regarded by most observers as the premier see on the island, because it surpassed the other dioceses either in terms of its financial resources, or the relative order and sophistication of its institutional fabric. Many aspects of this construct – including the political and social authority attached to the archbishop's office, the recruitment and training of his leading officials and the constitutional and liturgical forms adopted by his secular cathedral, St Patrick's – were, by the sixteenth century, long established expressions of the political and socio-cultural heritage of English Ireland, having originated and evolved through conscious imitation of English church structures, and their societal contexts, throughout the Middle Ages.[2] Thus, on the eve of the Reformation, the ecclesiastical landscape of the heartland of the diocese – effectively, the modern county of Dublin – would have presented a generally recognisable picture to those familiar with the pattern of ecclesiastical life in Tudor England and, as such, it is arguable that it fitted broadly within the mainstream of the Western Church.

Throughout most of Ireland, however, the church operated in a markedly divergent political and socio-cultural milieu, the Ireland of independent

---

[1] S. Duffy (ed.), *Atlas of Irish history* (Dublin, 1997), pp. 54–5; Ellis, *Ireland in the age of the Tudors*, p. 386.

[2] On the anglicisation of Dublin see M. Murphy, 'The Archbishops and administration of the diocese and province of Dublin, 1181–1298' (Ph.D. thesis, Trinity College, Dublin, 1988) and 'Archbishops and anglicisation: Dublin, 1181–1271', in Kelly and Keogh (eds.), *Catholic diocese of Dublin*, pp. 72–91; Mason, *History of St Patrick's*, pp. 1–146; G. J. Hand, 'The medieval chapter of St Patrick's Cathedral, Dublin', *RN* 5 (1964), pp. 229–48.

Gaelic and 'degenerate' English lordships. The prevailing conditions in the independent lordships – they were highly militarised, economically under-developed and culturally self-assured – created very considerable difficulties for the institutional church. The most notable of these was a deep-rooted and systemic poverty, which was frequently exacerbated by the laity's encroachment upon, or despoliation of ecclesiastical property. The same set of conditions also ensured that the church was suffused with a range of customary practices that not only departed from European ecclesiological norms but, in some instances, also contravened particular aspects of the Roman canon law. Although countervailing forces, such as the Observant reform movement amongst the mendicant friars, and the effectiveness of the provincial and diocesan administrations of the archbishops of Armagh in Ulster, determined that its mission was not completely undermined as a result of these difficulties, and that late medieval Catholicism was not without some genuine vitality,[3] the church in the independent lordships was still considered by many observers to be in a decayed state.[4] While it is true that some of their reports exaggerated the level and extent of this decay, they did create a backdrop, albeit impressionistic, against which Dublin's pre-eminence bore witness to the perceived inadequacies of the Gaelic and Gaelicised church, rather than to any uniquely meritorious qualities inherent within itself. Thus the contrast between the diocese, the central ecclesiastical unit in English Ireland, and the majority of Irish sees was important, because it provided a definite context through which contemporaries perceived and judged it as a functioning entity.

I

The most quantifiable element of Dublin's ecclesiastical pre-eminence was its superior wealth. This was particularly evident in relation to the archbishop's own benefice. Worth some IR£534 15s. 2½d. net c.1539, the see of Dublin was the most valuable in Ireland. Excepting Meath, which at IR£373 12s. 0½d. was the closest in value to Dublin, the Tudor archbishopric boasted a living at least three and up to forty times greater than the remaining episcopal livings extended during the sixteenth century (Table 1.1, p. 22).

---

[3] On Observantism and its significance see Bradshaw, *Dissolution of the religious orders*, ch. 1; Ellis, *Ireland in the age of the Tudors*, pp. 196–7; T. S. Flynn, *The Irish Dominicans 1536–1641* (Dublin, 1993), pp. 3–8; C. N. Ó Clabaigh, *The Franciscans in Ireland, 1400–1534* (Dublin, 2002), ch. 3. On Armagh see *Octavian's register, passim*; Jefferies, *Priests and prelates of Armagh*.

[4] J. Watt, *The church in medieval Ireland* (Dublin, 1972), pp. 181–3.

Table 1.1 *Sixteenth century valuations of Irish bishoprics*[5]

Bishopric	Province	Net value
Henrician valuations, c. 1537–40		
Dublin	Dublin	IR£534 15s. 2½d.
Meath	Armagh	IR£373 12s. 0½d.
Armagh	Armagh	IR£183 12s. 5¼d.
Ferns	Dublin	IR£108 13s. 4d.
Waterford & Lismore	Cashel	IR£72 8s. 1d.
Kildare	Dublin	IR£69 11s. 4d.
Ossory	Dublin	IR£66 13s. 4d.
Cashel	Cashel	IR£66 13s. 4d.
Leighlin	Dublin	IR£50 0s. 0d.
Elizabethan valuations c. 1584–91		
Elphin	Tuam	IR£138 10s. 8d.
Clonfert	Tuam	IR£106 13s. 4d.
Tuam	Tuam	IR£66 13s. 4d.
Cork & Cloyne	Cashel	IR£54 13s. 4d.
Limerick	Cashel	IR£53 6s. 8d.
Emly	Cashel	IR£35 11s. 5d.
Killala	Tuam	IR£31 2s. 3d.
Kilmore	Armagh	IR£26 13s. 4d.
Ross	Cashel	IR£25 6s. 8d.
Kilmacduagh	Tuam	IR£17 15s. 7d.
Ardfert	Cashel	IR£16 17s. 9d.
Ardagh	Armagh	IR£14 13s. 4d.
Achonry	Tuam	IR£13 6s. 8d.

Dublin's top-ranking position in the hierarchy of Irish ecclesiastical benefices, and the style of living that it entailed for its archbishops, did not go unnoticed by informed contemporaries. Francisco de Chierigatus, an Italian cleric who visited Dublin while serving as a papal nuncio in England during 1515–16, wrote favourably to Lady Isabella D'Este Gonzaga of his stay in the cathedral city, noting amongst other things the honourable entertainment afforded to him by Archbishop William Rokeby (1512–21). In a similar vein, Jean Du Bellay, the bishop of Bayonne and French ambassador in London, while notifying the Grand Master of France of the

[5] TCD, MS 567, ff. 1–22r; *Valor beneficiorum ecclesiasticorum in Hibernia* (Dublin, 1741), pp. 1–26; NLI, MS 474 (includes a copy of the printed *valor* with handwritten corrections by John Lodge, deputy keeper of the rolls 1754–74); 'A book of the proceedings against the clergy of Ireland upon certain informations in the exchequer there' (TNA: PRO SP 63/127, no. 18). For a critical introduction to the surviving versions of the Irish *valor* see Ellis, 'Economic problems of the church', pp. 245–8.

promotion of John Alen (1528–34) to the chancellorship of Ireland and the see of Dublin, described it as 'a good archbishopric in the country' ('une bonne archevesché au pays'). As a seasoned careerist cleric there is little doubt that Du Bellay was referring to the archbishopric principally as a source of remuneration.[6]

The inequality in wealth that existed between the Tudor prelates of Dublin and their fellow Irish bishops was a function of various factors. One of the most decisive was their inheritance of an endowment which greatly exceeded the patrimonies of the majority of the Irish episcopate, and which included over 50,000 acres in the territory of the old Hiberno-Norse diocese of Dublin, an area roughly coterminous with the modern county. The contrasting absence of comparable sources of wealth in all but a few of the other Irish dioceses was generally recognised by contemporary English observers, and was deemed by some to be a matter fraught with undesirable political consequences. Thus, according to one writer of the early 1520s, the fact that so many Irish bishoprics were of such 'small value' determined 'that no Englishman will accept them, so that Irishmen possess and enjoy them which be most apt and ready to make war and excite others to move war against the king and his deputy'. He thus exhorted Cardinal Wolsey to obtain a bull from the pope which would authorise him or his deputies to unite such poorly endowed sees 'after their discretion'.[7]

The advantage enjoyed by Dublin's archbishops was not confined solely to the greater size of their see's medieval endowments. It also extended to the favourable location of much of this property. Virtually all of the see lands in modern Co. Dublin were located in the Pale Maghery, the 'land of peace', an area defined by the network of defences – fortified bridges, dykes and tower houses – that insulated it from the depredation caused by Gaelic raiding in the outlying areas of the Pale. Thus it was notable for its tranquillity and a strongly accented English socio-cultural organisation, in

---

[6] A. Portioli (ed.), *Quattro Documenti D'Inghilterr ed uno di Spagna Dell' Archivio di Mantova* (Mantova, 1868), pp. 20–1; J.P. Mahaffy, 'Two early tours in Ireland', *Hermathena* 17, no. 40 (1914), p. 10; V.L. Bourilly and P. DeVaissière (eds.), *Ambassades en Angletere de Jean Du Bellay. La Première Ambassade (Septembre 1527-Février 1529). Correspondance Diplomatique* (Paris, 1905), pp. 461–2 (*LP* IV. ii, no. 4942).

[7] J. Otway-Ruthven, 'The medieval church lands of County Dublin', in J. A. Watt, J. B. Morrill and F. X. Martin (eds.), *Medieval studies presented to Aubrey Gwynn S. J.* (Dublin, 1961), pp. 54–73; W. Reeves, *Analysis of the united dioceses of Dublin and Glendalough* (Dublin, 1869), pp. 2–5; W. J. Smyth, 'Exploring the social and cultural topographies of sixteenth and seventeenth century county Dublin', in F. H. A. Aalen and K. Whelan (eds.), *Dublin city and county: from prehistory to present. Studies in honour of J. H. Andrews* (Dublin, 1992), pp. 132–4; 'A device how Ireland may be well kept in obedience', *c*.1521 (TNA: PRO SP60/1, no. 28), and see also 'Remembrances for Ireland', *c*.1520 (TNA: PRO SP 1/30, f. 89).

which the more developed practices of English husbandry, centred on the manor, had been best preserved following their introduction after the Anglo-Norman conquest.[8] In addition, about half of these Co. Dublin lands – the manors of Swords, Lusk, Portrane, Clonmethan and Finglas – lay on the Fingal plain to the north of the River Liffey which was part of the central lowlands, the most fertile region on the island. Such features, and the fact that the lands formed a substantial proportion of the immediate hinterland of the chief and most populous urban centre in Ireland, the city of Dublin, ensured that they were geared towards producing a grain surplus to feed the city's inhabitants.[9] Overall, then, they were quite attractive to prospective tenants, which determined that the Tudor incumbents of the see were not only the chief landlords in the Dublin region, with all of the attendant prestige and social authority that this entailed, but also assured of receiving what was by Irish standards a lucrative financial return, even allowing for the profligate letting policies of their fifteenth-century predecessors.[10]

Most of the Irish episcopate did not share such advantages. Apart from the bishops of Meath, whose lands were located within the Pale and the fertile central lowlands and, like Dublin, were also organised on the English manorial model, the majority of Irish bishops functioned as possessioners in a society where the prevailing cultural and socio-economic climate was not conducive to the exploitation of ecclesiastical property. Many bishops in the north and west of Ireland, for instance, had to contend with the customary Gaelic system of ecclesiastical land stewardship – a system which had its

[8] Ellis, *Ireland in the age of the Tudors*, pp. 31–3, 70–2 and *Reform and revival. English government in Ireland, 1470–1534* (Woodbridge, 1986), pp. 50–2; A. K. Davin, 'Tower houses of the Pale' (M. Litt. thesis, Trinity College Dublin, 1982), pp. 174–6; T. O'Keefe, 'Medieval frontiers and fortifications: the Pale and its evolution', in Aalen and Whelan (eds.), *Dublin city and county*, pp. 57–77; A. Simms and P. Fagan, 'Villages in County Dublin: their origins and inheritance', in ibid., pp. 79–119; R. Stanyhurst, *Holinshed's Irish chronicle*, ed. L. Miller and E. Power (Dublin, 1979), p. 13.

[9] E. Estyn Evans, *The personality of Ireland: habitat, heritage and history* (Belfast, 1981), pp. 23, 26; Smyth, 'Social and cultural topographies of county Dublin', pp. 122–32; F. H. A. Aalen, *Man and the landscape in Ireland* (London, 1978), pp. 10–14, 117–21, 137, 171; E. Hogan (ed.), *The description of Ireland . . . in anno 1598* (London, 1878), p. 43; Lennon, *Lords of Dublin*, pp. 23–4; G. MacNiocaill, 'Socio-economic problems of the late medieval Irish town', in D. W. Harkness and M. O'Dowd (eds.), *The town in Ireland: historical studies XIII* (Belfast, 1981), p. 19; K. Down, 'Colonial society and economy in the high middle ages', *NHI* II, pp. 453–7, 459–62, 467–72, 480–1; R. Stalley, 'The archbishop's residence at Swords: castle or country retreat', in S. Duffy (ed.), *Medieval Dublin VII. Proceedings of the Friends of Medieval Dublin Symposium 2005* (Dublin, 2006), pp. 152–76.

[10] For a general study of the social authority enjoyed by the Tudor episcopate see F. Heal, *Of prelates and princes. A study of the economic and social position of the Tudor episcopate* (Cambridge, 1980); on the letting policies of the fifteenth-century archbishops see J. Murray, 'Archbishop Alen, Tudor reform and the Kildare Rebellion', *PRIA* 89 C (1989), pp. 4–5.

roots in the exclusively monastic organisation of the early Irish Church – whereby church lands were invested in quasi-clerical and hereditary clans, who elected a coarb or erenagh from among their number to oversee them. In return the latter paid a very low fixed rent to the bishop and were obliged to provide annual entertainment or 'noxials', at least once and up to four times a year, when the bishop and his train went on progress. Though the noxials might be commuted for cash or provisions that exceeded the annual rent, it is probable that further research will reveal that the coarb and erenagh families benefited to a greater extent from their interest in ecclesiastical property than the bishops.[11]

Of much greater significance as a contributory factor to the poverty of Irish bishoprics, however, was the under-developed nature of the economy of Gaelic and Gaelicised Ireland. In contrast to the rest of Europe, which was then undergoing a demographic upsurge, Ireland was greatly under-populated throughout the sixteenth century, a feature particularly evident in the independent lordships beyond the more densely settled English Pale. Land as a result was chronically under-utilised, a situation which gave rise to a predominant, though not exclusive, bias towards pastoral farming among their inhabitants, as well as the associated practice of transhumance.[12] The combination of low utilisation of land and transient settlement meant, of course, that the bishops were unable to capitalise on whatever assets they possessed: neither the demand for land nor tithe yields – the bishops in the north and west of Ireland were entitled to the third or fourth part of all parochial tithes in their dioceses[13] – would have been very high. It is likely, then, that some bishops in Gaelic and Gaelicised Ireland functioned as economic beings in much the same way as secular Gaelic lords, maintaining herds of cattle in pasture, rather than as rentier landlords after the manner of English bishops, the model to which the Tudor archbishops of Dublin conformed. In this connection the comments of the clerical annalist Thady Dowling concerning Nicholas Maguire, bishop of Leighlin (1490–1512), seem indicative. Dowling commended him

---

[11] K. W. Nicholls, *Gaelic and Gaelicised Ireland in the Middle Ages* (2nd edn, Dublin, 2003), pp. 127–30; C. Mooney, *The church in Gaelic Ireland: thirteenth to fifteenth centuries* (Dublin, 1969), pp. 10–15; C. Lennon, *Sixteenth-century Ireland: the incomplete conquest* (Dublin, 1994), p. 127; Jefferies, *Priests and prelates of Armagh*, pp. 125–8.

[12] K. W. Nicholls, *Land, law and society in sixteenth century Ireland* (O'Donnell Lecture, Dublin, 1976), p. 9 and 'Gaelic society and economy in the high middle ages', *NHI* II, pp. 410–14; D. B. Quinn and K. W. Nicholls, 'Ireland in 1534', *NHI* III, p. 4; K. Simms, 'Nomadry in medieval Ireland: the origins of the Creaght or *Caoraigheacht*', *Peritia* 5 (1986), pp. 379–91; Lennon, *Sixteenth-century Ireland*, pp. 44–7.

[13] K. W. Nicholls, 'Rectory, vicarage and parish in the western Irish dioceses', *JRSAI* 101 (1971), p. 65.

for his 'hospitality', and 'the number of cows that he grazed without loss' so
well was he loved by his flock.[14]

Dowling's comments are instructive also in that they hint at another basic
feature of Gaelic and Gaelicised society that eroded the economic well-
being of the Irish episcopate. Bishop Nicholas was well respected in his
diocese, partly because he was a native of the area and partly on account of
his reputation as a learned pastor. He was thus allowed to graze his herd
free from the troublesome cattle raiding so widely and endemically practised in Gaelic Ireland.[15] Other bishops would not have been so fortunate.
Cattle raiding, in fact, was only one of a number of manifestations of a
general disorder which gripped Tudor Ireland, a disorder occasioned by the
political fragmentation of the island, and one which was particularly telling
for the church in the independent lordships. Other aspects included violent
disputes between rival clans or rival factions within the same clans and,
as the century progressed, the conflict engendered by the attempt of successive English viceroys to promote and enforce their reform policies in the
lordships.[16]

For most of the century, it was the internal fragmentation of Gaelic and
Gaelicised society that made the greatest impact upon the ecclesiastical
economy. In a society where so many petty lordships jostled with each
other to maintain or acquire power, military retaining was an inherent
characteristic and it was supported by the oppressive billeting of the lord's
soldiers upon the territories under his jurisdiction and the levying of a
range of exorbitant exactions. The system, known as 'coign and livery'
among English observers, was damaging to the economy in so far as it
discouraged agricultural improvement, and church lands were not exempt
from its effects. Thus, in 1493, the Irish parliament was forced to
reconfirm previous ordinances 'that no manner of extortion, coign or
livery should be taken or . . . imposed upon any man of Holy Church nor
upon any dweller in the glebe of Holy Church' because such acts of
parliament 'for the most part are broken and lost and despised by every

[14] *The annals of Ireland by Friar John Clyn and Thady Dowling, together with the annals of
Ross*, ed. R. Butler (Dublin, 1849), p. 32. Also suggestive in this regard is the fine of 200
cows imposed upon Cornelius MacArdle, 'the pseudo-bishop of Clogher', by Archbishop
Creagh of Armagh in 1567: C. Lennon, *An Irish prisoner of conscience of the Tudor era.
Archbishop Richard Creagh of Armagh, 1523–86* (Dublin, 2000), p. 87.

[15] *Annals of Clyn and Dowling*, ed. Butler, p. 32; H. F. Hore and J. Graves, *The social state of
the southern and eastern counties of Ireland in the sixteenth century* (Annuary of the Royal
Historical and Archaeological Association of Ireland for 1868–9), p. 144. On cattle raiding
and its adverse effects upon the Tudor Irish economy see Nicholls, 'Gaelic society and
economy', pp. 414–15.

[16] Quinn and Nicholls, 'Ireland in 1534', pp. 2–4; *SP* II, pp. 1–31; Nicholls, *Gaelic and
Gaelicised Ireland*, ch. 2; Brady, 'Court, castle and country', pp. 22–49 and *Chief Governors, passim*.

temporal person at war within this land'. Similarly, the author of an early sixteenth-century treatise advocating political reform in Ireland noted that 'the noble folk of Ireland oppresseth, spoileth the prelates of the church of Christ of their possessions and liberties; and therefore they have no fortune, ne grace, in prosperity of body ne soul'. We know, for example, that among the noble folk who levied 'coign' on the ecclesiastical properties in their territories were the earls of Desmond in Munster, the O'Neills in Ulster and the Fitzgerald earls of Kildare and their kinsmen and allies in Leinster.[17]

The political disorder of Tudor Ireland could lead to a more direct form of depredation upon episcopal estates however. Many Irish dioceses, including all of the dioceses that comprised the territories that made up the English Pale, straddled areas within the ambit of both Gaelic and crown influence. English-allied prelates possessing titles to property within the Gaelic areas of their sees were often prevented from levying their rents, as their rights to these estates were not recognised and sometimes forcibly usurped by militarily powerful and independent local Gaelic clans. The diocese of Armagh is perhaps the best known example of this. For long periods during its medieval history, the see lands in the parts '*inter Hibernicos*' were overrun by the O'Neills. But the problem also impacted heavily upon the late medieval archbishops of Dublin and their suffragans. Amongst the latter, the bishop of Kildare was particularly badly affected. In 1523 the Earl of Kildare informed Cardinal Wolsey that the 'substance' of the bishop's living lay 'in the Irishry, and will not be lightly had but by temporal power'.[18] In Dublin itself, the problem was confined to the southern part of the diocese. Dominated by the Wicklow mountains, and comprising about two-thirds of its total extent, these southern territories were ruled by the O'Toole and O'Byrne clans and 'degenerate' English marchers, and were effectively no-go areas for the archbishop and his officials. As a result, the latter exercised little or no authority within them, whether spiritual or temporal, and derived little or none of the rental

---

[17] *Statutes Ireland, Richard III – Henry VIII*, pp. 86–9; *SP* II, p. 10; K. Simms, 'The archbishops of Armagh and the O'Neills 1347–71', *IHS* 29 (1974–5), p. 52; *Octavian's Register* II, nos. 14, 43; C. A. Empey and K. Simms, 'The ordinances of the White Earl and the problem of coign in the later Middle Ages', *PRIA* 75 C, pp. 180–1; Jefferies, *Priests and prelates of Armagh*, pp. 58–9; Lyons, *Church and society in Kildare*, p. 73.

[18] Simms, 'Archbishops of Armagh and the O'Neills', p. 41; J. Watt, 'Ecclesia inter Anglicos et inter Hibernicos: confrontation and coexistence in the medieval diocese and province of Armagh', in J. F. Lydon (ed.), *The English in medieval Ireland* (Dublin, 1984), pp. 52–3; A. Lynch, 'Religion in medieval Ireland', *AH* 36 (1981), pp. 8–9; Jefferies, *Priests and prelates of Armagh*, pp. 58–9, 121–5; *SP* II, pp. 98–9; Lyons, *Church and society in Kildare*, pp. 73–4.

income and feudal dues to which they were entitled in English law.[19] Yet, as bad as the problem of depredation was in Dublin, it did not inflict the same level of damage as it did on other Irish dioceses, because it was counterbalanced by the positive effects of the stability and economic well-being of the see's Maghery heartland. Indeed, the relative order and prosperity of the diocesan heartland enabled Dublin to sustain a degree of wealth and institutional sophistication which ensured that it outshone all the remaining Irish sees, given that many of the latter were subject to a more all-encompassing and thoroughgoing poverty and turbulence. This contrast was particularly evident in relation to the see's secular cathedral, St Patrick's.

II

The 'four-square' secular cathedral, which consisted of a chapter presided over by the four dignitaries of dean, precentor, chancellor and treasurer and supplemented by a fixed number of canons holding endowed prebends, was a Norman innovation in Ireland. It was most successfully implanted in those areas where their settlements had made a lasting impact: namely, the south and east of Ireland or the ecclesiastical provinces of Dublin and Cashel.[20] The livings of Irish secular canons were financed almost exclusively by parochial tithe revenues and the favourable agricultural conditions which obtained within the environs of Dublin city ensured that there was a greater volume of tithable produce there than was common elsewhere in Ireland. These conditions not only ensured that Dublin's beneficed parochial clergy were the wealthiest on the island, with an average income per head of £22 8s. 8d., but also enabled the medieval archbishops of Dublin to construct the richest chapter on the island, endowing it 'with notable livings and diverse fat benefices'.[21] In the Tudor era, the combined net value of the livings of the chapter of St Patrick's Cathedral was nearly three to thirty-eight times greater than the combined values of the livings of the remaining cathedral chapters in the provinces of Dublin and Cashel (Table 1.2, p. 29).

[19] Quinn and Nicholls, 'Ireland in 1534', pp. 5–7; J. Murray, 'The sources of clerical income in the Tudor diocese of Dublin, c. 1530–1600', *AH* 46 (1991–2), pp. 144–5; below pp. 60–1.

[20] K. W. Nicholls, 'Medieval Irish cathedral chapters', *AH* 31 (1973), pp. 103–4. On the four-square secular cathedral generally see K. Edwards, *The English secular cathedrals in the Middle Ages* (2nd edn, Manchester, 1967).

[21] Ellis, *Ireland in the age of the Tudors*, pp. 201–3; Stanyhurst, *Holinshed's Irish chronicle*, p. 44.

Table 1.2 *Combined values of cathedral chapter livings in the provinces of Dublin and Cashel c. 1537–40, 1584–91*[22]

Chapter	Province	Net value
Dublin	Dublin	IR£667 15s. 3d.
Ferns	Dublin	IR£249 1s. 11d.
Ossory	Dublin	IR£131 3s. 4d.
Lismore	Cashel	IR£130 2s. 8d.
Kildare	Dublin	IR£86 15s. 6d.
Limerick	Cashel	IR£83 14s. 4d.
Waterford	Cashel	IR£70 17s. 0d.
Cashel	Cashel	IR£67 13s. 4d.
Cork	Cashel	IR£57 13s. 4d.
Cloyne	Cashel	IR£56 3s. 1d.
Leighlin	Dublin	IR£29 6s. 8d.
Ross	Cashel	IR£22 16s. 0d.
Emly	Cashel	IR£20 11s. 7d.
Ardfert	Cashel	IR£18 0s. 0d.

Apart from the wealth of its chapter, St Patrick's was also the most imposing cathedral institution in terms of both its physical and constitutional structure. Physically, it was the largest single ecclesiastical building in Ireland, measuring some 300 feet in length.[23] It also had the largest chapter membership, numbering twenty-seven canons in all (twenty-eight if the archbishop's honorary prebendal stall is included) as against figures for Cork of seventeen; Lismore and Limerick, sixteen each; Ferns and Cloyne, fifteen each; Waterford, fourteen; Killaloe, thirteen; Ossory, twelve; Emly, eleven; Cashel, ten; Leighlin, Kildare and Ross, eight each; and Ardfert, six.[24] Its college of vicars choral, numbering sixteen members in all, greatly surpassed the average membership of the other Irish vicars' colleges, which, if they existed at all, was generally set at four.[25] Finally, St Patrick's was the

[22] Sources as in note 5 above.
[23] E. C. Rae, 'Architecture and sculpture, 1169–1603', *NHI* II, p. 749.
[24] *Alen's register*, p. 297; E. Bolster, *A history of the diocese of Cork from the earliest times to the Reformation* (Shannon, 1972), pp. 226–33, 235; *Valor beneficiorum*, pp. 10–11, 13, 14, 17–20; G. J. Hand, 'The medieval chapter of St Mary's Limerick', in Watt, Morrill and Martin (eds.), *Medieval studies presented to A. Gwynn*, p. 76; J. B. Leslie, *Ferns clergy and parishes* (Dublin, 1936), *Ossory clergy and parishes* (Enniskillen, 1933), pp. 53–161, and *Ardfert and Aghadoe clergy and parishes* (Dundalk, 1940), pp. 15–48; D. F. Gleeson, *A history of the diocese of Killaloe* (Dublin, 1962), pp. 525–32; St J. D. Seymour, *The diocese of Emly* (Dublin, 1913), pp. 157–69 and *The succession of parochial clergy in the united diocese of Cashel and Emly* (Dublin, 1908), pp. 23–31.
[25] Nicholls, 'Medieval Irish cathedral chapters', p. 105. Strictly speaking there were seventeen vicars choral, but the prebendaries of Kilmactalway and Tipper shared a vicar in common.

only cathedral in Ireland that possessed a college of petty or minor canons.[26]

The elaborate constitutional structure and superior size of St Patrick's was not due solely to the greater availability of resources. It was also a distinctive element in the shaping and maintenance of Dublin's anglicised ecclesiastical identity throughout the medieval period, a process that went hand in hand with the establishment and preservation of the English crown's lordship in Ireland. From the beginning, Dublin and its environs, on account of the geo-physical advantages of the region, attracted heavy Anglo-Norman settlement and emerged as the focal point of the colony, containing in the city of Dublin the administrative and judicial centre of the same.[27] The politicisation of the local church swiftly followed the arrival of the Anglo-Normans. From 1181, with the appointment of John Comyn (1181–1212) under the aegis of Henry II, until the end of our period all the archbishops of Dublin were natives of England with the exception of one, Walter Fitzsimon (1484–1511), and he was a scion of an old Anglo-Norman family deeply loyal to the crown's interest in Ireland. The majority of them were royal nominees and were appointed either as a reward for service in the royal administration in England, or with a view to further service in a civil capacity in Ireland. By the Tudor era the latter feature was the norm: the archbishops being resident civil servants with ex officio membership of the Irish council and holders, generally, of high secular office, especially the chancellorship of Ireland.[28] The English origin of Dublin's medieval archbishops was an important factor in the formation of the character of the diocese, as it gave rise to a successful restructuring

Thus, there were only sixteen vicars' stalls and only sixteen actual appointees: RCB, D6/3, f. 150v (*Alen's register*, pp. 297–8); Call book of 1610 metropolitan visitation (TCD, MS 566, f. 31r).

[26] Nicholls, 'Medieval Irish cathedral chapters', p. 105 and below pp. 32–3.

[27] The region possessed a low-lying topography, comprised of largely fertile soils. Anglo-Norman settlement at the time of the Conquest was confined to relatively fertile lands below the 400-foot contour line, so it had inevitably emerged as the centre of the heaviest and most concentrated English colonisation during the Middle Ages. Although Gaelic migration into the region was not unknown after the Conquest, and actually accelerated in the late fifteenth and early sixteenth centuries, its small-holding population remained predominantly English in origin on the eve of the Reformation (Ellis, *Ireland in the age of the Tudors*, pp. 31–5).

[28] Watt, *Church in medieval Ireland*, pp. 116–17; A. Gwynn, *Anglo-Irish church life: fourteenth and fifteenth centuries* (Dublin and Melbourne, 1968), p. 70; J. D'Alton, *The memoirs of the archbishops of Dublin* (Dublin, 1838); J. R. O'Flanagan, *The lives of the lord chancellors and keepers of the Great Seal of Ireland, from the earliest times to the reign of Queen Victoria* (2 vols., London, 1870), i, *passim*; J. G. Crawford, *Anglicising the government of Ireland. The Irish privy council and the expansion of Tudor rule, 1556–1578* (Dublin, 1993), p. 42.

of the old Hiberno-Norse see according to the model of the Anglo-Norman church in England.

The cathedral of St Patrick emerged as the most potent symbol of the newly anglicised church. Before the Normans arrived Dublin already possessed a cathedral church, the priory of Holy Trinity, commonly known as Christ Church Cathedral, a regular institution staffed by Austin canons of the order of Arrouaise. It is not absolutely certain whether the founders of St Patrick's, Archbishops John Comyn and Henry of London (1213–28), intended it to supersede Christ Church. However, there is little doubt that they would have preferred a cathedral on the secular model, both because of its prebendal system, which enabled the diocesan to finance his administrative staff and household clerks, and because it was generally perceived to be more compliant to his will.[29] Thus, although Christ Church did not entirely succumb to St Patrick's – a situation which gave rise to the anomaly whereby the diocese contained two cathedrals in very close proximity, one regular, the other secular – and although it too underwent the process of anglicisation,[30] the elder cathedral was gradually displaced from the centre of diocesan power by its secular rival, its role in the administrative machine being reduced to purely formal and honorific functions. St Patrick's, by contrast, soon formed part of an administrative complex with the adjacent palace of St Sepulchre, the archbishop's main Dublin residence, in the southern suburbs of the city. It was from here, the effective nerve-centre of the diocese, demarcated by the stretch of city wall between St Nicholas's Gate and the Pole Gate and the three medieval streets of St Bride, St Kevin and St Patrick, that the archbishop's spiritual and secular jurisdictions were supervised and executed.[31] St Patrick's administrative role was concerned

---

[29] G. J. Hand, 'The rivalry of the cathedral chapters in medieval Dublin', *JRSAI* 92 (1962), pp. 195–8, *The church in the English lordship, 1216–1307* (Dublin and Sydney, 1968), pp. 9–10 and 'Medieval chapter of St. Patrick's', p. 231; Murphy, 'Archbishops and anglicisation', pp. 84–7; Edwards, *English secular cathedrals*, pp. 6–8, 21; H. J. Lawlor, *The Fasti of St Patrick's, Dublin* (Dundalk, 1930), pp. 9–10; C. H. Lawrence, *Medieval monasticism. Forms of religious life in Western Europe in the Middle Ages* (London and New York, 1984), pp. 121–3.

[30] For the early history and anglicisation of Christ Church see the following essays in K. Milne (ed.), *Christ Church Cathedral Dublin. A history* (Dublin, 2000): S. Kinsella, 'From Hiberno-Norse to Anglo-Norman, c. 1030–1300', pp. 25–52; R. Stalley, 'The construction of the medieval cathedral, c. 1030–1250' and 'The architecture of the cathedral and priory buildings, 1250–1530', pp. 53–74, 95–128; J. Lydon, 'Christ Church in the later medieval Irish world, 1300–1500', pp. 75–94.

[31] H.B. Clarke (ed.), *Irish historic towns atlas no. 11: Dublin, part 1, to 1610* (RIA, Dublin, 2002), p. 7, maps 4, 9. On the archbishop's secular jurisdiction see C. McNeill, 'The secular jurisdiction of the early archbishops of Dublin', *JRSAI* 45, 2 (1915), pp. 81–108; Wood, *Liberty of St Sepulchre*, pp. vii–xiii. For the palace of St Sepulchre generally see V. Jackson, 'The palace of St Sepulchre', *DHR* 28 (1974–5), pp. 82–92; D. O'Donovan, 'English patron, English building? The importance of St Sepulchre's archiepiscopal palace, Dublin',

exclusively with the execution of the archbishop's ordinary jurisdiction, the process of spiritual government, its main function being to provide financial support for his officials in the form of prebendal livings. To this end, Dublin's medieval archbishops had ensured that St Patrick's, rather than Christ Church, was the greater beneficiary of their largesse, being ever-ready to enhance its standing by continued and liberal endowment of its constituent parts with valuable rectorial tithes.[32] In addition, St Patrick's was also the site of the archbishop's consistory court. Sessions were held in *loco consistorii* by the west wall of the north aisle during term time.[33]

This policy of locating and financing the diocesan administration within the new secular cathedral was animated by the desire to imitate the practices prevalent in the English Church, especially the English secular cathedral. One of its major effects was that it bolstered the English identity of the diocese. A similar effect was achieved by introducing English liturgical forms into the cathedral. The performance of a daily cycle of masses and the divine offices, the *opus Dei*, was the primary function of the majority of clergy in a secular cathedral. In St Patrick's, the liturgical practices of Salisbury Cathedral, the Sarum Use, were adopted for this purpose, a process that began at the inception of the institution when Archbishop Comyn granted its canons those privileges enjoyed by their counterparts in the English foundation.[34] Thereafter, the way was open for the adoption of the full Sarum consuetude, and this was achieved by degrees throughout the thirteenth century.[35] Imitative construction was also apparent in the last major innovation affecting the cathedral's constitution before the Reformation – the erection of a college of petty canons – a development which clearly demonstrates the influence of the English backgrounds of Dublin's medieval archbishops upon the institutional evolution of their diocese. The

---

in S. Duffy (ed.), *Medieval Dublin IV. Proceedings of the Friends of Medieval Dublin Symposium 2002* (Dublin, 2003), pp. 253–78.

[32] Otway-Ruthven, 'Medieval church lands', p. 54. The tithe endowments are recorded in *Dignitas decani, passim.*

[33] 'Incipiunt statuta consistorii Dublinensis a Johanne Alano septimo . . . archiepiscopo anno Christi 1530', RCB, D6/4, pp. 36–40; *Alen's register*, pp. 274–5, 297; Marsh's Library, MS Z4.2.19, pp. 1–126 *passim* (Act book of the Dublin consistory court, Michaelmas 1596 to Michaelmas 1599); V. Jackson, *The monuments in St. Patrick's Cathedral, Dublin* (Dublin, 1987), p. 2.

[34] Edwards, *English secular cathedrals*, pp. 56–9; S. E. Lehmberg, *The reformation of cathedrals. Cathedrals in English society, 1485–1603* (Princeton, 1988), pp. 9–12; *Dignitas decani*, p. 41.

[35] Ibid., pp. 5–7, 12–16, 27–9, 38–9, 97–8; G.J. Hand, 'Cambridge University Additional MS. 710', *RN* 2 (1958), pp. 17–32; W. Hawkes, 'The liturgy in Dublin, 1200–1500: manuscript sources', ibid., pp. 33–8. The Sarum liturgy was also adopted in Christ Church Cathedral for which see A.J. Fletcher, 'Liturgy in the later medieval cathedral priory', and B. Boydell, 'Music in the medieval cathedral priory', in Milne (ed.), *Christ Church Cathedral*, pp. 129–41, 142–8.

college was erected in the 1430s under the aegis of Archbishop Richard Talbot. And it was his experience of ecclesiastical life in England which provided the precedent for his action: he served as precentor of Hereford, one of only two English secular cathedrals where minor or petty canons served in the choir during the Middle Ages. Like the dean and chapter and vicars choral before them, the English identity of the college of petty canons was further enhanced when, nearly one hundred years later in 1519, Henry VIII granted them royal letters of incorporation.[36]

The elaborate structure of Dublin's secular cathedral contrasted most strikingly with the cathedral system operating in the predominantly Gaelic provinces of Tuam and Armagh, in the west and north of Ireland respectively. In the western province the four-square pattern had been adopted in the twelfth and thirteenth centuries, but it underwent a general regression in the fifteenth century to a very simple pattern. This was due perhaps to a reduction in contact between the Gaelic west and English east of Ireland, though the more likely explanation is that it resulted from the relative poverty of the individual cathedrals. During the Tudor period, then, the common pattern of cathedral organisation in Tuam was that of a chapter consisting of a dean, archdeacon and sacrist and an unfixed number of canons – the latter feature being the most pronounced departure from the standard English model – though there was a fixed number of prebendal endowments. The endowments, themselves, did not consist of full rectories but very small portions of parochial livings, which, individually, would not have supported a single canon. From time to time they were arranged in different combinations, a single canon holding more than one, which meant that the number of canons making up the chapter varied accordingly. In the northern province of Armagh, the most remote from English political and ecclesiastical influence, the 'four-square' secular cathedral, consisting of secular canons with definite and fixed prebends, had made even less impact. In fact, there was a sizeable number of completely unendowed chapters in the northern province – Clogher, Derry, Raphoe and Ardagh – and even Meath, the diocese which in most other respects resembled Dublin, especially in regard to its wealth and anglicised ethos, possessed no cathedral foundation at all.[37]

The capitular and institutional simplicity of the cathedrals in the independent lordships of Ireland were also mirrored in the physical condition of the same, many of which would have been indistinguishable from the average English parish church. This was partly a legacy of the

---

[36] *Dignitas decani*, pp. 44–6, 171–2; Lawlor, *Fasti of St Patrick's*, pp. 32–4; J. H. Bernard, 'Richard Talbot, Archbishop and Chancellor', *PRIA* 35 C (1919), pp. 224–6; Hand, 'Cambridge University Additional MS. 710', pp. 31–2; Edwards, *English secular cathedrals*, pp. 258–9.

[37] Nicholls, 'Medieval Irish cathedral chapters', pp. 105–11.

celto-monastic organisation of the early Irish Church, which had given rise to the formation of a disproportionate number of dioceses relative to the size of the island. As a result the internal resources available in each diocese for the construction of cathedrals had been correspondingly restricted.[38] Furthermore, by the sixteenth century a number of these ecclesiastical sites had lost their original importance as settlement locations, and retained nothing more than their ancient religious associations.[39] The great Gothic cathedrals of England and the continent, of which Dublin's two cathedrals provided modest examples – both of them fit neatly into the pattern of early English Gothic – were associated with relatively large urban environments which contained sufficient concentrations of wealth and patronage for their construction and maintenance.[40] While much remains to be unearthed concerning the nature of Gaelic settlement in the medieval and Tudor periods, it is clear that permanent and recognisably urban settlements were not a prominent feature of the Gaelic landscape. Settlement was transient, in line with the pastoral-nomadic bent of Gaelic agriculture, and the church was predominantly rural in character.[41]

There were, however, more fundamental differences between the English Irish and Gaelic Irish ecclesiastical polities than the absence in the latter of much of the outward structural paraphernalia and splendour associated with local churches in more prosperous areas of Europe. It is clear that in Gaelic Ireland, as elsewhere throughout the Celtic fringes of Europe, Christianity had failed historically to supplant certain aspects of the Gaelic pre-Christian social system. One implication of this was that the church in Gaelic Ireland waived important areas of the canon law of Western Christendom, albeit with the tacit approval of Rome, in favour of its own traditional social codes, a feature particularly evident in the areas of marriage and sexuality.[42] This, in turn, gave rise to further divergence from the

---

[38] R. A. Stalley, *Architecture and sculpture in Ireland 1150–1350* (Dublin, 1971), p. 58, and 'Irish Gothic and English fashion', in Lydon (ed.), *English in medieval Ireland*, p. 67; T. B. Barry, *The archaeology of medieval Ireland* (London, 1987), p. 143.

[39] Nicholls, 'Gaelic society and economy', pp. 399, 403.

[40] R. A. Stalley, 'The medieval sculpture of Christ Church Cathedral, Dublin', in H. B. Clarke (ed.), *Medieval Dublin: the making of a metropolis* (Blackrock, 1990), pp. 202–26, *Architecture and sculpture in Ireland*, pp. 58–71, 'Irish Gothic and English fashion', pp. 65, 71–3, and his essays cited in note 30 above; E. C. Rae, 'The medieval fabric of the cathedral church of St Patrick in Dublin', *JRSAI* 109 (1979), pp. 29–73; M. O'Neill, 'Design sources for St Patrick's cathedral, Dublin, and its relationship to Christ Church Cathedral', *PRIA* 100 C (2000), pp. 207–56.

[41] Ellis, *Ireland in the age of the Tudors*, pp. 40, 193–4; Nicholls, 'Gaelic society and economy', pp. 403–4; M.J. Haren, 'A description of Clogher cathedral in the early sixteenth century', *Clogher Record* 12/1 (1985), pp. 48–54.

[42] Nicholls, *Gaelic and Gaelicised Ireland*, pp. 83–7; A. Cosgrove, 'Marriage in medieval Ireland', in A. Cosgrove (ed.), *Marriage in Ireland* (Dublin, 1985), pp. 28–34.

norms of European ecclesiastical practice and organisation, and is most strikingly illustrated in the hereditary nature of the clerical profession. Concubinage among the clergy was a widely accepted practice in a society where sexual expression was uninhibited. Many priests' sons followed their fathers into holy orders and many succeeded directly to their fathers' benefices, obtaining the necessary dispensations from Rome.[43] The problem with this system was that it sometimes led to a lessened sense of vocation in the profession, and a deeply ingrained secularisation of the church in which the cure of souls was neglected.

Secularisation was arguably the most pronounced characteristic of the church in Gaelic and Gaelicised Ireland during the late medieval and Reformation periods. At the parochial level it was apparent in the activity of unscrupulous benefice seekers at the Roman Curia, which caused immense problems when the papal court entertained the claims of manifestly unsuitable candidates for preferment.[44] At the level of the diocese it revealed itself where locally powerful clans controlled the nomination and admission of prelates to their sees.[45] The most damaging aspect of the phenomenon occurred where clerics, including bishops, shaking off the moral constraints and spiritual requirements of their offices, acted in the capacity of lay, warlord chieftains, an excess which could and did lead to ecclesiastical chaos and which certainly required some degree of reform. Early sixteenth-century Ardagh, as portrayed in the report presented by Henry VIII's proctors at the Roman Curia in 1517 to further the suit of his chosen candidate for the vacant bishopric, is the best known, though not unique, example of this. The king's witnesses deposed that the cathedral city lay in the mountains in the midst of woods, containing only four timber huts and few inhabitants on account of the 'continual enmities and quarrels' which prevailed there. The disorder was occasioned by the efforts of the late bishop, William O'Farrell (1479–1516), chief of the O'Farrells of Annaly, to exercise temporal lordship over the neighbouring peoples and brought ecclesiastical life to a virtual standstill. The cathedral itself was in ruins,

[43] Nicholls, *Gaelic and Gaelicised Ireland*, pp. 106–13; Watt, *Church in medieval Ireland*, pp. 185–7 and 'Confrontation and coexistence in Armagh', pp. 55–6; Lynch, 'Religion in medieval Ireland', pp. 4, 8; Ellis, *Ireland in the age of the Tudors*, pp. 194–5; K. Simms, 'Women in Gaelic society during the age of transition', in M. MacCurtain and M. O'Dowd (eds.), *Women in Early Modern Ireland* (Dublin, 1991), pp. 36–8; Lennon, *Sixteenth-century Ireland*, pp. 126–7; A. Cosgrove, 'Ireland beyond the Pale, 1399–1460', *NHI* II, pp. 587–8.

[44] Nicholls, *Gaelic and Gaelicised Ireland*, pp. 117–21; Watt, *Church in medieval Ireland*, pp. 188–92; Ellis, *Ireland in the age of the Tudors*, p. 199.

[45] On the deleterious effects that this entailed for one diocese, Elphin, see F. X. Martin, 'Confusion abounding: Bernard O'Higgin, O. S. A., bishop of Elphin', in A. Cosgrove and D. McCartney (eds.), *Studies in Irish history presented to R. Dudley Edwards* (Dublin, 1979), pp. 38–44.

containing only one altar under an open sky. It had no sacristy, bells, nor bell-tower and barely enough liturgical accoutrements to celebrate a single mass. Only one priest officiated there and even then, rarely. Even allowing for hyperbole the report reveals that the ecclesiastical condition of Ardagh was particularly wretched. The extent of the secularisation of the local church is apparent in the record of Bishop William's obit in the Annals of Connacht. He is described as the bishop of Annaly, the O'Farrells' lordship, and not Ardagh.[46]

Set against the poverty-stricken and, at times, severely disordered character of the church in the independent lordships of Gaelic and Gaelicised Ireland, the maintenance of basic standards in Dublin made it appear as the very apogee of ecclesiastical order and sophistication. The metropolitan cathedral of St Patrick in the suburbs of the city of Dublin offered a startling contrast to Ardagh. This was especially apparent in the care taken over the performance of the liturgy and the maintenance of the church fabric, as revealed by the annual administration of the revenues attached to the common fund or economy of the cathedral, which was overseen by its proctor.[47] Until the introduction of the English vernacular liturgy of the Elizabethan settlement of 1560, the cathedral's liturgy consisted of a daily series of Latin masses and divine offices, sung and performed according to the age-old and elaborate Sarum use.[48] The stalls in the choir were normally occupied by some nine to thirteen residentiary canons (out of a total of twenty-seven), four petty canons, sixteen vicars choral and six boy choristers.[49] An organist was hired to accompany them and paid at the rate of £3 6s. 9d. per annum. The boy choristers were trained by their master, one of the canons or petty canons, in the art of prick and part song, the latter receiving a stipend of four marks annually. Money was also spent to keep

---

[46] A. Theiner, *Vetera monumenta Hibernorum et Scotorum* (Rome, 1864), p. 521; A. Gwynn, *The medieval province of Armagh 1470–1545* (Dundalk, 1946), pp. 154–7; A. Martin Freeman, *Annala Connacht . . . A.D. 1224–1544* (Dublin Institute for Advanced Studies, 1944), pp. 632–3; Nicholls, *Gaelic and Gaelicised Ireland*, pp. 115–16.

[47] On this see the account of Sir John Andowe, general proctor of the economy, 24 June 1509–24 June 1510, RCB, C2, no. 106 (printed in Mason, *History of St Patrick's*, App. XVI, pp. xxvii–xxxi).

[48] The vernacular Edwardian Prayer Book services were never used in St Patrick's because the cathedral was suppressed for the duration of the reign. For a bibliography of printed versions of the Sarum liturgical texts used in St Patrick's see Hand, 'Cambridge University Additional MS. 710', pp. 19–20.

[49] *Alen's register*, pp. 297–8; Lawlor, *Fasti of St Patrick's*, pp. 32–3, 36. Very little information on the residence of the canons now survives. The figures supplied above are based on headcounts of the canons, derived from the signatures appended to the following leases granted by the dean and chapter: lease of the tithes of Malahide to Robert Yans, 1538 (Bodleian, MS Talbot b. 49/10); lease of the manor of Deansrath to Finian Basnet, 1546 (RCB, C2/2, no. 7); lease of a house in St Patrick's Street to Patrick Dowdall, 1562 (RCB, C2/2, no. 11).

the choir's hymn books in repair or to make new ones. In Proctor Andowe's account of 1509–10 it is recorded that Sir William Growe, one of the petty canons, was paid a fee of 6s. 8d. for writing and making the musical notation in the same, as well as 4d. to buy two ounces of vermilion to make the 'short notes' ('notulas'). A beadle or usher was employed to give the liturgy added solemnity. He acted as a kind of master of ceremonies – his duties including leading the dean and his clergy in the elaborate processions associated with the Sarum liturgy – and was paid at the rate of £4 per year.[50]

Another important officer was the sacristan who was in charge of the church plate and vestments, and who received an annual fee of four marks. A high premium was put on maintaining the church plate and clerical garb. In the year June 1509 to June 1510, for instance, a Dublin goldsmith was paid 4s. 7d. for gold and his labour in the gilding of the chalices and paten of the high altar, and one Margery Warde received 14s. for repairing twenty-one hoods belonging to the clergy. Concern was also shown to create a fitting ambience for worship. The proctor's account of 1509–10 reveals that a new image of the crucifix had been recently set up in the rood loft, that steps were taken to prevent pigeons entering the cathedral, and that £12 5s. 2d. was laid out upon $388\frac{1}{4}$ pounds of wax to light the church during the year. The proctor would also employ a host of tradesmen, including carpenters, tilers and masons, to carry out the more basic repairs upon the cathedral from year to year. Altogether some £139 7s. 10d. in tithe and land rents was set aside annually to meet these liturgical and main-tenance expenses, as well as casual revenues, which included receipts from the oblation boxes and church pardoners, worth £7 19s. 5½d. and £10 13s. 4d. respectively in 1509–10.[51]

III

While all of this was unremarkable in the context of the church in Europe as a whole, and in Tudor England in particular, it is worth dwelling upon to emphasise the fact that Dublin shared in this ecclesiastical conventionality and, in doing so, existed in a different ecclesiastical world to that obtaining in many of the independent lordships. Indeed, in the course of the Middle Ages, Dublin's ecclesiastical conventionality had come to be enshrined as a symbolic element within the English ethos of the local community, both

---

[50] RCB, C2, no. 106, mm. 1, 2 (Mason, *History of St Patrick's*, pp. xxviii, xxx). On the Sarum processions generally see T. Bailey, *The processions of Sarum and the western church* (Toronto, 1971).

[51] RCB, C2, no. 106, mm. 1, 2 (Mason, *History of St Patrick's*, pp. xxvii–xxxi).

because it had originated and developed out of the community's own adherence to the English ecclesiological norms that had been introduced after the Anglo-Norman conquest, and because of the parallel adoption by the local church of many of the attitudes that formed this English ethos, such as a pronounced Anglophile sentiment, a strong royalist sympathy and a deep aversion to the politics, social organisation, law and church life of Gaelic Ireland. By the early decades of the sixteenth century, the symbolic identification of church and communal ethos was evident in the formal links operating between Dublin's ecclesiastical establishment and the institutions of crown government in the lordship, in the espousal by the same of populistic royalism, and in the elitist and exclusivist attitudes it exhibited towards the Gaelic Irish, all of which were exemplified by Dublin's two cathedrals.

Christ Church Cathedral had a long-standing association with the political and judicial institutions of English Ireland. Parliaments and councils, for example, were often held within its precincts, while each year at the conclusion of the Michaelmas and Hilary terms the prior and his conventual brethren would close proceedings in the courts of Chancery, Exchequer and the two benches with the singing of hymns and antiphons. The cathedral also provided a focus for the expression of loyalty to the crown. When queens of England successfully bore royal progeny it was the custom of the people of Dublin to proceed to Christ Church where the *Te Deum Laudamus* would be sung 'to the laud and praise of God and honour of our said princes and princesses'.[52]

The less attractive face of the English Irish communal ethos was evident in the bias shown against the Gaelic Irish within the statutes of her sister cathedral, St Patrick's. In January 1515, for instance, in an agreement drawn up between Archbishop Rokeby and the cathedral chapter concerning the dean's jurisdiction and capitular discipline, it was enacted that the old custom denying membership of the cathedral to anyone 'of the Irish nation, manners and blood' should be specially approved. Significantly, the new statute was strictly enforced in St Patrick's, a fact that did not go unnoticed by ambitious clerics who wished to acquire a lucrative canonry in the cathedral. One such man was Christopher Lynam, a native of Co. Meath and a chaplain of Charles Brandon, the duke of Suffolk. In August 1516, Lynam moved to quash certain rumours and doubts that were then circulating about the Englishness of both himself and his brother, Richard,

---

[52] H. G. Richardson and G. O. Sayles, *The Irish parliament in the middle ages* (London, 1952), pp. 190–1; Vice-Treasurer Brabazon's account 1534–7 (TNA: PRO, SP 65/1, no. 2, f. 22v [*LP* XII. ii, no. 1310]); *SP* II, p. 545. See also Lydon, 'Christ Church in the later medieval Irish world', pp. 84–6.

through the holding of an inquisition in Mellifont Abbey. The findings of
the inquisition – that Christopher's father was truly English, that his sur-
name was 'Lynam, and not Lynnane, nor Leannane or Leannachan', and
that he had brought his two sons up in the English manner according to the
customs of Ireland – cleared the way for his later appointment to the
prebend of Mulhuddart in St Patrick's.[53]

The symbolic identification of church and communal ethos could also be
expressed in a more explicit manner. The tensions that were engendered by
particular aspects of the early Reformation campaign in Dublin – such as
the Tudor regime's attempt in 1537 to override the privilege of the chapter
of St Patrick's to freely elect a dean, and the threatened suppression of
Christ Church Cathedral during the period 1539–43 – forced the local
community, in endeavouring to protect the interests of the local church, to
formulate more direct articulations of the idea.[54] The defence of St Patrick's
privilege was propounded in a letter to Thomas Cromwell by six members
of the cathedral chapter – Henry Parker, James Humphrey, Simon Jeffrey,
Bartholomew Fitzsimon, John Wogan and Robert Fiablis (or Fiable) – all of
whom were of English Irish extraction, 'of this land's birth' according to
Lord Deputy Grey and the Irish council, and otherwise confirmed by the
Anglo-Norman and English provenance of their surnames. The prebendaries began by informing Cromwell of the historic links existing between
their cathedral and the English monarchy; stressing, with indignant pride,
the crown's ancient patronage – 'our church is of the king's foundation' –
and that their right to elect a dean was firmly rooted in the series of
'liberties, statutes and establishments commendable' granted by Henry VIII
and his progenitors. These privileges had ensured that good, grave and
learned men were appointed to the office whereby 'God hath been well
served' and, most importantly, 'the king daily prayed for'. If such men had
not been appointed, they continued, the king's grants for the 'maintenance
of good order' would not have been executed and

this his grace's church should or long since have been in such case as is the churches
in Irishry which churches digressing from the king's grants and privileges do take
unlearned, simpler and unmeet persons contrary their gifts and privileges whereby

---

[53] *Alen's register*, pp. 262–3; Mason, *History of St Patrick's*, pp. 143–4; *Octavian's register* II,
no. 146; Lawlor, *Fasti of St Patrick's*, p. 137. It appears that Lynam was later deprived of
the prebend by Archbishop Alen, probably on account of non-residence (NAI, RC 9/3,
p. 66; Lambeth MS 602, ff. 115rv (*Carew MSS, 1515–74*, p. 122).

[54] S. T. B. Percival, 'The Basnetts during the 16th and 17th centuries', *CNWAHSJ* 49 (1962),
pp. 29–30; Lord Deputy Grey to Cromwell, 19 January 1540 (*SP* II, pp. 544–5, misplaced
in 1538); the mayor and aldermen of Dublin to Cromwell, 23 January 1540 (ibid.,
pp. 545–6, misplaced in 1538); *SP* III, pp. 130–1, 414–16, 468, 484, 489–90.

not God is honoured neither the church ne kings prayed for nor yet any good service done to his grace as it appeareth many ways to them that hath here experience.[55]

The basic contention of the prebendaries, then, was that the church in Dublin, as manifested by St Patrick's Cathedral, stood for the maintenance of good ecclesiastical order because it existed, voluntarily and contentedly, within a stable temporal polity under the jurisdiction and protection of the English crown: the fountainhead of order and civility. The participation of their church as a corporate entity within the crown's lordship had been actively pursued: St Patrick's Cathedral had upheld with unremitting devotion those privileges – 'our old commendable grants' – bestowed by the crown in the centuries following the Anglo-Norman incursion into Ireland. Indeed these privileges formed the cornerstone of the church and had ensured that it was preserved free from the disorder and chaos which contaminated the 'churches in Irishry', whose habits and customs were perceived to be aberrant digressions from the civilising influence of royal ecclesiastical privilege. Thus, like their peers in the lay community – the nobility, gentry, and citizenry of the inner Pale and coastal towns of eastern Ireland – the canons of St Patrick's posed as protectors of English civility, in this case English ecclesiastical civility, on an island where all around them the disorder of Gaelic custom and practice held sway and threatened to swamp it.[56] In developing and presenting this argument they displayed a clearly defined sense of their own English identity, their loyalty to the crown and its lordship over Ireland, and a sense of superiority to the Gaelic Irish whose church, they argued, fulfilled no proper function and whose clergy they derided as 'unlearned, simpler and unmeet persons'. To override their liberties, therefore, would not only be an unjustified attack on the cathedral, but an affront also to everything that it represented. Ultimately, it would undermine the condition and health of English Irish society, for their cathedral church, as a symbol of English civility, was an important bastion of the same.

The defenders of Christ Church Cathedral, the mayor and citizens of Dublin, also advanced a similar argument.[57] The core of their defence was based on the contention that Christ Church Cathedral represented an important focus for the expression of civic pride and that its destruction 'would be a great desolation and foul waste and deformity of the said city'. Underpinning their argument, however, was the notion that the existence of the cathedral within the city – it was the only major religious foundation

---

[55] Prebendaries of St Patrick's to Cromwell, 20 Feb 1537 (TNA: PRO SP 60/4, no. 10).

[56] On the Palesmen's views of the Gaelic Irish see N. Canny, *The formation of the old English elite in Ireland* (O'Donnell lecture, Dublin, 1975), pp. 10–12.

[57] *SP* II, pp. 545–6.

within the old city walls – not only contributed to the formation of a corporate civic spirit, but was an indispensable element in the maintenance of a specifically English civic spirit. Thus they related how Christ Church stood 'in the midst of the said city and chamber in like manner as Paul's church is in London', a parallel which conveyed a sense of mutual participation by Dublin and London in a common English civic heritage. On one level, then, the mayor and citizens were arguing that the suppression of Christ Church Cathedral would have the same demoralising effect upon the citizens of Dublin as the destruction of St Paul's would have upon the London citizenry. However, it was also being argued implicitly that the disappearance of the cathedral would have a denuding effect upon the Englishness of their city, for the cathedral was a key element in the ordered civic landscape, a landscape which in turn formed an important layer in the composition of the fabric of English Irish society as a whole. To suppress the cathedral, then, would be to assault that fabric, an inference explicitly drawn by the mayor and citizens who warned that such an act would be 'a great comfort and encouraging of our sovereign lord's the king's Irish enemies'. Thus, like the prebendaries of St Patrick's, the mayor and citizens drew attention to their community's vision of the local church as an important bulwark in the maintenance of their English identity. Above all it was a symbol of order and civility and, as such, it offered a symbolic resistance to the perceived disorders and incivilities which obtained in the independent lordships wherein dwelt 'the king's Irish enemies'.

The indigenous perception of the institutional church in Dublin – as a symbol of the political, social and cultural order of English Ireland – and the accompanying belief that its ecclesiastical structures and societal contexts were superior to their Gaelic Irish equivalents, had been reciprocated and championed by Dublin's English-born archbishops throughout the Middle Ages. Their attitudes in this regard were most evident in the stand they adopted in their age-old dispute with the archbishops of Armagh concerning primatial titles and functions in the Irish Church.[58] At base this dispute was about ecclesiastical jurisdiction and, of course, its fiscal implications: the archbishops of Dublin were loath to admit the validity of ecclesiastical titles which might entail jurisdictional subjection to another Irish ecclesiastical authority and the loss of precious judicial business and fees. It also encompassed the archbishops' concern to maintain their 'honour' as spiritual noblemen in a feudal world: they were adamant, for

---

[58] The best accounts of the primatial dispute are J. Watt, 'The disputed primacy of the medieval Irish Church' in P. Linehan (ed.), *Proceedings of the 7th International Congress of Medieval Canon Law, Cambridge, 1984* (Vatican City, 1988; Monumenta Iuris Canonici, series C, Subsidia, viii), pp. 373–83; P. Talbot, *Primatus Dubliniensis, or the primacy of the see of Dublin*, ed. W. E. Kenny (Dublin, 1947), pp. lvii–lxii.

instance, that no ecclesiastic from outside the province of Dublin, saving the pope's envoys, should display the symbols and tokens which signified the dignity and authority of their offices within the archbishop's own domain. To this end they accumulated royal and papal grants forbidding other bishops, including Armagh, to have their crosses borne before them in Dublin.[59]

Underpinning all of this, however, was the politico-cultural dimension. Dublin's medieval archbishops refused to acknowledge the claim of Armagh to the primacy because it would have meant effectively that the political and cultural centre of Anglo-Norman Ireland was of inferior ecclesiastical status to an entity dominated by a pervasive Gaelic culture; for, despite the fact that the see of Armagh came into the possession of English archbishops in the later Middle Ages, virtually the entire province remained beyond the ambit of crown influence until the beginning of the seventeenth century.[60] Indeed Armagh's traditional seniority in the Irish Church and its claim to primatial status was intimately connected with its Gaelic heritage. The claim was based on the see's association with St Patrick and had been enshrined in the ancient celto-monastic organisation of the church: the archbishop of Armagh being primate because he was deemed to be the coarb or successor of Ireland's apostle. To counteract this claim Dublin's early Anglo-Norman archbishops had secured papal privileges, which made their diocese exempt from any assertion of a superior ecclesiastical jurisdiction. These grants – the first of which occurred in 1182 during the episcopacy of Dublin's first Anglo-Norman archbishop, John Comyn – were quite new in the context of previous papal grants to the see and, as such, undoubtedly represented politically motivated and precautionary measures aimed at denying Armagh the opportunity of exercising its traditional primacy in Dublin at a time when it was held by Gaelic bishops. Their advent also signalled the first step in Dublin's pursuit of primatial status for itself.[61]

Primatial status was 'quietly annexed' by the see of Dublin in the fourteenth century, an action which was legitimated by Edward III's proposal that the feuding prelates should adopt the compromise formula that he had

[59] J. Watt, *The church and the two nations in medieval Ireland* (Cambridge, 1970), pp. 109–10 and 'Disputed primacy', p. 376; *Octavian's register* II, no. 242; *Alen's register*, pp. 43, 207–8.

[60] John Watt cautioned against explaining the primacy dispute solely in terms of ethnic rivalries. He did concede, however, that Dublin's acquisition of primatial status may have been an 'aggrandisement' related to its growth 'into the colonial capital'. This clearly did have politico-cultural connotations, and these were seized upon by Archbishops Alen and Browne in the sixteenth century when promoting or reflecting upon Dublin's primatial claims (Watt, 'Disputed primacy', pp. 376, 380; below pp. 43–4, 202).

[61] Simms, 'Archbishops of Armagh and the O'Neills', pp. 42–3; J. Watt, 'Gaelic polity and cultural identity', *NHI* II, p. 341 and *Church and the two nations*, pp. 108–12.

successfully brokered between the archbishops of Canterbury and York in England. In this settlement, Dublin was to acquire the title 'primate of Ireland' and Armagh 'primate of all Ireland'. Dublin's archbishops adopted their title and, by the fifteenth century, it was in habitual use. The archbishops of Armagh, however, were unwilling to compromise and the dispute between the sees raged on throughout the fifteenth and sixteenth centuries and even into the seventeenth century where it survived both within the post-Reformation Catholic Church and the Protestant Church of Ireland.[62] In the sixteenth century the initiation of political and ecclesiastical reform policies in Ireland under the aegis of the Tudor regime gave the dispute added impetus. Despite the emergence of these new contexts, however, the Tudor archbishops of Dublin thought about the primacy in much the same way as their predecessors had done, either defending their own primatial style or casting covetous eyes upon Armagh's in order to maintain or magnify the identity and dignity of their anglicised see. One instance of the dispute from the period shows the traditional basis of their preoccupation and reveals how enduring it was.

Archbishop John Alen's concern with the primatial question was influenced by his involvement in Cardinal Thomas Wolsey's efforts to extend his legatine jurisdiction throughout Ireland in the 1520s. Objections had been raised against the constitutional proprieties of the cardinal's efforts – the bulls pertaining to his legacy contained no reference as to their validity in Ireland – and the resistance which this provoked, in conjunction with the restricted influence of crown authority in the lordship, an authority which Wolsey himself represented as the king's chief minister, determined they had met with little success for most of the decade.[63] In what was to prove his final and most determined bid to enforce his legateship in the lordship, the cardinal sent his trusted and pugnacious servant Alen to Ireland in February 1529, and designated him his vice-legate. As conceived by Wolsey and Alen, this title conferred on the latter a theoretical suzerainty over the Irish Church through which, it was hoped, some form of centralised and anglicised ecclesiastical administration would be effected in the same. However, only six months after Alen's arrival in Dublin the cardinal fell from grace having failed to secure Henry VIII's divorce from Katherine of Aragon and, in his wake, Alen's vice-legateship fell into abeyance. The interesting thing is that the archbishop still hankered after some form of overall leadership in the Irish church, a position which his vice-legateship had entailed and one which was implicit in the archbishop of Armagh's primatial style. Thus, in a

---

[62] Watt, 'Disputed primacy', pp. 379–82; *Primatus Dubliniensis*, pp. lx–lxxi.
[63] Murray, 'Archbishop Alen and reform', p. 8; P. Gwyn, *The King's cardinal. The rise and fall of Thomas Wolsey* (London, 1990), pp. 252–3.

terse note appended to a thirteenth-century deed transcribed into his register in which one of his predecessors in the see of Dublin was addressed as 'primate of all Ireland', Alen observed wistfully that this was a 'wonderful title' ('mirabilis . . . titulus'). Like many of the medieval archbishops of Dublin, then, Alen desired Armagh's primatial title, for it would have conferred upon him and his see a full and unambiguous suzerainty over the Irish Church.[64] While his view reflected a newly emerging confidence and expansionist outlook which was to characterise the new breed of English administrator in Tudor Ireland, his reasoning as to why Dublin should hold this position was firmly grounded in tradition.

It is clear from his writings elsewhere that Alen based his belief in the efficacy of Dublin acquiring the title of 'primate of all Ireland' upon the traditionally English politico-cultural orientation of the diocese. He spoke, for example, of his metropolitan see as the 'handmaid' ('ancilla') of the English Church and proudly enunciated that his secular cathedral of St Patrick was a 'notable follower' ('insignis pediseque') of the Church of Sarum in England. Inherent within these descriptions there were connotations of the see's Englishness and its adoption of English ecclesiastical mores. The Archbishop also perceived his own primatial title in bold politico-cultural terms. Writing to Thomas Cromwell in March 1532 he casually referred to himself as 'primate of his [the king's] church in Ireland', a description which indicates that he and others conceived his archiepiscopal dignity, and accompanying primatial title, as conferring upon him an ex officio leadership of that part of the Irish Church which, in political terms, showed allegiance to the English crown. Again, this conception was founded upon the Englishness and royalism of his see and, like the argument of the prebendaries of St Patrick's Cathedral, it contained an inherent and laudatory avowal of the see's preservation of ecclesiastical liberty through its participation in the beneficent English secular constitution, qualities which Alen believed the entire Irish Church should aspire to.[65] The political realities which prevailed in Alen's lifetime – royal influence in Ireland was confined to a small area around Dublin – determined that his thoughts and desires concerning the promotion of an anglicised disposition throughout the church in Ireland, under Dublin's natural leadership, remained nothing more than a pipe dream. Nevertheless, if he was unable to bring about any expansion in the area of English ecclesiastical influence he did fight vigorously to maintain and defend the dignity and status of his own diocese, a diocese in which that same influence still retained a noteworthy vitality. Thus, in regard to the question of the primacy, he was careful to ensure that

---

[64] Murray, 'Archbishop Alen and reform', p. 9.
[65] Ibid., p. 10; *SP* II, p. 159; *Alen's register*, pp. 281, 289.

there would be no admission of Armagh's dignity in his own province and, to this end, he engaged in a dispute with Archbishop Cromer in 1533 over rights of precedence in the seating arrangements for the parliament of that year held at Dublin.[66]

The value of exploring those views which were formulated and advanced in the 1530s by Archbishop Alen, the mayor and citizens of Dublin and the canons of St Patrick's Cathedral, lies in the fact that they depict the then predominant perception of the diocese of Dublin as an institutional entity. Taken together, they delineate the composite elements that formed the see's contemporary and definitively English character during the same period, a character forged in and inherited from its medieval past. This character was historically significant because it proved to be an enduring and potent manifestation of the political and religious culture of the Anglo-Norman colony in Ireland. With the initiation of state-sponsored religious reform in the sixteenth century, however, it was to take on an even greater significance, for it appeared to provide the Tudor administration in Ireland with a genuine and exploitable asset in its appointed task of implementing and enforcing the crown's religious innovations.

Dublin's character, and all that it encompassed, appeared advantageous to the Tudor regime in a variety of ways. In the first instance, the regime could expect that the oft-professed loyalty of the local ecclesiastical establishment to the English crown, so much in contrast to the attitudes of the ecclesiastical elites of Gaelic and Gaelicised Ireland, would facilitate the acceptance of the new religious dispensation amongst the local community, especially those aspects touching the royal prerogative, namely the crown's assumption of supremacy over the Irish Church. Secondly, the fact that the local ecclesiastical establishment and the royal administration were deeply intertwined in the person of the archbishop of Dublin, traditionally a royal appointee and an integral figure in the political community of English Ireland, meant that well-established points of contact between the two were in existence at the outset of the Reformation. Thus the archbishop was well placed, being a royal servant, a figure of political and social power, and the superior ecclesiastical authority in English Ireland, to assume the mantle of leadership in introducing and enforcing the crown's new religious policies. More importantly, the latter's prospects of success in this regard were considerably enhanced by the cultural traditions and institutional strength of his diocese. The fact that many of its inhabitants saw themselves as English and spoke the English language was a very important feature, given that many of the major innovations associated with the Reformation either concerned the introduction of vernacular forms of the liturgy or were

[66] Ibid., p. 300.

expected to be propagated or disseminated by preaching in the vernacular. Similarly, because the Tudors chose to implement reform through the pre-existing ecclesiastical structures, Dublin's superior wealth and the strength and sophistication of its institutional fabric were additional advantages.

These points are well exemplified in the opinion expressed by Sir Henry Sidney, one of the most committed reformers amongst the Elizabethan viceroys in Ireland, on the occasion of the translation of Adam Loftus from the see of Armagh to Dublin in 1567. Although Loftus was moving from the primatial see to Dublin, Sidney perceived his translation as a promotion to higher things, because it brought with it increased benefits and a much greater wealth. 'You shall find yourself advanced in honour or living', he wrote to Loftus. More significantly, Sidney noted that Dublin was the centre of English Ireland – 'the city of Dublin is the chief place within this realm' – and he believed it to be, on account of its central position in the English body politic in Ireland, and its English culture, a culture which rendered it capable of receiving the tenets of reformed religion as conveyed in the English vernacular, the 'most open for any good example, so it will grow (by your good and careful order) to reformation in religion'. Because of its politico-cultural traditions, then, Dublin was deemed to be the most fertile ground in Ireland for receiving the Reformation, as transmitted from England. Once this was done it would also provide the best foundation from which to launch a more general religious reformation throughout the island as a whole. All of this, of course, was in marked contrast to what Loftus might have expected in other Irish sees and to what he had actually encountered in Ireland's other primatial see, Armagh. Before his appointment to Dublin, he had petitioned Sir William Cecil to allow him to resign from the archbishopric of Armagh because 'neither is it worth anything to me, nor I able to do any good in it, for that altogether it lieth among the Irish'.[67]

Perceptions of the see of Dublin's cultural, structural and strategic advantages, and the favourable environment that they appeared to provide for the introduction, reception and enforcement of the crown's religious policies in Ireland, remained in being for the duration of the sixteenth century. Throughout, the English regime in Ireland, in the person of the archbishop of Dublin, hoped to capitalise on the inherent qualities that formed the see's medieval character to further the Reformation on the island. The logic and the assumptions that underlay such hopes were deeply compelling to contemporaries, a feature evident even as late 1600 when, in a set of instructions for the lord deputy and council, the queen commanded

---

[67] Shirley, *Church in Ireland 1547–1567*, pp. 278–80, 294.

Archbishop Loftus to redress the problem of recusancy in his cathedral city, because it was 'the metropolitan city of the realm' and the abode of her 'best subjects', and because it was expected 'to give example to all the other parts of the kingdom'.[68] Yet, despite all the evidence to the contrary, these hopes were to prove misplaced. Although there is no doubt that the see of Dublin was quintessentially English, this Englishness could not be reduced to purely abstract notions of political and cultural loyalty that were there to be exploited at will by successive regimes to promote the perennially changing religious ideologies of the Tudor monarchs. This was so for one very important reason. The Englishness of the diocese of Dublin also had a very pronounced, long-standing, deeply ingrained and inseparable religious dimension. In essence, this religious dimension was Catholic and Catholic in a very distinct way. One group in particular, both within the diocese of Dublin itself and elsewhere throughout the English Pale, espoused and embodied this identity of Catholic Englishness: the senior corporate clergy. It is to this group that we must now turn.

[68] TNA: PRO SP 63/207(3), no. 139.

2

Faithful Catholics of the English nation: patriotism, canon law and the corporate clergy

I commit my sinful soul to the grace and mercy of Jesus, my maker and redeemer, . . . to His mother, the most blessed Virgin Mary, and to all the saints; [and] my body [to be buried] in . . . [St Patrick's] cathedral before the feet of the image of St Patrick . . . I give and leave one messuage . . . that I have in Duleek . . . for the use and support of the poor and infirm in the house which I built lately in St Kevin's street, Dublin. I give and leave . . . all my messuages . . . in Thornton in the parish of Skreen, for the use of the poor in the said house, for the continual reparation of the same house and to buy clothes and other necessaries for the poor . . . Not any poor whatsoever, but faithful Catholics of good repute, honest conversation and of the English nation, especially of the nation of the Aleyns, Barrets, Beggs, Hills, Dillons and Rodiers living in the dioceses of Meath and Dublin . . . I will . . . moreover that the . . . admission . . . and also the removal . . . of the poor in this . . . house should be made diligently by the dean and chapter of the said cathedral church for the time being; . . . no exaction or receipt of money . . . should be made for the . . . admission . . . of any of the poor in this house . . . but . . . should be made altogether gratis, for the love of God and in respect of charity. (Extract from the will of John Aleyn, dean of St Patrick's Cathedral, 12 December 1505)[1]

The will of John Aleyn seems relatively innocuous on first sight. Although the document is of some historical interest – it supplies one of the few surviving testimonies of the spiritual world inhabited by a senior Dublin cleric at the end of the Middle Ages – its content is deeply conventional. In essence, it is a portrayal of the traditional religious culture which predominated in England and English Ireland on the eve of the Reformation, which was ubiquitous at all social levels and which comprised the liturgy, devotions, iconography and theology of medieval Catholicism.[2] Thus, apart

---

[1] The full Latin text is printed in Mason, *History of St Patrick's*, App. XII, pp. xiv–xv (calendared in *Alen's register*, pp. 258–9). Aleyn died on 2 January 1506 (Refaussé with Lennon, *Registers of Christ Church*, p. 40).

[2] The definitive study of traditional religion in England is Duffy, *Stripping of the altars*. For material relating to Dublin see Berry, *Register of wills*; M Murphy, 'The high cost of dying: an analysis of pro anima bequests in medieval Dublin', in W. J. Sheils and D. Wood (eds.),

from the observation that Aleyn was an active participant in this culture, it appears that nothing of any real import can be said based on an analysis of the will; nothing, that is, that would help explain why the Tudor Reformation failed to make its expected impact in the diocese of Dublin. Yet the will is more complex and informative than is apparent from an initial perusal. As befitting the educational and occupational backgrounds of its author – Aleyn was an Oxford graduate in canon law, a professional cleric and a royal and seigneurial official[3] – it is an articulate evocation of one man's understanding of traditional religion, and the meaning which it gave to the world around him. Full of personal and local nuance, the document defines much of the religious identity that animated Aleyn and the professional grouping to which he belonged, the corporate clerical elite of Dublin and the English Pale. This identity, which was both Catholic and English to the core, is important, for it is arguable that it was decisive in shaping the overall response of the Englishry to the Tudors' religious innovations during the sixteenth century.

I

The most striking aspect of John Aleyn's will was his attitude to the poor. Like many late medieval Catholics, the old dean believed that at his death he would be judged by Christ on his treatment of the poor in this life, rather than on any outward declaration of his Christian faith, no matter how devout and pious such a declaration may have been. This belief usually found expression in a desire to perform one or more of the seven corporal works of mercy and, as Aleyn approached the end of his life, he was determined that he would not be found wanting.[4] Thus in the year prior to the making of his will he was responsible for building an almshouse in St Kevin Street in the suburbs of Dublin for the indigent and destitute. The

---

The church and wealth, studies in church history xxiv (Oxford, 1987), pp. 111–22; Robinson, 'Churchwardens' accounts, St Werburgh's', pp. 132–42; M.V. Ronan, 'Religious life in old Dublin', *DHR* 2 (1939–40), pp. 46–55, 106–11 and 'Religious customs of Dublin medieval guilds', *IER*, 5th series, 26 (1925), pp. 225–47, 364–85; Lennon, 'St Anne's Guild', pp. 6–25; R. Gillespie, 'Catholic religious cultures in the diocese of Dublin, 1614–97', in Kelly and Keogh (eds.), *Catholic diocese of Dublin*, pp. 127–43.

[3] Aleyn was granted a licence of non-residence for four years in June 1464 to undertake his studies. He was elected dean of St Patrick's in 1467. In August 1494, already a royal chaplain, he was appointed a master of the Irish chancery and one of Henry VII's Irish council. Between *c.*1495 and 1504 he served as steward and general receiver to the earl of Ormond in the counties of Dublin and Meath (*Statutes Ireland, Edward IV*, i, pp. 373–5; *BRUO 1500*, i, pp. 22–3; Lawlor, *Fasti of St Patrick's*, p. 43; *Patent rolls, 1485–94*, p. 473; TNA: PRO, SP 46/183, ff. 112, 137; *Ormond deeds, 1509–47*, pp. 321–2, 342, 349–52, 355–6, 358–9).

[4] On the works of mercy and their significance see Duffy, *Stripping of the altars*, pp. 357–62; for the practice among Dubliners generally see Murphy, 'High cost of dying', pp. 121–2.

will itself was intended to be the culmination of the endeavour, as it stipulated that 'Christ's poor', especially the denizens of his almshouse, would be
his sole heirs and beneficiaries.[5] Yet Aleyn's attitude to the poor was
ambivalent. In his will, he made a distinction between what he considered to
be a deserving and undeserving poor. For him, the poor to be received and
preferred in his almshouse were not to be 'any poor whatsoever, but faithful
Catholics of good repute, honest conversation and of the English nation'.[6] It
is a proviso which begs a number of important and far-reaching questions.

The first of these questions is what exactly John Aleyn intended when he
penned the proviso. Ostensibly, he wished to create a ring-fenced refuge in
St Kevin Street for natives of the English Pale who had English forebears
and who had fallen on hard times, an intention otherwise confirmed by the
additional clause he affixed to the proviso: that a certain group of named
families – all of whom were of English origin and hailed from the predominantly English dioceses of Dublin and Meath – should receive pref-
erential treatment when it came to choosing the inmates of the almshouse.
But this was not his sole intent. Aleyn also stipulated that the dean and
chapter of St Patrick's Cathedral should have full control over the admission and removal of the residents of the house. The cathedral, it will be
remembered, had long upheld a ban on anyone of the Irish nation, manners
and blood becoming a member.[7] Thus we need not doubt that the proviso –
when viewed in the light of that institution's traditional antipathy towards
the Gaelic Irish, and Aleyn's own long-standing leadership of the same –
was also designed to place a positive embargo on the entrance of poor men
of the Irish nation. Aleyn, we can assume, not only harboured warm feelings
towards his own people, the Englishry of Ireland, but also a marked hostility towards the Irishry, a sentiment which jars dramatically with the
charitableness and concern for the poor evinced elsewhere in his will.

Why, then, did he uphold such attitudes? It is arguable that their formation was rooted in two distinct, but related, life experiences, the first of
which is hinted at in the list of families whom he singled out to receive
special treatment in the admission policy of his almshouse. All of these
families, including the Aleyns, came from the farming communities of north
Co. Dublin and east Co. Meath in the heart of the Pale Maghery. Of
relatively humble stock, what marked these and so many similar families
out was their pride in their English origins, which many of them claimed
stretched back to the earliest Anglo-Norman settlement of the region when,

---

[5] *Alen's register*, pp. 78, 254–5, 258–9.
[6] 'Non tamen quoscunque pauperes, sed fideles catholicos, bone fame, honeste conversacionis
   et Anglice nationis' (Mason, *History of St Patrick's*, App. XII, p. xv).
[7] Above, pp. 38–9.

in the words of Richard Stanyhurst, 'diverse of the conquerors planted themselves near to Dublin and the confines thereto adjoining'. The most evocative and telling piece of evidence concerning the English identity of these people is to be found in Stanyhurst's well-known description of Fingal in north Co. Dublin, a district which some of Aleyn's favoured families lived in and which flowed seamlessly into the bordering baronies of east Meath where the remainder dwelt.[8]

Fingal, in marked contrast to the outlying areas of the Pale, had enjoyed an unusual degree of peace and tranquillity in the centuries following the Anglo-Norman conquest, largely because it was so well ensconced within the Maghery. Apart from the unusual circumstances of the Kildare rebellion in the mid-1530s, it was, according to Stanyhurst, 'not before acquainted with the recourse of the Irish enemies'. Untroubled by the Irish, the district was able to sustain its English culture and social organisation without hindrance. This was done to such an extent that by the sixteenth century the term Fingal had become totally synonymous with its English inhabitants:

the word Fingal countervaileth in English, the race or sept of the English or strangers, for that they were solely seized of that part of the island, gripping with their tallants so firmly that warm nest, that from the conquest to this day, the Irish enemy could never rouse them from thence.[9]

This identification of land, people and culture was also enshrined in the nomenclature of the local townlands. The townlands that the Fingalians and their neighbours farmed bore their names, which would have been assigned by the early settlers. Thus, among Aleyn's group of favoured families, the Hill family was commemorated in at least three townlands in north Co. Dublin and east Co. Meath,[10] and the Beggs in two;[11] while the Aleyns certainly and the Rodiers possibly were each recalled in a single townland, both in Co. Meath.[12]

---

[8] Stanyhurst, *Holinshed's Irish chronicle*, p. 13. Although Stanyhurst wrote over fifty years after Dean Aleyn died, his description of the region highlighted the historical continuity in its social conditions and cultural traditions, which stretched back to the time of the conquest.

[9] Ibid., pp. 13, 267.

[10] 'Hylton' (1547) now Hilltown, parish of Swords, north Co. Dublin; 'Hilton' (1540) now Hilltown Great and Hilltown Little, parish of Duleek, Co. Meath; 'Hylton' (1540) now Hilltown, parish of Piercetown, Co. Meath: Survey of possessions 1547, RCB, C2/1/27, no. 2 (Mason, *History of St Patrick's*, pp. 78–9); White, *Monastic extents*, pp. 106, 314.

[11] 'Begeston' (1540) now Beggstown, parish of Ratoath, Co. Meath; 'Beggeston' (1540) now Beggstown, parish of Dunboyne, Co. Meath: G. MacNiocaill (ed.), *Crown surveys of lands with the Kildare rental begun in 1518* (IMC, Dublin, 1992), p. 60; White, *Monastic extents*, pp. 288–9.

[12] 'Aleyston' (1541), 'Alenston' (1560) now Allenstown Demesne, parish of Martry; 'Ridder' (1530s), 'Rydder alias Rodder' (1558), now Rudder, parish of Duleek Abbey: White, *Monastic extents*, pp. 115, 317; *Fiants, Mary*, no. 252; *Fiants, Elizabeth*, no. 206.

In practical terms the Fingalians' maintenance of an English culture meant two things: the preservation of the English tongue and the continued usage of the medieval strip farming practices which had been brought over from England at the time of the conquest. As far as language was concerned, Stanyhurst noted that they spoke 'the dregs of the old ancient Chaucer English', an archaic dialect which suggests that the cultural strength of the community stemmed from its ability to hold on to and maintain the attributes of earlier generations of settlers, rather than subsequent innovation and change. Such conservatism, in fact, was also implicit in their attachment to the farming life, which was wont to draw from the more sophisticated Stanyhurst and his fellow urbanites in Dublin a gentle chiding. 'Fingal especially', he wrote, 'from time to time hath been so addicted to all the points of husbandry, as that they are nicknamed by their neighbours, for their continual drudgery, Collonnes of the Latin word, *Coloni*, whereunto the clipt English word, Clown, seemeth to be answerable'.[13]

It was precisely these 'clowns', these upright, hard-working yeomen and husbandmen – men of 'good repute, honest conversation and of the English nation' – whom John Aleyn had in mind when he established his almshouse in St Kevin Street. These were his people and he wanted to show charity and good neighbourliness to those among them who had fallen, or would fall, into straitened circumstances. Thus the proviso in his will was an expression of local patriotism, and a form of social bonding in which he endeavoured to show his solidarity with a community that had upheld a way of life for centuries, of which he felt a part and was deeply proud. This sense of patriotism also goes some way towards explaining Aleyn's antipathy towards the Gaelic Irish. We know that in the early sixteenth century the people of Fingal and east Meath would have felt that their traditional way of life was under threat to a degree which they had never previously experienced. This was not just because of the continuing contraction of the English lordship in Ireland in the face of Gaelic political resurgence. This after all had been going on for well nigh two centuries. Rather, it was because the Pale Maghery itself was beginning to feel the winds of unwelcome social change, most evident in the replacement of English husbandmen by Gaelic peasants on the lands of the English Irish aristocracy, especially, and most worryingly of all, in the lordship of the most powerful magnate in Ireland, the earl of Kildare. The departure from Kildare of English farmers who were unwilling to labour under the burden of the Fitzgeralds' imposition of 'coign and livery', and the infiltration of this once largely English district by cheap Irish-speaking labour, would have signalled to Aleyn and his people the fearful prospect that social, cultural and

---

[13] Stanyhurst, *Holinshed's Irish chronicle*, pp. 13, 14.

economic degeneration, on a scale similar to that which had occurred in the outlying areas of the English lordship, was now an emerging reality in the hitherto sacrosanct Maghery.[14] Seen in this light, the dean's embargo on poor Irishmen entering his almshouse seems entirely explicable. It was yet another in a long line of measures stretching back to the mid-fourteenth century Statutes of Kilkenny through which embattled English colonials endeavoured to protect and preserve their social and cultural mores by controlling all forms of intercourse with the Gaelic Irish.

But this is not the whole story. Aleyn's proviso cannot simply be reduced to nor classified as an expression of English patriotism or English discrimination against the Gaelic Irish. While it certainly contained these ideas, the proviso also included another, arguably more important, concept, which was encapsulated in Aleyn's phrase 'faithful Catholics'. It was 'faithful Catholics', in fact, who Aleyn really wanted to inhabit his poorhouse. The other requirements – reputation, honesty and Englishness – merely defined the characteristics of faithful Catholicism or, more precisely, identified who faithful Catholics were in the Irish context. For John Aleyn, a man steeped in the laws and traditions of the medieval Catholic Church, this was a straightforward matter. Faithful Catholics were civil Englishmen like the farmers of north Co. Dublin and east Co. Meath. They would also have included the citizens of the 'regal city' of Dublin, of which Aleyn himself had been made a freeman in October 1471; or their near neighbours, the English farmers of the 'king's land', a district which lay to the south-west of the city, centred on the ancient royal manors of Crumlin, Esker, Newcastle Lyons and Saggart.[15] To Dean Aleyn, all of these groups would have been classifiable as law-abiding, trustworthy, hardworking and God-fearing Christians: faithful Catholics of the English nation. By way of contrast, faithful Catholics most definitely did not comprehend the Gaelic Irish clans or degenerate English marchers, groups whose lawless behaviour and corrupt social mores ensured that they were absolutely excluded from this category. There is little doubt that Aleyn had confidence in this judgement, so much so in fact that he was prepared to go to his grave upholding it. Indeed, he was even prepared to integrate it into the final spiritual act of his life, an act whereby he gave all his worldly possessions to the poor – the poor of the faithful Catholic variety – in return for eternal life. To understand why he had this conviction, to understand more fully why he classified the different inhabitants of Ireland as faithful or

[14] Canny, *Old English elite*, pp. 7–9; Hore and Graves, *Southern and eastern counties*, pp. 152–3; Ellis, *Ireland in the age of the Tudors*, pp. 33, 36.

[15] Stanyhurst, *Holinshed's Irish chronicle*, pp. 13, 39, 51; C. Lennon and J. Murray (eds.), *The Dublin City franchise roll, 1468–1512* (Dublin, 1998), p. 5.

non-faithful Catholics – the classification upon which he based his exclusion of the Irishry from his almshouse – it is necessary to turn to the second of those life experiences which formed his attitudes. Here we encounter the John Aleyn who emerged from the farming community of east Meath to become a canon lawyer and senior official of the church in Dublin.

II

Practitioners of canon law – those who had enough knowledge of the romano-canonical disciplines to participate in the workings of the many tribunals that administered ecclesiastical justice or issued ecclesiastical licences in the later Middle Ages – occupied a prominent position in the Irish Church. An anonymous political reformer writing from the Pale about 1515 complained that 'the church of this land use not to learn any other science, but the law of canon'.[16] Although the surviving sources do not allow us to quantify the numbers involved, there is little doubt that he was reporting on an objective fact. This was evident, for example, in the con-temporary demand for formal tuition in the canon and civil laws amongst aspiring clerics from the English Pale. Thus, at the University of Oxford there were at least two, and perhaps as many as four, halls – Aristotle and Eagle being the most prominent – which catered specifically for Irish legists at different times in the fifteenth century. The same demand was also reflected in the efforts of Archbishop Walter Fitzsimon of Dublin, a man with a very strong background in canon law, to establish a new university in his diocese at the end of the century.[17]

Yet while there is no doubting the proliferation and preponderance of canonists at this time, nor indeed their genuine need and desire for training and tuition, it would be wrong to assume that they represented the existence of a genuinely intellectual or academic movement in the Irish Church, at least not in the sense in which we normally understand such terms. On the contrary, the failure of Archbishop Fitzsimon's university scheme,[18] the

---

[16] *SP* II, p. 16. On the romano-canonical tradition, or *ius commune*, and the symbiotic relationship between canon and civil law see J.A. Brundage, *Medieval canon law* (London and New York, 1995), pp. 60–1, 176–7; A. García Y García, 'The faculties of law', in H. De Ridder Symoens (ed.), *A history of the university in Europe: volume I: universities in the Middle Ages* (Cambridge, 1992), pp. 388–406.

[17] T.H. Aston, 'Oxford's medieval alumni', in *Past & Present* 74 (1977), pp. 23–4; Gwynn, *Anglo-Irish church life*, pp. 73–5; *Alen's register*, p. 260. On Fitzsimon see Murray, 'Tudor diocese of Dublin', p. 73 nt. 19.

[18] The reason for the scheme's failure is unknown, but as it was hoped to raise funds for the faculty lectors by taxing the clergy of the province of Dublin over a seven-year period, it is possible that it foundered because of clerical reluctance to pay the yearly assessment (*Alen's register*, p. 260).

apparent reluctance of Irish graduates in canon and civil law to continue their studies to doctorate level and the almost complete absence of indigenous writing on canonical jurisprudence,[19] all suggest that the canonists were motivated by more basic concerns than the expansion of their knowledge of the philosophical and judicial principles which underpinned the law of the Western Church. This was certainly the view of the anonymous reformer of 1515. He attributed the predominance of canonists to nothing more than clerical greed, 'covetousness of lucre transitory'.[20]

On first sight this contention seems plausible. Even when we make allowances for the fact that it belonged to a tradition of moralistic writing that castigated all canonists as a cadre of avaricious and unscrupulous careerists,[21] there is a persuasive body of evidence available to support it. The career of Dean Aleyn of St Patrick's is a case in point. His incumbency of the deanery was dominated by a lengthy series of litigious disputes with his archbishop, John Walton (1472–84). These concerned the jurisdictional and financial rights of the deanery and, in terms of the bitterness they generated and the derogatory effect they had on day-to-day religious practice in the diocese, reflected poorly on the profession of canonists as a whole. The disputes began in the mid-1470s when Archbishop Walton annulled on appeal a sentence of excommunication that Aleyn had pronounced on one Thomas Browne, a Dublin notary. Thereafter they grew to encompass a variety of accusations and counter-claims, including Aleyn's charge that the archbishop had illegally dispossessed him of tithes in the decanal prebends of Tallaght and Clondalkin. They also led at one point to Aleyn's formal deprivation, although the sentence was never given effect. The most striking aspect of the disputes, however, was not the substantive points at issue between the parties, but the impact that they made on life in the close of St Patrick's Cathedral. According to Aleyn and his fellow canons the 'wrongful and unjust process' of the archbishop and his allies actually interrupted and curtailed divine service in their church; including, on the vigil of the feast of St Patrick in 1474, the complete omission of vespers, an event described in an act of the Irish parliament as 'a most piteous thing for any man to hear who is a native of this land'.[22]

It is little wonder, then, that moralists like the anonymous writer of 1515 could hold such a disparaging view of the canonists. For him, the fact that their litigious instincts could sow such scandalous discord between the clergy, even between the two most senior clerics in the best appointed diocese in the

---

[19] Gwynn, *Anglo-Irish church life*, pp. 32–8.   [20] *SP* II, p. 16.
[21] On this tradition see Brundage, *Medieval canon law*, pp. 179–80.
[22] *Statutes Ireland, Edward IV*, ii, pp. 195–203; *CPR, papal letters, 1471–84*, pp. 453–4, 462–3; *CPR, papal letters, 1484–92*, pp. 267–8; *Octavian's register* II, no. 221; Murray, 'Tudor diocese of Dublin', pp. 74–5 nt. 25.

Irish lordship,[23] was indicative of a much greater and more widespread malaise effected by them throughout the church at large. Contentious suits, which were often used as a device to secure ecclesiastical livings for the plaintiffs, and commenced by the procurement of papal bulls appointing judges-delegate to hear the issues in dispute, were very common on the eve of the Reformation and could be extremely disruptive of the church's pastoral and administrative functions.[24] Yet, for all its persuasive simplicity, the moralist's belief that the canonists were motivated merely by ambition and greed fails to explain satisfactorily the full significance and complexity of their activities on the eve of the Reformation. John Aleyn's decision, for example, to endow an almshouse and to make 'Christ's poor' the sole beneficiaries of his will alerts us to the dangers of labelling him, and by extension other active canonists, as a purely selfish and materialistic breed of clergyman, even when we take into account his litigation with Archbishop Walton. More significantly, the dean himself believed that when he undertook this litigation there was a much more profound principle at stake than the personal gain of a single ecclesiastic. This principle was, in fact, nothing less than the defence of the liberties of the English Irish ecclesiastical establishment, which were perceived by that establishment as being an integral and indispensable part of their community's historic role in Ireland: the reformation of Gaelic Irish society along conventional canonical lines according to the uses of the English Church.[25] It was this role, in fact, or at least the contemporary interpretation of it, which motivated Aleyn's actions as a canon lawyer and which informed his attitude towards the Irishry. Ultimately, it would inform the response of his community to the Tudor Reformation.

The Englishry's reforming imperative, and its canonical parameters, were believed by many contemporaries to have been established by Pope Adrian IV's infamous bull *Laudabiliter* of 1155, which granted lordship over Ireland to the English crown. 'You have indeed indicated to us', wrote Pope Adrian to King Henry II:

that you wish to enter the island of Ireland to make that people obedient to the laws, and to root out from there the weeds of vices. We therefore support your pious and

---

[23] The Aleyn–Walton dispute was not effectively settled until 1515 when their successors, Archbishop Rokeby and Dean Rochfort, agreed new statutes on their respective jurisdictions over St Patrick's Cathedral (*Alen's register*, pp. 262–3; Mason, *History of St Patrick's*, pp. 143–4; *Dignitas decani*, pp. 56–64).

[24] Cosgrove, 'Ireland beyond the Pale, 1399–1460', pp. 587–8; W.N. Osborough, 'Ecclesiastical law and the Reformation in Ireland', in R. Helmholz (ed.), *Canon law in Protestant lands* (Berlin, 1992), p. 227. For a general description of the process see Sughi's introduction to *Octavian's register* I, pp. liii–lx.

[25] On the growth of the English Irish community's sense of its historic role in Ireland see R. Frame, *The political development of the British Isles* (Oxford, 1990), pp. 179–87.

praiseworthy intention with the favour which it deserves and . . . we regard it as pleasing and acceptable to us that you should enter that island for the purpose of enlarging the boundaries of the church, checking the descent into wickedness, correcting morals and implanting virtues, and encouraging the growth of the faith of Christ.[26]

Although a significant body of historians now believe that the document may not be authentic, or that Henry II did not actually invoke *Laudabiliter* when he came to Ireland in 1171–2, the bull was still regarded by later generations, especially amongst the colonial community, as the ultimate sanction for the English conquest of Ireland, and as the ultimate source and proof of the reforming intentions which motivated the enterprise. To a large extent this viewpoint was promulgated by Gerald of Wales's influential history of the conquest, *Expugnatio Hibernica*, a work that was widely available in manuscript form, both in the original Latin and in various English adaptations, throughout the later Middle Ages.[27] Not only did the *Expugnatio* reproduce in full the text of *Laudabiliter*, and other key documents such as the reforming constitutions of the council of Cashel of 1172, but, through the author's commentaries on these documents, also provided a clear and unambiguous message that the English conquest of Ireland was a religious undertaking authorised by the papacy because of 'the monstrous excesses and vile practices of that land and people'. Indeed, some of these commentaries, whether through mistranslation or wilfully erroneous adaptation, attained the same force as the original documents themselves, especially in the fifteenth-century English versions of the *Expugnatio*. Gerald's comment on the constitutions of Cashel, for

---

[26] *Alen's register*, p. 1; F. X. Martin, 'Diarmait Mac Murchada and the coming of the Anglo-Normans', *NHI* II, pp. 56–61; M. Richter, 'The first century of Anglo-Norman relations', *History* 59 (1974), pp. 195–210; R. Frame, *Colonial Ireland, 1169–1369* (Dublin, 1981), pp. 11–14; the full Latin text of *Laudabiliter*, with an English translation, is printed in Giraldus Cambrensis, *Expugnatio Hibernica: the conquest of Ireland*, ed. A. B. Scott and F. X. Martin (Dublin, 1978), pp. 144–7. For discussions concerning its authenticity see M. P. Sheehy, 'The bull *Laudabiliter*: a problem in medieval diplomatique and history', *GASJ* 29 (1961), pp. 45–71; M. Richter, 'Giraldiana', *IHS* 21 (1979), pp. 430–1; B. Bolton and A.J. Duggan (eds.), *Adrian IV the English Pope (1154–1159). Studies and texts* (Aldershot, 2003), pp. 138–55.

[27] Richter, 'Giraldiana', pp. 423–31; H. Morgan, 'Giraldus Cambrensis and the Tudor conquest of Ireland' in H. Morgan (ed.), *Political ideology in Ireland, 1541–1641* (Dublin, 1999), pp. 22–44. For the Latin manuscript versions see *Expugnatio Hibernica*, ed. Scott and Martin, pp. xxxiv–xl. The first English version, from the early fifteenth century, appears to have been TCD, MS 592, printed in F.J. Furnivall (ed.), *The English conquest of Ireland A.D. 1166–1185, mainly from the 'Expugnatio Hibernica' of Geraldus Cambrensis* (London, 1896). The TCD text was the source for other medieval English versions of the 'Expugnatio', such as Bodleian, MS Rawlinson B. 490 (also printed in Furnivall's *English conquest of Ireland*); Lambeth MS 598 (printed in *Carew MSS. Book of Howth*, pp. 261–317) and BL, Additional MS 40674, which belonged to the Darcy family of Platten in Co. Meath.

example – that they were intended to bring the Irish Church into conformity with the observances of the English Church – was often rendered as an actual canon of the council itself. This development further reinforced the notion of the Englishry's reforming, canonical mission in Ireland, as it gave it a concise, forceful and pseudo-legal expression: 'The eight [constitution], that all men and women worship holy church, and oft go to church, and holy church be governed on all manner that it is in England'.[28]

For Dean Aleyn and the chapter of St Patrick's Cathedral – the leaders of an institution which had been founded under the auspices of the Anglo-Norman monarchy to give this reforming imperative practical effect – Gerald's words, and the words of the documents that he reproduced, were particularly resonant. Not only did they explain and justify historically the English presence in Ireland and the existence of their own church and corporation; but, despite their age, they remained the benchmark against which the cathedral and other religious corporations in English Ireland defined their contemporary *raison d'être* and set their current aspirations.[29] By the late fifteenth and early sixteenth centuries, however, the aspirations of the cathedral and corporate clergy had changed subtly from those that had existed at the time of the Anglo-Norman conquest. The incomplete nature of the conquest, the subsequent resurgence of the Gaelic lordships, the contraction of the English colony and the Gaelicisation of areas formerly under English rule, had all combined to create a situation in which the canonical standards of religious life and practice envisaged by *Laudabiliter* were confined largely to the four shires of the English Pale. Indeed, the possibility that the Irishry might make further advances, whether through direct military action or the corrosive effects of Gaelicisation, threatened to undermine these standards even within this circumscribed area. In these circumstances, the clergy of St Patrick's were less concerned with the outward-looking, proselytising dimension of their traditional reforming role. Rather, their aim was simply to defend and preserve intact its most tangible remnant, the ecclesiastical inheritance of the English Pale.

The threat that the Irishry posed to this inheritance was not imaginary, but a tangible, everyday reality. The conditions that prevailed within the borderlands and the areas *inter Hibernicos* of every single Pale diocese

---

[28] *Expugnatio Hibernica*, ed. Scott and Martin, pp. 97–101; *Carew MSS. Book of Howth*, pp. 285–6.

[29] Significantly, of course, the vast majority of the manuscript versions of the 'Expugnatio' were either produced or preserved in monastic scriptoria or libraries, both in England and in Ireland (*Expugnatio Hibernica*, ed. Scott and Martin, pp. xxxiv–xl). This tradition continued as late as the fifteenth century when Brother Stephen Lawless of St Mary's Abbey, Dublin, produced versions of Gerald's 'Topographia Hiberniae' and the 'Expugnatio', which are now in the John Ryland's Library, Manchester (MS 17).

demonstrated beyond all doubt that they remained committed – perversely in English Irish eyes – to customs and practices, which contravened some of the most fundamental principles and theories associated with the canon law and which, should they spread any further, would bring about the final and irrevocable ruin of all that the conquest had achieved and stood for in Ireland. The most important of these principles was the notion of the rule of law itself, the idea that no secular ruler, however powerful, could ever be above the existing laws.[30] In the diocese of Dublin this notion was openly flouted by the chiefs and petty captains who reigned over the Gaelic enclaves and marcher borderlands in Co. Wicklow, which formed the bulk of the territory that comprised the archdeaconry of Glendalough.[31] In essence, Glendalough was a zone of war and brigandage in the late fifteenth and early sixteenth centuries. Here, the force of arms, rather than spiritual influence or canonical dictate, was the only effective way of asserting and legitimising any claim to authority.

For the archbishop and his officials based in Dublin, this had very serious repercussions. It prevented them, for example, from appointing English priests to those benefices in the region that were in the archbishop's gift. One result of this was that Archbishop Fitzsimon had to seek parliamentary licences in the 1480s and 1490s to allow him to appoint Irish clergymen instead, because 'no Englishman can safely occupy the said benefices nor go to them nor come from them peaceably'. Equally seriously, the same difficulties also prevented the diocesan administration from maintaining a permanent presence and visibility in the region with the result that their ordinary jurisdictions ceased to have any foundation in reality. In 1468, for example, it was reported of the visitation of St Patrick's Cathedral by Archbishop Michael Tregury (1449–71) that 'all the prebends of the said church were visited except the prebends . . . situated in the Irish parts and also in the marches, which he had not dared to visit on account of the disturbances of the wars'. Tregury's fears were well founded, for some time before 1462 he had been captured by Geoffrey Harold, the captain of a Gaelicised marcher family in south-east Dublin, who imprisoned him 'and inflicted other great affronts and injuries upon him'.[32] Although few details of this incident have survived, it indicates what little respect was afforded to

---

[30] On the development of this notion see Brundage, *Medieval canon law*, pp. 104–5, 110–11.

[31] The only important exception to this was the deanery of Leixlip Co. Kildare, which formed a detached portion of the archdeaconry lying in the Pale Maghery (Reeves, *Analysis of the united dioceses of Dublin and Glendalough*).

[32] *Statutes Ireland, Richard III–Henry VIII*, pp. 64–7, 82–5; Berry, *Register of wills*, pp. 173–4; *Alen's register*, p. 242. On conditions generally in the Glendalough region see J. Lydon, 'Medieval Wicklow – "A land of war"', in K. Hannigan and W. Nolan (eds.), *Wicklow: history and society* (Dublin, 1994), pp. 151–89.

the Dublin diocesan administration amongst the inhabitants of the see 'in partibus hibernicanis et marchialibus'. So prevalent was this disposition, in fact, that it led to the complete collapse of archidiaconal jurisdiction and the virtual collapse of archiepiscopal jurisdiction in the late fifteenth century, the latter feature being evident in the fact that a partially successful attempt was made, on the part of the Gaelic Irish clans, to fill the void by reviving an independent see of Glendalough.[33]

The Irishry's disregard for the rule of law had other derogatory implications for the ecclesiastical establishment in Dublin. It underpinned, for example, their rejection of another basic canonical principle: the sacrosanct nature of ecclesiastical property. One effect of this was that the economic standing of the archbishop of Dublin was consistently eroded in the marcher and Irish districts of his diocese in the late medieval period. In the mid-1530s, for example, 89 per cent of the temporal revenues of the archbishopric were derived from property situated within the archdeaconry of Dublin in the Pale Maghery, while only 11 per cent was derived from archiepiscopal manors located in the archdeaconry of Glendalough.[34] This imbalance was due to the fact that much of the property which had accrued to the archbishopric after the unification of the sees of Dublin and Glendalough in 1216 had been overrun by the Gaelic Irish clans in the succeeding centuries, including the ancient and once lucrative manor of Castlekevin in north Co. Wicklow. Worth almost £90 per annum in the late thirteenth century, Castlekevin was lost to the O'Tooles in the fourteenth century and never again came into archiepiscopal hands. In fact, the crown formally recognised the O'Toole claim to the property in 1541, while endeavouring to woo the clan towards submission to royal authority.[35]

Moving out of the Gaelic enclaves and into the marches proper, the archbishop's property remained, nominally at least, within his own possession. However, the persistent depredation it suffered at the hands of the Irishry in the late fifteenth and early sixteenth centuries determined that much of it was wasted, depopulated and almost completely valueless; a feature particularly evident in relation to the manor of Ballymore, which lay

---

[33] On the ineffectualness of the archdeacon's office see Murray, 'Tudor diocese of Dublin', p. 79 nts. 35, 36; A. Coleman (ed.), 'Obligationes pro annatis diocesis Dublinensis, 1421–1520', *AH* 2 (1913), appendix, pp. 28–30.

[34] TNA: PRO, SP 65/1, no. 2, f. 14v; Reeves, *Analysis of the united dioceses of Dublin and Glendalough*, pp. 2–5. The manors located in the archdeaconry of Glendalough were Ballymore, Shankill and Dalkey.

[35] Pipe roll 7 Edward I, *Appendix to the 36th Report of the Deputy Keeper of the Public Records . . . Ireland* (Dublin, 1904), p. 42; *APC 1540–2*, pp. 92–3; Bradshaw, 'George Browne' (MA thesis), pp. 72, 374; below p. 32. For descriptions of other property withheld from the archbishops in the Gaelic enclaves of their diocese see Murray, 'Tudor diocese of Dublin', pp. 80–1 nt. 38.

on the border of Kildare and north-west Wicklow. Writing to the king in 1537, Dublin's first Reformation archbishop, George Browne, drew a sorry picture of this medieval inheritance, lamenting the fact that the 'lands thereunto appertaining' had been 'almost made waste' due to their proximity to the O'Tooles, O'Byrnes and the Kavanaghs, and that the rent of assize there was 'not leviable above £20 sterling where in times past it was 340 marks yearly, which we cannot study ne compass to have'. There was no lasting improvement in the conditions obtaining in Ballymore thereafter. In a poem written by the Gaelic Irish bard Fearganainm MacEochadha, entitled 'Ag So Caithréim Aodha Mhic Seaáin Ón Bhfear Gcéadna', the continuing problems experienced by the manor are thrown into sharp relief. The 'Caithréim' or battle-roll, an encomium of the military prowess of Aodh Mac Seán O'Byrne, chief of the Gabh Raghnaill branch of the clan from the mid-sixteenth century until his death in 1579, gives details of the latter's attacks on Ballymore and its constituent townlands – Dunlavin, Rathsallagh, Tornant and Barretstown – throughout this period. That this was no idle boast is otherwise confirmed by the records of the archbishop's own manorial court. In 1587 and 1590 the jurors declared that various properties known as 'the wastes of Ballymore', covering 446 customary acres, were let to various tenants free of rent; a result, no doubt, of their depressed condition following the attacks of the O'Byrnes and other Irish chiefs throughout the fifteenth and sixteenth centuries.[36]

The aberrant and uncanonical behaviour of the Irishry, characteristics which the ecclesiastical establishment in Dublin perceived in the lawlessness of such clans as the O'Tooles and the O'Byrnes, and which had made such a dire impact on its economic standing and administrative capacity in the Gaelic enclaves and borderlands of the see, were also evident in the sexually active lifestyles of its clergy. The eradication of this abuse, an abuse referred to as 'Nicolaitism' by the Gregorian reformers of the eleventh century and which was deemed to comprehend all sexual activity, whether in marital, concubinary or casual relationships, had lain at the heart of the Anglo-Norman reform mission at the time of the conquest.[37] Despite its centrality, however, little of practical consequence had been achieved, largely because of the decline of English rule in Ireland and the accompanying reduction of English influence in the Irish Church. Thus, as late as the latter end of the fifteenth and the beginning of the sixteenth centuries, clerical concubinage was a common, and socially acceptable, practice in Gaelic Ireland,

---

[36] Lambeth MS 602, f. 54v (*Carew MSS, 1515–74*, p. 161); Seán Mac Airt (ed.), *Leabhar Branach. The book of the O'Byrnes* (Dublin, 1944), p. 69, lines 1793–1816; Wood, *Liberty of St Sepulchre*, pp. 41, 74.

[37] Martin, 'Diarmait Mac Murchada and the coming of the Anglo-Normans', pp. 58–9. On Nicolaitism generally see Brundage, *Medieval canon law*, pp. 35–7.

especially in the provinces of Armagh and Tuam where it was an integral part of an ecclesiastical culture that upheld the markedly uncanonical principles of priestly succession to, and dynastic control of, every kind of ecclesiastical benefice. It is not known how prevalent clerical concubinage was in the marcher and Gaelic areas of the diocese of Dublin at this time, as the lack of authority that the archbishop and his officials exercised in these districts precluded them from investigating it. Yet if the diocesan administration had little personal experience of dealing with the problem, they would certainly have been aware of its existence in the Gaelic enclaves of other Pale dioceses, at the very least through the tales of ecclesiastical officials from dioceses like Armagh and Kildare.[38]

There is little doubt, then, that the Irishry were perceived to constitute a real and live danger to the entire English Irish ecclesiastical order on the eve of the Reformation. The fundamental lawlessness and inherent canonical deviancy of Gaelic Irish politics and society – both of which had been experienced with increasing vividness by the English colony as the area under crown rule receded in the fourteenth and fifteenth centuries – seemed to threaten the existence or, at the very least, the corruption, of the one part of Ireland where the standards of religious life required by *Laudabiliter* were still reasonably intact. This threat was most keenly felt by the senior corporate clergy of the Pale, a group who, in their guises as diocesan officials, as judges of their own peculiars, or as papal judges delegates, were traditionally responsible for administering canon law and upholding English Irish ecclesiastical mores. At the forefront of this group were the dean and chapter of St Patrick's Cathedral, a corporation which, through its maintenance of ecclesiological and canonical customs that dated back to the time of the conquest, embodied the English Irish ecclesiastical order in its purest form.[39] Thus it was they who had the fullest appreciation of the extent to which the Irish deviated from the standards of *Laudabiliter* and the actual and potential damage it could unleash upon the Pale. Led by canonically literate men like John Aleyn, it was they who were prevented from exercising the ordinary jurisdiction of their bishops, as well as their own peculiar jurisdictions, in the borderlands and *in partibus Hibernicos*

---

[38] Sources as in note 43 above p. 35; on Kildare see Lyons, *Church and society in Kildare*, pp. 77–8. For a different view of concubinage and its significance see Jefferies, *Priests and prelates of Armagh*, pp. 79–82.

[39] Above pp. 23–33. This was particularly manifest in the cathedral's active involvement in diocesan administration, which contrasted markedly with the other major Pale dioceses, Meath and Armagh, where cathedrals played a more peripheral role. In Meath there was no cathedral at all, while in Armagh the cathedral lay among the Irish and governed the diocese *inter Hibernicos* rather than the diocese *inter Anglicos* (Cosgrove, 'Ireland beyond the Pale, 1399–1460', p. 584; Watt, 'Confrontation and co-existence in Armagh', pp. 47–50; Jefferies, *Priests and prelates of Armagh*, pp. 84–90).

because Gaelic and Gaelicised clans had turned them into bandit country. It was they who had lost valuable revenues and property rights because those same militarily powerful clans had elected to usurp or destroy ancient ecclesiastical endowments. It was they who, in opposition to all of this, had embodied for centuries the Gregorian standards of canonical correctness that Pope Adrian IV and King Henry II had wished to implant amongst the Irishry. It is no real surprise, then, that it was they who felt the strongest impulse to defend and preserve English ecclesiastical order and canonical rectitude where it still had some lifeblood. In fine, the medieval experience of the English colony had transformed the dean and chapter of St Patrick's, and the corporate clerical elite of the Pale generally, from being missionaries of the *Laudabiliter* settlement into being its most committed and most conservative guardians.

It was in this role of guardianship over the *Laudabiliter* settlement that Dean Aleyn of St Patrick's Cathedral was moved to classify the Irishry as unfaithful Catholics in December 1505, and to exclude them from his almshouse. As a legist, a patriotic Palesmen and someone who had seen up close the harm wrought by the Irishry on the English ecclesiastical order in Ireland, Aleyn perceived them as a people who ignored or rejected at every turn the basic Christian standards of behaviour enshrined in canon law – hence their classification as unfaithful Catholics – and who corrupted all whom they came into contact with. By the late fifteenth century it seemed that the only group left to be corrupted in this way were 'the faithful Catholics … of the English nation' in the Pale, the last repository of the virtuous Christian values that had been brought into Ireland at the time of the conquest. It was largely on this basis, therefore, the desire to preserve the *Laudabiliter*-inspired and intrinsically English version of Catholicism free from Gaelic Irish corruption, that the dean chose to maintain his almshouse as an exclusively English domain.

Yet it was in this context too that Aleyn undertook his lengthy litigation with the English-born archbishop of Dublin, John Walton. For Aleyn and his colleagues in St Patrick's, Walton's attack on his decanal jurisdiction and property rights was as great an affront to the English Irish ecclesiastical order – indeed it was directly comparable – as anything that the deviant Irishry had done or would do. This was so for one simple reason. These jurisdictional and property rights had been granted, with royal and papal approval, at the time of the cathedral's foundation in the early days of the conquest, and were regarded thus as a fundamental, *ab initio* component of the original *Laudabiliter* settlement. That the dean and chapter thought in this way is evident from an act passed by the Irish parliament in 1474 at the height of the controversy. This act was actually procured by Dean Aleyn and his colleagues as a legal device to be employed directly in the battle against their archbishop. At the time, Aleyn had a sentence of deprivation hanging over him from Walton, which he was in the process of appealing at the Roman Curia. To ensure that this sentence would not be given effect, he not only placed his benefice under the protection of the pope pending the appeal, but also got the Irish parliament to place it under the protection of King Edward IV. In addition, the same act also confirmed and approved the foundation and liberties of the cathedral; and made it a statutory offence, punishable by a £20 fine, to act contrary to them.[40]

The most interesting aspect of the act, however, is the justification that was given for these actions. It was stressed repeatedly that the cathedral was of the king's foundation and that its 'liberties, statutes, ordinances, constitutions and lawful customs, and especially the constitution *dignitas decani et omnium canonicorum*' dated back to the time of the conquest, having been 'granted first by . . . King John when he was Earl of Morton and Lord of Ireland'. Furthermore, it was also stressed that these consitutions had been 'confirmed, ordained and established by the Holy Fathers Innocent and Nicholas, Popes, at the court of Rome'. All of this, of course, was shorthand for a message that would have been instantly recognisable to an English Irish audience. In essence, the act was contending that the liberties of St Patrick's Cathedral had been granted by the same authorities that had sanctioned and undertaken the conquest, and not simply by coincidence, but as an integral part of that hallowed enterprise. For this reason, they were regarded as an indispensable part of English Irish political and ecclesiastical culture generally, and would have to be defended stoutly; not only by the dean and chapter of St Patrick's themselves, but by the entire English Irish community assembled in parliament.

That what was essentially a matter of competing ecclesiastical jurisdictions could take on, in the context of the late medieval Irish lordship, this wider cultural meaning is confirmed in another related act passed by the same parliament in 1474. It is evident from this statute that Dean Aleyn and the chapter of St Patrick's believed that Archbishop Walton had commenced his 'unjust and wrongful process' after receiving counsel from one Marcellus of Rome, a doctor of laws, who appears to have been operating as a freelance jurisconsult in the English Pale at the time.[41] Worse, 'Doctor Marcel' was also reckoned to have 'caused . . . great variance' – 'by deceitful promises, perjury and false administration of the law of Holy Church' – amongst other Irish clergy 'especially in the counties of Uriel, Meath, Dublin and Kildare'. Apart from the Aleyn–Walton feud, he was held

---

[40] *Statutes Ireland, Edward IV*, ii, pp. 197–203.
[41] Ibid., pp. 195–7; Murray, 'Tudor diocese of Dublin', p. 86 nt. 44.

responsible for a dispute between Archbishop Bole of Armagh and Bishop Sherwood of Meath 'which by his means and false counsel had very nearly utterly destroyed the clergy of Meath and Uriel', and another fracas involving Dean Aleyn and one Thomas Clinton, a fellow canon of St Patrick's.[42] For Aleyn, the cathedral clergy of St Patrick's and other senior ecclesiastics in the Pale, Marcellus's actions were worrying in the extreme. It had become clear that his innovatory and sharp legal practices, which had obviously impressed and appealed to many of the clergy when he first arrived in Ireland, were capable of doing irreparable damage to the English Irish ecclesiastical polity. Not only did they threaten to destroy the rights and liberties upon which this polity was built, but they even threatened to undermine the solidarity and unity of purpose that had traditionally characterised the clergy of the Pale. Without this solidarity, *Laudabiliter* and all that it stood for would become a dead letter, a situation which demanded from them firm leadership and the strongest of defensive actions to neutralise the danger. Thus, with the help of the laity, it was enacted in parliament 'that proclamation be made that the said Doctor for his manifest falsity shall quit this land of Ireland within one month after the said proclamation made . . . and never to return to this said land'. Failure to do so on his part would make it lawful 'for anyone to take him as an enemy or traitor to the king'.[43]

The actions taken in parliament in 1474 over the Aleyn–Walton feud were very significant. They showed, for example, the depth of commitment of the dean and chapter of St Patrick's to maintaining their *Laudabiliter*-based ethos, and how sensitive they could be in recognising and identifying any force or individual which threatened to undermine it. They also showed, in the closing of clerical ranks against 'Doctor Marcel', that this ethos was embraced by the senior clergy elsewhere in the Pale, and that it was respected and upheld by the English Irish community generally. Above all, however, the parliamentary actions showed how deeply conservative this ethos was, and how resistant it would be to any form of innovation or change, whether such change resulted from the actions of the deviant Irishry, a foreign jurisconsult or, as would happen in the next generation, an English monarch intent on revolutionising the relationship between church and state. Given all this, it is worth exploring the nature and basis of these conservative clerical instincts in more detail; for it is clear – even from the impact they made on church life in the late medieval lordship – that they

---

[42] *Statutes Ireland, Edward IV*, ii, pp. 195–7; *Octavian's register*, nos. 223, 231. On the dispute between Aleyn and Clinton see *CPR, papal letters, 1458–71*, pp. 294–5; *CPR, papal letters, 1471–84*, pp. 312–3; Murray, 'Tudor diocese of Dublin', p. 86 nt. 45.

[43] *Statutes Ireland, Edward IV*, ii, pp. 195–7. See also *Octavian's register*, nos. 259, 352–4.

would play a crucial part in the formulation of the Englishry's response to state-sponsored religious reform in the sixteenth century.

III

The origins of the conservative ethos of the dean and chapter of St Patrick's Cathedral, and their peers amongst the Pale clerical elite, lay, as we have seen, in the events and thinking that surrounded the Anglo-Norman conquest of the twelfth and thirteenth centuries. Thereafter it was moulded and refined by the largely negative experiences of the English colony in the fourteenth and fifteenth centuries. Yet the feature that really sustained it and gave it an enduring strength and tenacity that would last right through to the eve of the Reformation, was its institutional character. The *Laudabiliter* settlement lived on in the hearts and minds of the Pale clergy not simply because they believed in and supported the values which it contained, but because those same values were embodied in the ecclesiastical institutions over which they presided, and implicit in many of their activities; and because the institutions themselves managed to retain the respect and support of the English Irish community throughout the Middle Ages.

The institutional embodiment of the *Laudabiliter* settlement, and its continuing attractiveness for the English Irish community, was a subtle and complex phenomenon, which manifested itself in a variety of ways. On one level it was purely symbolic. For the Englishry, the reforming mission enunciated in *Laudabiliter* was perceived both as the harbinger of English civility in Ireland and the underlying motive behind the foundation of many of the religious corporations of the Pale. Thus these corporations – whether they were original Anglo-Norman foundations or 'normanised' versions of those which had existed before their coming – stood out as monuments of English civility and, as such, were a source of communal pride. One of the most striking instances of this perception was evinced in the attitude of the citizenry of Dublin to the proposed dissolution of Christ Church Cathedral in the late 1530s and early 1540s. The Dubliners argued against this proposal and defended the cathedral on the grounds that its loss would have a denuding effect on the Englishness of their city, that it would undermine the fabric of English Irish society as a whole and that ultimately it would encourage 'the king's Irish enemies'.[44]

The clergy, for their part, were keenly aware of the symbolic link between their churches and the heritage of the English Pale, and did their utmost to sustain and cultivate it. This was evident, for example, in the efforts of bodies like St Patrick's Cathedral to preserve the status and standing of their

---

[44] Above pp. 40–1.

churches in a manner which approximated to, or fabricated, their condition at the time of their foundation. Thus in 1468 Archbishop Tregury and Dean Aleyn united the safe and lucrative Maghery churches of Lusk and Newcastle Lyons to the livings of the precentor, treasurer and archdeacon of Glendalough in St Patrick's Cathedral because their prebends in the marches and amongst the Irishry had 'fallen in decay' on account of 'the continual war had in this land of Ireland by Irish enemies and English rebels'. At least part of the reason for this action would have been the need to maintain St Patrick's standing as the one, truly impressive example of the English 'four-square' secular cathedrals which had been introduced by the Anglo-Normans at the time of the conquest. And there is little doubt that the action had the desired effect. As late as the reign of Elizabeth, Richard Stanyhurst, in his description of the churches of Dublin, commented explicitly on its rich endowment, which he attributed to the 'liberality of King John'.[45] The same desire to maintain this symbolic link with the past was evident in other actions taken by the cathedral at this time. In the parliament of 1467–8, for example, the dean and his clergy also secured the passage of a statute which gave new chapter acts concerning the extension of divine service and hospitality the same force as if they had been 'made, ordained and established, by authority of the king at the first foundation of the said church'.[46]

But more was expected of the religious corporations of Dublin and the English Pale than simply reminding the English Irish community of its past glories. They also had wide-ranging and contemporary social and political roles, which were dedicated to keeping English civility alive in Ireland in the present. One of the most important of these roles was the education of the young, as was attested to by a letter of the Irish council to the government in England on the eve of the dissolution of the monasteries. The council requested that six houses should be let stand – including, in the province of Dublin, Christ Church Cathedral, St Mary's Abbey, the nunnery of Grace Dieu and the priory of Greatconnell – because 'in them young men and childer, both gentlemen childer and other, both of man kind and women kind, be brought up in virtue, learning and in the English tongue and behaviour'.[47] Nor did this list represent the full extent of the corporate clergy's involvement in the education of the youth of the Pale. One important omission, because it was not threatened with suppression at the time, was St Patrick's Cathedral. The cathedral had its own choir school which had been established in the early fifteenth century and which looked

---

[45] *Alen's register*, p. 244; *Statutes Ireland, Edward IV*, i, pp. 477–81; Stanyhurst, *Holinshed's Irish chronicle*, p. 44.
[46] *Statutes Ireland, Edward IV*, i, pp. 639–41.   [47] *SP* III, pp. 130–1.

after the education of the six boy choristers who sang daily in the choir. In addition, individual dignitaries in the cathedral are known to have taken young boys into their households and provided for their schooling. Amongst those educated in this way was John Browne, a member of a freeholding family from Clondalkin, who as a boy was a member of the household of Dean Aleyn. Thereafter, he served Deans Rochfort, Ricard, Sutton and Darcy, and eventually took orders, after which he secured a prebend in St Patrick's himself. They also included John Plunket of Dunsoghly, who as a boy was educated in the household of Robert Fitzsimon, the precentor of St Patrick's (1508–42). Plunket later went on to the Inns of Court in London, and became chief justice of the Queen's Bench in Elizabeth's reign.[48]

The religious corporations' dedication to keeping English civility alive in Ireland was also evinced in their active participation in the government and administration of the Pale. The clergy of St Patrick's, for example, armed with their training in, and experience of, administering the romano-canonical law, often served in the Irish court of chancery. In the first two decades of the sixteenth century, three deans – Thomas Rochfort, John Ricard and Thomas Darcy – served as keeper of the rolls of chancery; while another, John Aleyn, took up a mastership in chancery in the mid-1490s, as did the aforementioned Robert Fitzsimon in the 1530s.[49] As well as providing personnel for the political and judicial institutions of English Ireland, the corporate clergy also provided facilities for the conduct of their business. Christ Church Cathedral, as we have seen, was the main site for the holding of parliaments and councils, while St Mary's Abbey was the 'common resort of all such of reputation, as hath repaired hither out of England'. In addition, the religious corporations were regular and reliable contributors to the hostings against the Irishry in the later Middle Ages, finding 'on their proper costs . . . many men of war as they are appointed by the king's deputy and council for the same'. And they also supported the defence of the Pale through the clerical subsidy levied by parliament.[50]

Perhaps the most striking aspect of the corporate clergy's participation in the government and administration of the Pale was their contribution – through their representatives, the lords spiritual[51] and clerical

---

[48] *Dignitas decani*, pp. 44–6, 123–4; Lawlor, *Fasti of St Patrick's*, p. 36; F.E. Ball, *The judges in Ireland, 1221–1921* (2 vols., London, 1926), ii, p. 208.

[49] Ellis, *Reform and revival*, p. 220; Lawlor, *Fasti of St Patrick's*, pp. 43, 56; TNA: PRO, SP 65/1, f. 19r; *Patent rolls 1485–94*, p. 473.

[50] *SP* III, p. 130; Ellis, *Reform and revival*, pp. 69–72; Richardson and Sayles, *Irish parliament*, pp. 185, 234–43.

[51] Evidence for the summoning and attendance of spiritual peers is scanty for the fifteenth century. Those who regularly attended from the diocese of Dublin included the abbot of the Cistercian abbey of St Mary by Dublin, the prior of the Knight's Hospitallers at

proctors[52] – to the work of the Irish parliament; a body which in the late medieval period dealt almost exclusively with matters of local concern to the Pale community.[53] Although precise details are lacking, their very active involvement in the parliament's deliberations is evident from the fact that a large number of ordinances were passed – no doubt as a result of their own lobbying – which confirmed existing or granted new corporate rights and privileges. These ranged, for example, from Thomas Court Abbey's right of possession of the priory of St Katherine at Leixlip, through the abbot of St Mary's right to present to the vicarage of Skreen in Co. Meath and the exemption of the prior and convent of All Hallows from paying taxes on their lands, to the priory of Holmpatrick's right to receive poundage on fishing vessels in order to complete a harbour near Skerries.[54]

More significantly, the parliament also acted as a useful forum for upholding, and reinforcing amongst the community at large, the corporate clergy's own *Laudabiliter*-inspired ethos. This was evident, for example, in the acts secured by the dean and chapter of St Patrick's Cathedral concerning the Aleyn–Walton dispute in 1474, or in provisions like the act from the 1494–5 parliament which stipulated that no person should be made prior of the Knight's Hospitallers at Kilmainham 'but of the English blood'.[55] Above all, however, it was evident in the parliament's attempts to curb the ill-effects of the Irishry's propensity towards 'Rome-running'. 'Rome-running' – the initiation of ecclesiastical causes at the Roman Curia, usually for the purpose of securing or retaining for the plaintiffs titles to ecclesiastical benefices – was a very common practice in Gaelic Ireland, probably because there was no effective judicial infrastructure in place to

---

Kilmainham, and the abbot of the regular canons of Thomas Court Abbey, Dublin (Richardson and Sayles, *Irish parliament*, p. 127).

[52] The clerical proctors represented the interests of the cathedral chapters and diocesan clergy of about thirteen dioceses in the fifteenth century, including proctors for St Patrick's Cathedral, Christ Church Cathedral and the lower clergy of the diocese of Dublin. It is difficult to quantify the numbers that actually attended individual parliaments, but it is reasonable to assume that the four Pale dioceses – Dublin, Kildare, Armagh *inter Anglicos* and Meath – were regularly represented (Richardson and Sayles, *Irish parliament*, pp. 183–6).

[53] On the late medieval Irish parliament generally see S.G. Ellis, 'Parliament and community in Yorkist and Tudor Ireland', in A. Cosgrove and J.I. McGuire (eds.), *Parliament and community: historical studies xiv* (Belfast, 1983), pp. 43–68; Richardson and Sayles, *Irish parliament*, pp. 174–281.

[54] *Statutes Ireland, Edward IV*, i, pp. 451–5, 727–9; *Statutes Ireland, Richard III – Henry VIII*, pp. 138–43; D.B. Quinn (ed.), 'The bills and statutes of the Irish parliaments of Henry VII and Henry VIII', *Analecta* 10 (1941), p. 85.

[55] Quinn, 'Bills and statutes', p. 92; A. Conway, *Henry VII's relations with Scotland and Ireland, 1485–98* (Cambridge, 1932), p. 210.

deal with the causes locally.[56] It was thus a painful reminder to the Pale clergy of the failure of the *Laudabiliter* reform mission to establish in Gaelic Ireland the English system of courts Christian that had been put in place in the heartland of the colony at the time of the conquest and, as such, was particularly despised. In reality, there was little the corporate clerical elite could do to improve this situation generally, but they were certainly determined to prevent the practice spreading to, or harming, the inhabitants of the Pale. Thus, at their behest, the Irish parliament attempted on a number of occasions in the late fifteenth century to control the situation by outlawing, under the fourteenth century statutes of provisors, all papal delegates and their substitutes, especially 'Irish prelates, beneficers and clerks not obedient to the commands of the king nor to his laws', who presided over any ecclesiastical cause that injured or troubled 'the king's subjects'.[57]

There is little doubt, then, that the corporate clergy played a very full and active part in the political, cultural and social life of the English Pale in the later Middle Ages. Nor is there any doubt that in doing so they were able to promote, integrate and maintain their own conservative, *Laudabiliter*-inspired ethos as a permanent and unquestioned fixture in the thought and culture of the local community. This was hugely significant, for it gave the senior corporate clergy almost total freedom to express this ethos in the workings of their own corporate bodies without any fear of outside interference; and, intermittently, when external forces did threaten it, it ensured that they were able to secure the backing of the Pale community, in the shape of organs of the Dublin administration, to fend them off. Yet the unquestioned support of their community was not the only factor which helped sustain the conservative ethos of the senior Pale clergy. Equally important was the attitude of English-born bishops in Ireland, the one group who in theory would have had the capacity to alter, however subtly, the institutional basis of the Pale clergy's ethos. Generally, however, they adopted a policy of non-interference, a policy that was particularly evident in relation to Dublin's late medieval archbishops, all of whom, with the exception of Archbishop Fitzsimon, were natives of England.

[56] Cosgrove, 'Ireland beyond the Pale, 1399–1460', pp. 587–8; Osborough, 'Ecclesiastical law', pp. 227–30. Very little evidence survives on the existence and activities of the Gaelic Irish church courts in the later Middle Ages, but the fact that litigants resorted to Rome directly in so many ecclesiastical causes suggests that if such courts were in operation on a consistent basis, their rulings were to a large extent ineffective. However, the situation was not entirely static. Mario Sughi has recently shown that the clergy of Armagh *inter Hibernicos* began to appreciate the importance of the archbishop of Armagh's metropolitical court in the late fifteenth century and began to frequent it either to make accusations against rival clerics or to lodge appeals to Rome (*Octavian's register*, pp. lviii–lix).

[57] *Statutes Ireland, Edward IV*, i, p. 767, ii, pp. 541–5.

The capacity of Dublin's English-born archbishops to alter the institutional basis of the local clergy's value system was centred on the recruitment of the chapter of St Patrick's Cathedral and, more particularly, the recruitment of their diocesan officials from within this body. It was the archbishop who held the right of advowson in the vast bulk of the cathedral canonries, 24 out of a total of 27,[58] and thus whenever any of these livings became vacant – whether a major cathedral dignitary, an administratively important benefice like the archdeaconry of Dublin,[59] or an ordinary prebend – he could present the cleric of his choice, including clerical associates from his own land. In addition, he also had the right to bestow the other key administrative post, the diocesan chancellorship or official generalship, upon anyone from within this group of cathedral presentees, including once again natives of England.[60] The latter possibility, however, was rarely utilised by the archbishops. Although English appointees to cathedral prebends were not unknown in the later Middle Ages, the vast majority of those presented in the period were natives of the Pale, while those who went on to secure appointment as diocesan officials were exclusively so.

This patronage policy was most visible in regard to the appointments made to the diocesan chancellorship, being especially evident in the backgrounds of the five men who held the post during the period 1482–1534. The first of these, John Waren, was a Dubliner by birth. He was admitted to the franchise of the city in 1481, as were his kinsfolk Alice (in 1472); Walter, a merchant's apprentice (in 1481) and another John, a point maker (in 1482). Waren was succeeded by Geoffrey Fyche in the early 1490s, who hailed from a leaseholding farming family based to the north of the city of Dublin in Glasnevin. It was through their landlords, Christ Church Cathedral, that this family established its links with the local church, which were otherwise revealed in the keeping of the obits of seven members of the family, including Geoffrey, by the prior and convent. Robert Fitzsimon succeeded Fyche as chancellor early in the new century and was a member of a merchant and patrician family from the city of Dublin, which had

---

[58] Two prebends, Yago and Maynooth, were in the gift of the earl of Kildare, while the deanery was an elective dignity (*Alen's register*, pp. 279–80, 297–8; White (ed.), 'Reportorium Viride of John Alen', pp. 180–217 *passim*).

[59] On the duties and role of the archdeacon generally see Murphy, 'Archbishops and administration of Dublin', pp. 199–213; Murray, 'Tudor diocese of Dublin', pp. 94–5 nt. 62; A.H. Thompson, 'Diocesan organisation in the Middle Ages: archdeacons and rural deans', *PBA* 29 (1943) and *The English clergy and their organisation in the later Middle Ages* (Oxford, 1947) pp. 57–63.

[60] The chancellorship was a combination of two distinct offices, the vicar generalship and official principalship. For the duties attached to these offices see *CCD*, no. 1034; Thompson, *English clergy*, pp. 46–56; Murray, 'Tudor diocese of Dublin', p. 95, nt. 63.

moved out into the north Co. Dublin countryside. His brother Thomas, of Corduff, served Archbishops Inge and Alen as the lay seneschal of their manorial courts and was recorder of the city of Dublin *c.* 1530–54. The last two men who held the chancellorship of the see prior to the Reformation were born outside the diocese – Thomas Darcy and Walter Cusack – but were both very much part of the Pale community, being younger sons of gentle families based within the Maghery in Co. Meath. Darcy held the position in the second decade of the sixteenth century and perhaps even longer. He was probably the third son of John Darcy IV of Platten and brother of Sir William Darcy, who was undertreasurer in the Irish administration for a period in the 1520s. Cusack was the second son of Christopher Cusack of Tara and served as chancellor under Archbishop Alen in the early 1530s until his death in 1534.[61] Why the English-born archbishops of Dublin always patronised such locals is not entirely certain. The probable reasons for the policy – lack of interest on the part of English clergymen in following careers in the Irish church, the archbishops' concern to win the support of their flocks by ensuring that episcopal rule was brought to bear upon them through their own representatives – are less important than the impact it had upon the course of episcopal government and diocesan administration. In effect, it gave the local clergy a complete stranglehold over the entire process, which was exploited from generation to generation to maintain a canonical culture dedicated to sustaining their own *Laudabiliter*-inspired ethos.

The dean and chapter's controlling influence over the process of church government, and the manner in which they exploited it to promote their own ideological interests, is easily identifiable, especially in the content of local canonical ordinances. In January 1515, for example, Dean Rochfort and his chapter secured a new agreement with their archbishop, William Rokeby, which formally renewed the dean's ancient jurisdictional rights over the chapter of St Patrick's. Significantly, as if to underline the cathedral's desire to protect its *Laudabiliter*-inspired ethos, the new statutes also confirmed the ancient custom which denied membership of the cathedral to

---

[61] Lennon and Murray (eds.), *Dublin city franchise roll*, pp. 6, 15, 16–17; CCD, nos. 359–60, 366–7, 386, 422, 956, 1003, 1034; Refaussé with Lennon, *Registers of Christ Church*, pp. 42–3, 49, 52–3, 55, 61; *Alen's register*, p. 253; TNA: PRO, SP 65/1, f. 19r; RIA, 12.S.28, no. 831 (exemplification of the will of Alexander Beswick by Robert Fitzsimon, official principal of the metropolitan court of Dublin *sede vacante*); RCB, D6/113, no. 2 ('An abstract of inquisitions taken in Henry VIII's reign, relating to the archbishopric of Dublin'); Morrin, *Patent rolls*, i, pp. 326–7; Lennon, *Lords of Dublin*, pp. 14, 59, 73; *Ormond deeds, 1509–47*, p. 23; *Octavian's register* II, no. 146; PRONI, D 430, no. 59 (Will of William Hoggison, late mayor of Dublin, 1519); S.B. Barnewall, 'Darcy of Platten, Co. Meath', *IG* 6, no. 4 (1983), pp. 408–9; H. Gallwey, 'The Cusack family of Counties Meath and Dublin. Pt V: Cusack of Gerardstown', *IG* 6, no. 2 (1981), p. 134.

anyone of the Irish nation, manners and blood, a ruling which was confirmed by Pope Leo X in the following July.[62] Another similarly motivated
ordinance was passed in 1518 by the Dublin provincial council, the
body which was responsible for making local canon law and which was
comprised of the archbishop, his suffragan bishops, and representatives of
the religious and cathedral chapters of the province. In this instance,
the local ecclesiastical establishment, including the dean and chapter of
St Patrick's, reaffirmed its long-standing commitment to preventing the
worst excesses of the Irish clergy's canonical deviancy taking a hold in
the parishes of Dublin and its suffragan sees. The council enacted that
priests from Ulster and Connacht were not to be admitted unless, in the
judgement of the ordinary, they were found to be fit pastors, a stipulation
which would have demanded from them the unquestioned acceptance of the
principle of priestly celibacy.[63] Yet while the cathedral clergy's continuing
commitment to sustaining and promoting their traditional notions of
English canonical rectitude is obvious, less so was the mechanism through
which they transmitted these ideas from one generation to the next. Here
too, however, the process was 'institutionalised', being centred on the
training of prospective canon lawyers for the Dublin and other Pale
diocesan administrations.

In each generation, a handful of Pale clergymen acquired degrees in
canon or civil law from the University of Oxford, some of whom went on to
take up senior positions in the diocesan administrations in the Pale. These
included Robert Fitzsimon and Walter Cusack who served as chancellors of
the diocese of Dublin in the early decades of the sixteenth century.[64] The
degree courses on offer, however, were largely theoretical in scope and did
not really equip prospective ecclesiastical judges and lawyers with the skills
or experience that were needed to preside over, or practise in the courts
Christian, with the result that they were not thought to be necessary for

---

[62] *Alen's register*, pp. 262–3; Mason, *History of St Patrick's*, pp. 143–4; *Dignitas decani*, pp. 56–64.

[63] 'Presbyteri Conactenses et Ultoniensis non admittantur, nisi judicio ordinarii inveniantur idonei': D. Wilkins (ed.), *Concilia Magnae Britaniae et Hiberniae* (4 vols., London, 1737), iii, p. 660, calendared in H.J. Lawlor (ed.), 'Calendar of the Liber Ruber of the diocese of Ossory', *PRIA* 27 C (1908–9), p. 165.

[64] Of the five men who occupied the chancellorship of Dublin in the period 1482 to 1534 – John Waren, Geoffrey Fyche, Robert Fitzsimon, Thomas Darcy and Walter Cusack – only two of them, Fitzsimon (Bachelor of Civil Law) and Cusack (Bachelor of Canon Law), are known with certainty to have held degrees in law, although Thomas Darcy studied at Oxford and acquired an MA. Similarly, Walter Cusack was the only formally qualified canonist amongst the five men who held the archdeaconry of Dublin in this period (*BRUO 1501–40*, pp. 157, 160; *BRUO 1500*, i, p. 544, ii, p. 695; Lawlor, *Fasti of St Patrick's*, pp. 78–9).

anybody intent on pursuing such careers, even in England.[65] Nor, more importantly, would these degree courses have instilled in budding Pale canonists the ideological mores that were associated with the practice of ecclesiastical law in their own land. From the perspective of the Dublin diocesan establishment, then, what was required, and what was actually provided by them to make good these deficiencies, was a less formal, indigenous, more broadly based and more vocationally oriented system of education to train and form prospective canon lawyers in their own image. The medium through which this was achieved was the family.

Although sparsely documented, there is little doubt that there existed a very strong, family-based and markedly practical tradition of legists in Dublin in the later Middle Ages. Amongst these clerical, canonical dynasties, for example, were the Warens. Three different Warens served in the Dublin diocesan administration throughout the latter half of the fifteenth century, comprising Robert, who served as official principal of Dublin, and Thomas, who served as commissary of the dean of St Patrick's, both in the 1460s; and John, who served as diocesan chancellor (1482–c. 92).[66] John Waren's successor as chancellor, Geoffrey Fyche, came from a very similar family. Before he succeeded to this office in the 1490s, a probable kinsman and formally trained canonist, Richard Fyche, served as official principal of Dublin in the 1470s. In addition, one Thomas Fyche, probably Geoffrey's elder brother, was sub-prior of Christ Church Cathedral from the 1480s until his death in 1518.[67] Fyche's successor as chancellor was Robert Fitzsimon. The Fitzsimon family too, in all its various branches, was very prominent in the local church, and notable for a strong legist bent. One of their number, Walter, was the only native of Ireland to hold the archbishopric of Dublin in the centuries following the Anglo-Norman incursion into Ireland. His elevation to the episcopate, in fact, followed an earlier career as a diocesan administrator, which included a stint as official principal of the diocese in the 1470s. Connections with the canon law and the local institutions which administered it were also evident in Robert's more immediate family. His brother Richard, like Robert himself, attended Oxford, where he supplicated for a degree in canon law in 1526. Thereafter he was appointed, under archiepiscopal patronage, to the valuable vicarage

[65] J.L. Barton, 'The legal faculties of late medieval Oxford', in J.I. Catto and R. Evans (eds.), _The history of the University of Oxford. Volume II: later medieval Oxford_ (Oxford, 1992), pp. 307–8.

[66] CCD, nos. 298, 1034; Lennon and Murray (eds.), _Dublin City franchise roll_, pp. 54, 56, 57, 60, 67.

[67] CCD, nos. 308, 342, 359; Berry, _Register of wills_, pp. 13–196 _passim_; DNB sub nomine 'Thomas Fyche'; _BRUO 1500_, ii, p. 735; Refaussé with Lennon, _Registers of Christ Church_, p. 42.

of Swords and it was probably only his premature death in 1534 which prevented him from succeeding to a senior administrative post. In addition, one other probable kinsman, Bartholomew, was a fellow canon in St Patrick's Cathedral.[68]

It is reasonable to assume that this family-based tradition of practising legists had a very strong formative effect on the young canon lawyers of Dublin and the Pale. For some, it would have provided the sole source of their education. There is no record, for example, that Geoffrey Fyche attended university or that he held a formal qualification in either canon or civil law. Thus it is likely that he gained his training and knowledge of ecclesiastical law from his kinsman Richard, perhaps through a combination of access to a family library and observation of the elder Fyche presiding over the consistory court in St Patrick's Cathedral.[69] For those who did attend university, the tradition would have provided a spur to seek out practical experience of the church courts, with a view to fleshing out the more academic knowledge of the decretals that they acquired from their lectures and reading. It is noticeable, for example, that the two graduates who went on to practise in the Dublin church courts in the early sixteenth century, Robert Fitzsimon and Thomas Darcy, took on the positions of principals in their academic halls. As principals, both men would have been utilised by the university as agents in the preservation of discipline among the students who lodged in their halls, a role which would have involved both Fitzsimon and Darcy liaising with the university chancellor's court in the prosecution of office cases against delinquent scholars.[70] It also gave Fitzsimon practical experience of such matters as the probate and administration of wills, for he was chosen by fellow students resident at Beke's Inn to administer their goods after their decease.[71]

The most important legacy of the dynastic tradition of canon law in Dublin, however, was its role in the preservation of the *Laudabiliter*-based ethos of the senior Pale clergy. Given the canonical basis of this ethos, and

---

[68] CCD, no. 386; *BRUO 1500*, ii, p. 695, iii, pp. 2175–6; Berry, *Register of wills*, p. 27; *BRUO 1501–40*, p. 206; NAI, RC 9/2, pp. 194–200; Morrin, *Patent rolls*, i, pp. 21, 28; *Fiants, Edward VI*, no. 77.

[69] For a later example of this 'observational' mode of training in the ecclesiastical law in Dublin see the case of Thady Dowling discussed below pp. 284–5.

[70] Fitzsimon was admitted principal of Beke's Inn in June 1502, while Darcy was admitted to two successive principalships – St Mildred's Hall and Beam Hall – in June and December 1505 respectively: *BRUO 1500*, i, p. 544; ii, p. 695; W.T. Mitchell (ed.), *Registrum Cancellarii 1498–1506* (Oxford Historical Society, New Series, 27, Oxford, 1980), pp. 70, 84, 144, 229–30. On the disciplinary role of the principal see A.B. Cobban, *The medieval English universities: Oxford and Cambridge to c. 1500* (Aldershot, 1988), pp. 146–8.

[71] Mitchell (ed.), *Registrum Cancellarii*, pp. 70, 229–30.

the known facts that the local canonists upheld it and that it survived right through to the eve of the Reformation, it is difficult to conceive that the legist families were not instrumental in preserving and transmitting it down the generations. Their involvement in this process would also help explain the non-academic basis of the local canon law tradition. For historical reasons – above all, because of the contraction of the English colony in medieval Ireland – the legist families, especially those based in Dublin, would have been primarily concerned with defending the remnants of the old Anglo-Norman ecclesiastical settlement in Ireland, which was most perfectly realised in bodies like St Patrick's Cathedral and which of itself was thought to embody all the finest aspects of canon law. Thus, although an occasional interest was shown in establishing a university in the Pale to provide easier access to formal training in the romano-canonical laws and other disciplines – as in the parliamentary plan of 1465 to found one at Drogheda,[72] or Archbishop Fitzsimon's plans for a similar body in Dublin – there was no real impetus for such innovation and change. Rather, the aim of the legist families and their peers was simply to maintain the status quo, including, above all, the preservation of their ideology and its ecclesiological basis. This was an aim, as experience had shown, which could be easily realised by invoking the tried and trusted methods of training canon lawyers.

Once trained, and once they had fully absorbed the ideological mores of previous generations of Pale canonists, the new diocesan officials and their colleagues in St Patrick's Cathedral played a very full part in transmitting their *Laudabiliter*-based ethos to the other corporate clergy of the diocese and, ultimately, to the clergy and laity of the diocese as a whole. The main media used for transmitting their ethos amongst the religious would have been formal bodies like the Dublin provincial council and the Irish parliament, which as we have seen were frequently used to give it practical effect through a wide variety of acts and ordinances. However the canonists also had available to them less formal means of inculcating the same ethos. As the acknowledged experts in canon law in the diocese, and in the English Pale generally, the clergy of St Patrick's were called upon to act as jurisconsults, a service which was no doubt provided complete with the full *Laudabiliter* gloss. Thus, in the early 1520s, All Hallows Priory and Thomas Court Abbey retained Robert Fitzsimon, the precentor of St Patrick's and a former official principal of Dublin, to advise on the canonical modes for electing their heads. While ostensibly such advice would have dealt solely with the technical details of electing a monastic head – by scrutiny, compromise or inspiration – we may also assume that

[72] *Statutes Ireland, Edward IV*, i, p. 369.

more local concerns, such as the confinement of the candidates to those born of English blood, were also raised or, at the very least, tacitly understood.[73] The same understanding and acceptance of the Pale clergy's ethos would also have underpinned Dean Aleyn's decision on the eve of his death to donate his books on canon law – the Repertorium of Peter, bishop of Brescia, and Panormitanus's commentary on the decretals – to Christ Church Cathedral; or the decision of Richard Ellerkar, prebendary of Castleknock, to act as the prior of Kilmainham's steward from the 1520s until the priory was dissolved in 1540.[74]

The dean and chapter's capacity to radiate their canonical culture amongst the corporate clergy generally was hugely important, for with it came a much greater capacity to extend that same culture into the parishes of their diocese and of the Pale as a whole. The foundation upon which it was built was the corporate clergy's almost total control of the parochial system, which was derived from their position as the appropriators of the vast majority of parochial rectories. Thus on the eve of the Reformation, *c.* 1530, 163 rectories out of a total of 192 in the diocese of Dublin – just over 84 per cent – were appropriated to the two Dublin cathedrals and eighteen religious houses. Of these 163 appropriated parishes only thirty-four, or 21 per cent, had endowed vicarages which meant that the corporate clergy, either as individuals or as collective entities, had the ultimate responsibility for appointing curates and chaplains to 129, or 67 per cent, of all Dublin parishes.[75] This was an extremely powerful position because the vast majority of the curates and chaplains were totally dependent upon the corporate clergy for their economic well-being. All of them could be removed at will from their posts by the corporate rectors, because they possessed no freehold interest in the livings in which they served. It would be wrong, however, to assume that this relationship of economic dependency was built upon fear. On the contrary, it was paternalistic in nature. Some of the corporate clergy, especially the richly endowed clergy of St Patrick's Cathedral, were sufficiently indulgent to allow their curates portions of their parochial possessions, usually the altarages and occasionally the glebelands, in recompense for serving the cures.[76] With these

---

[73] BL, Additional Charters, nos. 7043, 7044; Griffith, *Exchequer inquisitions*, p. 76. On the canonical modes of election generally see Lawlor, *Fasti of St Patrick's*, pp. 22–8.

[74] Berry, *Register of wills*, p. 199; *The miscellany of the Irish Archaeological Society* (Dublin, 1846), pp. 81–3; TNA: PRO, E 344/18, f. 29r.

[75] Below Appendix 2.

[76] On this see the survey of the cathedral's possessions taken after its dissolution in 1547: RCB, C2/1/27, no. 2 *passim* (printed in Mason, *History of St Patrick's*, pp. 28–99). On the glebelands and altarages generally see Murray, 'Sources of clerical income' pp. 146–57.

grants, the curates would normally receive warranties from their masters that their possession of the properties would be automatically defended in the church and secular courts against intrusions, or the refusal of their parishioners to pay the customary parochial dues.[77] In this way the corporate clergy appeared as the beneficent defenders of the lower clergy, a pose which occasionally evoked gestures of genuine affection from individual parish priests towards their employees;[78] but which, above all, would have demanded from them a full acceptance of their masters' dearly held notions of English civility and canonical rectitude. In turn, the parochial clergy attempted to promote and disseminate these ideas themselves amongst the wider community through the parochial schools that they kept on the eve of the Reformation.

Very little information now survives on individual parochial schools from the late fifteenth and sixteenth centuries. The incidental reference to the school that was kept in the 'priest's chamber' by Sir Richard Roger, chaplain of the north county Dublin parish of St Margaret, Dunsoghly, in the early sixteenth century, is almost unique.[79] Nevertheless, a number of such schools – the equivalent of the English petty or ABC schools – do seem to have been in operation in this period, and were very much involved in the work of preserving and maintaining English cultural mores. Some evidence for this can be found in a statute passed by the Irish parliament in 1537, the act for the English order, habit and tongue. Framed with the intention of extending into Gaelic and Gaelicised Ireland the cultural mores and practices that were already current in the Pale, the act provided that all beneficed clergy were to keep 'a school for to learn English' in their parishes, in just the same manner, the act implied, that was then in operation throughout the Maghery.[80] And there is further evidence that the early application of the act was extremely successful, at least in Co. Dublin. Thus, of the forty-eight or so beneficed clergymen who, under the terms of the act, were bound to keep schools in the county, only five – Thomas Hallynge, vicar [sic] of Baldongan, Patrick Long, vicar of Bray, Gilbert Rose, vicar of Swords, John Wogan, vicar of Balrothery and Thomas Cruise, vicar of Balscaddan – were found by the barons of the exchequer in February 1548 to have neglected

---

[77] For some later examples of such warranties coming into effect see the Act book of the Dublin Consistory, 1596–99, Marsh's Library, MS Z4.2.19, pp. 102–3, 110.

[78] One such priest was Patrick Law, chaplain of Glasnevin, who, on his death in 1514, left all his goods to Christ Church Cathedral, the corporate rector of his parish (*CCD*, no. 1117; Refaussé with Lennon, *Registers of Christ Church*, p. 77).

[79] *CCD*, no. 429.

[80] *Statutes Ireland, Richard III–Henry VIII*, pp. 236–44. The act stated that the parish priest/ school keeper should take for his pains 'such convenient stipend or salary as in the said land is *accustomably used* to be taken' (p. 243, my italics).

this duty.[81] Overall, then, it would seem that the corporate clergy were not only successful in keeping their ethos alive in their own cloisters and precincts, and amongst the political community whom they were responsible for educating; but also – through the influence they exerted on the parochial clergy – in the community of lowly artisans and humble farmers who inhabited the parishes of the English Pale. It is no surprise, therefore, that representatives of these groups, men like John Aleyn of the farming community of east Co. Meath, would enter the ranks of the corporate clergy themselves, and make their own deeply motivated contribution towards preserving English culture, and the notion of canonical rectitude that it encompassed, from one generation to the next.

IV

At the time of his death, in January 1506, John Aleyn believed that the main danger to the survival of the Pale clergy's anglocentric, *Laudabiliter*-based, communal identity was the influence of the deviant Irishry. It was this fear – which had animated many generations of the English Irish clerical elite since the original Anglo-Norman conquest – that led him to establish an almshouse dedicated to preserving an overtly English and canonically correct version of the Catholic religion. Yet within a few decades of his death, a new and potentially more damaging enemy would emerge to threaten the existence of the culture which he and his contemporaries had done so much to preserve and pass on to the next generation of corporate clergy. Most disturbingly for the successors of Dean Aleyn, the new enemy was one of the bedrock institutions upon which their culture was founded and to which they had traditionally looked for its continued sustenance, the English monarchy.

The Tudor monarchs, who ushered in what was once thought of as 'The English Reformation', are now reckoned by many modern historians to have presided over the introduction of more than one Reformation or, at the very least, a number of theologically distinct religious settlements, which provoked many and varied local responses throughout the Tudor dominions during the sixteenth century.[82] This view has much to commend it and, in the wake of Brendan Bradshaw's pioneering work on the Reformation in Ireland, has found its way into the mainstream of Irish historiography, where it is now generally accepted that sections of the indigenous

---

[81] NAI, RC 9/2, pp. 300, 304–7; Griffith, *Exchequer inquisitions*, pp. 120–1; *Valor beneficiorum*, pp. 9–10.

[82] The fullest and most explicit use of this 'various (and varied) Reformations' interpretative framework is Haigh, *English reformations*. See especially pp. 12–21.

population, however nominally, were willing to conform to certain aspects of these reformed settlements, especially under Henry VIII.[83] Yet the point can obscure another reality that there was at least one highly influential group in Irish society that found the Reformation in its different guises difficult to come to terms with: the corporate clerical elite of Dublin and the English Pale. For this group, in particular, the fact that there were dissimilarities between the various Tudor religious settlements – that some were liturgically or doctrinally less radical than the others – was of little concern or little consolation, in the light of those traits which all of them held in common. The most important of these traits – the crown's abolition of papal authority in its dominions, its rejection of the authority of Roman canon law, and its disregard for the independence and liberties of the clerical estate – undermined or threatened to destroy virtually every element of the clerical elite's ethos; including the political basis of the original *Laudabiliter* settlement, the intellectual and legal foundations of their cherished notions of canonical correctness, and even their own hallowed position in Pale society. Thus, from the outset, the Reformation was a source of great discomfiture to the corporate clerical elite. Inevitably, it would arouse opposition from within its ranks.

The individual who would experience this opposition most intensely was the archbishop of Dublin; for, given that the Tudors chose to retain the traditional, episcopally based governmental structures of the medieval church, a major part of the responsibility for promoting and enforcing religious change in the archbishop's own domain rested firmly upon his shoulders. In addition, the same ecclesiological policy also meant that the archbishop would be expected to enlist the support of the corporate clerical elite – the traditional judicial and administrative caste of his diocese and province – in undertaking this task. It was to be in the working out of these administrative imperatives, primarily, that divisions and discord would arise between the archbishop and his senior clergy.

These interactions between the archbishops of Dublin and their senior clergy, however, did not take place in a vacuum. The enforcement of the crown's religious policies, and the reactions it provoked, were also a major concern of crown government in Ireland and, more particularly, of the head of the royal administration, the viceroy. Like the archbishops of Dublin, the Tudor viceroys also bore a significant part of the responsibility for implementing the crown's religious policies and, in this connection, had to engage with the archbishop and his clergy on a range of religious and ecclesiastical matters on an ongoing basis. The following chapters, then, will attempt to chart – in both the contexts of the

[83] Murray, 'Church of Ireland: critical bibliography', pp. 347–9.

archbishops' efforts to enforce the Tudors' religious settlements in Dublin, and of the viceroys' parallel efforts to elaborate and implement religious and ecclesiastical policy more generally – the course of clerical opposition, and to analyse its impact and significance on the fate of the Reformation in Ireland.

3

Rebellion and supremacy: Archbishop Browne, clerical opposition and the enforcement of the early Reformation, 1534–40

The Reformation began in the diocese of Dublin in an atmosphere of crisis, provoked by the outbreak of the Kildare rebellion in the summer of 1534. Although motivated initially by secular concerns – the Fitzgeralds' desire to force the abandonment of the political and administrative reforms of the king's chief minister, Thomas Cromwell[1] – the revolt swiftly assumed a religious dimension. From an early stage, Silken Thomas and his supporters claimed that they were 'of the pope's sect and band and him will they serve against the king and all his partakers'.[2] For the Tudor regime, and for many historians subsequently, the most striking aspect of this claim was the possibility that it might secure for the Kildare cause military or financial support from the papacy and the Holy Roman emperor, thus turning what was a domestic disturbance into an international Catholic crusade against a schismatic English king.[3] In practice its repercussions were less dramatic. Yet it still proved to be damaging to the fate of the Henrician Reformation in Ireland. In justifying their decision to play the papal card, the Fitzgeralds drew heavily upon the thinking, and sought the support, of the clerical elite of the English Pale, especially amongst the Dublin diocesan establishment based in St Patrick's Cathedral. Thus, even as the Tudor regime prepared to implement its ecclesiastical revolution, the Kildare revolt had already crystallised the issues that were at stake for the local clergy and, as a result,

---

[1] L. McCorristine, *The revolt of Silken Thomas* (Dublin, 1987), ch. 2; S.G. Ellis, 'Tudor policy and the Kildare ascendancy in the lordship of Ireland', *IHS* 20 (1976–7), pp. 235–71 and 'Thomas Cromwell and Ireland', *HJ* 23 (1980), pp. 497–518; B. Bradshaw, 'Cromwellian reform and the origins of the Kildare rebellion', *TRHS*, 5th series, 27 (1977), pp. 69–93.

[2] Robert Cowley to Cromwell, *c.* June 1534 (*SP* II, pp. 197–8).

[3] *LP* VIII, no. 957; Edwards, *Church and state*, pp. 1–5; McCorristine, *Revolt of Silken Thomas*, pp. 71–8; W. Palmer, *The problem of Ireland in Tudor foreign policy 1485–1603* (Woodbridge, 1994), ch. 3; M. O'Siochrú, 'Foreign involvement in the revolt of Silken Thomas', *PRIA* 96 C (1996), pp. 49–66.

ensured that the Reformation was greeted by a well-informed and organised culture of indigenous clerical resistance.

I

The task that Kildare and his supporters set themselves, in attempting to persuade the clerical elite of the diocese of Dublin to withdraw their allegiance from Henry VIII, was formidable. Centuries of habitual loyalty to the monarchy, allied to a fundamental belief and trust in the crown's essential contribution to the maintenance of their English identity and canonical ethos – and the hope, at this early stage of the Reformation, that it might still be restored – ensured that the clergy were profoundly wary of taking such a precipitate step. Indeed, the problem of overcoming such inherent conservatism was made even more difficult for Kildare and his supporters by the dramatic and shocking event that heralded the outbreak of their revolt: the murder of Archbishop John Alen of Dublin. Although the archbishop was not a very popular figure amongst his clergy, a feature evinced in the fact that he was left buried in a pauper's grave after his death, his murder at the hands of Lord Thomas Fitzgerald and a small band of supporters at Artane in July 1534 was still regarded as a heinous crime and a poor advertisement for a movement that claimed to defend the old religion, including clerical privilege, from the ravages of a heretical king. Not surprisingly, it resulted in the custodians of the see's spiritual jurisdiction – Dean Geoffrey Fyche of St Patrick's Cathedral and Prior Thomas Hassard of Christ Church – issuing a very strongly worded ecclesiastical censure against its perpetrators. While the custodians' 'curse' had been eagerly sought by Lord Deputy Skeffington and the Dublin administration for propagandist purposes, there is no reason to doubt that it was an authentic expression of the diocesan administration's feelings on the matter, nor that it caused deep embarrassment to the supporters of Kildare who were seeking to portray his rebellion as a religious crusade.[4]

Yet the situation was not entirely discouraging for the Geraldines. As the patron of two prebends in the cathedral, Maynooth and Yago, Kildare had his own representatives within the chapter of St Patrick's, and would have been aware that Dean Fyche and his fellow canons had very deep misgivings about the crown's developing religious policy, especially its attack on the wealth and independence of the English church in the early 1530s. One manifestation of this – the punishment of Archbishop Alen in 1531 for

---

[4] Murray, 'Archbishop Alen and reform', pp. 1–2; *LM* II, pt. 5, p. 97; Lord Deputy Skeffington to Henry VIII, 11 November 1534 (*SP* II, pp. 205–7, at p. 206); the custodians' 'curse' (*SP* II, pp. 217–19).

committing offences against the English statutes of *praemunire* and pro-visors – had already made a devastating impact in the diocese of Dublin itself. Fined the massive sum of £1,466 13s. 4d. sterling for his involvement in the exercise of Cardinal Wolsey's legatine jurisdiction, Alen was a victim both of the 'aristocratic *putsch*' that had brought about his former master's demise, and of the king's general *praemunire* manoeuvres, which were conducted against the Canterbury clergy to cow the bench into submission to his divorce plans and to display his power and resolve to the Roman Curia. Standing at four times the annual revenue of the see of Dublin, the fine imposed upon Alen sent out a very chilling warning to the local clergy about the king's determination to secure the full submission of the clerical estate to his will, and provided a vivid preview of the financial ramifications that such a submission might entail for them.[5]

Any doubts that were still harboured on this matter were resolved late in 1533 or early in 1534, with the arrival in Dublin of Dr John Travers, an English theologian, who took up the post of chancellor of St Patrick's Cathedral, and who confirmed for his new colleagues the full and unwel-come extent of the Henrician revolution in England. The exact circum-stances surrounding Travers's appointment are obscure. His living was in the gift of the archbishop of Dublin, which suggests that Archbishop Alen – attracted possibly by the Oxford-educated Travers's academic attainments – was responsible for making it. Arguably of more significance, however, were Travers's own reasons for coming to Dublin. For someone with his qualifications, the move to the relative obscurity of St Patrick's Cathedral was unusual and certainly not undertaken to advance his career. Rather, given his later actions – he is thought to have written a book in defence of the papal supremacy and is known to have joined the Kildare rebellion on religious grounds – it is likely that he came to Dublin because of his disillusionment with the crown's onslaught on the liberties of the English Church, and in the knowledge that his own religious preferences would find a more receptive audience in Ireland.[6]

Travers's hopes were soon confirmed. From the moment he arrived in Dublin, there was a genuine meeting of minds between himself and the cathedral clergy, so much so in fact that Geoffrey Fyche was prepared to

---

[5] Murray, 'Archbishop Alen and reform', pp. 11–12. On the praemunire manoeuvres and the submission of the clergy generally see J. A. Guy, 'Henry VIII and the praemunire manoeuvres of 1530–1531', *EHR* 97 (1982), pp. 482–503, and *Tudor England* (Oxford, 1988), pp. 127–8; G. W. Bernard, 'The pardon of the clergy reconsidered', *JEH* 37 (1986), pp. 258–82, and *The King's Reformation. Henry VIII and the remaking of the English Church* (Yale, 2005), pp. 30–50.

[6] Lawlor, *Fasti of St Patrick's*, p. 63; R. D. Edwards, 'Venerable John Travers and the rebellion of Silken Thomas', *Studies* 23 (1934), pp. 687–99; *BRUO 1501–40*, p. 575.

resign the deanery – a living which was normally reserved as a reward for existing and senior members of the chapter who had made a significant contribution towards the administration of the diocese – to enable the canons to elect him as their leader ahead of the impending struggles over the implementation of the Reformation.[7] The favourable impression that Travers made in St Patrick's soon spread beyond the cathedral precincts. Once the Kildare rebellion broke out, he was identified – on account of his popularity in the close, his theological expertise and his abilities as a negotiator[8] – as the figure most likely to convince his fellow clergymen in St Patrick's of the necessity of supporting the revolt on religious grounds. With the experience of the English clergy's capitulation to the king so fresh in his mind, Travers himself was easily prevailed upon to join the rebels. The only question that remained unanswered was whether Kildare and his supporters could provide him with sufficiently strong arguments to convince his ultra-loyalist colleagues that they should do likewise.

The Geraldines were advised on the religious question by a group of 'learned counsellors', amongst whom were Cormac Roth, the archdeacon and official principal of Armagh; Edward Dillon, the dean of St Brigid's Cathedral, Kildare, and prebendary of Maynooth in St Patrick's Cathedral, Dublin; and Charles Reynolds, the archdeacon of Kells and official principal of Meath. Although it is well known that all of these men had Kildare connections which pre-dated the outbreak of the revolt, it has been too readily assumed that they acted out of purely factional motives.[9] What has not been appreciated generally is the extent to which they were part of the senior clerical establishment of the Pale and how much their political attitudes were influenced by the traditional values of this group. In essence, all of them upheld the *Laudabiliter*-inspired, canonical ethos of the senior English Irish clergy, a set of beliefs that they had been either born into, or had bought into to further their ecclesiastical careers. It was this culture which informed their own attitude to the Reformation, and upon which the appeal of Chancellor Travers to their peers in St Patrick's would ultimately be based.

Cormac Roth personified more than most the defining characteristics of his caste. A native of the diocese of Meath, he belonged to a family which

---

[7] Lord Deputy Grey and the council to Cromwell, 11 February 1537 (*SP* II, pp. 420–1).

[8] After he joined the rebellion Travers was employed by Lord Thomas as an emissary in discussions with the citizens of Dublin over gaining entrance to the city to take over the castle (Edwards, 'Venerable John Travers', p. 691).

[9] John Alen to Cromwell, 26 December 1534 (*SP* II, pp. 219–24, at pp. 221–2); Gwynn, *Medieval province of Armagh*, pp. 48, 56–7, 61, 68, 71–2, 127–30, 153, 182–5; Lawlor, *Fasti of St Patrick's*, p. 128; S.G. Ellis, 'The Kildare rebellion and the early Henrician Reformation', *HJ* 19 (1976), pp. 820–1.

had been anglicised for a couple of generations. The family also had a strong legist bent: a near kinsman, William, was a chaplain to the bishop of Meath in the 1490s and later served as official of the diocese in the 1520s. Roth himself studied at Oxford where he graduated in canon law. Thereafter he was a very active archdeacon and official principal in Armagh *inter Anglicos* until his death *c*.1539.[10] Edward Dillon was the personal chaplain of Gerald, ninth earl of Kildare and the son of Sir Bartholomew Dillon, who, in the early decades of the sixteenth century, had served successively as chief remembrancer of the Exchequer, undertreasurer and chief justice of the King's Bench. In 1523 Kildare described Edward as a man of 'virtuous living, and of English name and condition'. All of this, as well as his membership of the most quintessentially English of Irish religious corporations, St Patrick's Cathedral, suggests that he too subscribed fully to the traditional canonical culture of his peers.[11] Charles Reynolds was initially a less typical member of the group, but he did acquire the traits of his peers as his career progressed. A member of the Gaelic Irish family of MacRaghnaill from Co. Leitrim, Reynolds adopted the cultural mores of the clergy of English Ireland by securing a grant of English liberty in 1531. Like Roth, he was both a canonist and graduate of Oxford, and worked very actively as a diocesan and provincial administrator, sometimes in conjunction with the archdeacon of Armagh, prior to his involvement in the rebellion. There was also a legist tradition in his family. A near kinsman, Thady, undertook legal studies at Oxford and became a doctor of canon and civil law, serving later as a papal and royal bishop in the 1540s.[12]

As canon lawyers, senior ecclesiastical officials and upholders of the traditional justification for the English presence in Ireland – they believed that the English were there under papal sanction to reform the Irishry along conventional canonical lines – Kildare's 'learned counsellors' quickly recognised how fundamental an attack the Reformation was on all of their values, from the intellectual and legal bases of their dearly held notions of canonical correctness, to the very foundations of the original *Laudabiliter* settlement itself. Thus, spurred on by the political ambitions and anxieties of their Fitzgerald masters, the onset of the Reformation provided them with sufficient justification to think the most radical of thoughts and to make the most radical of decisions. Quite simply, if the king of England was prepared to reject both the papal authority upon which his own sovereignty

---

[10] Gwynn, *Medieval province of Armagh*, pp. 56, 72, 81; *BRUO 1501–40*, pp. 492–3; Jefferies, *Priests and prelates of Armagh*, pp. 45, 47, 92, 136, 139.

[11] Lyons, *Church and society in Kildare*, p. 94; Ellis, *Reform and revival*, pp. 221–3; Kildare to Wolsey, 8 February 1523 (*SP* II, pp. 98–9).

[12] Gwynn, *Medieval province of Armagh*, pp. 127–31, 153; Morrin, *Patent rolls*, i, p. 2; *BRUO 1501–40*, pp. 477–9.

over Ireland rested, and the orthodox canonical religion which he and his people were traditionally bound to promote and spread amongst the Irishry, then it was legitimate for his subjects to deny the validity of, and to rebel against, his own authority.

But they did not stop there. The group also employed this essentially traditionalist argument as a propagandist tool in all of their efforts to secure support for the Kildare cause. In December 1534, for example, Archdeacon Reynolds undertook a diplomatic mission to Rome, during which visit he portrayed the rebellion as an almost exclusively religious enterprise, that is, as an orthodox canonical protest against a heretical monarch. Hence, he took with him 'diverse old muniments and precedents, which should prove that the king hold this land of the see of Rome' and alleged 'the king and his realm to be heretics digressed from the . . . faith catholic'. Amongst these documents was King John's acknowledgement from 1213 that he held his dominions as fiefs of the apostolic see, a selection which showed that *Laudabiliter* and all that flowed from it still held a deep contemporary resonance for senior clerical figures in the English Pale.[13] In addition, the archdeacon also sought a papal absolution for Lord Thomas for the murder of Archbishop Alen, to ensure that the rebellion's image as a canonically legitimate and orthodox Catholic enterprise would remain unsullied.[14] It follows, then, that when John Travers set about the task of persuading the chapter of St Patrick's to support the Geraldine cause in the late summer of 1534, he not only had at his disposal a ready made and powerful argument, but one which would have struck a particularly strong chord with the cathedral canons, given that it originated in and encapsulated a set of values that were an essential part of their own corporate identity. In effect, Travers and Kildare's 'learned counsellors' sought to portray the revolt as a defence of the traditional canonical ethos of the chapter of St Patrick's and their peers amongst the English Irish clerical elite.

Yet while it is possible to identify the core issue that the cathedral clergy wrestled with following the outbreak of the revolt, the precise details of how their deliberations unfolded are not now on record. That said, there remain good grounds for arguing that the debate was a close run thing. In the aftermath of the rebellion, the Dublin administration certainly felt that Dean Fyche and his chapter were tainted with the same treasonable intent

---

[13] *SP* II, p. 222; Ellis, 'Rebellion and the early reformation', pp. 813–14; O'Siochrú, 'Foreign involvement', pp. 57–8; *CSP Spain* V, pt. 1, no. 164; M.P. Sheehy (ed.), *Pontificia Hibernica: medieval papal chancery documents concerning Ireland, 640–1261* (2 vols., Dublin, 1962–5), i, nos. 83–4.

[14] Gwynn, *Medieval province of Armagh*, pp. 69–70; F. M. Jones, *The Counter Reformation* (Dublin and Melbourne, 1967), pp. 1–2; O'Siochrú, 'Foreign involvement', p. 58; *CSP Spain* V, pt. 1, no. 164.

that Travers had openly exhibited, which was stimulated wholly by their distaste for the crown's reforming intentions. Similarly, the five-month delay in pronouncing the excommunication against the murderers of Archbishop Alen – it was not made until at least the middle of November – suggests that the dean and chapter may well have been considering their position as late as the autumn of 1534. In the end, however, the canons' traditional loyalty to the crown, and that of their community generally – shown, for example, in the resistance of the citizens of Dublin to the rebels' siege of their city – just about stood firm. Although they undoubtedly sympathised with the religious justification put forward by Travers for the Kildare revolt, Dean Fyche and his colleagues stopped short of joining him in open rebellion against their sovereign. Thus, only Travers amongst the cathedral canons was subsequently indicted and convicted of treason.[15]

Despite this outcome, the crown still had to pay a not insignificant cost. The debate inaugurated by Dillon, Roth, Reynolds and Travers at the outset of the Kildare rebellion had clarified for all of the senior clergy of the Pale just how threatening and offensive the crown's religious innovations were. And it had done so not for any abstruse theological reasons, but for reasons to which every English Irish clergyman could relate. The Reformation challenged their very *raison d'être*: their traditional role of reforming Ireland, under papal sanction, according to conventional canonical stand- ards and according to English ecclesiological norms. It was no surprise, therefore, that when the rebellion was eventually crushed, Thomas Crom- well, the king's chief minister, endeavoured to ascertain from the captured Silken Thomas 'what spiritual persons in Ireland did denounce unto him that the king was an heretic, and that it was lawful therefore . . . to digress from his obedience'. The fact that this notion was current amongst senior ecclesiastical officials in Ireland was not only disturbing for the Tudor regime in political terms, but it also spelled out, in the most emphatic manner, that the impending task of extending the Henrician ecclesiastical revolution to the lordship would pose a very considerable challenge.[16]

If further confirmation was needed regarding the extent and particular nature of this challenge, it was soon found in the proceedings of the Irish parliament that met in 1536–7 to enact Henry VIII's Reformation legisla- tion. It is now well established that the clergy, represented by their proctors, provided the sole opposition to the passage of the crown's ecclesiastical acts. Traditional characterisations of the clerical proctors, however – that they represented the voice of a heroic lower clergy who courageously

---

[15] *SP* II, pp. 206–7, 217–19, 420–1. On the siege of Dublin see McCorristine, *Revolt of Silken Thomas*, pp. 88–90; Edwards, *Church and state*, p. 109.
[16] Ellis, 'Rebellion and the early reformation', pp. 813–14.

resisted the dictates of Henry VIII – are wide of the mark.[17] Rather, they represented predominantly the voice of the cathedral chapters and diocesan administrations of English Ireland,[18] the clerical elite of the Pale, which had so recently flirted with rebellion because they felt that the onset of the Reformation would destroy all that they stood for. Thus the parliamentary opposition of the proctors was a direct continuation of the clerical resistance that had emerged during the rebellion. Nor is it surprising that such opposition was confined exclusively to this group. According to the canonical theory of representation, the dean and chapter of a diocese were thought to hold a mandate to speak on behalf of the entire population.[19] It may well be that the original idea behind the proctors sitting in parliament was to enable them to exercise this voice when the institution had to deal with religious and ecclesiastical matters. Certainly, this would help explain why the proctors' activities in the medieval Irish parliaments were concerned almost exclusively with such matters, and why it was they alone who resisted the imposition of the Reformation legislation. The bishops, monastic heads and laity who objected to this legislation but who for political reasons were in no position to oppose it, could content themselves in the knowledge that their objections were being raised literally by proxy.[20]

The actions of the proctors in parliament, coming so soon after the dissidence displayed by the clergy during the Kildare rebellion, confirmed to Cromwell and the Tudor regime that there was a serious problem of clerical resistance to the Reformation in the English Pale. In the short term, they attempted to combat it by instituting a number of punitive actions against those held responsible for the most notorious instances of disobedience. Amongst the measures undertaken were the execution, c. July 1535, of Chancellor Travers,[21] and an attempt, early in 1537, to force the resignations of Geoffrey Fyche, the dean of St Patrick's, and Thomas Hassard, the prior of Christ Church who, as custodians of the see of Dublin's spiritual jurisdiction during the Kildare revolt, were deemed to have lent an unacceptably sympathetic ear to the treasonous promptings of Travers.[22] Yet Cromwell was disinclined to continue with these admonitory

---

[17] Bradshaw, 'Irish reformation parliament', pp. 292, 298–9; G. A. Hayes-McCoy, 'The royal supremacy and the ecclesiastical revolution, 1534–1547', *NHI* II, pp. 57–8; Ellis, *Ireland in the age of the Tudors*, pp. 206–7; Lennon, *Sixteenth-century Ireland*, p. 135.
[18] Above pp. 68–70. [19] Brundage, *Medieval canon law*, pp. 106–8.
[20] Edwards, *Church and state*, p. 9; Ellis, 'Parliament and community in Yorkist and Tudor Ireland', p. 49, and *Ireland in the age of the Tudors*, p. 47. Significantly, Lord Deputy Grey and Vice-Treasurer Brabazon contended that the proctors were simply doing the bidding of their 'masters', the bishops (*SP* II, pp. 437–9).
[21] Edwards, 'Venerable John Travers', pp. 693–6.
[22] Murray, 'Tudor diocese of Dublin', pp. 117–18.

proceedings on an indefinite basis and, after he brought them to a close at the end of 1537 with the silencing of the clerical proctors' voice in parliament,[23] the problem of clerical dissidence in English Ireland was given only indirect attention in Whitehall.

Cromwell's stance at this point was reflective of the general manner in which he oversaw the affairs of Ireland in the period of his ascendancy. The government of the lordship was traditionally regarded as a matter of secondary importance amongst the crown's responsibilities. Thus, ever mindful of this reality, and the fact that he was personally burdened with an extensive and extraordinarily demanding range of political and administrative functions – including the delicate task of leading a radical programme of religious change in England, before an unpredictable monarch who prided himself on his theological expertise and Catholic orthodoxy – Cromwell had neither the will nor the capacity to engage with Irish matters in anything other than a fitful manner. Indeed, on the intermittent occasions when the lordship did exercise his mind, his decisions and actions were generally influenced by secular considerations, most notably, the desiderata of propagating his own personal patronage network, and of maintaining a low-cost system of government.[24] As far as the problem of clerical dissidence in Ireland was concerned, then, he tended to the view that it was a matter that would be best addressed as part of the broader implementation of the crown's programme of ecclesiastical and religious reform. The expectation was that the gradual rolling out of this revolutionary reform programme in all of its aspects – juridical, devotional and evangelical – would eventually win the clerical doubters over to the new religious dispensation, if not through the force of the reformers' message itself, then at least through administrative familiarity and inertia.

For Cromwell, then, the issue to be addressed was not the development of an understanding of the particular nature of clerical resistance in the Pale and the devising of a specific strategy to combat it. Rather, what he faced was the essentially bureaucratic problem of finding a group of loyal and able agents who would be capable of managing the implementation of the Henrician reform programme in Ireland on his behalf. An early opportunity to commence the formation of this group, and to provide it with an

---

[23] *Statutes Ireland, Richard III – Henry VIII*, pp. 213–14; Bradshaw, 'Irish reformation parliament', pp. 298–9 and 'Beginnings of modern Ireland', p. 74; Edwards, *Church and state*, pp. 9–10 and *Ireland in the age of the Tudors. The destruction of Hiberno-Norman civilisation* (London, 1977), p. 46.

[24] The most convincing evaluation of Cromwell's role in Irish affairs is Brady, *Chief Governors*, pp. 14–16; on his management of the enforcement campaign in England see G. R. Elton, *Policy and police. The enforcement of the Reformation in the age of Thomas Cromwell* (Cambridge, 1972).

ecclesiastical leader, arose with the need to replace the murdered John Alen in the see of Dublin. Significantly, the man Cromwell chose for the position of archbishop, George Browne, was both a close personal ally and an experienced agent of the Henrician Reformation in England.

II

George Browne began his career in the early 1520s as an Augustinian friar.[25] An Englishman by birth, he remained a relatively obscure figure until, in 1532, he emerged as prior of the Augustinian Friars' London convent at Throgmorton Street. His rise to prominence within his order was quickly followed by the achievement of commensurate academic attainments. In July 1532, after ten years of study, he supplicated for his baccalaureate in theology at the University of Oxford. In the following October, he received a royal licence to travel overseas and, although abroad for only a short time, he appears to have acquired a doctorate in theology from a foreign university, for which he was incorporated at Oxford on 20 July 1534 and at Cambridge in 1535–6.

It was as prior of the Augustinian friars in London that Browne first came into contact with Thomas Cromwell, the executive authority behind the king's emerging ecclesiastical revolution.[26] Cromwell owned a house within the precincts of the convent, and he soon entered into negotiations with Browne over the purchase of additional land for the purpose of constructing a more grandiose abode. Through these dealings he also learned that Browne was eager to lend his support to his plans for breaking the impasse surrounding Henry VIII's divorce from Queen Katherine. This was a particularly welcome fact for Cromwell for the prior was not only a professional preacher, but one who had access – on account of Throgmorton Street's position as a fashionable residential district in the city – to a politically and socially influential audience.

Browne, then, was first employed as an agent of the Henrician Reformation as a pulpit propagandist and, over the next three years, acted as a mouthpiece for Cromwell in disseminating the official news and ideology of

---

[25] The following paragraphs on Browne's early career are based on Bradshaw, 'George Browne', pp. 301–9; *BRUO 1501–40*, p. 76.

[26] Historical opinion on Cromwell's role in the English Reformation is sharply divided. Some historians view him as an ideologue who led an 'evangelical' faction in its efforts to introduce radical religious ideas and policies into mainstream English politics during the 1530s; others see him as the quintessential civil servant who dutifully did his royal master's bidding at every turn. For recent restatements of both of these positions see (for Cromwell as ideologue) R. McEntegart, *Henry VIII, the League of Schmalkalden and the English Reformation* (Woodbridge, 2002), and (for Cromwell as loyal bureaucrat) Bernard, *The King's Reformation*.

the new political and ecclesiastical order. In his Easter Day homily in 1533, for instance, he was the first person to reveal in public that the king had married Anne Boleyn, while in January 1535 he expounded on the theme that the bishops derived their power of jurisdiction exclusively from the king as supreme head.[27] Yet Browne was also employed by Cromwell to give the Henrician settlement more practical effect, especially in relation to the mendicant friars. For this purpose, the king appointed him provincial of his own order in April 1534, and granted him a commission, in conjunction with Dr John Hilsey, provincial of the Dominicans, to carry out a general visitation of the mendicant orders which, through the administration of the first oath of succession, was intended to secure their obedience to the new settlement.[28] It was no surprise, therefore, that when Cromwell turned his attention to the task of extending the Reformation to Ireland, Browne's recent experience marked him out as a potential contributor. He was regarded by the regime as someone who 'dedicated himself . . . to the setting forth and preaching the sincere word of God' and to procuring 'the good furtherance' of the king's affairs, and was therefore deemed to be a suitable candidate to fill the vacant see of Dublin.[29] Browne was formally nominated to the position on 11 January 1536. On 19 March he received the pallium from Archbishop Cranmer of Canterbury, and in the following July he landed at Dublin.[30]

Browne's prior involvement in the enforcement campaign in England did more, however, than simply convince Cromwell that he was a sufficiently able and trustworthy person to be given the task of spearheading religious and ecclesiastical change in Ireland. The experience also provided him with the essential frame of reference for developing an approach to his new role. Since the 1970s, and the appearance of Brendan Bradshaw's pioneering research on the archbishop, the generally accepted view of Browne is that he emerged from England as a worldly wise civil servant, whose efforts on behalf of the Reformation were inspired primarily by a sense of duty and service to the crown rather than any personal commitment to the new, reformed theologies emerging from continental Europe. Thus, Browne's career in Ireland is explicable in terms of him exercising the

---

[27] *LP* VI, no. 391; *LP* VIII, no. 121. Eustace Chapuys, the Imperial ambassador, later claimed that Browne presided over the secret marriage ceremony of the king and Anne Boleyn in January 1533: E. Ives, *The life and death of Anne Boleyn* (Oxford, 2005), p. 169.

[28] On Browne's visitation of the mendicants see F. Roth, *The English Austin Friars 1249–1538* (2 vols., New York, 1961–6), ii, pp. 445–8; Bernard, *The King's Reformation*, pp. 156–7.

[29] The quotations are from a letter of the king to Browne from July 1537 in which he recalled, *inter alia*, the reasons why the prior had been appointed to the archbishopric of Dublin (*SP* II, p. 465).

[30] *LP* X, nos. 80, 226 (grant 6), 597 (grants 20, 23, 47); *LP* XI, no. 120.

same unquestioning devotion to fulfilling the often changing, and sometimes contradictory religious demands of Henry VIII and Edward VI.[31] Yet,
while there is no doubting the fact that many elements of this thesis retain
their validity – particularly the contention that Browne was a long way off
from conforming to the type of the radical, continental reformer – there is
also a need, prompted by the surviving evidence, to redress the balance and
to allow for the possibility that his thinking and actions, both in England
and Ireland, were not completely devoid of ideological motivation.
Although the historical record does not allow us to reconstruct his spiritual
biography in any great detail, it is evident that, like many of the evangelically minded clerics promoted by Cromwell to the episcopal bench in the
period 1534–6, the new archbishop of Dublin came to Ireland imbued with
a strong and fervent attachment to the notion of the royal supremacy, and
that a proper recognition of this attachment is crucial to any understanding
of his subsequent career.

At its most basic level, Browne's attachment to the supremacy implied a
simple acceptance of the Erastian principle that the two parts of the body
politic, the 'spiritualty' and 'temporalty', were subject to one ruler, the king
of England. But the supremacy was not simply about abstract matters of
jurisdiction, or the particular quarrel between Henry VIII and the pope
regarding the question of who ruled the churches in England and Ireland. It
also had a strong doctrinal dimension. From the outset, Henry VIII adopted
the rhetoric of the Erasmian humanists in defence of his supremacy, and
equated it absolutely with the advancement of the Gospel and the sincere
and true understanding of God's word. Thus, those who promoted the
supremacy were also engaged in an enterprise to promote the Gospel and
the truth, a point which Archbishop Browne frequently alluded to in his
correspondence with Thomas Cromwell.[32] As well as having this doctrinal
dimension, Browne's attachment to the supremacy was also underpinned by
strong, English nationalist sentiments, which found expression both in
worshipful feelings directed towards the sacred kingship of Henry VIII, and
in a desire to defend Henry's honour and dynastic interests against any
foreign prince or potentate which offended or threatened them, as was the
case with the pope and the Holy Roman emperor during the crisis surrounding the 'king's great matter'.[33] These sentiments, which were shared

---

[31] The classic and most influential statement of this thesis remains Bradshaw, 'George
Browne', *passim*.
[32] Bernard, *The King's Reformation*, pp. 225–43; Browne to Cromwell, 21 May and 27 July
1538 (*SP* III, pp. 10–11; TNA: PRO SP 60/7, no. 27).
[33] This nationalist sentiment was articulated in the preambles to various statutes passed in the
English Reformation parliament in 1533–4, especially the act in restraint of appeals, for
which see *SR* III, pp. 427–9.

by the other evangelically minded bishops in the Henrician Church, were implicit in their efforts to promulgate, through their preaching activities, a sincere acceptance of the supremacy amongst the wider populace and in their desire to extirpate all traces of the papacy from the English Church.[34] Browne, no less than any of his peers based in England, was a proponent of this monarchical, anti-papal ideology, and sought inevitably to secure a similarly heartfelt allegiance to the new royal style amongst his flock in Dublin.

The second feature of Browne's approach that derived from his English experience was directly related to his commitment to the doctrine of the royal supremacy. He maintained the view that the successful promotion and enforcement of the supremacy would ultimately be dependent upon him establishing direct and regularly repeated displays of the new prerogative in action. Such displays – whether they came in the form of ad hoc royal commissions to exercise particular aspects of, or to demand allegiance to, the king's spiritual authority;[35] or in the establishment of a permanent office, like Cromwell's position of vicegerent in spirituals to the king,[36] to exercise it in a more overarching and formal manner – had the effect in England of making the supremacy a visible and, at times, awe-inspiring reality for the inhabitants of its parishes and religious houses, and had thus contributed to the success of the early Reformation campaign there.[37] Moreover, on the basis of his own participation in or observation of these processes, he also assumed that an identical course of action would be required to advance the supremacy in Ireland. Thus he was a reformer who was not only ideologically driven but someone who also conceived his mission in narrowly functional terms. For him, the form, if not the end, of Reformation was an instrumentalist concern. He sought nothing less or, indeed, nothing more, than the full replication in Ireland of the existing

---

[34] On this general point see the succinct account in R. Rex, *The Tudors* (Stroud, 2003), pp. 78–80.

[35] A good example of such an ad hoc commission was that granted to Archbishop Cranmer's official in June 1534 to obtain the subscription, during the metropolitan visitation of Canterbury, of the corporate and parochial clergy to an article concerning 'the bishop of Rome's authority within this realm' (M. Bowker, 'The supremacy and the episcopate: the struggle for control', *HJ* 18 (1975), pp. 229–30).

[36] On the vicegerency and its operation in England see S.E. Lehmberg, 'Supremacy and vicegerency: a re-examination', *EHR* 81 (1966), pp. 225–35; C. J. Kitching, 'The probate jurisdiction of Thomas Cromwell as vicegerent', *BIHR* 46 (1973), pp. 102–6; F. D. Logan, 'Thomas Cromwell and the vicegerency in spirituals: a revisitation', *EHR* 103 (1988), pp. 658–67; D. MacCulloch, *Thomas Cranmer. A life* (Yale, 1996), pp. 133–6, 165–6, 185–92.

[37] A good example of one such display of the supremacy in action was the administration of the oath of succession to the citizens of London in April 1534. It appears that none of the citizens refused to take it: Brigden, *London and the Reformation*, pp. 222–4.

English model of reform in all of its juridical and administrative detail, for it was in this operational detail that the supreme headship of the distant king would be most clearly seen by his Irish subjects.

Browne's initial experiences in Ireland did little to challenge any of the assumptions he carried with him from England. Having witnessed in person the resistance of the clerical proctors to the religious changes that were being effected in the later sessions of the Irish Reformation parliament, he quickly became convinced that the 'usurped power of the bishop of Rome' was 'a thing not a little rooted amongst the inhabitants here',[38] and that there was a clear need to enforce the new religious settlement in the same rigorous manner, and with the same administrative and judicial infrastructure, that had been applied in England. Yet, while the broad thrust of this approach was supported by Browne's political masters in England, its practical implementation was to prove particularly problematical in Ireland. From the moment he set foot in his see in July 1536, Browne encountered a host of difficulties in enforcing the Reformation, all of which were attributable to two fundamental and related impediments: the fitful nature of the king and Cromwell's interest in Ireland, and the restricted nature of royal authority there. Although the Irish parliament had proclaimed Henry VIII supreme head of the Irish Church just two months previously,[39] the fact that the king's writ did not run in many of the independent Irish lordships determined that the claim was largely theoretical at this juncture, and that the crown had a very limited capacity to promote the new style throughout the island, or to secure anything but the most nominal acceptance of it. For the king and Cromwell, the repercussions of this situation were clear if undesirable: without too much anxiety they resigned themselves to accepting it, and to taking the entirely pragmatic decision to postpone, until some more propitious time, the establishment of much of the judicial and administrative infrastructure that had been associated with the introduction and enforcement of the supremacy in England. For Archbishop Browne, in contrast, its consequences were wholly deleterious. It ensured, in the first instance, that his favoured approach to reform was largely inoperable because he was deprived of the basic administrative template that he had worked with in England. Worse, it also provoked an ill-considered response on his part, the main effect of which was to expose him as someone who would struggle at every turn to develop an alternative reformist strategy that would adequately address the circumstances he faced in Ireland.

[38] Browne to Henry VIII, 27 September 1537 (*SP* II, pp. 512–14).
[39] *Statutes Ireland, Richard III – Henry VIII*, pp. xxxii, 172–3; Bradshaw, 'Irish reformation parliament', pp. 290–2; *LP* XI, no. 120.

Evidence of Browne's struggle emerged most clearly in relation to the crown's inability to activate in Ireland one of the most important bureaucratic tools utilised in the English Reformation: the royal visitation. This procedure, which had been employed in Browne's own visitation of the English mendicants in 1534, and in the general royal visitation of the English Church in 1535–6, lay at the heart of the enforcement strategy employed by Cromwell in the immediate aftermath of the establishment of the royal supremacy. It amounted, in effect, to a spectacular, annunciatory, display of Henry VIII's new powers – in particular, his acquisition of the pope's position as the supreme ordinary in the local church – and contributed, in a very tangible manner, to the realisation of a truly national church in England, because it made the supremacy a visible reality within the parochial and religious communities of the ecclesiastical provinces of Canterbury and York.[40] Yet, while the possibility of conducting a similar, national visitation of the Irish clergy was actively considered by the Tudor regime on the eve of Browne's departure for Ireland, the decision to proceed was postponed because there were no immediate prospects that any royal visitors would be admitted into substantial areas of the four Irish ecclesiastical provinces.[41] The adjournment of the proposed visitation was highly significant. It determined, in effect, that there were would be few visible signs – apart from Henry VIII's exaction of new taxes from the clergy – that a national church, subject to the spiritual jurisdiction of king, had been founded in Ireland.[42]

For Archbishop Browne, this was an outcome which he not only regarded as unacceptable, but one which he also was determined to remedy. Thus, in the absence of the requisite administrative and judicial structures, he endeavoured to make the supremacy more perceptible by demonstrating publicly that his own episcopal authority and jurisdiction were derived solely from the king as supreme head, and that he was not therefore bound by any of the conventions associated with the papistical canon law. To this end, he collated William Body, a lay agent of Cromwell who had accompanied him to Ireland, to the prebend of Swords within days of his arrival, notwithstanding the facts that the benefice was supposed to be preserved for ordained priests, and that the anti-canonical act scandalised observers,

---

[40] On the royal visitation of the English church generally see Elton, *Policy and police*, pp. 247–51; MacCulloch, *Thomas Cranmer*, pp. 129–35; Bowker, 'Supremacy and the episcopate', pp. 235–40; W. H. Frere and W. M. Kennedy (eds.), *Visitation articles and injunctions of the period of the Reformation* (Alcuin Club, 3 vols., London, 1910), i, pp. 119–23.

[41] *SP* II, p. 369.

[42] In September 1537, Browne informed the king that he was 'the first spiritual man that moved the 20th part and first fruits' (*SP* II, p. 513).

including the king's deputy, Lord Leonard Grey.[43] Yet, as offensive as this act of iconoclasm was, it marked only the beginning of his efforts to give the supremacy the kind of exposure that he believed was necessary if the new religious dispensation was to make a genuine impact. Ceremonial acts and homilies soon followed which highlighted what Browne believed to be the special nature of his mission in Ireland – that he had, in effect, some form of delegated authority from the crown to exercise the supremacy on its behalf – but which to his critics appeared to be nothing more than braggadocio. He 'boasteth himself', according to one critic, 'to rule all the clergy under our sovereign lord', and endeavoured to give this self-appointed 'rule' an appropriate stature and air of formality by surrounding it in what were dismissively described as 'foolish ceremonies'.[44] This aggressive and generally injudicious approach to the promotion of the king's supremacy ultimately erupted in an unseemly dispute between Browne and his fellow English bishop, Edward Staples of Meath when, following Browne's imprisonment of one of Staples's suffragans – on the charge that the latter had upheld papal and imperial authority in a sermon – the pair engaged in a damaging 'battle of the sermons' during Lent 1538. In the heat of this battle, the generally diplomatic Staples was moved to publicly denigrate Browne as a 'heretic and beggar'.[45]

Browne's actions, and the responses they provoked, clearly showed his determination to breathe life into the supremacy in Ireland, and his desire that his flock would be made aware of the new ecclesiastical order in as stark and uncompromising a manner as the laity and clergy of the provinces of Canterbury and York had been in the years preceding his arrival in Dublin. But they also displayed a startling political naiveté. While there is little doubt that Cromwell had indeed intimated to Browne that he would exercise some kind of leadership role in relation to the implementation of religious change, most probably through the promise of a commission to act as his deputy vicegerent,[46] the artless way in which the archbishop

---

[43] *SP* II, pp. 396–402 (at p. 399). Browne's aggressive and iconoclastic attitude to the niceties of traditional canon law had also been evident in his preaching prior to his arrival in Ireland – in a 'solemn sermon' made in January 1535 he reportedly maintained that all bishops who failed to burn their papal bulls of appointment, and get new ones from the king, deserved very severe punishment and could not discharge any episcopal duty (*LP* VIII, no. 121).

[44] Henry VIII to Archbishop Browne, 31 July 1537 (*SP* II, p. 465), Bishop Staples to St Leger or, in his absence, Moyle, 17 June 1538 (*SP* III, pp. 29–30); on the link between the two letters see Murray, 'Ecclesiastical justice and the enforcement of the Reformation', pp. 38–9, 231 (nt. 27).

[45] *SP* III, pp. 1–3; the 'battle of the sermons' is reconstructed in Ronan, *Reformation in Dublin*, pp. 108–11.

[46] Cromwell's own vicegerential commission extended to Ireland and allowed him to appoint deputies (Logan, 'Cromwell and the Vicegerency', p. 661, 665–6). Significantly, Browne's travelling companion, William Body, had a similarly elevated view of his standing which

attempted to fulfil it – steadfastly ignoring the fact that he had not actually been given any formal authority or commission to act in such a manner – served only to alienate his peers, including Bishop Staples, who were broadly supportive of Henry VIII's acquisition of the supreme headship of the Irish Church. The resultant complaints – that in his 'dream' he compared himself 'so near to a prince in honour and estimation', and that 'every honest man . . . reckoneth that pride and arrogance hath ravished him from the right remembrance of himself' – would haunt the archbishop throughout the opening years of his episcopacy, for they not only damaged his credibility in Ireland but, more significantly, they quickly eroded his reputation in the corridors of power in Whitehall and the English court.[47]

The opening phase of his episcopacy, then, had not gone the way Browne would have hoped or anticipated. His desire to replicate the English pattern of reform in Ireland had been frustrated by the crown's inability to establish those administrative and judicial structures that he believed were necessary to give effect to its claims that it was the supreme authority in the Irish Church. And his own clumsy and ill-considered efforts to overcome this difficulty had backfired spectacularly, because he succeeded only in raising the ire of fellow members of the English political establishment in Ireland. Such pronounced failings, especially coming from someone of who so much had been expected, could not easily be overlooked and, at an early stage, Cromwell and the king felt it necessary to intervene directly to put the reform process back on track. Thus, at the end of July 1537, a letter was despatched to the archbishop from the king which severely castigated him for his shortcomings, highlighting, in particular, his arrogant behaviour and the inflated notions he held of his own importance.[48] The message contained in the letter was not simply one of rebuke however. It was also intended to instruct Browne on the manner in which his political masters expected him to comport himself and to perform his duties from here on in. Thus, he was commanded to 'reform' himself by doing first his duty towards God 'in the due execution of your office', and then by doing his duty 'towards us in the advancement of our affairs there'. In effect, he was being told to stop thinking of himself primarily as a special agent of the royal supremacy. Instead, he was to look upon himself as someone who had been advanced to the 'order, dignity and authority' of an archbishop, a role which, if it was executed properly, would encompass Browne's responsibilities regarding the implementation of the Henrician Reformation in Ireland.

---

would appear to have originated in the promptings of their master Cromwell: according to Grey, after he taken him on a journey to Munster, he named himself 'the king's high commissioner' in every place they visited (*SP* II, p. 399).

[47] Sources as in nt. 44 above.   [48] *SP* II, p. 465.

This message was important for it reflected a subtle shift in the regime's thinking on the nature of the episcopal office from that which had existed in the immediate aftermath of the enactment of the royal supremacy, and from that which Browne had initially absorbed and carried with him on his succession to the see of Dublin. In 1535 the royal visitation of the English Church had been preceded by the inhibition of the powers and jurisdiction of the English bishops. These powers, which included the right to visit, were only returned gradually by royal commission in the succeeding years. Originally, this policy was instituted to undermine the notion that the bishops derived their authority from the pope, its main effect being to transform the episcopate into a body of royal functionaries who served as ecclesiastics at the king's pleasure. But it also acted as a strong political pressure on the bishops to conform to the king's religious dictates, and to ensure that those same dictates were implemented throughout their own dioceses, for the more a bishop conformed, the more speedily he would recover his powers to hold visitations and to grant probate on wills, with their attendant and lucrative fees.[49] By the time George Browne arrived in Dublin, the policy had achieved its desired ends and the gradual restoration of episcopal authority was growing apace.[50] In fact, it was gradually becoming clearer that there was no absolute need for the king to intervene directly in the administration of ecclesiastical discipline. The reconstructed episcopacy could be called upon to do the job for him through the operation of their individual ordinary jurisdictions. In this, the archbishop of Dublin was not to be excepted, especially as he was a prelate whose loyalty to the new settlement was beyond question. He, no less than any of his fellow English bishops, was expected to use his episcopal authority, including the right to visit and correct his clergy and flock, to enforce the settlement.

Yet, despite the severity of the criticism in the king's letter, Archbishop Browne made no immediate moves to take up the challenge presented by his sovereign. Part of the reason for this was his inexperience as a conventional diocesan administrator. An academic theologian by training, Browne's theoretical and practical experience of the administration of traditional canonical procedures had been necessarily limited, and he certainly lacked the confidence to adapt them for the enforcement of the Henrician religious settlement. His reticence, however, was also due to the fact that the legislative output of the Reformation parliament had failed, up to the point the

---

[49] Haigh, *English Reformations*, pp. 123–4; Bowker, *Diocese of Lincoln under John Longland* (Cambridge, 1981), pp. 76–8; MacCulloch, *Thomas Cranmer*, pp. 133–5.
[50] In February 1537, for example, Bishop Longland of Lincoln recovered all his powers by licence from the king (Bowker, 'Supremacy and the episcopate', p. 242).

king wrote to him, to make any provisions for the enforcement of religious change which could be easily absorbed into the traditional disciplinary machinery of the church. Although the ecclesiastical legislation enacted in the opening session of the parliament had established the central principle of the Henrician settlement that the king, rather than the pope, was the supreme ecclesiastical authority in the Irish Church; and had set out pro-cedures through which the crown could put into immediate effect certain limited aspects of its new prerogative – these included, for example, a process to enable it to hear the appeals of its subjects from the decrees of local ecclesiastical courts – not a single statute defined any offences against the new settlement which Archbishop Browne or his diocesan officials would have been empowered to detect and correct.[51] Nor, on account of the fall of Anne Boleyn, and in stark contrast to what had transpired in England at the outset of its Reformation, was there any usable legislation enabling the archbishop to impel positive statements of loyalty to the settlement in the form of a corporal oath upholding new succession rights to the crown.[52] Mindful, then, of the need to eschew any actions that would further damage his reputation, and hopeful, still, that parliament might establish the kind of clear legal directives that had pre-figured and sanc-tioned all the major reformist activities in England, the archbishop chose to defer his inaugural diocesan visitation until such time as his enforcement role was more precisely defined.

Such definition finally came in the form of two statutes that were enacted in the closing session of the Reformation parliament in the autumn of 1537. The first of these was 'the act of succession betwixt the king and Queen Jane', the primary purpose of which was to legitimate the progeny of Henry VIII's marriage to Jane Seymour. To the chagrin of papal loyalists, however, the act also reaffirmed that the marriage of Henry and Katherine of Aragon was 'unlawful' and that its issue was illegitimate, and instituted a formal procedure for positively binding the king's subjects to the new dispensation. A corporal oath upholding the succession could now be administered by the king, his heirs or any duly appointed deputy, to any of his subjects living in Ireland who were of full age. Refusal to take this oath was adjudged to be

---

[51] Murray, 'Ecclesiastical justice and the enforcement of the Reformation', pp. 37, 230–1 (nts. 18, 19).

[52] An 'act of succession of the king and Queen Anne', incorporating a provision for the administration of a corporal oath, had been passed in the opening session of the Irish Reformation parliament, but had immediately fallen into abeyance following the queen's conviction and execution on trumped-up treason charges: *Statutes Ireland, Richard III – Henry VIII*, pp. 158–65; Bradshaw, 'Reformation parliament', pp. 290–2. On the use and importance of the first succession oath in the campaign to enforce the Henrician ecclesiastical revolution in England see Elton, *Policy and police*, pp. 222–7.

high treason and punishable by death.[53] Here, at last, was something tangible that Archbishop Browne could implement, even within the context of a diocesan visitation. Indeed, the archbishop now had a choice of oaths to administer, for the other reformist measure passed in the final session of the parliament – 'an act against the bishop of Rome's power' – laid down that a separate oath upholding the king's supremacy, and rejecting papal authority, should be taken by all ecclesiastical and temporal officials on entering office, by all clergy and laymen suing livery out of the king, and by all secular clerks and religious taking their orders or vows. As with the oath of succession, refusal to take the oath of supremacy was also decreed to be a treasonable offence and punishable by death.[54]

The significance of the act against the bishop of Rome's power extended well beyond the institution of a procedure for eliciting statements of support for the new religious order. Although virtually identical to an English statute enacted in the preceding year – which had had the more limited purpose of closing a legal loophole that allowed supporters of the papacy to escape prosecution as long as they avoided publicly criticising the king[55] – it provided, in its Irish context, the overall basis for a coherent, though necessarily restricted, strategy for enforcing reform which, at the very least, could be applied in the loyal territories of the Pale, including Archbishop Browne's diocesan and metropolitan jurisdictions. This was achieved in two distinct ways. First, it confronted in a direct and unambiguous manner the essential problem facing the Tudor regime with regard to the implementation of religious change in the Pale: the need to wean the indigenous clergy away from their deep and culturally rooted attachment to the papacy. To this end, it forbade any act or deed, including printing, writing, teaching or preaching, which set forth, maintained or defended the authority, jurisdiction or power of the pope after 1 November 1537. It thus provided the supporters of reform with a legal instrument which entitled them not only to demand positive statements of compliance to the new order – in the form of the oath of supremacy – but also empowered them to seek out and punish most forms of resistance to it, whether covert or overt.

---

[53] The act is printed in *Statutes Ireland, Richard III – Henry VIII*, pp. 193–209 (the oath is on pp. 206–7).

[54] I have used the title of the act coined by William Brabazon, as it is more descriptive than the title given on the statute roll, 'the act for the bishop of Rome': Vice-Treasurer Brabazon's note of acts passed in the first, second and final sessions of the Reformation parliament (TNA: PRO SP60/5, no. 53(i); *SP* II, pp. 526–7); *Statutes Ireland, Richard III – Henry VIII*, pp. 220–6 (the oath is on p. 224).

[55] For the text of the English act for extinguishing the bishop of Rome's authority see *SR* III, pp. 663–6; for an analysis of its purpose see S.E. Lehmberg, *The later parliaments of Henry VIII, 1536–1547* (Cambridge, 1977), pp. 25–8.

The second way in which the act provided for an enforcement strategy was by setting out explicit arrangements regarding the policing of the law. In essence, the act vested this responsibility in the local secular and ecclesiastical authorities and thus went some way towards filling the administrative vacuum that had been created by the crown's inability to activate in Ireland the key enforcement structures it had utilised during the early Reformation campaign in England. In terms of the secular authorities, for example, the justices of the peace and assize were empowered to inquire into all offences against the act. Any such offences detected by them were to be certified into King's Bench for their hearing and determination, the penalty for conviction being the same as those of the medieval statute of *praemunire*. The other side of the detection process fell to the ecclesiastical ordinaries. The act authorised all archbishops, bishops, archdeacons and other ecclesiastical judges to inquire during visitation into offences specifically committed by the clergy. Clergymen suspected of such crimes or actually found guilty in the ecclesiastical courts were to be handed over to the secular arm – either to the next gaol delivery or to the deputy and council at Dublin Castle – where their case would receive a further hearing; or, if they had already been found guilty by an ecclesiastical tribunal, where they would be subjected to the penalties of *praemunire*. To ensure that this enforcement procedure would not be subverted, ecclesiastical visitors who knowingly concealed or hid any knowledge of a clergyman's offence were to be subject to a fine of IR£40.

It is clear from these arrangements, just as with the provisions defining the offences against the act, that the crown considered it a vital undertaking to secure the conformity of the local clergy. Although the secular authorities had a general brief in the act to detect and punish instances of support for the papacy amongst the community at large, the special provisions made for detecting clerical offences indicate that it had a higher priority. There were two important reasons for this. The first concerned the actions of the clergy during the Kildare rebellion. Cromwell and the Tudor regime were fully aware of the extent to which the clergy had attempted to subvert the Reformation during the revolt and recognised thus that securing their allegiance would be a vital aspect of preventing any further outbreaks of dissidence. But this was not to be an end in itself. Once clerical obedience was achieved, it was envisaged by the Tudor regime that they would become enforcement agents themselves by promoting the Henrician religious settlement through their traditional teaching and preaching functions.[56] Fully aware of this prerequisite of the Henrician scheme of reform,

---

[56] On the important role of pulpit propaganda in the enforcement of the Henrician settlement in England see Elton, *Policy and police*, pp. 211–16; Rex, *Henry VIII*, pp. 29–31.

then, the passage of the act against the authority of the bishop of Rome firmly placed the onus on Browne to meet his clergy head on, and to attempt by the formal procedures of episcopal visitation to win them over to his way of thinking.[57]

III

The archbishop's inaugural visitation took place in the winter of 1537. With his train in tow, Browne travelled on horseback to pre-selected parish churches in the rural deaneries *inter Anglicos*, and to the chapter houses of the religious, where he presided over specially convened visitation courts. Here, the assembled secular clergy and the inmates of the monasteries were examined on pre-prepared visitation articles.[58] The actual business of the visitation was a mixture of old and new concerns. The clergy were examined on a number of traditional disciplinary matters such as their frequenting of common taverns and ale-houses or, in the case of dispensed non-resident beneficed clergy, whether they had found able curates to serve the cure of souls in their stead.[59] The main thrust of the proceedings, however, concerned the enforcement of clerical obedience to the new religious settlement which, tactically, Browne approached in a hierarchical manner, by concentrating his efforts on the numerically small, but highly influential, senior corporate clergy. This involved swearing in cathedral and monastic chapters to the supremacy in writing under their seals, using his servants to remove the pope's name from their service books, and attempting to institute a preaching programme on behalf of the settlement amongst abbots, priors, cathedral dignitaries and prebendaries and masters of hospitals.[60]

There were a number of compelling reasons for adopting such an approach, the first being the fact that advanced clerical learning was concentrated in the senior corporate clergy. One of the main implications of this was that ecclesiastical judges, whether they administered diocesan or peculiar jurisdictions, were invariably recruited from the grouping or held

---

[57] The following reconstruction of Browne's visitation is based on his visitation 'articles', which are printed in J.P. Collier (ed.), *The Egerton papers* (London, 1840), pp. 7–10; and his report to Cromwell of 8 January 1538 (*SP* II, pp. 539–41). For an analysis of the documentation and its significance see Murray, 'Ecclesiastical justice and the enforcement of the Reformation', pp. 40–1, 231–2 (nts. 33–8).

[58] The visitation commenced after 1 November 1537 when the act against the bishop of Rome's power came into effect, and was completed by 8 January 1538, when Browne drafted a report on the proceedings for Cromwell. For a description of the itinerary generally see Murray, 'Ecclesiastical justice and the enforcement of the Reformation', p. 41.

[59] *Egerton papers*, pp. 9–10 (articles 13 and 14).

[60] *Egerton papers*, pp. 7–9 (articles 1, 2, 4, 5, 7, and 8); *SP* II, pp. 539–41.

their positions by virtue of their membership. In effect, it was this grouping which would assume the major responsibility for the day-to-day enforcement of the new religious dispensation in the times between the archbishop's own triennial visitations. Securing the conformity of the senior corporate clergy, therefore, was essential if the reform project was ultimately to be a success.

As learned clerks, moreover, the senior corporate clergy played an important social role either as educators of youth, or as men of affairs. This could be a particularly influential role if the cleric in question was related to families of good social standing, which was often the case in a tightly knit and endogamous society like the English Pale.[61] A man who embodied all of these qualities when Archbishop Browne arrived in Dublin was Robert Fitzsimon, the precentor of St Patrick's Cathedral and official principal of his consistory court.[62] Fitzsimon belonged to an eminent family amongst the Dublin city merchant oligarchy. His brother Thomas, for example, was recorder of the city. Robert, himself, was an Oxford MA and graduate in civil law, which virtually guaranteed him a career as a senior administrator in his native diocese. The range of his interests did not stop there however. He also acted as a freelance legal adviser to monastic houses on canonical matters, was a broker of monastic leases, served as a master in the Irish chancery, and kept a household which made provision for the education of young boys from leading Pale families, like John Plunket, of Dunsoghly, who later became chief justice of the Queen's Bench in Elizabeth's reign.[63] It was clear that senior corporate clergymen like Fitzsimon, if they were not well-disposed towards the reform project, had the capacity to inflict great damage on its progress by mobilising their extensive networks of familial and social contacts against it.

The final reason why Browne concentrated his efforts upon the senior corporate clergy had to do with the fact that they exercised a controlling influence over the vast majority of Dublin parishes. 84 per cent of Dublin parishes, in fact, were appropriated to the two cathedrals and eighteen religious houses, fourteen of which were based within the English Pale, including eleven within the diocese of Dublin itself. This controlling influence gave the local corporate clergy the authority to appoint curates and chaplains to nearly two-thirds of all Dublin parishes. Thus they had the

---

[61] On the endogamous pattern of marriage in Dublin city and county see Lennon, *Lords of Dublin*, pp. 78–83.

[62] Lawlor, *Fasti of St Patrick's*, p. 56; RIA, 12.S.28, no. 831 (exemplification of the will of Alexander Beswick by Robert Fitzsimon, official principal of the metropolitan court of Dublin *sede vacante*); Murray, 'Tudor diocese of Dublin', p. 130 nt. 54.

[63] Above pp. 67–8, 71–6; on Fitzsimon's brokering of monastic leases see Morrin, *Patent rolls*, i, pp. 312–13.

power to sway the majority of the parochial clergy towards their way of thinking, whether on political or religious matters, because most of these curates and chaplains were totally dependent upon them for their livelihood.[64]

Archbishop Browne's decision to concentrate his attentions on this grouping, then, was well founded. They controlled the government of the local church, they commanded the loyalty of the parochial clergy and their influence reached into the very heart of the local political community. Yet it was among the corporate clerical elite that he found the most organised and ingrained resistance to the new religious dispensation. Although most of the cathedral and monastic chapters took the oaths of succession and supremacy as administered by the archbishop, the experience of visiting them convinced Browne that they were 'borne against' him. He believed, as he reported to Cromwell, that they 'seduceth' the rest of his flock, and 'hindereth and plucketh back amongst the people' all his work in promoting the crown's supremacy. This was particularly evident in the clergy's obdurate refusal to preach on behalf of the king's supremacy. Browne noted that before 'our dread sovereign' was declared to be supreme head over the Irish Church, the clergy 'would, very often even till the right Christians were weary of them, preach after the old sort and fashion', but that now they would not 'open their lips in any pulpit for the manifestation of the same'.[65]

The difficulties posed by the clergy's unwillingness to preach were also exacerbated by another related form of resistance: the refusal of exempt religious orders, like the Knights Hospitallers of Kilmainham and the Observant Friars in Dublin, to admit the archbishop into their jurisdictions. Browne's surprise at this refusal, in particular, was indicative of his inexperience as an episcopal administrator. A cursory examination of the records of his predecessors' episcopacies would have revealed to him that these orders, if for no other reason than to maintain their peculiar jurisdictions inviolate, would inevitably present a tough legal challenge to any enforcement campaign run by the archbishop of Dublin on behalf of the crown. Even his immediate predecessor, the pugnacious canonist John Alen, who rarely flinched in the face of conflict and who dedicated much of his episcopacy to strengthening his authority over the regular clergy, had not dared to challenge the Observants and the Knights Hospitallers. Browne, himself, soon learned that he had been mistaken in his assumption that he had the legal authority to enter their jurisdictions. Shortly after he issued his visitation injunctions in the early spring of 1538, he was forced to abandon article 10 which stipulated that 'in places exempt' he could 'punish such as

---

[64] Above pp. 77–8; Appendix 2 below.   [65] *SP* II, p. 539–41.

been culpable' of offences against the settlement 'no liberty, grant, ne licences withstanding'.[66]

All of this dismayed Archbishop Browne because he could not see any way in which the situation would be improved using the conventional diocesan administrative system, even with the coercive backing of the statute against the bishop of Rome's power. Because so many of his clergy were patently guilty of offences against the statute, it would have been politically and administratively impossible to prosecute and inflict the penalties of *praemunire* upon them all. Thus in his own visitation he tried to persuade his clergy to row in behind the settlement 'by gentle exhortation, evangelical instruction' and 'threats of sharp correction'.[67] Yet even the exertion of this much pressure could not be guaranteed once the archbishop ceased his visitation. From that point on the responsibility for disciplinary proceedings in the heartland of the diocese would devolve for three years upon the archdeacon of Dublin, William Power, and the official principal, Robert Fitzsimon, both of whom were long-standing and conservatively inclined members of the cathedral chapter of St Patrick's.[68] Browne was of the opinion that these men would be slow to detect and correct offences against the settlement. In his report on his visitation in January 1538 he urged Cromwell to issue a letter to the Irish treasurer, the chief justice and the master of the rolls giving them authority over all ecclesiastical persons, which he believed would help him 'prick other forthwards that been underneath me' to execute their offices. In making this request Browne revealed his true instincts. The experience of his primary visitation had reaffirmed his belief that direct displays of the supreme head's power, like those in which he had participated in England, were the only truly effective means of furthering the reformist cause amongst a stubborn clergy who were determined to undermine his best efforts. Indeed, Browne was so convinced of this fact that he sought to have the full apparatus of the royal supremacy erected in Ireland, including the appointment of a separate vicegerent and a master for faculties. He believed that such offices would make the supremacy visible on the ground, buttress his little-regarded authority and counteract the nefarious influence of the papacy, which manifested itself in the too easily available papal indulgences and dispensations.[69]

Despite the passionate nature of Browne's appeal, however, it went unheeded. In the same way that they had shied away from commissioning a royal visitation of the Irish clergy in 1536, the king and Cromwell were

---

[66] *SP* II, pp. 539–41; *SP* III, pp. 1–3; *Egerton papers*, p. 9 (article 10 is struck out in the original). On Archbishop Alen's campaign against the regulars see Murray, 'Archbishop Alen and reform', pp. 6–7.

[67] *SP* II, p. 539.   [68] On Power see Lawlor, *Fasti of St Patrick's*, pp. 63, 79, 117.

[69] *SP* II, p. 540.

reluctant to erect new supremacy structures in Ireland, because they knew that that they would have no effect throughout much of the lordship, given the limited reach of royal authority. Instead, the archbishop was commanded to issue his visitation injunctions or articles of reformation to the clergy of Ireland at large, an action which would, at the very least, expose most of the clergy within the English-ruled areas of Ireland to the basic tenets of the Henrician settlement. The articles, eighteen in all, dealt with the taking of the corporal oaths concerning the succession and supremacy, the rejection of papal authority and with a variety of reformed practices to be undertaken at different clerical levels. In effect, it was a handbook for Henry VIII's new model Irish clergy.[70] Yet, although it finally gave some credence to Browne's claim that 'under his grace' he was 'chief over the [Irish] clergy', the order from the crown to promulgate his visitation injunctions more widely was regarded by the archbishop as a wholly inadequate response to the situation he faced, because all it did was create a new set of official rules and observances that, in the case of his own diocese, required monitoring by a diocesan administration which he knew lacked any commitment to the principles lying behind them. Who, for example, Browne must have wondered, would ensure that the parsons, vicars and curates of the diocese would read the archbishop's new bidding prayers – 'The Form of the Beads' – after the gospel every Sunday and holy day? Who would ensure that they would teach the people their Paternoster and Creed in English, or that they would teach the people what the communion was, why they should receive it and what profit would come from receiving it?[71]

IV

Given the crown's continued reluctance to establish an Irish vicegerency, or to appoint any other formally authorised deputies to exercise different aspects of the supremacy on its behalf, one of the few options open to Browne – apart from attempting to reconstitute his diocesan administration with pro-reformist officials[72] – was to turn to the local secular authorities for succour and support, if for no other reason than that the same authorities, like the ecclesiastical ordinaries, had an officially designated enforcement role enshrined in the act against the bishop of Rome's power. Yet here too Browne ran into difficulties, mainly because his vision of

---

[70] *Egerton papers*, pp. 7–10.

[71] *SP* II, p. 539; Articles 6, 15 and 16 (*Egerton papers*, pp. 8–10). Browne's bidding prayers, 'The Form of the Beads', are printed in *SP* II, pp. 564–5.

[72] On Browne's largely failed efforts to achieve this see Murray, 'Ecclesiastical justice and the enforcement of the Reformation', p. 45.

reform was not shared by the leading secular authority in the lordship, the king's deputy, Lord Leonard Grey.

The viceroy had assumed office in 1536 in the very difficult circumstances of post-rebellion Ireland, and had had to cope with the great political void and instability that followed the destruction of the house of Kildare, as well as with the unreasonable demands placed upon him by the royal administration in Whitehall. Thus, obliged on the one hand to operate within the very tight financial constraints that Cromwell had laid down for his own administration – these included a substantially reduced garrison – and desirous on the other to retain the hard-won independence that the victory over the rebels had entailed for the viceregal office, Grey chose to govern the lordship by assuming the mantle of the overthrown earl of Kildare, and by seeking to exploit on behalf of the crown the vast, Geraldine network of alliances, which spanned much of English and Gaelic Ireland.[73]

For Archbishop Browne, the deputy's rapprochement with the Geraldines was by definition suspect because the latter's cause was indelibly linked with a treasonable attachment to the papacy. The Geraldines had openly rejected Henry VIII's right to rule in Ireland because they believed that it had been founded upon an ancient papal grant, and that it had subsequently been rendered invalid because the king had withdrawn his allegiance from the pope and proclaimed himself supreme head of the English Church. By seeking an accommodation with them, therefore, Grey appeared to be endorsing an ideology which ran counter to that which Browne had been sent into Ireland to promote. Nevertheless, it is doubtful that such an analysis of Grey's governmental strategy would have held any sway, had not the deputy's own behaviour and actions revealed that he had little sympathy for the new religion, or the forward, evangelical mode of religious reform favoured by Browne. Thus, although he had played a full part in securing the passage of the Henrician religious settlement through parliament,[74] and although he generally sought and secured formal acknowledgements of the royal supremacy from the bishops, dynastic lords and civic officials he encountered during his vice-regal progresses,[75] Grey was unwilling to press for anything more than an outward show of conformity to the new religious dispensation, for fear of alienating his prospective Geraldine allies and jeopardising, in consequence, the achievement of his main political objectives. Indeed, on occasion, the deputy neither baulked at the prospects of protecting or defending the interests of the

---

[73] On Grey's viceroyalty see Brady, *Chief governors*, pp. 13–25.

[74] For example, Grey initiated the moves which led to the abolition of the clerical proctors (*SP* II, pp. 437–9).

[75] Ronan, *Reformation in Dublin*, p. 39; *Carew MSS, 1515–74*, pp. 136–8.

opponents of religious change, or of staging public demonstrations of his own affection for the 'old religion', if he thought that some political advantage might be gained from doing so. Such actions – which ranged from his protection of the Observant friars in Galway from the attentions of the reformers in August 1538, to his very pointed and devout hearing of 'three or four masses' before the statue of the Blessed Virgin in St Mary's Abbey, Trim, in the following October – fuelled the suspicions of Browne and fellow supporters of the reformist cause that Grey was a papist.[76]

In Archbishop Browne's eyes, then, Grey's governmental strategy was not only papistical in intent but, in practice, it also hindered the advance of the new religious dispensation in the lordship. Indeed, Browne himself experienced the impedimentary effect of Grey's strategy in its most direct and unremitting form, for, as the leading exponent of religious change in Ireland, he had been identified early by the viceroy as someone whose words and deeds were likely to complicate or even impair his own efforts to secure a rapprochement with the Geraldines and their sympathisers. Thus, from the outset of Browne's episcopacy, Grey endeavoured systematically to undermine his prelatical status and authority, and to render inconsequential the political effects of all his exertions on behalf of the Reformation. A variety of measures were utilised by Grey to achieve these ends, including treating the archbishop contemptuously in public forums and regularly and peremptorily appropriating his goods and property. And Browne believed that they encouraged the corporate clergy, especially the Observant friars, in their opposition to him.[77] The measure that aggrieved Browne most, however, and which did the greatest damage to his enforcement campaign, was the intervention the viceroy made on behalf of James Humphrey – a native-born member of the chapter of St Patrick's Cathedral and the chief fomenter of conservative religious dissidence in his diocese – who, in May 1538, the archbishop had resolved to bring to book.[78]

Humphrey's conservative leanings first appeared on record in 1537 when he signed the letter of protest to Cromwell from the prebendaries of St Patrick's against the Irish council's attempted removal of their aged dean, Geoffrey Fyche.[79] Thereafter he resisted the imposition of the oath of supremacy and Browne's articles for reforming the clergy.[80] He was also

[76] Archbishop Browne to Cromwell, 10 August 1538 (*SP* III, pp. 65–7); Thomas Alen to Cromwell, 20 October 1538 (*SP* III, pp. 102–3).

[77] Archbishop Browne to John Alen, 15 April 1538 (*SP* III, pp. 1–3) and to Cromwell, 8 January 1538, 16 February and 21 May 1539 (*SP* II, pp. 539–41; *SP* III, pp. 9–11, 122–4).

[78] On Humphrey's background generally see Murray, 'Ecclesiastical justice and the enforcement of the Reformation', p. 47.

[79] TNA: PRO SP 60/4, no. 10.

[80] Archbishop Browne to Cromwell, 8 May 1538 (*SP* III, pp. 6–7, at p. 7).

involved in stirring up ill feeling between Browne and his fellow reforming bishop, Edward Staples of Meath, during their contretemps in Lent 1538.[81] However, it was an incident which took place during the patronal feast day mass in Humphrey's prebendal church of St Audoen that finally provoked the archbishop to attempt to bring him down. Humphrey was the main celebrant and, after reading the gospel, he declined to recite the special bidding prayers composed by Browne – the 'Form of the Beads' – which upheld the king's supremacy and denigrated papal authority, and which had been enjoined upon the clergy by the archbishop's articles of reformation. Humphrey's curate tried to remedy this omission but he was stopped in his tracks by his superior who began the preface of the mass to the accompaniment of the clerks in the choir.[82]

A formal presentment of Humphrey's offence was made by some of the parishioners to the archbishop. It is unclear whether this was a spontaneous gesture on their part or whether it was solicited by Browne's registrar, William Mowesherst, who would have been the usual conduit for receiving such extra-visitation presentments.[83] In any case, Browne was determined to make the most of the incident and quickly incarcerated the offending cleric in the episcopal gaol at St Sepulchre's. He also wrote in haste to Cromwell to inform him of the incident and to seek his advice on how he should proceed. It appears that the archbishop believed he had a prima facie case against the prebendary for offences under the act against the bishop of Rome's power. Humphrey's adamant refusal to read the 'Form of the Beads' could be interpreted as an act of defiance against the royal supremacy and in favour of papal authority, and Browne let it be known that he intended to hand him over to the deputy and council for prosecution as stipulated by that act.[84]

Yet, while Browne awaited Cromwell's reply, Grey freed Humphrey from prison against the archbishop's will. Although the surviving records give no indication as to why the deputy acted in this way, the circumstantial evidence suggests that it was an attempt to pacify all those adherents of the 'old religion' who had been politicised by the tumultuous events of the mid-1530s. James Humphrey was one of these figures. Like his former superior, Dean Geoffrey Fyche of St Patrick's – a man whose position he had defended when it came under attack from Cromwell in 1537 – Humphrey had come close to joining the rebels in 1534, because of his objections to the crown's religious policies. Moreover, neither the subsequent collapse of the

[81] SP III, pp. 1–2; Ronan, *Reformation in Dublin*, p. 103.
[82] SP III, pp. 6–7; *Egerton papers*, pp. 8–9 (article 6).
[83] SP III, p. 7; R. O'Day, 'The role of the registrar in diocesan administration' in O'Day and Heal (eds.), *Continuity and change*, pp. 81–4.
[84] Archbishop Browne to Cromwell, 20 May 1538 (SP III, pp. 8–9).

revolt or the passage of the Henrician ecclesiastical legislation in parliament had lessened in any way his aversion to the new religious dispensation, or dissuaded him from becoming a mouthpiece for the disaffected. Thus, although Grey had followed Cromwell's line in 1537 and pressed for the punishment of the dissident canons of St Patrick's by removing Fyche from office – on the grounds that the old dean's actions had come perilously close to being treasonable – Humphrey's predicament in 1538 afforded him an opportunity to rebuild in a small way the crown's relationship with the alienated clergy and laity that the prebendary represented. The freeing of Humphrey, then, was designed to gain the deputy credit with all those religious conservatives who had been involved on the margins of the Kildare uprising, including the canons of St Patrick's Cathedral. As such, it formed a logical strand in the ongoing development and implementation of his pro-Geraldine governmental strategy, and was of a type with other, similarly motivated, ecclesiastical interventions that he made during this period, such as his promotion of a 'Grey friar, one of the holy confessors of the late Geraldines' to the bishopric of Cork and Cloyne;[85] or his recruitment of Prior George Dowdall of Ardee as his principal emissary amongst the Ulster Irish, despite the facts that Dowdall had been a protégé of the Kildare counsellor-cleric, Cormac Roth, and that he was known to hold 'papistical' views.[86]

It is impossible now to determine what benefit, if any, Grey achieved by his sympathetic handling of Humphrey's case. What is certain, however, is that the entire episode was a deeply humiliating experience for Archbishop Browne, especially within the confines of the cathedral close of St Patrick. The act of arresting Humphrey in the first place would have soured Browne's already poisoned relationship with the cathedral chapter. But the viceroy's intervention robbed him of all credibility in the canons' eyes. He said so much when he informed Cromwell of the matter on 20 May, lamenting the fact that the simplest holy water clerk was better esteemed than he in his diocese. Indeed, he went much further, begging Cromwell that he should either 'cause my authority to take effect, or else let me return home again unto the cloister'.[87]

---

[85] *SP* III, pp. 122–4.

[86] Depositions of the baron of Slane and Sir George Dowdall, late prior of Ardee, concerning the treasons and misdemeanours of Lord Leonard Grey, 23 October 1540, TNA: PRO, SP 60/9, no. 62, printed in T. Gogarty (ed.), 'Documents concerning Primate Dowdall', *AH* 2 (1913), pp. 251–3; 'The extent of all the abbeys within the Pale', TNA: PRO SP 60/3, no. 87 (*LP* XI, no. 1416). On Dowdall's relationhip with Roth see H. Jefferies, 'Primate George Dowdall and the Marian Restoration' in *Seanchas Ard Mhaca* 17, no. 2 (1998), p. 2.

[87] *SP* III, pp. 8–9.

The archbishop's plea fell on deaf ears however. The reality was that Ireland occupied a position of secondary importance in the crown's affairs and Cromwell was unwilling to check the deputy's religious indiscretions on the expediential grounds that he was successful in delivering the one thing that the king desired above all else for the lordship: an inexpensive and relatively ordered system of government. With only a small retinue at his disposal, Grey had proven to be an adept governor in the preceding two years, for he had not only managed to protect the Pale from the ravages of Gaelic clans like the O'Mores, O'Connors and MacMurroughs, but had also begun, by means of a series of 'journeys' into the provinces, to assert the crown's authority over powerful dynastic lords like the O'Neills in Ulster and the O'Briens and O'Carrolls in Munster.[88] Browne, in contrast, had failed to deliver any comparable results for the reformist cause and, although, in ideological terms, he was closer to Cromwell than Grey, this was not enough to win him the support of his master when the two parties vied for his favour.

By the summer of 1538, then, Browne's plans for the reform of the Irish Church had fallen into disarray, for the king and Cromwell had not only remained steadfast in their refusal to establish the institutional structures that the archbishop had persistently sought as being essential for the successful extension of the Reformation in Ireland, but had also failed to support him when he attempted to implement the more limited enforcement strategy that they had enjoined upon him, and which required him – as stipulated by the act against the bishop of Rome's power – to effect religious change by utilising and working through the existing ecclesiastical structures and the organs of the state. The archbishop emerged from the events of the summer, therefore, not only bruised and humiliated after his unsuccessful brush with the viceroy, but also unsure as to what his next move should be, for he realised now that he had taken on what seemed like a virtually impossible task: the leadership of a reform process that was being subverted from within because the agencies responsible for its implementation were untrustworthy and because nobody was willing to call them to account.

Nothing symbolised this strangely inverted world that Browne now inhabited more graphically than the spectacle of Vicegerent Cromwell – the man who only a few short years before had pursued Bishop Fisher and Sir Thomas More to their graves to advance the royal supremacy – endorsing Lord Deputy Grey's abhorrent policy of rebuilding the crown's relationship with Ireland's papist clerics. Hard on the heels of the Humphrey affair, Browne suffered one further indignity when Cromwell issued letters

---

[88] Brady, *Chief governors*, p. 22; SP II, pp. 349–56, 440–5, 468–70, 528–32, 541–2; *Carew MSS 1515–74*, pp. 94–5, 96.

directing him to promote Thomas Creef, a vicar choral of St Patrick's, to a prebend in the same church, notwithstanding the facts that Creef had previously been sacked by Browne from his office of archiepiscopal steward on account of 'his popishness' and that, while in England seeking Cromwell's patronage, he had displayed his full conservative leanings by going on pilgrimage to the great shrines at Canterbury and Walsingham. All Browne could do in response was to request, with resigned politeness, that Cromwell should 'hire my simple advice' in making future appointments within his jurisdiction, especially concerning 'them that shall come out of these parts'.[89]

Yet, despite all these difficulties, Browne's situation was not completely hopeless. There were some substantial figures in Ireland who looked on his plight sympathetically, all of whom shared one characteristic: distaste for the viceroy and his pro-Geraldine governmental strategy. More importantly, they also considered that the deputy's attitude and approach to religion remained, despite his triumphs over Browne, a potential weakness, and believed that significant political advantages might still be gained if the archbishop's reputation could be rehabilitated and the forward, evangelical mode of religious reform re-energised and reactivated. Thus the ensuing years of Browne's episcopacy were characterised by the enmeshment of the reformist cause in local politics, as those who were discontented with the viceroy's conduct rallied round the archbishop and sought to repair the damage that Grey had inflicted on him. This development also had a wider significance, however, for it led to a gradual, but inexorable, alteration in the archbishop's vision of reform, in which he ceased to think of the reform process in Ireland simply as a matter of replicating what had occurred in England, but as something that would need to be adapted and framed to meet the particular circumstances he encountered locally.

v

Support for the archbishop came from two sources. One of these was the Butler family and their affinity, headed by Piers earl of Ossory, and his son and heir, Lord James, and advised and abetted by the Kilkenny lawyers, Robert and Walter Cowley.[90] With the collapse of the house of Kildare in the mid-1530s, the Butlers had expected to augment their power and influence in Irish affairs at the expense of their embattled Geraldine

---

[89] Archbishop Browne to Cromwell, 27 July 1538 (TNA: PRO, SP 60/7, no. 27).
[90] Ossory succeeded to the earldom of Ormond in February 1538; on the background to the succession and the Cowleys see D. Edwards, *The Ormond Lordship in County Kilkenny 1515–1642* (Dublin, 2003), pp. 40–1, 79–90.

enemies. But Lord Deputy Grey was unwilling to allow another powerful aristocratic family to fill the void left by the Fitzgeralds, and thus, determined to maintain the independence of his own office, he actively sought to curb Butler ambitions by befriending many of Kildare's former clients.[91] The Butlers, then, had a major political grievance with the deputy which, in itself, would have made them natural bedfellows of Browne. However, the relationship was also reinforced by the Butlers' pro-reformist religious sympathies. The family had, uniquely in the Irish context, signed up to the new religious dispensation at an early stage: on Trinity Sunday 1534 Ossory bound both himself and his son to Henry VIII 'to resist with all their possible powers, everywhere under their rules . . . the bishop of Rome's usurped jurisdiction'. Thereafter, Lord James, in particular, displayed a marked enthusiasm for the new religion, which was evident in his procurement of anti-papal books through contacts like Bishop Latimer of Worcester, and in the fulsome praise he bestowed on Archbishop Browne's preaching.[92]

The other source of Browne's support was a small cadre of officials in the Dublin administration, which was led by John Alen, the master of the rolls,[93] and whose adherents also included William Brabazon, the vice-treasurer, and Gerald Aylmer, the chief justice of King's Bench. The efficient execution of Cromwell's administrative reforms by Alen and his circle in the mid-1530s had been one of the main factors that precipitated the Fitzgeralds' revolt, and thus they automatically rejected any initiatives, including Grey's rapprochement with the traitorous Geraldine rebels, that threatened to roll back the political gains the crown had achieved in overcoming them.[94] Yet while the primary focus of the officials' opposition to Grey was political, it also had a discernible religious dimension. Alen, in particular, was a strong proponent of the royal supremacy, and had previously advocated – in a submission to the royal commissioners sent to Ireland in 1537 to investigate and reform abuses in the government of the lordship – that the oath of supremacy should be tendered to all the king's subjects in every county in Ireland. Thus he would have had little truck with the temporising attitude to religious matters displayed by the viceroy. In a similar vein, Alen was also anxious to counteract the popular notion, ultimately attributable to the bull *Laudabiliter*, that the king's lordship over Ireland was contingent upon the continuing sanction of the papacy, and had therefore proposed to the commissioners, as a means of weakening its hold on the popular imagination, that parliament should enact a statute

---

[91] Brady, *Chief governors*, pp. 17–20.
[92] *SP* II, pp. 194–7 (at pp. 196–7); Edwards, *Ormond Lordship*, pp. 164–5.
[93] Alen was appointed lord chancellor of Ireland on 18 October 1538 (*LM* I, pt. ii, p. 14).
[94] Brady, *Chief governors*, pp. 18–20.

recognising Henry VIII as king of Ireland. The same pro-papal notion, of course, had also been adopted and promoted by the Fitzgeralds during their revolt, and Alen's concern to eradicate it suggests that his opposition to the Geraldines generally, and to Lord Deputy Grey's rapprochement with them in particular, arose, in part, from his commitment to the supremacy and the anti-papal ideology associated with it.[95]

It is clear, then, that while all of Grey's opponents had particular political agendas for opposing him, the one factor that united them, and that brought Archbishop Browne into their orbit, was their allegiance to the Henrician religious settlement. Writing to Cromwell on 5 April 1538, Thomas Agard observed that only 'the archbishop of Dublin . . . my good Lord Butler, the master of the rolls, Master Treasurer, and one or two more' were prepared to speak out against the 'abusions' of 'that monster, the bishop of Rome, and his adherents'.[96] Moreover, amongst these adherents, as Lord Butler wrote in the following June, they accounted the deputy to be 'the chief and principal in this land',[97] and let no opportunity pass to highlight his religious indiscretions in the many critiques of his governorship that they sent to Cromwell in the late 1530s.[98] This chorus of complaint against Grey reached a crescendo in the late spring and summer of 1538, culminating in a concerted attempt on the part of his enemies to secure his recall from Ireland. Though ultimately unsuccessful, the attempted coup against Grey was significant because it forced his enemies, including Archbishop Browne, to reappraise the manner in which they operated politically, and to develop a more effective strategy to achieve their political and religious ambitions.

The chief spokesmen for the conspirators were John Alen and Gerald Aylmer who, in the company of the returning royal commissioners, undertook a visit to court in the early summer of 1538.[99] This visit was intended to be the defining moment of their campaign against Grey, the moment when the hated viceroy's misdemeanours would be fully revealed to the king and Cromwell and when the latter would be left with no choice but to remove him from office.[100] But although they provided Cromwell with an extensive series of articles setting out the 'enormities and abuses' of Grey's conduct of government,[101] and were confident that their claims

---

[95] *SP* II, pp. 480–6 (at p. 480). On the mission of the royal commissioners generally see Bradshaw, *Irish constitutional revolution*, pp. 117–21; Ellis, *Ireland in the age of the Tudors*, pp. 145–6.

[96] *SP* II, pp. 569–70.   [97] *SP* III, pp. 32–5 (at p. 34).

[98] For some examples see *SP* III, pp. 50–2, 65–7, 94–6, 102–3.

[99] Alen and Aylmer left Ireland in April and were back in Dublin by July (*SP* II, pp. 550–5, 566; *SP* III, pp. 1–3, 17–9, 46–7, 55–7).

[100] For the campaign generally see Brady, *Chief governors*, pp. 20–1.

[101] *SP* III, pp. 36–43.

would be verified by the royal commissioners, Alen and Aylmer's attack on the deputy came to nothing. While they conducted their politicking in England, Grey successfully countered the charges against him with reports sent from Ireland, which detailed *inter alia* his successes in cutting passes in the countries of Offaly and Farney and in brokering agreements with O'Carroll and O'Neill.[102]

The survival of Grey at this juncture was an undoubted blow to his opponents, but it did, at least, open their eyes to the prevailing political realities. They now realised that the king and, more particularly, Cromwell had little time for their constant sniping at the deputy. Instead, the continued support that was given to Grey indicated that what the busy chief minister really wanted to hear were the kind of success stories that the deputy regularly served up in the reports he submitted on his provincial journeys, and which acted, in effect, as rebuttals to the accusations of his detractors. By comparison, their purveyance of political tittle-tattle and innuendo lacked real substance, a point that was affirmed again and again during the summer of 1538, especially when Alen attempted, on behalf of Archbishop Browne, to widen the attack on Grey to include Bishop Staples of Meath, who was then engaged with the archbishop in a war of words from the pulpit, and who the archbishop had insinuated was an adherent of the viceroy's party. As in the case of Grey, Cromwell was not prepared to listen to this gossip, and on 31 May wrote a stinging letter to Browne in which he rebuked him for the 'malice' of his preaching and writing.[103] The lesson to be gleaned from all of this was that if their views were to gain any credibility with Cromwell and the king, Grey's opponents would have to prove that they were as capable as the viceroy of producing results, and that they could offer a genuinely viable alternative to his governmental strategy.

Immediately on their return from England, then, Alen and Aylmer consciously set about trying to achieve this objective by ensuring that all unnecessary disputes between their circle and Grey and his supporters were brought to an end, and by taking care to record and promote their own particular achievements. Thus in August 1538 they prevailed upon Archbishop Browne to end his unseemly dispute with Bishop Staples of Meath and, together with Vice-Treasurer Brabazon, made strenuous efforts – all of which were reported to Cromwell in the most minute detail – to broker a deal between Grey and the Butlers which aimed to 'pacify' their long-running dissentions.[104] As well as these conflict management exercises, Alen and Aylmer also encouraged Archbishop Browne to include reformist success stories in his correspondence with Cromwell, rather than simply

---

[102] *SP* III, pp. 7–8, 15–17.   [103] *SP* III, pp. 1–3; TNA: PRO, SP 60/7, no. 27.
[104] *SP* III, pp. 65–7, 71–86.

regaling him with tales of the viceroy's efforts to impede the Reformation. Thus, in November 1538, the archbishop was moved to report something that he had omitted from previous despatches, namely, that he had successfully concluded a campaign to integrate the Observant friars within the jurisdiction of their conventual brethren. According to the archbishop, the campaign had driven the 'papish, obstinate Observants' to 'such desperation, that where there hath been twenty in an monastery, there been now scarcely four'.[105]

It was not until the closing month of 1538, however, that an opportunity arose for the anti-Grey faction to fully prove its mettle. Letters addressed to the viceroy and council from Cromwell, which were received on 1 December, and which appear to have been accompanied by the second set of royal injunctions that Cromwell issued in his capacity as vicegerent in spirituals to the king, called amongst other things for a renewed effort touching 'the setting forth of the word of God, abolishing of the bishop of Rome's usurped authority, and extinguishing of idolatry'.[106] This challenge, as Grey's enemies well knew, was something that the viceroy was unlikely to embrace with any enthusiasm, and the way was therefore left open to them to demonstrate that they were the only servants of the crown in Ireland who were both genuinely predisposed to, and capable of fulfilling the crown's religious dictates. Thus, in a response to Cromwell, penned on 12 December by a group of councillors which included Chancellor Alen, Archbishop Browne and Vice-Treasurer Brabazon, but not Lord Deputy Grey, they let it be known that the process had begun 'well' already, presumably in Browne's jurisdiction, and that they intended to 'persevere with all industry and diligence'.[107] What they meant by this soon became apparent. Under separate cover, Alen and Brabazon also informed Cromwell that they, together with Archbishop Browne and Chief Justice Aylmer, intended to undertake a journey in the ensuing Christmas vacation through the 'four shires above the Barrow', with the express aim of publishing the new injunctions, advancing the supremacy, 'together with plucking down idols, and the extinguishing of idolatry'. Moreover, they also intended to levy the first fruits and twentieth part in these territories and to keep sessions and redress the peoples' complaints. Their underlying purpose, therefore, was not simply to promote the new religious dispensation. Rather, what they aimed to show was how an integrated approach to the secular and ecclesiastical aspects of crown government in the lordship might

---

[105] *SP* III, pp. 103–5; the campaign appears to have been prompted by the English officials in the Dublin administration (*SP* III, pp. 5–6). On the campaign generally see Bradshaw, *Dissolution of the religious orders*, pp. 92–7.

[106] *SP* III, pp. 108–11.   [107] *SP* III, pp. 108–11 (at p. 110).

operate, and how they, rather than the papistical pro-Geraldine viceroy, were the best people to administer it.[108]

In implementing this strategy, however, the officials were also conscious that there was still some work to be done with regard to rehabilitating the reputation of their principal ecclesiastical affiliate, Archbishop Browne. Thus, the two despatches on the journey that were sent to Cromwell early in 1539 – dated 18 January[109] and 8 February[110] respectively – emphasised his effectiveness as an agent of the supremacy. A careful report of the proceedings was compiled which showed that Browne preached to great audiences 'in advancing the king's supremacy, and the extinguishment of the bishop of Rome' in Kilkenny (on 1 January), in Ross (on 5 January), in Wexford town (on 6 January), in Waterford (on 13 January) and in Clonmel (on 20 January). They also highlighted how, unencumbered by the un-cooperative viceroy, Browne was capable of propagating the latest reformist thinking and doctrine with great celerity. In Kilkenny, for example, he published the new royal injunctions, and delivered English translations of the Pater Noster, Ave Maria, the Articles of the Faith and the Decalogue to the bishop of Ossory and other local prelates, in order that they, and the clergy generally, might meet their teaching responsibilities under the fourth injunction. Thereafter, he instituted the same programmes in the other towns visited by the officials. These detailed notices of Browne's activities were designed, of course, to win the approbation of Cromwell, in much the same way that Lord Grey's reports on his activities in the provinces had created a favourable impression of his deputyship. However, just in case the message failed to hit home, the officials also requested Cromwell 'by your next letters, to give thanks to my lord of Dublin for his pains and diligence he hath used in this journey with us in the setting forth of the word of God'.[111]

The same detailed reporting was also employed by the officials in support of the primary purpose of their journey: to show how the administration of royal justice could and should be integrated with the process of ecclesiastical reform. Thus it was noted that in every venue the archbishop preached, Alen, Aylmer and Brabazon kept sessions on the following day, where they heard presentments for redress from the king's subjects and put to death 'certain malefactors, some for felonies, others for murders'. Two of the recorded incidents, in particular, drew attention to their views on the

---

[108] This letter, which is not extant, is referred to in *SP* III, pp. 111–16 (at p. 111). For the second set of royal injunctions see H. Gee and W.J. Hardy (eds.), *Documents illustrative of English church history* (London, 1896), pp. 275–81.

[109] Alen, Brabazon and Aylmer to Cromwell (*SP* III, pp. 111–16)

[110] Alen, Browne, Brabazon and Aylmer to Cromwell (*SP* III, pp. 116–18).

[111] *SP* III, pp. 111–16 (at p. 116).

complementary nature of the crown's secular and ecclesiastical jurisdictions, and how they should at all times operate in tandem. The first concerned a friar who was put to death at Waterford for thieving. Although his offence was of a secular nature, the crown officials were determined that his punishment should be exemplary in a religious manner. They therefore commanded, and here the contrast with Grey's modus operandi was evident, that the unfortunate friar 'be hanged in his habit, and so to remain upon the gallows, for a mirror to all other his brethren to live truly'.[112] The second incident, which took place in Clonmel, was also a showpiece event and brought the officials' journey to a spectacularly successful close. Following an anti-papal sermon given by Archbishop Browne, ten bishops from the region, including two archbishops, and 'diverse others there present' took the oaths touching the king's succession and supremacy before the king's chief legal officer, Lord Chancellor Alen, and the assembled congregation. Here was a most shining example of how, once the right officials were in charge, the temporal and spiritual polities might function in perfect unison under the crown.[113]

There was one final aspect of the officials' journey which, above all others, confirms that it was a calculated undertaking conceived by Lord Deputy Grey's opponents. This was the involvement of the Butlers of Ormond in the enterprise. Although the officials themselves were relatively discreet in what they revealed about this involvement, there were enough telltale signs in their reports to reveal that the Butlers were not merely participants in the process, but that they effectively stage-managed it from behind the scenes. The first such sign was the choice of location. All the venues that were visited were either in the heart of the Butlers' territories or within the ambit of their influence. This, of course, enabled the earl of Ormond and his family and clients to provide Archbishop Browne with the audiences he required to hear his preaching, as well as the protection that he and his colleagues needed to move from venue to venue. Indeed, it is likely that the detailed itinerary they followed was actually worked out with the Butlers' assistance, for Browne and his colleagues began their journey by spending Christmas time with them – first with Lord James Butler at Carlow, and then with his father, the Earl of Ormond, at Kilkenny – where they were they 'very well entertained'.[114]

Not surprisingly, then, the officials portrayed the Butlers as 'earnest and conformable' in all things touching 'the king's honour, defence of the country, and the quiet and tranquillity of the king's subjects', and beseeched

---

[112] *SP* III, p. 114. For the contrasting support that Grey showed for the friars see *SP* II, pp. 539–41; *SP* III, pp. 103–5, 122–4.
[113] *SP* III, p. 117. [114] *SP* III, p. 111.

Cromwell to give thanks, on the king's behalf, for their efforts to ensure that the yearly subsidy due to the king would be paid within their territories. Equally unsurprisingly, they had nothing favourable to say about the local Geraldine interest. They criticised James Fitzjohn, the 'pretended' earl of Desmond, and his kinsman, Gerald MacShane, for failing to answer a summons to meet them at Clonmel. They also lambasted Gerald's mischief-making and disobedience, which were identified as the chief causes of the crown's inability to collect a subsidy from Waterford. Finally, they also reiterated the by now traditional link between Geraldinism and papism by accusing Gerald McShane of openly maintaining the bishop of Rome against the king's supremacy, and preventing the levying of the first fruits and twentieth parts anywhere under his rule.[115]

Overall, then, the Munster journey represented a deliberate attempt on the part of Lord Grey's opponents to undermine the credibility of what they regarded as his pro-Geraldine, and papistically inclined, governmental strategy, and to show that they were capable of instituting an alternative mode of government that was more in tune with the reformist values of the Tudor regime in England. And it had the desired effect. For the king's chief minister Thomas Cromwell, the achievements registered by Alen, Browne, Brabazon and Aylmer in the aftermath of their failed coup against Grey – not just in relation to the journey in Munster, but also in relation to the restoration of amity with Bishop Staples, the subduing of the Observant friars and the promotion of the royal injunctions of 1538 in Dublin – were both welcome and timely. The chief minister was beginning to experience, for arguably the first time since his rise to prominence, real political pressure at the hands of an emerging conservative religious faction at court. Taking advantage of Cromwell's failure to secure a much desired diplomatic and theological accord between the Schmalkaldic League and England in the summer of 1538, the conservatives had persuaded the king to enshrine his traditionalist views on clerical marriage – one of the main issues that had stood in the way of an agreement with the Lutherans – in a royal proclamation, issued on 16 November 1538, which was aimed primarily at eradicating sacramentarian and anabaptist heresies. In the context of this shift to the theological right, which would eventually culminate in the passage of the act of six articles in the following June, news of the reform party's successes in Ireland was a source of some relief to Cromwell, especially as he was about to extend the campaigns to suppress the religious shrines and the monasteries to Ireland.[116] He could now feel confident that

---

[115] *SP* III, pp. 111–18.

[116] For the shift generally see McEntegart, *Henry VIII, the League of Schmalkalden and the English Reformation*, pp. 115–66; Haigh, *Tudor reformations*, pp. 136–7, 152–67.

he had the right men in place to manage these campaigns and thus, in the opening months of 1539, he responded positively to the anti-Grey alliance's demonstration of its reformist capabilities by appointing Browne, Alen and Brabazon as his deputies in his capacity as vicegerent in spirituals of the king,[117] and by naming them on two new high-powered ecclesiastical commissions for the suppression of images,[118] and for the dissolution of the monasteries.[119]

The appointment of this triumvirate to the three commissions represented a significant political coup for the anti-Grey faction, especially for Archbishop Browne who, only nine months previously, had been moved to request his recall to England because he believed his authority was being undermined by the viceroy. Indeed, the establishment of a vicegerential commission represented a particular vindication of Browne's views on reform, for he had persistently called for the setting up of this and similar offices in the belief that they would give the supremacy much needed visibility in Ireland, and force its opponents, especially the corporate clerical elite, to submit themselves to the crown's spiritual jurisdiction. In contrast, the same developments amounted to a significant political reversal for Lord Deputy Grey. While it would be wrong to claim that Grey had lost the confidence of Cromwell, and that Cromwell wished specifically to undermine his position, his exclusion from all three ecclesiastical commissions indicates that the chief minister was endeavouring to achieve a more balanced system of power – between his ideological affiliates on the one hand, and the pragmatic, soldier-governor on the other – so that the advancement of the new religious dispensation, and not just security matters, would feature in the crown's government of the lordship.

Such an effort to rebalance the system of power, however, necessarily curtailed Grey's room for manoeuvre. It would not now be possible for him to be so cavalier in his treatment of the reformers, and so disdainful of what they were trying to achieve, simply because political expedience demanded it. That said, Grey was loath to let Archbishop Browne's involvement in the Munster journey go unpunished and, before his return to Dublin at the end of January 1539, Grey undertook one final retaliatory act against him by entering into his palace of St Sepulchre, and taking much of the

---

[117] The vicegerential commission was granted on 3 February 1539 (Morrin, *Patent rolls*, i, p. 55).

[118] Issued on 3 February 1539, Browne, Alen and Brabazon were joined on this commission by another close ally, Robert Cowley, the master of the rolls, and Thomas Cusack (C. McNeill, 'Accounts of sums realised by sales of chattels of some suppressed monasteries', *JRSAI* 52 (1922), pp. 11–14).

[119] The commission for the suppression of the monasteries had the same membership as the commission for the suppression of images and was issued on 7 April 1539 (Bradshaw, *Dissolution of the religious orders*, pp. 110–11).

'household stuff' with which it was furnished.[120] But, in the main, the viceroy became noticeably more circumspect in his dealings with the reformers, and with the indigenous religious conservatives whom they wished to convert. Where before the Munster journey complaints about his leniency to papists had been frequent and explicit, the concluding year of Grey's deputyship, which effectively ended with his recall in April 1540, was notable for a perceptible decline in both the number and precision of such criticisms.

In the months that followed the Munster journey, then, Archbishop Browne was, for the first time in his career in Ireland, able to assert his authority as a reformer in an unfettered manner, and quickly set to work to make up for the unproductive years that preceded it. Through the commission for the suppression of the monasteries, for example, Browne was able to strike a near mortal blow at the corporate clergy who had so staunchly resisted his reformist efforts during his primary episcopal visitation. Not only did he finally rid himself of those exempt religious orders that had previously refused to admit him into their jurisdictions, such as the Knights Hospitallers of Kilmainham, but, through their destruction, he also sent out a chilling warning to the surviving corporate clergy in his diocese – now confined to the two cathedrals of St Patrick and Christ Church – that a continued refusal on their part to submit wholeheartedly to the royal supremacy, and all that it entailed, might lead to similarly dire consequences.[121]

In conjunction with this attack on the corporate clergy, Browne also set about remodelling the traditional religious culture of his diocese, and that of the English Pale more generally, in line with the new Henrician spiritual orthodoxies. Thus, through the commission for suppressing images, he and his fellow reformers sought to purify the old religion of 'idolatry' and 'superstitious' practices. Specifically, they stripped some of the most venerated shrines in English Ireland of precious jewels and ornaments, including the *Baculus Jesu*, or staff of Jesus, in Christ Church Cathedral and, with symbolic resonance, the statue of the Blessed Virgin at Trim, which not long previously Lord Deputy Grey had utilised to demonstrate his sympathy for the old religion.[122] In a similar vein, through the vicegerential commission, Browne, together with Alen and Brabazon, altered Christ Church Cathedral from a monastic to a secular institution, which not only propagated, through the abrogation of a hated monastic rule, classical

[120] *SP* III, pp. 122–4.
[121] On Browne's part in the dissolution campaign see Bradshaw, *Dissolution of the religious orders*, pp. 110–45 *passim*.
[122] McNeill, 'Accounts of chattels of some suppressed monasteries', pp. 11–16; *SP* III, pp. 102–3; Bradshaw, *Dissolution of the religious orders*, pp. 100–9.

Henrician dogma,[123] but also placed the king more firmly at the centre of the cathedral's votive devotions, through the institution of a new mass, dedicated to his well-being, which was to be celebrated three times a week at the high altar by the newly constituted vicars choral.[124]

Clearly, then, the freedom and authority that Browne acquired after the Munster journey resulted in the Henrician Reformation making significant headway in the period from the spring of 1539 to the spring of 1540. Moreover, Browne and his allies could look forward with some confidence to consolidating and extending these gains in the following months and years, given that their patron, Thomas Cromwell, had apparently overcome his conservative enemies at this juncture, and once again stood high in the king's favour. On 18 April 1540 Henry VIII created him Earl of Essex and Lord Great Chamberlain of England.[125] Yet such confidence was to prove misplaced. In June 1540, the political and religious landscape altered dramatically when Cromwell's enemies, bolstered by the failure of the Cleves marriage, finally got their man in a sudden and deadly coup at court.[126] The chief minister's fall cast a great shadow of uncertainty over the future of the reformist cause in Ireland and its chief proponent, Archbishop Browne. In its immediate aftermath, it was difficult not to imagine that the religious changes which had been so recently effected might be reversed, and that more conservative religious legislation, along the lines of the English act of six articles, might be introduced and enforced in both England and Ireland. Indeed, one of the most important gains the reformers had made in Ireland was lost straightaway. Barely a year after they had received it, and before they had had a chance to operate it fully, the commission granted to Browne, Alen and Brabazon to act as Cromwell's deputy vicegerents lapsed with the latter's attainder for treason.[127]

---

[123] For the development of the Henrician regime's increasingly negative attitude towards monasticism in the 1530s see Bernard, *The King's Reformation*, pp. 228–92, 433–42.

[124] RCB, C6/1/6, no. 3 (Registrum Novum of Christ Church), p. 1117. It has generally been assumed by historians that Alen, Browne and Brabazon altered the cathedral's constitutional status in their capacity as commissioners for the suppression of the monasteries (for example, Bradshaw, *Dissolution of the religious orders*, pp. 118–19; R. Gillespie, 'The coming of reform, 1500–58', in Milne, ed., *Christ Church Cathedral*, p. 165). A close reading of the preamble to their alteration device, however, reveals that they took this action on foot of the much more extensive commission to act as Cromwell's deputy vicegerents, which gave them powers *inter alia* to hear and determine ecclesiastical causes, to visit the clergy and people throughout all Ireland and to correct and reform their morals (RCB, C6/1/6, no. 3, pp. 1104–21, at p. 1104).

[125] *LP* XV, no. 541.

[126] Guy, *Tudor England*, pp. 184–9; Haigh, *Tudor reformations*, pp. 153–4; D. Starkey, *Six wives. The queens of Henry VIII* (London, 2003), pp. 617–43; McEntegart, *Henry VIII, the League of Schmalkalden and the English Reformation*, pp. 167–202.

[127] Cromwell's own commission as vicegerent ended at the time of his attainder, and he was never replaced (Lehmberg, 'Supremacy and vicegerency', p. 234; Logan, 'Cromwell and the

Cromwell's fall, of course, also had wider repercussions for Ireland: the same factional struggle that led to the chief minister's demise also brought down the viceroy, Lord Leonard Grey.[128] Viewed from this perspective, it was evident that the future course of the crown's religious policy in Ireland would depend greatly on who the king would choose as Grey's successor, and upon what approach the latter would adopt both in the contexts of the new, post-Cromwellian era of religious politics in England and of his own priorities for the government of Ireland. A new deputy, Sir Anthony St Leger, was appointed to replace Grey on 7 July 1540.[129] The following chapters will explore the impact of St Leger's viceroyalty on the Reformation in Ireland, focussing, in particular, on his relationship with Archbishop Browne.

vicegerency', p. 667). Much of Browne, Alen and Brabazon's time, after their receipt of the deputy vicegerential commission, was taken up with the dissolution of the monasteries – the alteration of Christ Church is the only recorded use of the vicegerential commission discovered thus far.

[128] Brady, *Chief Governors*, pp. 23–5; Grey was committed to the Tower two days after Cromwell's arrest (*LP* XV, nos. 765–7, 775).

[129] *LP* XV, no. 943 (31).

4

'God's laws and ours together': Archbishop Browne, political reform and the emergence of a new religious settlement, 1540–2

The fall of Thomas Cromwell in June 1540 has traditionally been viewed by historians as a watershed in George Browne's episcopate. It is thought to have closed the active phase in his career as a reformer, and to have marked the beginning of a period of quiescence that would last until at least the end of Henry VIII's reign. On first sight this judgement seems plausible for, in the aftermath of his master's demise, the archbishop not only desisted from the aggressive enforcement campaigns that he had previously waged against his clergy in support of the Henrician Reformation, but his voice was also silenced in the historical record because he was left without an influential English patron with which to correspond. The Browne of the 1540s was certainly a less vocal and controversial figure than the ardent activist of the 1530s.

Yet the case for the quiescent Browne has generally been overstated. The prevailing image of the archbishop that it has given rise to – that of a 'spent force' who, bereft of Cromwell's protection, was left exposed to the forces of a gathering conservative religious reaction, or who was cast into the political wilderness because his brand of authoritarian religious reform did not fit in with the 'liberal' approach favoured by the new lord deputy, Sir Anthony St Leger – has tended to obscure the reality of his public life after 1540.[1] As the surviving records of the St Leger administration show, Browne moved seamlessly, even confidently, into the post-Cromwellian era in Ireland, becoming not only an enthusiastic and favoured supporter of the viceroy, but one who engaged wholeheartedly with the political reform project that the latter launched in Ireland in the early 1540s.

---

[1] On this image see Edwards, *Church and state*, pp. 75–7 and *Ireland in the age of the Tudors*, p. 67; Murray, 'Ecclesiastical justice and the enforcement of the Reformation', pp. 49–51; Bradshaw, *Irish constitutional revolution*, pp. 245–51.

St Leger's reform project would dominate the Irish political scene throughout the succeeding decade and beyond, and subsume and mediate all aspects of the crown's religious policies. Indeed, for a brief period, it even held out the prospect of overcoming the dichotomy between church and state that had stymied the enforcement of the early Reformation in Ireland, and which had contributed to the souring of relations between Browne and Lord Deputy Grey. It thus provided a welcome opportunity for the archbishop to redefine the nature of his episcopacy, and to retain and reinforce his position in the new, conservative religious climate that prevailed after Cromwell's sudden eclipse. To gain a full understanding, then, of how the Reformation fared in Dublin and, indeed, elsewhere in Ireland, it is necessary to explore in some detail the impact of St Leger's reform project on religious and ecclesiastical matters in the 1540s.

I

George Browne's progress from Thomas Cromwell's protégé to proponent of Lord Deputy St Leger's reform project was a logical development in his career in Ireland. While Cromwell's fall was undoubtedly a traumatic event for the archbishop, there was one particular aspect to it that eased his transition to the new political order: the convulsions at court that brought about his master's fall also engulfed, and ultimately destroyed, his great adversary of the 1530s, Lord Deputy Grey. The chief architect of Grey's downfall, and the man who replaced him as the king's deputy in Ireland, was Sir Anthony St Leger. As Grey's nemesis, St Leger's standing was inevitably high among those who had avowed themselves to be the stricken viceroy's enemies and, initially at least, he could count upon their unstinting political support.[2] This was certainly the case with Archbishop Browne, who responded positively to the new deputy's succession, if for no other reason than that St Leger had rid him of a hated enemy who to the last had disparaged his authority and ridiculed him as a 'poll shorn friar'.[3]

Yet there was more to the coming together of Browne and St Leger than the vagaries of crude personality politics. Throughout the period of Grey's deputyship, the archbishop and his allies had represented themselves as 'the king's true subjects' being 'neither of the Geraldine band ne papists'. What they meant by this was that they espoused a set of political principles in which unquestioned obedience to the will of Henry VIII was

---

[2] On the circumstance surrounding Grey's fall and St Leger's part in it see Brady, *Chief Governors*, pp. 23–5.

[3] On the lasting enmity between the pair see Browne's final letter to Cromwell of 19 May 1540 (*SP* III, pp. 208–9).

paramount – in his capacity both as sovereign of Ireland and as supreme head of the Irish Church – and which demanded, as an essential step in fostering this acquiescent loyalism more generally, the dismantling of the faction-ridden and Geraldine-dominated system of politics that had prevailed in the late medieval lordship.[4] In broad terms, Lord Deputy St Leger was also an advocate of these principles and, through the development and implementation of his general reform strategy, was committed to embedding them in the local political culture. Indeed, in working out the detail of his reform strategy, he recognised that the anti-Grey coalition had a valuable contribution to make. Thus he was neither adverse to borrowing ideas from the group, or to elaborating upon or exploiting particular aspects of the reformist work that its various members had undertaken under the previous regime, including, in particular, their efforts to advance the royal supremacy and to suppress monasticism. The alliance that was formed between St Leger and the anti-Grey coalition, then, was founded not only upon a mutual antipathy towards Lord Leonard Grey, but also upon a shared commitment to a reform strategy which enshrined many of the group's basic values, and which, in certain crucial respects, sought to build upon the reforms that the group had introduced in the 1530s.

Historians have identified two distinct strands in St Leger's reform strategy – one grounded upon constitutional innovation, the other involving an attempt to foster island-wide political support for the crown – and, in each, the imprint of the anti-Grey coalition was readily detectable. At the heart of the first, the constitutional strand, was the alteration of Ireland's status from lordship to kingdom, through the enactment of the act for the kingly title in the 1541 parliament. An important intent of this act was to create a unified polity in Ireland and to break down the old ethnic divisions between the English Irish and Gaelic inhabitants of the island by treating them as equal subjects under the English crown. It thus served as the basis for one of the main initiatives in St Leger's general reform strategy, the policy of 'surrender and regrant', through which the viceroy attempted to negotiate, in a conciliatory and gradualist manner, the incorporation of the independent Gaelic lordships into the new unified polity.[5] Yet, as fundamental as the assimilation of the Gaelic lordships was to both the

---

[4] The description, written in August 1538, is from a letter of Thomas Alen, brother of the lord chancellor, to Robert Cowley, one of the Butler's most trusted clients (*SP* III, pp. 67–9, at p. 69). For some other examples of the group's espousal of these principles see Robert Cowley to Cromwell, 19 July and 5 August 1538, 8 September 1539 (*SP* III, pp. 50–2, 63–5, 145–9); Alen, Brabazon and Aylmer to Cromwell, 24 July 1538 (*SP* III, pp. 55–7); Archbishop Browne to Cromwell, 16 February 1539 (*SP* III, pp. 122–4); lord deputy and council to the king, 18 January 1540 (*SP* III, pp. 175–9).

[5] On this strand of St Leger's reform strategy generally see Bradshaw, *Irish constitutional revolution*, chs. 7–8, and 'Beginnings of modern Ireland', pp. 75–80.

conception and implementation of the viceroy's reform strategy, the act for the kingly title was also designed with a more pressing purpose in mind. This was the need to buttress the crown's authority in the face of the claim – advanced, among others, by the conservative clergy during the recent crises of the Kildare rebellion and the Geraldine League – that Henry VIII's right to rule in Ireland was conditional, and that it ultimately depended upon the assent of the papacy.[6] No group was more perturbed by the diffusion of this contention than the anti-Grey coalition, because it not only had the potential to incite rebellion, but it also flew in the face of the monarchical, anti-papal creed that the group had been trying to disseminate in Ireland since the enactment of the royal supremacy. Thus, throughout the late 1530s, and with ever growing trepidation, the king's 'true' subjects repeatedly voiced their concerns on the matter, a chorus of alarm that ultimately moved St Leger to press ahead with the enactment of the act for the kingly title, following his succession as viceroy in the summer of 1540.

The contention that the 'regal estate' of Ireland resided in the papacy, and that the king's lordship was 'but a governance under the obedience of the same' was, as Archbishop Browne's ally Sir John Alen averred in 1537, 'of long continuance', being attributable to various ancient papal grants such as the bull *Laudabiliter*.[7] However, it became a source of disquiet for the king's 'true' subjects soon after Henry VIII completed the abolition of papal authority within his dominions, because all manner of malcontents – whether Fitzgerald loyalists, disenchanted religious conservatives or ambitious Gaelic lords – could utilise it to argue that the king had relinquished his right to rule in Ireland. Significantly, this concern had been raised directly with the future viceroy, St Leger, as early as 1537, when the latter came to Ireland as one of a group of special royal commissioners. Indeed, in a formal submission to the commissioners, which was drafted by Alen, they not only defined the nature of the problem for Leger, but also proposed a possible solution which would extinguish any hint of conditionality about the king's authority in Ireland: namely, 'that his highness be recognised here, by act of parliament, supreme governor of this dominion, by the name of the king of Ireland'. As well as removing all doubts about the king's right to rule in Ireland, Alen also maintained that the use of the kingly title would serve as an inducement to the Irishry to recognise Henry VIII, and that over time it would be 'a great motive' to bring them to full obedience.[8]

---

[6] On the claim generally see Ellis, 'Kildare rebellion and the early reformation', pp. 813–14; Sheehy, 'The Bull *Laudabiliter*', pp. 52–3; Bradshaw, *Dissolution of the religious orders*, pp. 210–11 and *Irish constitutional revolution*, pp. 180–1.

[7] *SP* II, p. 480; Sheehy, 'The Bull *Laudabiliter*', pp. 52–3.

[8] *SP* II, p. 480. On the mission of the royal commissioners generally see Bradshaw, *Irish constitutional revolution*, pp. 117–21; Ellis, *Ireland in the age of the Tudors*, pp. 145–6.

Although the commissioners took no action on Alen's recommendation in 1537, the concerns which motivated it did not diminish thereafter. On the contrary, they grew in intensity as the threat of a major rebellion – in support of the surviving Geraldine heir and involving powerful provincial families like the Desmond Fitzgeralds in Munster and the O'Neills and O'Donnells in Ulster – emerged in 1539–40.[9] For the master of the rolls, Robert Cowley, one of the most vocal adherents of the king's 'true' subjects, the causes of this 'traitorous conspired treason' were plain for all to see. Writing in September 1539, he noted that the would-be rebels were motivated by the convictions 'that the king's highness is an heretic against the faith, because he obeyeth not and believeth not the bishop of Rome's usurped primacy' and that he 'hath no right or title to this land but usurpation'.[10] The same viewpoint was also shared by other members of his circle and found expression in a letter written to the king by the deputy and council in January 1540. Signed, among others, by Cowley, Archbishop Browne, Lord Chancellor Alen, Vice-Treasurer Brabazon and Chief Justice Aylmer, the letter briefed the king that the 'tyrannous purposes' of the rebels were 'to destroy all your grace's true and faithful subjects ... to subdue the whole land to them, to erect and glorify the bishop of Rome's usurped primacy and to elevate and fortify the Geraldine sect'. While the immediate threat of such calamities occurring may have been exaggerated by the councillors, there is little doubt that they were expressing a genuinely held fear that the prevailing uncertainty about the king's 'title to this land' was undermining his authority in the present and that, if left unchecked, would lead inevitably to its overthrow in the future.[11]

It was in this atmosphere of apprehension and uncertainty that St Leger arrived in Ireland and set about the task of formulating policy.[12] Significantly, the group of advisors that he gathered round him at this juncture was dominated by the very same figures – Alen, Browne, Brabazon, Aylmer and Cowley – who had opposed his predecessor Lord Grey, and who had been most perturbed by the aspersions that had been cast on the king's right to rule Ireland in the years following his assumption of the supremacy. Inevitably, then, their anxieties featured prominently in the elaboration of policy, especially in relation to the act for the kingly title. The decisive

---

[9] For the Geraldine League see Bradshaw, *Irish constitutional revolution*, pp. 174–81; Ellis, *Ireland in the age of the Tudors*, pp. 148–9.

[10] *SP* III, pp. 145–9, at p. 147.   [11] *SP* III, pp. 175–9.

[12] St Leger landed in Dublin *c.*12 August 1540 (*SP* III, p. 235). On the general atmosphere at this time see the letter which he and the council wrote to the king in October 1541, and which alluded to the fact that, prior to the enactment of the act for the kingly title, 'most wise and expert men' in Ireland had feared that the country would not be pacified for many years as a result of the Kildare revolt and the attempted insurrection of the Geraldine League (*SP* III, pp. 339–44, at p. 341).

discussions on the matter took place in the last two weeks of December 1540 when, following his receipt of a licence from the king to hold his first parliament, St Leger hastily assembled the Irish council to prepare the draft legislation. The resultant bill on the royal style was clearly framed with the concerns of the king's 'true and faithful' subjects in mind, for it not only provided for Henry's establishment as king of Ireland, but did so in exactly the same terms, and for precisely the same reasons, as Lord Chancellor Alen had outlined in his proposal to St Leger and his fellow commissioners three years earlier. Thus, in a letter written to the king on 30 December, the deputy and council justified the proposed act on the grounds that the Irishry would more gladly obey 'your highness by name of king of this your land, then by the name of lord ... having had heretofore a foolish opinion amongst them that the bishop of Rome should be king of the same'. It was for the 'extirping' of this 'foolish opinion', they stressed, that Henry VIII and his successors 'should be named kings of this land'.[13]

In its initial framing, then, the act for the kingly title owed much to the thinking of the circle in which Archbishop Browne had moved in the preceding years. Although, from the outset, the group had recognised that the act would provide a clear legal basis for incorporating the independent Gaelic lordships into a unified polity under the English crown, its primary purpose was to buttress the Erastian principle which they had worked so hard to establish after Henry VIII had been proclaimed supreme head of the Irish Church in 1536. This principle – that the king was supreme governor of both the spiritual and temporal polities in Ireland – had been consistently opposed throughout the 1530s by the supporters of the papacy and the 'Geraldine band', who maintained that the crown had not only no right to rule the church but, through its treatment of the papacy, had also forfeited its secular dominion over Ireland. St Leger's willingness to undertake an initiative that counteracted these charges, in the very way that the anti-Grey coalition had originally proposed, represented a strong endorsement of the group's values, and served also to encourage its wholehearted participation in his administration in support of his reform strategy.

The second strand of this strategy – the attempt to construct a new political interest in Ireland, the 'king's party' – was also animated by the monarchical ideology that Browne and his allies had promoted in the 1530s. However, where the act for the kingly title sought to reinforce the crown's authority in law, the attempt to build a new, island-wide loyalist interest was intended to give it practical effect on the ground. Specifically, St Leger aimed to bind to the crown the many and diverse

---

[13] *SP* III, pp. 277–8. The letter was signed by Alen, Browne, Brabazon, Aylmer and Cowley among others.

interest groups that existed on the island through the liberal distribution of crown property and, by these means, to transcend and ultimately neutralise the destructive factionalism that had traditionally dogged Irish politics, and which had undermined all previous attempts to achieve a lasting and peaceful political settlement on the island.[14]

As with the constitutional strand of his reform project, the intentions underpinning St Leger's attempt to build a strong, loyalist political bloc were very much in tune with the political aspirations of the various members of the anti-Grey coalition. They, like the deputy, were committed to advancing the crown's authority in a real and tangible manner and, as they had continually reminded Lord Grey and Cromwell in the 1530s, they were also staunch opponents of the faction-ridden system of politics that the construction of the 'king's party' was intended to overcome. In addition, the group also appreciated the viceroy's tactical nous. Archbishop Browne, in particular, was alive to the possibilities of exploiting the property market to achieve political ends and, in anticipation of St Leger, had already begun building alliances with key figures in the local political community, such as the Barnewalls of Grace Dieu, through the strategic alienation of some attractive archiepiscopal estates in north Co. Dublin.[15] For these reasons alone, the anti-Grey coalition would have been predisposed to support this aspect of the viceroy's reform project. However, the fact that St Leger also intended to use property that had been confiscated from the Geraldine rebels and the papist monasteries to achieve such laudable ends gave it an added attraction, especially as many of the coalition members, including Archbishop Browne, had been personally involved in procuring much of this property for the crown.[16] St Leger's attempt to create a loyalist interest through the exploitation of the crown's largesse thus represented a development of the reforming work that Archbishop Browne and his colleagues had begun under Cromwell and explains why the archbishop was prepared to give such an enthusiastic endorsement to the viceroy and his regime. St Leger's plans for the government of Ireland were hugely attractive to him because they were grounded upon the monarchical dogma that he and his allies had propounded in the 1530s, and because they presented an opportunity to build upon the work that he had previously undertaken to make this ideology a reality in Ireland. It was no surprise, therefore, that

---

[14] On this aspect of St Leger's reform strategy see Brady, *Chief Governors*, pp. 29–40.

[15] Griffith, *Exchequer inquisitions*, p. 136.

[16] On the involvement of the various members of the anti-Grey coalition in the campaign to suppress the monasteries see Bradshaw, *Dissolution of the religious orders*, pp. 110–45 *passim*. Alen, Aylmer and Brabazon were also granted a commission, in conjunction with St Leger, to dispose of the houses and possessions of the Irish friars in September 1541 (Morrin, *Patent rolls*, i, p. 90).

from the autumn and winter of 1540–1 the archbishop figured prominently in many of the activities undertaken by the new administration.

At this early stage of his viceroyalty St Leger was anxious to strengthen the security of the Pale because, in the hiatus between Lord Deputy Grey's departure and his own arrival, the region and its inhabitants had been subjected to 'burning, murders and spoils' at the hands of the Irishry.[17] Thus he undertook a series of military and diplomatic initiatives in eastern Ireland which were designed to secure the submissions of the Leinster Irish, including the O'Tooles, whose chief, Turlough, was deemed by the deputy and council to have 'done more hurt' to the English Pale 'than any man in Ireland'.[18] A deal was struck with the family in November 1540. In return for royal grants of the lands they claimed in Co. Wicklow, Turlough and his brother, Art Óg, agreed to submit themselves to Henry VIII's rule, and to release his subjects in the Pale from the tributes, estimated at 400 or 500 marks annually, that hitherto had provided a substantial part of their living. There was one difficulty with the plan however. The property that Art Óg claimed – Castlekevin and Fertire – belonged in English law to the see of Dublin. To solve it, therefore, St Leger entered into negotiations with Archbishop Browne, and requested him to assign the see's ancient title in the property to the crown so that it could be passed on to the O'Tooles. Browne, for his part, was 'contented liberally' to oblige and, by the following August, the legalities of the transaction had been completed to the satisfaction of all the parties.[19]

The appeasement of the O'Tooles in 1540–1 was directly advantageous to Browne, as it held out the prospect of ending the cycle of depredation and economic dislocation that the clan had traditionally inflicted upon the archbishop and his tenants in the marcher manors of Tallaght and Ballymore.[20] Yet Browne's participation in St Leger's administration, and the support which he accorded to the viceroy's reform strategy, was not contingent upon him receiving such benefits, or upon the immediate relevance of specific reforming initiatives to his own local situation. On the contrary, as far as the reform project was concerned, Browne's perspective was truly national, and he was quite prepared to move outside his own sphere of influence to advance St Leger's plans. An early instance of this occurred in

---

[17] On this see the lord justice and council to the king, 25 July 1540 (*SP* III, pp. 223–5).

[18] *SP* III, pp. 235–45, 266–71.

[19] Griffith, *Exchequer inquisitions*, p. 92; RCB, D6/113, no. 2 ('An abstract of inquisitions taken in Henry VIII's reign, relating to the archbishopric of Dublin'); *Fiants, Henry VIII*, no. 548; Morrin, *Patent rolls*, i, pp. 81–2; *SP* III, pp. 266–71, 390. For a detailed discussion of the O'Toole settlement and its broader political significance see C. Maginn, '*Civilizing' Gaelic Leinster. The extension of Tudor rule in the O'Byrne and O'Toole lordships* (Dublin, 2005), pp. 58–76.

[20] See above, pp. 60–1.

January 1541, when he and other councillors accompanied the deputy on progress in Munster. The main purpose of the journey was to obtain the submission of James FitzJohn Fitzgerald, in return for which the viceroy intended to pardon him for past misdemeanours and to recognise him as the legitimate earl of Desmond. The initial negotiations were tense and held at a distance. It was eventually agreed, however, that Fitzgerald would meet the deputy face to face in Cashel, providing that St Leger would put in suitable pledges for him. St Leger accepted the proviso, and those who were finally chosen as pledges included the deputy's brother Robert and, significantly, Archbishop Browne. As with the scheme for the O'Tooles, the combined efforts of the deputy and the archbishop proved fruitful. On 16 January 1541 Desmond submitted to the king's authority in the presence of 200 Irish gentlemen, after which St Leger delivered to him the king's 'most gracious pardon, which he most joyfully accepted'.[21]

By the spring of 1541, then, Archbishop Browne had established himself as an integral member of the viceroy's administration, and would remain so for the remainder of Henry VIII's reign. Indeed, as a letter written by St Leger and the council to the king in the following year testifies, the viceroy clearly thought highly of the contribution that the archbishop was making. St Leger and the council noted that Browne 'hath at all times been conformable to any thing that hath been to him moved on the behalf of your majesty', highlighting, in particular, his assistance in the scheme for the appeasement of the O'Tooles.[22] These were not idle words. As a mark of his favour and gratitude, the deputy also ensured that Browne was included in the distribution of the monastic spoils. Thus, on 13 March 1541, he was granted a twenty-one year lease of the site and appurtenances of the priory of Fethard in Co. Tipperary at the knockdown rent of £3 6s. 8d. per annum.[23] Moreover, another, more substantial favour was not long following. In the summer of 1542 St Leger successfully petitioned the king to remit a debt of £250 sterling which Browne had originally owed to Anne Boleyn's brother, Lord Rochford, but which was then due to the king as a result of Rochford's attainder.[24]

As welcome as these material benefits were to the archbishop, however, they were not the only rewards that he secured through his involvement in St Leger's administration. Browne also had the satisfaction of seeing and participating in something that he had consistently campaigned for in the 1530s. This was the introduction of a properly co-ordinated effort between

---

[21] *SP* III, pp. 285–90. [22] *SP* III, pp. 385–91 (at p. 390).
[23] *Fiants, Henry VIII*, no. 168. The friary had been valued at £6 7s. 10d. gross in January 1541 (White, *Monastic extents*, pp. 329–30).
[24] *SP* III, pp. 390, 396–7; Morrin, *Patent rolls*, i, p. 81.

the organs of the church and state to advance the king's authority in Ireland, especially the royal supremacy. Browne's sense of satisfaction was all the greater, in fact, because the new, integrated approach to reform bore immediate and impressive results. The Desmond submission was a case in point. As part of his agreement with the crown, the newly created earl undertook to 'deny and forsake the bishop of Rome, and his usurped primacy and authority' and to 'resist and repress the same, and all that shall by any mean use and maintain the same'. This, of course, was in stark contrast to what had transpired on the previous occasion that Browne had attempted to engage with James FitzJohn Fitzgerald. Then, during a journey into Munster in the winter of 1538–9, he would not even deign to meet Browne and his fellow royal emissaries.[25] As well as binding aberrant provincial lords like Desmond to the supremacy,[26] the pursuit of a more integrated approach to the political and ecclesiastical aspects of reform also ensured that papally appointed bishops were brought into the king's fold. In the year 1541 alone, for example, at least three such bishops – Thady Reynolds in Kildare, Florence Kirwan (Gerawan) in Clonmacnoise, and Roland De Burgo in Clonfert – surrendered their bulls, and were subsequently granted royal patents to their livings or, at the very least, were made suffragans of their local metropolitan.[27]

Symbolically, at least, the highpoint of the St Leger regime's merger of political and ecclesiastical reform occurred in June 1541 when the act for the kingly title was formally enacted by the Irish parliament in a blaze of ceremony and celebration. Although, ostensibly, the act was only concerned with the king's secular jurisdiction, the viceroy and his administration were also intent on ensuring that no one amongst the lords, bishops and gentlemen who attended the parliament, or who partook in the subsequent celebrations, would be left in any doubt that the king's new regal status also comprehended his mastery of the spiritual polity in Ireland. Thus the key roles in the proceedings, such as the speakership of the commons, were preserved for reliable adherents of the administration like Sir Thomas Cusack, a man who had worked with Archbishop Browne on the commissions to suppress the monasteries and the shrines, and who could be guaranteed to stay 'on message'.[28] He did not disappoint. In his opening

---

[25] *SP* III, pp. 286–7; above, p. 120.

[26] For similar anti-papal provisions in the submissions St Leger secured from various Gaelic lords in 1541–2 see *Carew MSS, 1515–74*, pp. 183–90.

[27] *Fiants, Henry VIII*, nos. 187, 262–3; Bradshaw, *Irish constitutional revolution*, p. 248.

[28] McNeill, 'Accounts of sums realised by sales of chattels of . . . monasteries', pp. 11–14; Bradshaw, *Dissolution of the religious orders*, pp. 110–11. On Cusack's relationship and involvement with Lord Deputy St Leger and his administration see Bradshaw, *Irish constitutional revolution*, pp. 189–96.

address to parliament, Speaker Cusack provided a solemn and laudatory meditation on the merits of Henry VIII's kingship which, by extolling the king's extirpation of papal authority from the realm, highlighted the continuity between what had gone before (the enactment of the act for the royal supremacy) and what was about to come (the enactment of the act for the kingly title). Less explicitly, though no less effectively, the same message was also reiterated in the formal ceremonies surrounding the proclamation of the act for the kingly title. Here again a veteran of the Henrician Reformation was placed centre stage – on this occasion Archbishop Browne himself – to show that what was being celebrated was Henry VIII's kingship in both its temporal and spiritual aspects. Thus, on Sunday 18 June 1541, the lords and gentlemen of the parliament rode to St Patrick's Cathedral 'where was sung a solemn mass by the archbishop of Dublin' – the man most identified with the promotion of the royal supremacy in the 1530s – 'and after the mass, the said act proclaimed there in the presence of 2,000 persons, and *Te Deum* sung, with great joy and gladness to all men'.[29]

That the occasion of the enactment of the act for the kingly title would be exploited to reassert the king's supremacy over the church was entirely predictable, given that the primary purpose of the act was, as the viceroy and council informed the king once again in October 1541, to 'put many fantasies and opinions out of Irishmens' heads', especially the 'abominable error' whereby they 'reputed the bishop of Rome as head and king of this land'.[30] What was not predictable, however, was the surprisingly muted response that this new trumpeting of the king's ecclesiastical authority evoked from the local clergy, especially from within that great bastion of religious conservatism in the diocese of Dublin, the cathedral chapter of St Patrick. While it is doubtful that the cathedral prebendaries shared, on account of its association with the supremacy, the same enthusiasm for the new royal style that the citizens of Dublin demonstrated in their exuberant participation in the festivities that accompanied the proclamation of the act for the kingly title, neither were they prepared to upset the celebrations by indulging in the kind of subversive actions that had previously characterised their disapproving attitude to the king's spiritual claims. To a man, the prebendaries of St Patrick's remained silent in the summer of 1541, and sat compliantly in their stalls while their archbishop led the religious ceremonies in honour of the newly proclaimed king of Ireland.[31]

The acquiescence of the clergy at this time can be explained, in part, by a greatly increased sense of vulnerability, which had been brought on by the dissolution of the monasteries. While many individuals in the chapter of St Patrick's would still have harboured strong objections against the

---

[29] *SP* III, pp. 304–5. [30] *SP* III, pp. 339–44 (at p. 341). [31] *SP* III, p. 305.

supremacy, there would also have been a marked reluctance to express them openly for fear of subjecting their cathedral to the wrath of the crown, and the same dire fate that had befallen the abbeys and priories in the Pale in 1539–40. But the clergy's conformity in 1541 reflected another important development in their attitudes: a recognition that the religion that was now being canvassed by the St Leger regime in the name of the king of Ireland was much more conservative in nature, and thus more palatable, than the aggressive evangelical religion which had accompanied the original pro-motion of the royal supremacy in the 1530s. The changing face of the Henrician religious settlement in the early 1540s was to prove significant in two respects. First, it provided the basis for a hitherto undreamt of accommodation between Archbishop Browne and his erstwhile enemies, the conservative clergy of his cathedral of St Patrick and the wider diocese. Second, it created a comparatively more congenial atmosphere which served not only to encourage the same clergy to engage in a positive manner with the monarchical ideology advanced by Lord Deputy St Leger's regime, but also to begin to identify clear points of contact and continuity between that ideology and their own cultural heritage. Thus, for the first and only time in the sixteenth century, and under the umbrella of St Leger's reform project, the Tudor regime began to make some genuine headway in the task of establishing the Reformation, albeit a distinctly conservative Reforma-tion, within the heartland of English Ireland.

II

The movement towards a more conservative religious settlement in Ireland in the early 1540s was driven by two distinct, but complementary, forces: the personal religious inclinations of Henry VIII, and the political needs of St Leger's reform project. The former was the first to manifest itself. Since the winter of 1538, and the burning of the Anabaptist, John Lambert, the king had signalled his intent that he would tolerate no further flirtation with radical religious thinking and practice within the confines of the state church, a stance which culminated in the passage of the act of six articles in the English parliament during the summer of 1539. This ordinance – which endorsed the traditional doctrines and practices of transubstantiation, communion in one kind, priestly celibacy, vows of chastity, private masses, and auricular confession, and made their denial penal offences – affirmed in the strongest possible terms the strict Catholic orthodoxy that Henry VIII upheld and which he wished all his subjects to adhere to.[32] Yet, although

---

[32] For the act of six articles and the conservative religious reaction generally see Haigh, *English reformations*, pp. 136–7, 152–67; G. Redworth, 'A study in the formulation of

the enforcement clauses in the act of six articles had indicated that it might be executed not only in England and Wales, but also 'in any other the king's dominions',[33] no attempt was made at the time to extend any of its provisions across the Irish Sea. On the contrary, the period in which the conservative religious reaction took a hold in England was to witness a marked increase in reformist activity in Ireland, as Archbishop Browne and his allies set about the tasks of securing the submission of the Munster bishops to the royal supremacy, disseminating the second set of royal injunctions, dismantling hallowed religious shrines and dissolving the religious houses of the English Pale.[34] In effect, and at the instigation of the king's vicegerent, Thomas Cromwell, the chief protector of religious radicalism in the Henrician regime, Ireland was being deliberately shielded from the conservative religious reaction at this juncture, so that the nascent reform movement would have an opportunity to establish a foothold there.[35]

The situation changed, however, when Cromwell fell from power in the summer of 1540. With his vicegerent removed from the scene, the king was able to intervene in the affairs of the Irish Church in a direct and unimpeded manner, and to begin the process of stamping it with his own personal brand of Catholic orthodoxy. A perfect opportunity for such intervention

policy: the genesis and evolution of the Act of Six Articles', *JEH* 37 (1986), pp. 42–67; MacCulloch, *Thomas Cranmer*, pp. 237–58; McEntegart, *Henry VIII, the League of Schmalkalden and the English Reformation*, pp. 131–66. For the text of the act of six articles see Gee and Hardy (eds.), *Documents illustrative of English church history*, pp. 303–19.

[33] Ibid., pp. 311–13.

[34] Above, pp. 117–23. The conventional notion of a conservative religious reaction in the 1540s, with the act of six articles at its heart, has recently been challenged by Alec Ryrie, *The Gospel and Henry VIII. Evangelicals in the early English Reformation* (Cambridge, 2003), especially pp. 13–57. However, while Ryrie has argued convincingly that the act was primarily directed against sacramentaries, and that it was only enforced in a limited manner and never used as the legal basis for a 'general purge' of reformist sympathisers, he also concedes that it constituted a 'body blow' to their hopes for future reformation and that it remained a potential threat to their cause throughout the remainder of Henry VIII's reign. See also G.W. Bernard's argument that there was no conservative religious reaction in the 1540s because there was no need for one, given that the king, the sole and determining mover of the religious change, had consistently and successfully striven to preserve religious unity in England through maintaining a middle way between Lutheranism and unreformed Catholicism. In this context, the act of six articles was simply a reflection of the king's existing beliefs and a reaffirmation of the middle-way position (Bernard, *The King's Reformation*, especially pp. 475–606). Bernard's argument is forcefully made, but not entirely persuasive, particularly in its outright dismissal of the significance of religious factionalism and the capacity of the king's advisers to influence him.

[35] Cromwell also succeeded in stymieing the widespread enforcement of the act of six articles in England in the immediate aftermath of its enactment (MacCulloch, *Thomas Cranmer*, p. 257; Ryrie, *Gospel and Henry VIII*, p. 40). On Cromwell's role as the protector of religious radicalism generally see, for example, Brigden, *London and the Reformation*, pp. 308–16.

quickly presented itself, following his decision in November 1540 to grant Lord Deputy St Leger a licence to hold a parliament in Ireland.[36] The particular issue that Henry VIII chose to focus his attention upon in the upcoming parliament was one of his most enduring preoccupations: the need to protect and reaffirm the principle of priestly celibacy.[37] Thus, in a letter written on 26 March 1541, the king informed the deputy and council that – in addition to the bills that they had already submitted to him for his approval – he wished the parliament to pass a number of other acts, including one 'for the restraint of prelates and priests for the keeping openly of concubines, according the last act of parliament in England'.[38]

The act referred to here was 'an act for moderation of incontinence for priests', which had been passed by the English parliament in 1540.[39] In essence, it was a piece of amending legislation that related to the act of six articles or, more specifically, to three clauses in the act which had set out the punishments that would be incurred by priests who, after 12 July 1539, were convicted of the offences of maintaining carnal relations or keeping company with women to whom they currently were or had been married or, in cases where they were not married, of having entered into concubinary relations with them. All such offences, whether after one or two convictions, were adjudged to be felonious and punishable by death.[40] Yet, almost as soon as they came into force, the Henrician regime began to have misgivings about these provisions. The punishments established in them, especially the death penalty, were considered to be 'very sore and too much extreme' for priests who failed to live up to the demands of the celibate life, and the amending act was introduced with the intention of moderating them. Thus where, under the act of six articles, a priest who was convicted of taking a concubine would, for the first offence, suffer imprisonment, forfeiture of goods and deprivation of all his livings, and for a second offence a felon's death; under the act for moderation of incontinence for priests, a first offence would lead only to forfeiture of goods and the loss of the revenues from all ecclesiastical benefices over and above one, and for a second offence, loss of

---

[36] *SP* III, p. 277.

[37] For the king's antipathy to priestly marriage, as well as the theological basis of his views, see MacCulloch, *Thomas Cranmer*, pp. 171–2, 219–20, 233, 245; H.L. Parish, *Clerical marriage and the Reformation. Precedent, policy and practice* (Aldershot, 2000), pp. 27–38; McEntegart, *Henry VIII, the League of Schmalkalden and the English Reformation*, pp. 124–7, 139–40, 160.

[38] *SP* III, pp. 293–4; Quinn, 'Bills and statutes', p. 158.

[39] 32 Henry VIII, c. 10 (*SR* III, pp. 754–5).

[40] For the relevant clauses in the act of six articles, which also stipulated the punishments that would be incurred by the women involved in relationships with priests, see Gee and Hardy (eds.), *Documents illustrative of English church history*, pp. 310–11, 318–19.

all goods and forfeiture of all the revenues of all benefices held. It was only after conviction for a third offence that a priest would suffer imprisonment, while the death penalty was removed altogether as a punishment for priests involved in concubinary relationships.[41]

The real significance of the king's desire to extend this act to Ireland, however, lay not in the particular detail of its provisions but, rather, in the fact that, as a piece of amending legislation, it was inextricably bound to its parent statute, the English act of six articles. This implied that the king considered the act of six articles to be applicable to Ireland – as, indeed, the wording of the enforcement clauses in the act had already indicated – and, more importantly, that he intended to proceed with its execution, at least in relation to the matter of priestly incontinence. Thus, in line with the act of six articles, it could be expected that once his bill for the continent living of clergy had gone through the Irish parliament, the king would move to appoint special commissions for the Irish shires, which would be led by the bishops and their commissaries, and which would necessarily inquire into all offences against priestly celibacy that had taken place since 12 July 1539. Further, those clerics who would be appointed to lead the commissions might also be expected to take the oath stipulated by the act of six articles that each of them would 'to your cunning, wit and power . . . truly . . . execute the authority to you given by the king's commission . . . without any favour, affection, corruption, dread or malice to be borne to any person or persons'.[42] In effect, the appearance of the king's bill at the council board in the late spring or early summer of 1541 seemed to herald the launch of an official campaign against clerical incontinence in the Irish Church that was rooted ultimately in the act of six articles.[43]

That Henry VIII was determined to proceed against Ireland's incontinent clergy at this juncture would have come as no surprise to Lord Deputy St Leger. He had been fully exposed to the monarch's trenchant views on the matter prior to his appointment as viceroy: at the very time the king clarified and defined his theological objections to clerical marriage – during the summer progress of 1538 and in the context of diplomatic negotiations with the Schmalkaldic League – St Leger had personally served him as one

---

[41] SR III, pp. 754–5 (the act also reduced the punishments for women convicted of concubinary offences); Gee and Hardy (eds.), Documents illustrative of English church history, pp. 310–11, 318–19; Lehmberg, Later parliaments of Henry VIII, p.119; MacCulloch, Thomas Cranmer, p. 274.

[42] Gee and Hardy (eds.), Documents illustrative of English church history, p. 316.

[43] The anticipation and fear that such a campaign would take place in England immediately after the enactment of the act of six articles had moved some married priests to abandon their wives (Parish, Clerical marriage and the Reformation, pp. 35–6; Ryrie, Gospel and Henry VIII, p. 27).

the gentlemen of his privy chamber.[44] Indeed, given St Leger's prior and intimate knowledge of the king's views on clerical marriage, Henry himself would have expected his deputy to move swiftly to set the campaign in motion by enacting his bill 'for the restraint of prelates and priests for the keeping openly of concubines'. But this is not what transpired. Instead of initiating the campaign, it soon became apparent that the viceroy and his administration lacked all enthusiasm for it, for no attempt was made to introduce the king's bill in the opening five sessions of the parliament that took place between June 1541 and June 1542. The reason for their reluctance was revealed in the following August when St Leger and the council wrote to the king to inform him that the bill had been 'stayed', on the grounds that if it was passed it would only apply to

English men and a few others of English blood, inhabited in a small circuit under the obedience of the law, which been already of far more honest living then the multitude of the residue that should be at liberty unpunished.[45]

Ostensibly, the argument advanced by the viceroy and council for staying the king's bill was entirely reasonable. It was generally known at the time that many of the king's clerical subjects in Gaelic Ireland kept concubines and that, had the bill for the continent living of clergy gone through parliament in its existing form – that is, as a piece of amending legislation linked to the act of six articles – they would have been liable for prosecution in far greater numbers than their English counterparts.[46] Add to this the fact that most of these priests inhabited districts in which the king's writ did not run and it was evident that, even with the new act in place, it would not have been feasible to proceed against incontinent Irish clergy in any meaningful way, because it would have been well nigh impossible to establish the kind of commissions envisaged by the act of six articles outside the four shires of the English Pale.[47]

As convincing as this argument was, however, it was not the only, let alone the main, reason for the staying of the bill. When the deputy and council spoke of it as being applicable only to 'Englishmen and a few others of English blood', they were thinking of a reality that was of much greater

---

[44] *LP* XIII.2, no. 1280 (pp. 534, 537); McEntegart, *Henry VIII, the League of Schmalkalden and the English Reformation*, pp. 115–27.

[45] *SP* III, pp. 404–9 (at p. 406).   [46] See above, pp. 61–2.

[47] Gee and Hardy (eds.), *Documents illustrative of English church history*, pp. 311–17. Even in England there were legal and technical difficulties associated with the enforcement of the act, for which see Ryrie, *Gospel and Henry VIII*, pp 24–6; for some examples of 'six articles' inquisitions in operation in England and Calais see MacCulloch, *Thomas Cranmer*, pp. 255–6; Brigden, *London and the Reformation*, pp. 320–2; Elton, *Policy and police*, p. 298; *LP* XV, nos. 362, 460, 473, 485; *LP* XVI, nos. 8, 234, 349, 420, 422, 988; *LP* XVII, no. 537.

import, and much closer to home than the essentially bureaucratic concern of preventing the enactment of an unenforceable statute. This was the emerging revelation that senior clerical figures at the heart of St Leger's own regime were married, and that they would be the first in line to suffer the punitive provisions of the act. Two of these figures were English ecclesiastics, who had served St Leger as members of the Irish council since his appointment as viceroy in 1540, and who had also given their assistance to him in the prosecution of the treason charges against his predecessor, Lord Leonard Grey: Edward Basnet, the soldier dean of St Patrick's Cathedral, and Edward Staples, the bishop of Meath.[48] But the most high profile and most senior of the married clerics was St Leger's principal ecclesiastical ally, Archbishop Browne of Dublin.

Detailed information about Archbishop Browne's marriage is not readily accessible in the historical record. Rather, the surviving data has to be mined and pieced together from a range of disparate documents, which post-date the commencement of the marriage by some years, which refer to it in only the most oblique manner and which reveal little beyond the barest facts about it: namely, that at some point in the late 1530s, the archbishop wed a young, local woman called Katherine Miagh;[49] that Miagh was related to one of the priests of Browne's diocese, Nicholas Miagh;[50] and

---

[48] *LP* XVI, no. 304 (ii), (iii); for the surviving evidence on the marriages of Basnet and Staples see *Pembroke deeds*, pp. 77–8; 'Matters' against St Leger (TNA: PRO SP 61/2, no. 53), printed in C. Maginn, 'A window on mid-Tudor Ireland: the 'Matters' against Lord Depuy St Leger', *Historical Research* 78 (2002), pp. 465–82; Shirley, *Church in Ireland 1547–67*, pp. 87–9. On their careers generally see Percival, 'The Basnetts during the 16th and 17th centuries', pp. 28–33; Scott, *Tudor diocese of Meath* (Dublin, 2006), *passim*.

[49] For the fact of Browne's marriage and the identity of his wife see Nicholas Harpsfield, *A treatise of the pretended divorce between Henry VIII and Catharine of Aragon*, ed. N. Pocock (London, 1878), p. 276; John Bale, *The Vocacyon of Johan Bale*, ed. P. Happé and J.N. King (Binghamton, New York, 1990), p. 68; M.V. Ronan, 'Cardinal Pole's absolution of George Browne', *IER* 72, 5th series (1949), pp 193–205; CCD no. 1220. Katherine's exact age at the time she married Browne is unknown, but she would have been quite young, given that she lived until *c.*1593, the year in which she made her will: 'Index to the act . . . books and . . . original wills of . . . Dublin', p. 591; GO MS 48, f. 26; NAI, Salved Chancery Pleadings, N/147.

[50] Nicholas was in Dublin before Archbishop Browne arrived in Ireland, having acted as collector of the clerical subsidy for the land of St Patrick's Cathedral for the year 27 Henry VIII (22 April 1535–21 April 1536). This, and the fact that he rented a garden in Dublin near St Bride's Church from the earl of Ormond, suggests that he was a vicar choral of St Patrick's Cathedral and a serving chaplain in one of the cathedral's city churches on Browne's succession. It is not known now how precisely he was related to the archbishop's wife, but it is likely that he was either her brother or uncle. Branches of the Miagh family resided in Dublin, Maynooth and Leixlip in the late fifteenth and early sixteenth centuries (Vice-Treasurer Brabazon's account 26–29 Henry VIII: TNA, PRO SP65/1/2 (f 25v); CCD, no. 1220; *Ormond deeds, 1509–47*, p. 180; Lennon and Murray (eds.), *Dublin City franchise roll*, pp. 16–17; G. MacNiocaill (ed.), *Crown surveys of lands 1540–41 with the Kildare rental begun in 1518* (Dublin, 1992), pp. 247–8).

that she subsequently bore the archbishop three sons: Alexander, Anthony and George junior.[51]

Despite these difficulties, however, the nature of the surviving evidence does point towards one further and notable feature of the marriage. Like Archbishop Cranmer's union with Margarete, the niece of the Nuremburg reformer, Andreas Osiander, the marriage of Archbishop Browne and Katherine Miagh was, initially at least, concealed from public view.[52] This is indicated not only by the generally imprecise and retrospective references to the marriage in the surviving sources, but is otherwise substantiated by the fact that none of the many enemies that Browne made in the 1530s, who ranged from Lord Deputy Grey to the conservative prebendaries of St Patrick's Cathedral, raised any objections against it at this time. Had they been aware of its existence, it is inconceivable that they would have failed to exploit the marriage to undermine the archbishop's position, especially after the act of six articles, which came into force in July 1539, gave 'full power and authority' to all ecclesiastical ordinaries in England, Wales 'or in any other the king's dominions' to enquire into all offences against it, including all transgressions against the rule of priestly celibacy.[53]

What altered this situation, of course, and what forced Archbishop Browne to lift the veil of secrecy that had previously hung over his marriage, was the appearance in Ireland of the king's bill against clerical incontinence, a fact otherwise confirmed by the near contemporary observation of Nicholas Harpsfield, the Marian archdeacon of Canterbury, that Browne was one of many married priests who 'put over' their wives in response to the 'very sharp laws' introduced by Henry VIII 'in his latter days'.[54] Linked

---

[51] For the identity of Browne's children see *CCD*, no. 1220; abstract of will of Alexander Browne, 1578 (Fisher Abstracts: Dublin Consistorial Wills, GO MS 290, pp. 18–19). On the basis that it is most unlikely that the conception of all three of Browne's sons took place after the early summer of 1541, when Henry VIII's command to enact the bill for the continent living of priests would have been received by the viceroy and council, it is safe to assume that Browne's marriage with Katherine Miagh, and indeed the births of some or all of their sons, took place in the late 1530s, probably before the act of six articles was enacted in England in the summer of 1539.

[52] On Cranmer's marriage see MacCulloch, *Thomas Cranmer*, pp. 72, 75, 249–50. Like Cranmer, Browne must have kept his wife in a remote location. A possible candidate for this location is the small estate that he rented from the priory of Fethard in Co. Tipperary, before it was dissolved in April 1540, and before he was granted a lease of the entire priory by Lord Deputy St Leger in March 1541 (White, *Monastic extents*, pp. 329–30, *Fiants, Henry VIII*, no. 168). In Fethard, Browne could have put his wife and young sons under the protection of the Butlers of Ormond, who were not only known admirers of the archbishop at this time but, rather suggestively, are also known to have had a business relationship with Katherine Miagh's kinsman, the priest, Nicholas Miagh – in June 1538 the earl of Ormond leased Nicholas a garden in Dublin (above, pp. 113–14, *Ormond deeds, 1509–47*, p. 180).

[53] Gee and Hardy (eds.), *Documents illustrative of English church history*, pp. 312–13.

[54] Harpsfield, *Prentended divorce*, p. 276; Parish, *Clerical marriage and the Reformation*, pp. 35–6; Ryrie, *Gospel and Henry VIII*, p. 27.

as it was to the English act of six articles, the king's bill appeared to herald the launch of an official campaign against married and concubinary clergy in the Irish Church, and thus not only signalled that the archbishop's own marriage would now be at greater risk of being exposed than hitherto, but, equally discomforting, also raised the prospect that he would have to lead one or more of the commissions that would be appointed to discover married priests within the English Pale. Whether viewed from the perspective of preserving his reputation, then, or simply as a matter of conscience, the archbishop's decision to keep his marriage secret looked increasingly untenable from the late spring or early summer of 1541. The reality was that he had few options other than to tell the truth about it, and to seek the assistance of a figure powerful enough to extricate him from the predicament in which it now placed him. The person that Browne turned to was his new patron, Lord Deputy St Leger.

Whether St Leger was aware that Browne was married before the king issued his command to enact the bill for the continent living of clergy is not known. However, once the bill did appear, and its implications had been fully digested, the deputy stood by the archbishop and determinedly set out to protect him. The most visible way in which he assisted the archbishop was the decision he took to stay the king's bill. But St Leger did much more than simply halt the passage of the bill. He also chose not to inform the king that he harboured such an intention for a period of some fifteen months.[55] This evasive use of silence was a tactic that St Leger employed throughout his career in Ireland and earned him a contemporary reputation as a discreet and wily politician.[56] In relation to the staying of the king's bill against clerical incontinence, however, we can identify its precise purpose: it was done with the intent of purchasing the archbishop sufficient time to regularise his marital status in a manner that would comply with the king's general views on clerical marriage – that is, by arranging for his separation and divorce from Katherine Miagh and for his return to the celibate life. Thereafter, St Leger envisaged using the terms of such a settlement as a basis for drafting an alternative act on clerical marriage which, as he and the Irish council informed the king in August 1542, would be 'in such a sort, as we think shall be reasonable, and possible to be performed; for surely, as it is penned after the act of England, it is not in some part beneficial for this realm'.[57] What the viceroy and council meant by this, although they were not at liberty to say so at the time, was that their act would not be linked to

---

[55] The king's command to enact the bill was dated 26 March 1541 (*SP* III, pp. 292–300, at pp. 293–4), and would have been received by the viceroy and council around four to eight weeks later, that is, in April or May 1541. St Leger did not inform the king that he intended to stay the bill until 24 August 1542 (*SP* III, pp. 404–9, at p. 406).

[56] Brady, *Chief Governors*, pp. 25–6. [57] *SP* III, p. 406.

the English act of six articles, and that it would not therefore lead to the prosecution of valued political allies like Archbishop Browne who had neglected to separate from their wives and to refrain from carnal relations after 12 July 1539.

St Leger's efforts to decouple the prospective Irish act on priestly incontinence from the English act of six articles, although absolutely necessary, represented only one of the elements in the equation that was required to solve the difficulties associated with Archbishop Browne's marriage. The other key element was the need to secure the support of the local clergy, particularly the clergy of St Patrick's Cathedral, in regularising Browne's marital status. Such support was needed in two distinct ways. Although St Leger and Browne were intent on preventing the strict legal application of the act of six articles in Ireland, on the grounds that it would necessarily lead to Browne's prosecution and conviction, they were also keenly aware that, in order to satisfy the king, the regularisation of the archbishop's position would ultimately have to comply with the basic requirements of that act. One of these requirements related to the proced-ures for formalising the separation of married priests. The act of six articles had declared in 1539 that all marriages and marriage contracts involving priests were 'utterly void and of none effect'. However, it had also stipu-lated that the ordinaries within whose jurisdictions the married priests were resident were from time to time 'to make separations and divorces' of these marriages and contracts. It was here that the clergy of St Patrick's Cathedral had a role. As the possessors of the chief judicial offices in the diocese in which Browne resided, the task of overseeing the separation and divorce of the archbishop from his wife would necessarily fall to them.[58] The second area in which the clergy's support was needed followed directly on from this. Once he was divorced from his wife, the archbishop would also need to make some provision for the upkeep of his young family. If, as seemed likely, given its ready availability, this was to involve the alienation or leasing of property that belonged to the see of Dublin, then the sanction of the clergy of St Patrick's would be required, for, in their role as custodians of the see's temporalties, they, along with their colleagues in Christ Church Cathedral, had to sign off on all transactions involving the disposal of diocesan property.[59]

Identifying where and how the support of the clergy would be needed in regularising Browne's marital status was a relatively easy task. It was quite another thing, however, to secure it. The problem here, of course, was that

---

[58] On this aspect of the act of six articles see Gee and Hardy (eds.), *Documents illustrative of English church history*, p. 310.
[59] On this custodianship role see Appendix 1.

the archbishop's relationship with the cathedral canons had been badly damaged in the 1530s, as a result of his reforming proclivities and the aggressive manner in which he had pursued them. Thus, in the early summer of 1541, Browne found himself in the unenviable position of having to open discussions with the cathedral clergy in order to secure their assistance in extricating himself from a marriage that would have symbolised all that they found most abhorrent about the reformed religion. Indeed, by the very act of opening this dialogue – an act which would not only have uncovered the existence of his marriage, but also the political and legal circumstances that were hastening its demise – the archbishop even ran the risk of alerting the cathedral clergy to the possibility of seeking immediate revenge for the hurts of the past, through the initiation of proceedings against him for offences under the act of six articles. While it cannot be determined now that this was ever a serious risk, it was certainly the case that the impending negotiations would present real difficulties for the archbishop, because he knew he would have to face and overcome the legacy of years of bitter religious and ideological division between himself and the canons, if they were to deliver an acceptable outcome.

That said, it was also the case that Archbishop Browne came to the negotiating table with something tangible to offer to the cathedral clergy. His acceptance of the need to terminate his marriage and to live the life of a celibate once again was an acknowledgement that he was willing to readopt a basic precept of canon law that had long been an integral part of the traditional canonical ethos of the clerical elite of the English Pale. This turnabout was, if nothing else, a vindication of the conservative religious position the cathedral clergy had maintained during the archbishop's reforming heyday, and contrasted markedly with the actions of those English reformers, like John Bale, who responded to the king's prohibition on clerical marriage by writing polemical literature in favour of it.[60] But the archbishop's return to the celibate fold, as the cathedral clergy well knew, also had a much wider significance. The fact that it was the king's thinking and actions that had forced Browne, the strident reformer of the 1530s, to follow such a course implied not only that the canons' traditionalist views on religion were once again deemed to be legitimate, but that they would also have to be absorbed into the official thinking of the royal administration in Ireland. Lord Deputy St Leger and, in his wake, Archbishop Browne, recognised this as a new and unchallengeable political reality and quickly appropriated the king's position as their own, trusting that, in

---

[60] On Bale and the other English reformers who voiced their hostility to clerical celibacy after the enactment of the act of six articles see Parish, *Clerical marriage and the Reformation*, pp. 15–17.

return, the clergy would be prepared to extend their cooperation in the business of regularising the archbishop's marital status. Thus, almost as soon as the discussions about Browne's marriage settlement had begun in the early summer of 1541, it was apparent that, apart from the non-negotiable matter of the king's supremacy, there were no major points of religious principle dividing the parties. The only question to be resolved, in fact, was whether the viceroy and the archbishop could persuade the cathedral clergy that their newfound adoption of the king's religious conservatism was genuine, and that it would not evaporate once the crisis surrounding Archbishop Browne's marriage had passed.

To address this issue, the deputy and archbishop moved quickly to establish a bond of trust between themselves and the cathedral clergy, by demonstrating their awareness and appreciation of the cathedral's heritage as an ancient and venerable royal foundation. The association between St Patrick's and the crown had long been treasured by its clergy, and was identified by St Leger and Browne as something that might be exploited as they strove to build bridges with them. Thus, pointedly, St Patrick's was chosen ahead of Christ Church Cathedral, the traditional venue for state and civic occasions requiring religious ceremonial, to host the liturgical celebrations surrounding the proclamation of Henry VIII's kingly title on 18 June 1541. It was a decision which served not only as an acknowledgment of the historic link that existed between the crown and the cathedral, but also showed that, despite the recent opposition of the cathedral canons to the crown's religious policies, the regime had no desire to bring about any diminution of St Patrick's status as 'his grace's church'. Rather, given the alteration that parliament had made to the king's style, the cathedral's position as a royal foundation would now be greatly augmented.[61]

The kingly title celebrations did more, however, than simply reaffirm or augment St Patrick's status as a royal foundation. They were also designed to show that the ancient bond between the cathedral and king would be maintained within its customary religious setting. Thus, significantly, and it was a point that St Leger set great store upon in his correspondence with Henry VIII, the liturgy chosen for the occasion was unambiguously traditional in nature.[62] Its centrepiece, a 'solemn mass', was particularly resonant for the cathedral clergy, because it was sung by Archbishop Browne, a man who, through his recently disclosed intentions to divorce his wife and

---

[61] TNA: PRO SP 60/4, no. 10 (Prebendaries of St Patrick's to Cromwell, 20 Feb 1537); *SP* III, pp. 304–5. It is clear that St Leger appreciated St Patrick's status as a royal foundation for in his report to the king about the proclamation of the act for the kingly title he referred to St Patrick's as 'your church' (*SP* III, p. 305). On Christ Church's position as the traditional ecclesiastical location for state and civic occasions see above p. 38.

[62] *SP* III, pp. 304–5.

resume a celibate life, had effectively rededicated himself to the pre-Reformation ideal of the priestly office, including all of its ancient sacrificial and mediatory functions.[63] Overall, then, the placing of St Patrick's Cathedral at the centre of the kingly title celebrations, and the liturgy selected to honour the king on the occasion, sent out a strong message about the regime's religious orientation. Notwithstanding the fact that the act for the kingly title had originated in the regime's desire to buttress Henry VIII's right to rule in Ireland against the claims of those who maintained that temporal authority on the island was ultimately in the gift of the papacy, it was evident from the celebrations surrounding the proclamation of the king's new style that the regime was no less determined, in line with the king's own inclinations, to maintain a form of religion that predated the monarch's break with Rome; and that it viewed the cathedral clergy – the avowed protectors of the old religion – as valued members of the political community, who would be accorded the same honoured place within the newly established kingdom of Ireland that they had held within the old medieval lordship.

This attempt to build bridges with the cathedral clergy yielded immediate dividends. It persuaded them that they should accept the king's new style, notwithstanding its association with the royal supremacy;[64] and – as revealed by the diplomatic silence they maintained on the subject of his marriage – it also encouraged them to give serious consideration to the possibility of supporting the deputy's plans for the regularisation of Archbishop Browne's position. Despite these positives, however, the gesture was not in itself sufficient to establish the conservative religious credentials of the regime. On the contrary, the contemporaneous involvement of St Leger and his officials in the final act of destruction of corporate religious life in the English Pale – the disposal of the sites and properties of the dissolved monasteries[65] – and in the ruthless pursuit of the viceroy's predecessor, the pronounced religious conservative and former friend of the cathedral chapter, Lord Leonard Grey, to his death on trumped-up treason charges,[66] implied that the regime's religious position was equivocal at best; an assessment otherwise corroborated by the fact that some members of St Leger's administration, such as Sir Thomas Cusack and John Travers, the

---

[63] On these functions generally see P. Marshall, *The Catholic priesthood and the Reformation* (Oxford, 1994), especially chs. 1 and 2.

[64] See above, pp. 35–6.

[65] The best account of the distribution of the monastic properties and its broader political significance is Brady, *Chief Governors*, pp. 34–40.

[66] Grey was beheaded at the Tower of London on 28 July 1541; on the regime's involvement in his destruction see the book of evidence which it compiled against him (TNA: PRO SP 60/9, nos. 59–62; *LP* XVI, no. 304).

master of the ordnance, continued to maintain openly evangelical religious opinions.[67] Mindful of all this, the clergy of St Patrick's remained reluctant to give their wholehearted support to the deputy's plans for the settlement of the archbishop's matrimonial affairs, at least until such time as they received greater assurances that his administration's appropriation of the king's religious conservatism had real substance and was likely to endure.

Initially, neither St Leger nor Browne were able to give these assurances for, having elected to prevent the passage of Henry VIII's bill against concubinary clergy, it was difficult to demonstrate in an authoritative and public manner that they and the king were of one mind on religious matters. Indeed, the related decision they took to withhold all knowledge of the archbishop's marriage from Henry VIII made the problem even more intractable, because it prevented them from bringing the king into their confidence and from enlisting his support directly in their cause. These complications, together with the regime's absorption with other concerns such as the management of parliament, and the institution of an extensive programme of 'surrender and regrant' settlements with the independent Gaelic lords, ensured that the problem of Archbishop Browne's marriage remained unresolved throughout the remainder of 1541 and into the following year.[68] Faced with these circumstances, the viceroy and archbishop had to look again at the nature of their engagement with the cathedral clergy, and to identify why, precisely, despite the grand gesture they had made during the kingly title celebrations, their efforts to strike a deal with them had run aground. The conclusion they reached, and which informed their subsequent actions, was that they had failed to substantiate their claim that they shared the same religious values as the king with the high standard of proof that a body of canon lawyers, like the chapter of St Patrick's, would have considered obligatory.[69] Thus, at some point in the opening half of 1542, the deputy and archbishop resolved to make good this deficiency by seeking a written testimonial from the king, which would bear witness to the fact that the king considered his English religious policies to be applicable to Ireland, and that he expected St Leger and Browne to be the principal agents for their execution there. Such a testimonial, once obtained and promulgated, would belie any notion that the regime was equivocal in its support for the religious settlement ushered in by the act of six articles and establish the conservative religious credentials of the regime.

---

[67] For the views of Cusack and Travers see their 'Devices' for the reformation of Ireland (*SP* III, pp. 326–30, 431–2).

[68] On the 'surrender and regrant' arrangements generally see Bradshaw, *Irish constitutional revolution*, ch. 7; Brady, *Chief Governors*, pp. 25–30.

[69] On the standard of proof required in the judicial processes of the canon law generally see Brundage, *Medieval canon law*, pp. 93–5, 132–3, 142–3, 145, 148–50, 177.

But the decision to proceed in this manner, as the viceroy and archbishop well knew, was also fraught with risk. Any attempt to initiate a dialogue with the crown on the matter of the testimonial would require that the king be reminded of his spiritual responsibilities towards Ireland. And this, in turn, raised the prospect that he would be alerted to the regime's failure to implement the principal measure that he had already deemed necessary for the maintenance of the spiritual wellbeing of his Irish subjects: his bill for the continent living of the Irish clergy. Indeed, it was even possible that the solicitation of the testimonial might lead to the full discovery of the scheme St Leger had instituted to protect Archbishop Browne from prosecution for his offences under the act of six articles. To minimise these risks, therefore, the viceroy and archbishop also resolved to seek their testimonial on grounds that would excite no suspicions about their underlying intentions. The pretext which they eventually fixed upon, and which enabled them in June 1542 to reactivate their plans to extricate Browne from his illegal marriage, was chosen with precisely this purpose in mind, for it came in the form of an apparently innocuous petition to the king from the Irish council to remit a debt of £250 which the archbishop had owed to the king's attainted brother-in-law, Lord Rochford.[70] What the regime set out to do, in effect, was to shape and exploit for its purposes the anticipated response of the king to the council's petition and, in the process, acquire an authoritative text that would clearly demonstrate that there was a seamless and unbreakable link between the king's conservative religious policies in England and its own policies in Ireland.

III

That such a complicated stratagem could realistically be pursued at this juncture was due to the fact that the main elements of the king's response to the council's petition were predictable. Given the large sum of money involved, the council's request would require, if it was to be granted, a substantial expression of royal munificence, and would therefore place the archbishop and, indeed, the viceroy and council, under a strong obligation to the king, especially in relation to the performance of the duties of their offices.[71] Following on from this, it could also be expected that, in return for his liberality, Henry VIII would exhort the principal beneficiaries to

---

[70] The petition was contained in a letter from the deputy and council to the king dated 2 June 1542 (SP III, pp. 385–91, at pp. 390–1); see also above, p. 133.

[71] The council's petition intimated as much when it noted that the remission of Browne's debt would ensure that he would 'be the more able to serve your majesty' and that he would be obliged 'according his most bounden duty to pray to Almighty God for the long preservation of your most royal estate' (SP III, pp. 390–1).

strive harder to fulfil their duties towards God and himself. It was on this prospective exhortation that the deputy and archbishop pinned their hopes. If it was properly worded, it would provide the perfect medium for transmitting the kind of nuanced message that St Leger and Browne required to convince the canons of St Patrick's that the regime adhered to the same religious values as the king. The task at hand, then, was to ensure that the king would not only accede to the council's request on the archbishop's behalf, but that he would accompany this grant with a religious admonition couched in suitably conservative language.

The man entrusted with the task of procuring the required text was the deputy's brother, Robert St Leger, who served the regime in a variety of capacities during this period, including acting, in conjunction with Archbishop Browne, as a pledge in the negotiations surrounding the submission of the earl of Desmond in January 1541.[72] Indeed, it was his involvement in the latter business that provided him with the perfect cover for undertaking this particular assignment. On foot of his submission, Desmond had promised to do homage to the king in person, and plans for the earl's visit to court were put in place in the late spring or early summer of 1542. One of Desmond's requirements, according to the viceroy and council, was that Robert St Leger should 'conduct him thither to your majesty', and thus the deputy's brother was conveniently included in the earl's party that attended on the king at Hampton Court on 29 June 1542 and on the days immediately following. While there the younger St Leger not only delivered the council's letter of 2 June to the king that contained the petition to remit Archbishop Browne's debt, but he was also perfectly positioned to work in the margins with Henry VIII's advisors – most notably, the king's secretary, Sir Thomas Wriothesley – on the drafting of a response that would fulfil the wider needs of the St Leger regime.[73]

Given their nature, no formal records were made of Robert St Leger's deliberations with Secretary Wriothesley in mid-summer 1542. However, it is evident from the king's response to the council's petition that St Leger completed the assignment in an assured and largely successful fashion. Finalised on 5 July, and included in a lengthy minute to the Irish council which the deputy received at the hands of the earl of Desmond in early

---

[72] Above, p. 133; *SP* III, pp. 285–90. Robert also served *inter alia* as sub-constable of Carlow Castle and oversaw the transporting of treasure from England into Ireland on behalf of his brother's administration (*Carew MSS 1515–74*, p. 186; *LP* XVII, no. 880, p. 483).

[73] *LP* XVII, nos. 340, 368, 376, 453, 460, 468 and 728–9; *SP* III, pp. 389–90, 394–7. The attendance of Wriothesley and the English privy council at Hampton Court is confirmed in *APC 1542–47*, pp. 15–17.

August,[74] the response revealed that Robert St Leger had not only negotiated Henry VIII's agreement to remit the archbishop's debt, but that he had also succeeded in prompting the king and his advisors to issue an admonition to the archbishop and viceroy and council which, unbeknownst to the king, doubled up as a testament to their religious orthodoxy. There were two distinct parts to the admonition. First, Archbishop Browne was directed to 'better apply his charge and office' and to 'provide that there may be some good preachers to instruct and teach the people their duties to God and us'. Second, and more importantly, the king enjoined the viceroy and the council to make all necessary provision so that the people of Ireland

> may learn by good and catholic teaching, and the ministration of justice, to know God's laws and ours together, which shall daily more and more frame and confirm them in honest living and due obedience, to their own benefits and the universal good of the country.[75]

Combined, these directions confirmed that the king of Ireland was as stout a defender of 'good and catholic teaching' as any of his predecessors had been, and that he expected his deputy and archbishop to do likewise.

Yet, as artfully as Robert St Leger had handled his brief, it had not proved possible, as the regime had feared, to obviate all discussion regarding the fate of the king's bill on priestly incontinence. Rather, in the course of the general political dialogue between St Leger, Desmond and Wriotheseley, it had emerged that that bill, and two other bills which the king had previously instructed the viceroy and council to enact – a bill relating to the division of the shire of Meath and a bill for the establishment of Annaly as a shire – had not yet gone through parliament. As a result of this revelation, an additional article was inserted in Henry VIII's letter of 5 July, in which he let it be known that he had been 'informed' about the viceroy and council's tardiness and that he expected them 'either to pass the same, or else signify upon what grounds they be stayed, that we may ascertain you of our further pleasure'.[76] Overall, then, as far as the matter of Archbishop Browne's marriage was concerned, the king's letter of 5 July was a mixed blessing for the St Leger regime. On the one hand, it provided a much

---

[74] *SP* III, pp. 394–7 (at pp. 396–7), 404–12. Desmond landed in Waterford on 31 July and, following notification from the viceroy, who was 'in the country of Ossory, for pacifying of certain variances depending between the earl of Ormond and the lord of Upper Ossory', he proceeded to Kilkenny to meet him and deliver the king's letter. If we allow some time for the notification to have reached Desmond, and for the journeys of both parties to Kilkenny, then the likely date for the receipt of the letter would be 1 or 2 August 1542.

[75] *SP* III, pp. 394–7 (at pp. 396–7).

[76] *SP* III, pp. 293–4, 394–7 (at p. 397). Following discussions with the Desmond delegation, the article on the acts, and another relating to a suit by Desmond for the bishopric of Emly, were added by Wriothesley to an existing draft of the king's minute (*LP* XVII, no. 460).

needed lever for breaking the deadlock between the regime and the canons of St Patrick's Cathedral regarding the dissolution of the marriage. On the other, it greatly intensified the pressure to achieve a speedy settlement of Browne's affairs, because the king had reiterated his determination to have his act against concubinary clergy enacted by parliament.

The first matter that St Leger and Browne had to address in finalising this settlement was the identification of an appropriate format in which to present the king's admonition to the audience for whom it was principally intended, the chapter of St Patrick's Cathedral. As things stood, the text was out of bounds to the clergy because it was contained in a private minute from Henry VIII to the council that dealt with a number of politically sensitive matters, including the king's demand that his bill for the continent living of clergy should be enacted forthwith.[77] To overcome this difficulty, therefore, the council extracted the admonition from the more extensive memo in which it had originated and certified it into chancery where it was enrolled on the patent rolls, most probably on 8 August 1542.[78] The act of enrolling the king's admonition was, of course, no mere bureaucratic exercise. As the cathedral canons well knew – given the historic association of many of their predecessors with the court of chancery and the office of keeper of the rolls[79] – it conferred upon the admonition the nature and status of a public notice which was expressly designed to communicate the king's wishes to his Irish subjects, and which had the same legal force and authority as other royal ordinances, such as royal proclamations or formal royal letters patent.[80] It thus provided a standard of proof about the regime's religious orthodoxy that could not be easily gainsaid by the cathedral clergy. Indeed, so confident were the viceroy and council that the cathedral canons would accept this reality, and that they would be attuned to all the nuances of the enrollment process, that they exploited the exercise in every conceivable way to strengthen the message that they were sending out to them. In particular, to emphasise the point that the king's words were being directed primarily at the viceroy and archbishop, and that the pair

---

[77] *SP* III, pp. 394–7.

[78] Morrin, *Patent rolls*, i, p. 81; *SP* III, pp. 394–7 (at pp. 396–7); *LP* XVII, no. 460. Morrin gave the date of the certification and enrollment as 8 July, which is incorrect, given that the letter which contained the king's admonition was only brought into Ireland by the earl of Desmond on 31 July and received by St Leger around 1 or 2 August (*SP* III, pp. 409–10, above nt. 74). The council's certification and the enrollment would have taken place on the viceroy's return to Dublin, which suggests that Morrin's date of 8 July was an error for 8 August.

[79] Above p. 68; Ellis, *Reform and revival*, p. 220.

[80] The device was employed by St Leger on more than one occasion: eleven letters written by Henry VIII were enrolled (including one which was enrolled twice) on the patent rolls during the course of his deputyship (Morrin, *Patent rolls*, i, pp. 74–5, 78–81, 86–7, 95, 99–100, 112–13, 125–6). The letter of 5 July 1542 was the only one enrolled in extract form.

had now been given the main responsibility for realising the king's 'Catholic' vision within the church and kingdom of Ireland, both men deliberately withheld their signatures from the council's certification.[81]

But it was the text itself that most impressed the cathedral canons.[82] Set in the context of his desire to defend the principle of priestly celibacy within the Irish Church, as well as his avowed support for the traditional doctrines and practices enshrined in the act of six articles, the 'Catholic' vision enunciated by Henry VIII in July 1542 struck a particularly strong and reassuring chord for the cathedral canons. In emphasising the requirement that his officials should dedicate themselves to imparting 'good and catholic teaching', and administering English law, in order to create a good and just society, the statement came as close as anything could at this time to being an official endorsement of the traditional ethos of the English Irish clerical elite, because it reaffirmed their core belief that the purpose of English rule in Ireland was the reform of its inhabitants through the dissemination of canonically sound, Catholic doctrine.[83] It thus created a context in which the regime's scheme for the regularisation of the archbishop's marital status could be viewed as a genuine act of Catholic orthodoxy, and permitted the cathedral canons to lend their assistance to the viceroy and archbishop in bringing it to a conclusion.

Yet the viceroy and archbishop remained cautious and, even at this late stage, they instituted one final confidence-building measure that effectively set the seal on their agreement with the clergy. The opportunity to institute this measure arose on the back of a vacancy that occurred in the cathedral chapter. On 14 June 1542, while the Desmond delegation was making its way to England to attend on the king, Robert Fitzsimon, the aged precentor of St Patrick's Cathedral, died.[84] The patronage of this living, which in seniority and wealth was second only to the deanery, was vested in the archbishopric of Dublin.[85] Fitzsimon's death thus opened the way for the

---

[81] The certification was signed by Lord Chancellor Alen, Bishop Staples of Meath, Chief Justice Aylmer, Vice-Treasurer Brabazon, Chief Justice Luttrell, Sir Thomas Cusack, master of the rolls, John Travers, master of the ordnance, and Dean Basnet of St Patrick's Cathedral (Morrin, *Patent rolls*, i, p. 81). For the enrollment process generally and the significance and authority of the patent rolls see R.D. Edwards and M. O'Dowd, *Sources for early modern Irish history, 1534–1641* (Cambridge, 1985), pp. 16–20; Wood, *Guide to the records deposited in the Public Record Office of Ireland* pp. 6–7, 14–15; *Guide to the contents of the Public Record Office* (3 vols., London, 1963–8), iii, pp. 14, 22–3.

[82] The text was easily accessible for consultation, or publication through exemplification, as it was written on the dorse of the last membrane of the patent roll for 32–33 Henry VIII.

[83] On this point see Chapter 2.

[84] Fitzsimon's obit is recorded in an antiphonal that belonged to the parish church of St John the Evangelist, Dublin (TCD, MS 79, f. 84v).

[85] *Alen's register*, pp. 239, 279–80, 297–8; RCB, C.2.1.27, no. 2 (survey of St Patrick's possessions, 1547).

archbishop to make an appointment that would stand as a guarantee to his erstwhile clerical enemies that his newfound regard for the old religion would endure. His choice of candidate was instructive. In a remarkable turnabout, Browne promoted the man who had led the clergy's resistance to religious change in Dublin during the opening phase of the Reformation, his *bête noire* of the 1530s, James Humphrey, the prebendary of St Audoen.[86] Doubtless, Humphrey's appointment was conditional upon him backing the regime's efforts to secure Browne his divorce and upon him assisting the archbishop in making provision for the upkeep of his family. Nevertheless, Browne remained reluctant to entrust the settlement of his affairs entirely to his old foe. To ensure therefore that his concession to the conservative clergy would indeed result in a settlement that would protect his own interests and the interests of his children, he also appointed Nicholas Miagh, his wife's kinsman, as Humphrey's successor in the prebend of St Audoen.[87]

The preferments of Humphrey and Miagh in the late summer of 1542, then, marked the terminal point of the negotiations that took place between the cathedral clergy and the deputy and archbishop on the matter of Browne's marriage. Thereafter, most likely before the end of August 1542, the archbishop got his divorce from Katherine Miagh, who was subsequently remarried to one of his servants, Robert Bathe.[88] The completion of these arrangements also gave the go-ahead to St Leger and the council to inform the king of their intention to stay his bill on clerical incontinence, which was duly communicated to him in a letter dispatched on 24 August.[89]

Initially, the king reacted to this news in a less than positive manner. 'We think it meet', he observed tartly in his response of 8 October, 'that seeing we have passed here the act for continency of priests, you should in like manner follow and do the same there'.[90] But St Leger stood high in Henry VIII's favour at this juncture, having recently secured the submission to the

---

[86] Lawlor, *Fasti of St Patrick's*, p. 56; above pp. 109–11. Due to lacunae in the sources, the earliest surviving notice of Humphrey as precentor dates from 15 June 1545 (Griffith, *Exchequer inquisitions*, p. 293). However, there is no evidence to suggest that Archbishop Browne displayed any tardiness in appointing him to the living. On the contrary, he is known to have filled another living vacated by Robert Fitzsimon – the prebend of Shareshill in the College of Penkridge, Staffordshire – by 14 July 1542 (W.N. Landor, 'Staffordshire incumbents and parochial records (1530–1680)', in *Collections for a history of Staffordshire edited by the William Salt Archaeological Society* (London, 1915), pp. 204, 209). We also know that Humphrey's successor as prebendary of St Audoen was *in situ* by 4 March 1544 (Mason, *History of St Patrick's*, p. lxxviii). Late July or early August 1542 is, therefore, the most likely date for Humphrey's promotion.

[87] Lawlor, *Fasti of St Patrick's*, p. 148; Mason, *History of St Patrick's*, p. lxxviii.

[88] Harpsfield, *Pretended divorce*, p. 276; *Vocacyon of Johan Bale*, ed. Happé and King, p. 68; CCD, no. 1220.

[89] *SP* III, pp. 404–9 (at p. 406).   [90] *SP* III, pp. 427–30 (at p. 428).

crown of the most powerful Gaelic lord in Ulster, Con Bacagh O'Neill, and the king was loath to make his failure to enact the royal bill against clerical concubinage a major point of contention between them.[91] Instead, he praised St Leger's efforts 'to train those folks [the Irish] to the knowledge of their duties', and conceded that he and the council could legitimately devise policy in the area of priestly morality on his behalf.[92] Thus, as a possible alternative to the enactment of his bill, the king called on the deputy and council 'upon consideration of the state of the country' to 'cause such a reasonable book to be devised and sent hither for that purpose, as may be to God's pleasure in the avoiding of that sin, and to the advancement of the honest name and fame of our clergy of that realm'.[93]

The apparent softening of Henry VIII's position provided all the encouragement the viceroy needed to press ahead with his plans to enact his own ordinance against clerical incontinence. Thus, instead of producing a 'reasonable book', St Leger and his advisors prepared a draft bill, which was sent to the king for his approval in December 1542.[94] While the text of this bill is not now extant, we know from the covering letter that it was drafted in a manner that reflected and sought to address the concerns that the deputy and council had previously raised about the king's bill on clerical incontinence. In particular, they reaffirmed the point that the new bill was not 'in such sort' as the act that had been passed in England – in other words, it was to be kept entirely separate from the act of six articles – because the 'more part' of the inhabitants of Ireland were not yet 'in so perfect obedience that the same could in all places be observed, nor yet could be executed', and because they did not want it to be visited exclusively 'upon those few your English subjects here inhabited'. In effect, then, though once again they studiously avoided saying so, the deputy and council were intent on establishing a law that would free them from the obligation of proceeding against clerical allies, like Archbishop Browne, who, in breach of the act of six articles, had neglected to separate from their wives after 12 July 1539. The upshot of this was that their bill had a much more limited purpose than the bill that the king had originally commanded them to enact. Unlike the latter, it was not envisaged as a mechanism for bringing about a general purge of concubinary behaviour amongst the Irish clergy. Rather, as St Leger and the council put it, the new bill was a 'little beginning' that over time would 'give light to the rest [of the clergy] to follow the same'.[95]

[91] *SP* III, pp. 350–9.
[92] St Leger took great delight in receiving the king's approbation and had the letter enrolled on the patent rolls (Morrin, *Patent rolls*, i, pp. 78–9).
[93] *SP* III, pp. 427–30 (at p. 428).   [94] *SP* III, pp. 432–40 (at p. 433).   [95] Ibid.

St Leger's persistence with this line ultimately eroded Henry VIII's resolve to pursue the enactment of a bill for the continent living of the Irish clergy. The king had already conceded the principle, in his letter of 8 October 1542, that the deputy should take the lead in formulating policy on the issue, which meant, in effect, that his own original bill on clerical incontinence was not likely to be resurrected. Yet it was also the case that the king did not consider the 'little beginning' envisaged in St Leger's bill to be the best solution to a problem, about which he had long maintained such deeply held and theologically grounded views. He declined, therefore, to give the go-ahead to the deputy to proceed with a watered-down bill and instead chose to equivocate. Responding to the receipt of the viceroy's bill in early March 1543, the king declared that he would have to give further consideration to it before determining what course of action would be 'most convenient for God's honour and the wealth of the realm'.[96] Whether, in fact, the king ever turned his mind to the bill again is doubtful, for he issued no more instructions to St Leger and the council to proceed with its enactment before parliament was prorogued in November 1543, with the result that no act on 'the incontinency of priests' was ever passed in what turned out to be the last Irish parliament of the reign.[97]

Despite this denouement, however, the king's attempt in the early 1540s to advance 'the honest name and fame' of the Irish clergy by means of a statute against priestly incontinence was still hugely significant. Not only did it force his leading ecclesiastical official in Ireland, Archbishop Browne, to reveal the existence of his own secret marriage, but it also compelled Lord Deputy St Leger and his administration, in a bid to regularise the archbishop's position and to protect him from the rigours of the act of six articles, to engage and negotiate with the largest, extant body of conservative religious clerics in the English Pale, the cathedral chapter of St Patrick's Cathedral. As part of this engagement, the regime went to great lengths to clarify its religious position and to demonstrate that it held the same 'Catholic' values as the king. This conciliatory approach, which came hard on the heels of the demoralising destruction of monasticism in English Ireland, was a great relief to the canons of St Patrick's and many other conservative ecclesiastics in the Pale, and went a considerable way towards assuring them that the religious settlement associated with Lord Deputy St Leger's reform project, and the establishment of the kingdom of Ireland was, and would remain, decidedly conservative in nature. Thus, from 1541–2, many of the clerics who had previously opposed the crown's

---

[96] *SP* III, pp. 404–9 (at p. 406), 440–3 (at p. 442).
[97] For a full list of the acts passed in the 1541–3 parliament see Quinn, 'Bills and statutes', pp. 164–9.

religious policies, including the doctrine of the royal supremacy, began to give their allegiance to the same policies on the basis of St Leger's assurances, a process that was most clearly visible in relation to the canons of St Patrick's Cathedral, who not only effected a reconciliation with their old adversary Archbishop Browne, but were also willingly reintegrated into the political establishment as fully paid-up members of the 'king's party'.[98]

But the developments of 1541–2 had wider repercussions. One unintended effect of the king's effort to instigate a campaign against married clergy in the Irish Church was that it lessened Lord Deputy St Leger's dependence on the old anti-Grey alliance. Indeed, one of the leading figures associated with the group, Archbishop Browne, was now greatly indebted to the viceroy, as a result of St Leger's efforts in 1541–2 to protect him from the legal difficulties arising from his illicit marriage. St Leger could now expect that Browne would give his unquestioning loyalty and obedience to him in return and that he would put all his energies, and the ecclesiastical resources he had at his disposal, firmly in the service of the viceroy's reform project. It would not take long, therefore, before St Leger came calling to Browne to release some of the riches of the see of Dublin to strengthen his regime and to support the ongoing growth of the 'king's party'.[99]

The lessening of St Leger's dependence on the anti-Grey alliance also had a broader ramification. Prior to the king's intervention in 1541–2, the deputy had needed the support of figures like Archbishop Browne, Lord Chancellor Alen and even the Butlers, because they were the most reliable upholders of the royal supremacy in Ireland. After 1541–2, however, as new supporters of the supremacy came on board and joined the 'king's party', St Leger's support base broadened, giving him a greater flexibility and manoeuvrability on political and religious matters than he had when he commenced his deputyship in August 1540. As a result, he chose to detach himself from the political and ideological agenda that the anti-Grey alliance had pursued in the 1530s, which had sought to enhance royal authority by crushing the 'Geraldine band' and by marginalising all those religious conservatives who had lined up behind the Fitzgerald cause. Instead, St Leger moved to wean the old religious conservatives away from the Geraldine cause and to redirect their allegiance to the 'king's party', by giving them ever-increasing space, within the context of the new constitutional settlement, and on a firmly non-papal basis, to express the essential elements of their religious and cultural ethos. This enabled the deputy to engage with indigenous and conservative religious figures like George

---

[98] The assimilation of the cathedral clergy into the 'king's party' is discussed in more detail in Chapter 5.
[99] See below, pp. 170–81.

Dowdall, the former head of the priory of Ardee in Co. Louth and erstwhile ally of Lord Leonard Grey who, unlike the English officials based in Dublin, were able to use their local knowledge and experience to assist St Leger in extending his political reform project into the independent Gaelic lordships.[100]

Like the negotiations which he conducted with the chapter of St Patrick's Cathedral in 1541–2, then, St Leger's ideological disengagement from the anti-Grey alliance had the effect of further developing and solidifying the conservative nature of the religious settlement associated with his reform project, and reinforcing its acceptance amongst the indigenous clergy and population at large. As a result, the years immediately following the developments of 1541–2 would prove to be the high watermark of the Henrician Reformation in the diocese of Dublin and the English Pale generally. This achievement was, in large measure, due to Lord Deputy St Leger's stewardship. But whether it would be sustained over the long term was contingent upon a variety of different factors, some of which were out of the viceroy's control, such as the continuing refusal of the crown to permit any further experimentation with radical reformist doctrines within the state church; and some of which were in his control, such as his continuing capacity to manage an increasingly complex set of political relationships in Ireland. The following chapter will explore in detail how St Leger oversaw the development of his religious settlement in the 1540s, and examine how it fared as the political and religious landscape evolved and changed as the decade wore on.

---

[100] St Leger's engagement with Dowdall and its significance is discussed in detail in the following chapter.

5

The rise and fall of the viceroy's settlement:
property, canon law and politics during the St Leger era, 1542–53

In the late summer of 1542 the Henrician Church of Ireland acquired a new religious settlement. This settlement was not enshrined in any legislation enacted by the Irish parliament. Nor was it set out in any formularies or injunctions issued in the name of the king. It rested instead upon the word and authority of the viceroy, Sir Anthony St Leger who, in dealing with the fallout from Henry VIII's sudden call in March 1541 for a statutory prohibition on clerical concubinage, had shifted the crown's religious policy away from the radical reforming agenda of the late 1530s, by affirming royal support for traditional forms of doctrine, liturgical practice and clerical behaviour. In plotting this change of direction, St Leger was attempting to do more than simply satisfy the theological demands of his capricious sovereign. He was equally determined that it would address two of his most pressing, domestic political concerns: his need to attract native, and locally influential, conservative clergymen into the ranks of the 'king's party', in support of his plans to make Henry VIII's kingly rule a political reality in Ireland; and his need to protect, on account of their dependability as supporters of the royal supremacy, the married ecclesiastics in his own administration. The settlement that emerged in 1542, then, was not the product of rigid, confessional design. It was a pragmatic and flexible construct which, while clearly signalling that the Henrician Church of Ireland would be grounded upon 'good and Catholic teaching', was also intended to cater for the basic beliefs and most immediate needs of Ireland's reform-minded clerics.[1]

Yet, while the 1542 settlement had its origins in a particular set of political circumstances, and represented an immediate and expediential response to them, it also tells us much about how its principal architect,

---

[1] Morrin, *Patent rolls*, i, p. 81; on the construction of the settlement see Chapter 4.

Lord Deputy St Leger, estimated the importance of religious affairs in public life, and how these affairs were regulated and managed in Ireland under his watch. Although his political instincts prevented him from committing anything to paper that would betray, and help historians explain, his underlying motivations, it is evident from his behaviour that he considered religious and ecclesiastical matters to be of secondary importance to political affairs. Indeed, he generally acted in accordance with the principles that religion should be subject to the imperatives of politics and that, wherever possible, religious policy should be utilised to assist the civil authorities achieve their political objectives. Nowhere did he put these principles into operation in a more ambitious manner than in the conception and design of the 1542 settlement. St Leger's overriding political objective at this time was to establish the kingdom of Ireland as a meaningful political entity; and every single feature of the settlement – especially, the way it was constructed to appeal to conservative and reform-minded clerics alike – was made to serve this objective. Specifically, on the back of what was agreed in 1542, the viceroy sought to build a broad measure of religious consensus in Ireland, and to unite the religious conservatives and religious reformers – who in their different ways were loyal subjects of the crown – in the common pursuit of extending and deepening Henry VIII's kingship throughout the length and breadth of Ireland.

Had St Leger undertaken only a short, single tour of duty as viceroy of Ireland, these observations would be of limited historical interest, and confined to a footnote in this book. However, St Leger served as viceroy for over twelve years during three distinct periods between July 1540 and May 1556, and governed Ireland not just during the latter years of Henry VIII's reign, but also during the critical periods of religious change under his successors, Edward VI and Queen Mary.[2] Throughout, St Leger dealt with religious affairs in exactly the same manner and on precisely the same basis that he had approached them in the early 1540s. Again and again, he strove to make religion, including the crown's religious dictates, a subordinate part of his general political strategy, and to ensure that the religious concerns of all the different interest groups in Ireland were made to serve or, at the very least, not obstruct, the attainment of his political goals. What this meant, in practice, was that he attempted to keep in place as much of the 1542 settlement as was possible in the later period, on the grounds that it had been deliberately constructed, and was thus best suited, to support his great

---

[2] In broad terms, the St Leger viceroyalties covered the periods July 1540 to May 1548, August 1550 to May 1551, and September 1553 to May 1556; but they were also punctuated by several periods of absence in England, during which times a lord justice deputised for him (Ellis, *Tudor Ireland*, p. 368).

project of making the Tudors' claim to kingship over Ireland a political reality.

The maintenance of the viceroy's settlement in a form that remained close to the original was an ambitious and challenging task in the changing circumstances of the late 1540s and 1550s. As St Leger and his administration moved to establish the crown's authority throughout the island, it was inevitable that they would face new demands and challenges that would require them to modify the contours, or test the limits of what had been agreed in the summer of 1542. Some of these changes were instigated by St Leger himself and arose, in the main, from his own repeated attempts to expropriate all manner of ecclesiastical property in order to bankroll his political activities. Other modifications to the settlement were necessitated by the demands of the crown, including, most critically, the abrupt attempt made by Edward VI to imbue the state church with a Protestant theology and liturgy during the late 1540s and early 1550s.

Local secular politics also played their part in reshaping the settlement. There were few parts of the island that did not feel the effects of the viceroy's political reform programme, and there were few men of power that did not conduct a political relationship with him. Many of these relationships were new and untested, and some, even, were intrinsically unstable. The fluctuating nature of St Leger's interactions with individual Irish lords, no matter how distant the latter were from the centre of English power, not only affected his political reform programme, but frequently impinged or impacted upon his religious settlement, even in the diocese of Dublin. Two such connections, in particular, will feature heavily in the ensuing story as they concern two lords who not only loomed large on the viceroy's political horizons, but who also cast large shadows on the political and cultural life of the English Pale. The first of these was Con Bacagh O'Neill, the chief of the great and militarily powerful Ulster clan, who, potentially, posed a significant security threat to the Palesmen throughout the St Leger era. The other was James Butler, the tenth earl of Ormond, whose political influence reached into the heart of the Pale and who possessed an equal capacity to destabilise the viceroy's political and religious programmes.

The constant alteration or reinvention by St Leger of what had been agreed in 1542 in order to accommodate or absorb the crown's religious dictates, his own despoliation of ecclesiastical property, or the fluctuations in his political relationships with the great Irish lords, was not always appreciated by his clients. At different times, particular changes to the settlement were perceived to have breached it, and gave rise to tensions and stresses amongst clerical adherents on both sides of the religious divide, which St Leger had to work hard to control and assuage. The viceroy's efforts at containment, whether they proved to be successful or unsuccessful, and his attempt to preserve intact the religious consensus that had been achieved in 1542, form a crucial, though often overlooked, component of Ireland's Reformation story during the 1540s and 1550s. They provide an essential key to understanding the dynamics of the Reformation in the mid-Tudor period and will be explored in detail in the course of this chapter.

I

The viceroy, himself, was the first to test where the boundaries of the 1542 settlement lay. At the end of August 1542, only days after Archbishop Browne's marriage had been terminated and only days after he and the council had informed the king that they were intent on staying his bill on clerical incontinence, it emerged that St Leger had already hatched a radical plan to secure some additional ecclesiastical resources to finance his political endeavours. What he had in mind was revealed in a letter to the king, dated 27 August. St Leger proposed that, if the king was in agreement, he would proceed with a scheme to downgrade one of Dublin's two cathedrals, Christ Church, to the status of a parish church, and that he would sequester its ancillary buildings and the bulk of its revenues in order to house and finance a resident council in the chief city of the realm.[3]

The appearance of St Leger's scheme for Christ Church requires some explanation for, at the outset of his viceroyalty in 1540, he had initially considered it advantageous to make a public avowal of his support for the cathedral. Having come to power on the back of a coup directed against Lord Deputy Grey, St Leger had been acutely aware of the need to establish a solid power base by retaining the allegiance of the anti-Grey faction on the Irish council, and saw in Christ Church and its affairs an important avenue through which he could pursue this objective. That St Leger perceived the cathedral in this way was due to the fact that three leading members of the anti-Grey faction – Archbishop Browne, Lord Chancellor Alen and Vice-Treasurer Brabazon – had been instrumental, as Vicegerent Cromwell's deputies, in preserving the cathedral in an altered secular state when it was threatened with suppression during the attack on the monasteries in 1539.[4] Moreover, following Cromwell's sudden fall in June 1540, and the resultant loss of their deputed vicegerential authority, the triumvirate stood by their earlier work and, together with the cathedral clergy, sought to secure confirmation of the legal validity of the alteration. It was in relation to this particular matter that Lord Deputy St Leger espied an opportunity. In the

---

[3] *SP* III, pp. 412–16 (at pp. 414–16).   [4] Above, pp. 121–3.

full expectation that it would strengthen their allegiance to him, the viceroy decided that he would facilitate Archbishop Browne and his allies in their efforts to copper-fasten the cathedral's reformed constitution. Thus, in September 1540, while seeking a licence from the king to hold a parliament, he permitted the former vicegerential commissioners and the rest of the Irish council to seek royal approval for the enactment of a statute to establish 'Christ's Church of Dublin to be a cathedral church or college with a dean, certain prebendaries and vicars chorals'.[5]

Had the crown sanctioned this legislation, it is doubtful that St Leger would ever have contemplated and conceived his scheme for the downgrading of Christ Church. Instead, Christ Church's new constitution, as drafted by Cromwell's deputy vicegerents in 1539, would have been put on a statutory footing and the cathedral's status assured.[6] But this is not what happened. On 26 March 1541, a letter from the king was issued to St Leger and the Irish council which belatedly approved the legislation for the upcoming parliament, and which contained two instructions that led ultimately to the viceroy formulating his scheme to downgrade the cathedral.[7] The first of these instructions informed the recipients that, following current English practice, the cathedral's new constitution was to be confirmed by letters patent issued under the great seal of Ireland, rather than by statute.[8] This not only put a break on the parliamentary process that St Leger had originally envisaged for the confirmation, but presented him with an unanticipated opportunity to think again about what Christ Church might contribute to his own political agenda.

The second instruction – Henry VIII's command to enact a statute against clerical incontinence in the Irish Church – was less obviously concerned with the cathedral's constitutional position. However, as we have seen, the appearance of the king's bill set in motion a process in which the viceroy and his administration were compelled to enter negotiations with the clergy of Dublin's other cathedral, St Patrick's, in order to extricate Archbishop Browne from his illegal marriage.[9] One significant by-product of this development was that it focussed the viceroy's mind on the administrative structures of the see of Dublin, and on the place and relationship of the two

---

[5] *SP* III, pp. 241–4 (at p. 244); 'The titling of the acts of parliament' (TNA: PRO, SP 60/10, no. 7); Quinn, 'Bills and statutes', pp. 157–8.

[6] The text of the constitution is in RCB, C6/1/6, no. 3 (Registrum Novum of Christ Church), pp. 1104–21.

[7] *SP* III, pp. 292–300 (at pp. 293–4); Quinn, 'Bills and statutes', p. 158. Parliament was originally meant to have sat from Candlemas (2 February) 1541 (*SP* III, p. 277).

[8] *SP* III, pp. 293–4; Quinn, 'Bills and statutes', p. 158. On the general practice for refounding monasteries as secular cathedrals in England under Henry VIII see Lehmberg, *Reformation of cathedrals*, pp. 81–100.

[9] Above Chapter 4.

cathedrals within those structures. Inevitably, too, it highlighted the uncomfortable fact that the diocese occupied a deeply anomalous position in the broader Henrician ecclesiastical polity, where the number of cathedrals had been reduced to one secular institution per diocese.[10] Thus, as the negotiations with the clergy of St Patrick's got into full swing in the early summer of 1541, St Leger began not only to question the validity of his earlier decision to proceed with the confirmation of Christ Church's secular status, but also to question its right to exist as a cathedral body.

In deliberating on these matters, St Leger was well positioned to make comparisons on the relative value of the two Dublin cathedrals, especially in relation to his own immediate political needs. And on most counts Christ Church came off second best. In the context of his efforts to promote Henry VIII's kingship, for example, it was an undoubted disadvantage to Christ Church that, unlike St Patrick's, it was not a royal foundation. It was no surprise, therefore, that when it came to choosing a venue to host the liturgical celebrations surrounding the proclamation of Henry VIII's 'kingly title' in June 1541, Christ Church was overlooked in favour of 'his grace's church'.[11] In a similar vein, Christ Church was also found wanting because its clergy had no substantial legal responsibilities or functions within Dublin's ecclesiastical courts. As a result, it was with St Patrick's, and not Christ Church, that St Leger had to do business, when the need to regularise Archbishop Browne's marital status became an immediate priority for his administration in 1541.[12]

These failings were significant enough in themselves, but they were compounded, in St Leger's eyes, when he considered the poor financial state of the cathedral. Indeed, he did not think that Christ Church was sufficiently well endowed to maintain the bearing of a cathedral at all. In his letter to the king of 27 August 1542, in which he first broached his scheme to downgrade the church, St Leger bemoaned the fact 'as the revenues thereof pass not £260 de claro' all that could be established there was 'a dean, three canons, and four vicars . . . which is but a small number for a cathedral church in a city'.[13] St Patrick's, in contrast, as he observed in a subsequent letter to the king, was 'more fairer than the said Christ's Church'.[14] Its abundant tithe revenues enabled it to support '20 or 30 dignities and canons with other ministers according' and was therefore 'meet to be preserved and maintained'.[15] The upshot of all this was that the viceroy could foresee no place for the 'late abbey' within the new kingdom

---

[10] To accomplish this, the Henrician regime had dissolved the monastic cathedrals at Coventry and Bath (Lehmberg, *Reformation of cathedrals*, p. 82).

[11] Above, pp. 146–7.   [12] Above, pp. 144–5.   [13] *SP* III, p. 415.

[14] St Leger to the king, 4 June 1543 (*SP* III, pp. 465–9, at p. 468).   [15] *SP* III, p. 415.

of Ireland. It would be far better, he concluded, that it should be 'converted' to offset the expense of maintaining a standing council in Dublin 'three days in the week'. What he had decided to do, in effect, was to expropriate the old priory complex with a view to turning it into the administrative centre of the new kingdom of Ireland.[16]

When, precisely, St Leger made this decision to convert Christ Church into a permanent residence for the council is not now on record. However, we do know that in the summer of 1541, over a year before he wrote to the king about his scheme, he took a step that indicates he had already made his mind up about the cathedral's future at this juncture. At some point in June or early July, and in line with the king's instruction to the council, St Leger's administration was approached by Dean Castle and the clergy of Christ Church to issue letters patent under the great seal confirming the alteration of the former priory into a secular cathedral. Yet, despite the fact that they came to the chancery armed with a warrant signed by the king, which had been solicited and procured in England on 10 May, St Leger 'stayed' the delivery of the sealed patent.[17] That he was prepared to obstruct, not for the first time during his viceroyalty, what was, in effect, a direct command from the king to proceed with the confirmation, indicates that he had already learned enough about the relative merits of the two cathedrals to determine that the conversion of Christ Church into a permanent residence for the council should be pursued as a political priority. However, it is also evident that St Leger decided to keep his intentions under wraps at this point, until such time as the negotiations with the clergy of St Patrick's on Browne's marriage settlement were concluded, for fear that such a revelation might destabilise them. As things turned out, St Leger had to wait some fifteen months before these discussions bore fruit, and it was only at this point, at the end of August 1542, that he showed his hand on the matter of Christ Church in his letter to the king.[18]

This delay in proceedings was not entirely unwelcome. The spirited attempt made by the clergy of Christ Church to force St Leger's hand on the issuing of the patent had drawn his attention to the fact that there would inevitably be some opposition to his scheme from those who identified with the cathedral's interests. Thus, while he awaited a positive conclusion to the negotiations with the clergy of St Patrick's, he was able to take steps to neutralise this potential opposition at source. The first of these steps was to call in some of the key individual players for face-to-face meetings, during

---

[16] *SP* III, p. 468.

[17] *SP* III, pp. 415–16; *CCD*, no. 432; Morrin, *Patent rolls*, i, p. 88. As a default position, the clergy of Christ Church secured the enrollment of the king's mandate on the patent rolls.

[18] *SP* III, pp. 414–16; above Chapter 4.

which he revealed his plans for Christ Church and 'commoned and persuaded' with them to give their support to the scheme. Dean Castle of Christ Church was one such figure who received the viceroy's attention in this manner. And it had the desired effect. The dean was prevailed upon by St Leger to give a commitment – after being promised that he would receive an annual pension of £50 sterling until he was preferred to an English benefice – that he would surrender his cathedral voluntarily once the scheme had received royal sanction.[19] Other key figures who bowed to the viceroy's persuasions at this time included two of the former vicegerential commissioners, Lord Chancellor Alen and Vice-Treasurer Brabazon, who had effected the alteration to the cathedral's status in 1539.[20] Like Dean Castle, their endorsement of the viceroy's scheme was influenced by the promise of future rewards which, in their particular case, would materialise in the form of further shares of the booty from the dissolved religious houses.[21]

As well as seeking the support of figures like Dean Castle, Lord Chancellor Alen and Vice-Treasurer Brabazon, St Leger was also conscious of the need to make his scheme for Christ Church an attractive proposition for the civic community in Dublin. The mayor and citizens had very strong and ancient bonds with the cathedral. Not only had they come out strongly in support of the institution when it was threatened with suppression during the campaign to dissolve the monasteries in 1539–40,[22] but it was likely that they would do so again once they became aware of St Leger's plans to downgrade it. In anticipation of such opposition, therefore, the viceroy included some additional provisions in his scheme which were calculated to meet and overcome the main objections that would arise from that quarter. One of these provisions related to the cathedral church itself. Although St Leger intended to downgrade it in terms of its status, he did recognise that it would be necessary to maintain the church as a parochial entity, as this would enable the citizens of Dublin to continue to attend religious services there.[23] He planned, therefore, to unite 'four little churches' that adjoined Christ Church, and to establish a new

---

[19] *SP* III, pp. 415–16; see also *SP* III, p. 468. St Leger guaranteed Castle that this preferment would be effected within two years of the surrender.

[20] Alen and Brabazon co-signed the letter to the king on 27 August 1542 which outlined the deputy's plans for downgrading Christ Church's status (*SP* III, pp. 412–16).

[21] For the monastic grants received by Alen and Brabazon in the period after St Leger decided to proceed with the conversion of Christ Church see Bradshaw, *Dissolution of the religious orders*, p. 237.

[22] *SP* II, pp. 545–6

[23] The former cathedral priory at Bath, which had also been the major place of worship for its citizens, served as a precedent: it was preserved as a parochial entity after its surrender in January 1539 (Lehmberg, *Reformation of cathedrals*, p. 82).

parish centred on the old cathedral. Further, to support the new parish, provision was to be made for the appointment of 'such ministers . . . as shall be necessary', including one who would act as a schoolmaster in the city. St Leger believed that the latter provision, in particular, would 'much please the citizens that have no school now here'. He also took comfort in the facts that by keeping the church going as a parochial entity, and by using the priory buildings as an official meeting place for the king's councillors, both would be 'preserved and maintained from ruin'. Thus, unlike in 1539–40, when the cathedral was threatened with outright suppression, he had cause for optimism that the citizenry would have no reason to fear that his scheme would despoil their city, and that, overall, it would not face the same level and intensity of opposition that had arisen in the earlier period.[24]

Such optimism, however, was to prove unfounded for, as soon as it was made public, his scheme for the conversion of Christ Church ran into difficulties. The first problem that it encountered was the reaction of the king. As far as Henry VIII was concerned, he had already signed a warrant to confirm Christ Church's alteration into a secular cathedral, and saw no pressing need for an alternative course of action. Thus, while he did not reject St Leger's scheme out of hand, and conceded that it 'hath a good appearance', he displayed little genuine enthusiasm for it. Indeed, he only responded to St Leger's initial letter about the conversion of Christ Church, and then only after a further reminder, in August 1543, a year after the scheme was first broached. Moreover, when it finally arrived, his response was distinctly non-committal: he ordered St Leger to send him a 'true extent' of the cathedral's income with a 'particular declaration' of how it would be spent, whereupon he would make a final judgement on the matter 'as we shall then think most expedient'.[25]

The lukewarm response of the king to St Leger's plans, although not fatal, did embolden others to question whether they were expedient, including, most notably, Archbishop Browne of Dublin. The reformed secular constitution of Christ Church Cathedral was the only legacy of the vicegerential commission, that he, Lord Chancellor Alen and Vice-Treasurer Brabazon had been granted by Thomas Cromwell in February 1539 and, as such, represented for the archbishop one of the few positive and tangible outcomes of the reformers' efforts in the 1530s to imbue the Irish Church with an ideology grounded in the doctrine of the royal supremacy.[26] Browne had been the most committed devotee of this cause in the 1530s and thus, unlike his former vicegerential associates, who had been persuaded ahead of time to endorse the scheme to turn Christ Church to secular uses,

---

[24] *SP* III, pp. 414–16, 468.   [25] *SP* III, pp. 465–9 (at p. 468), 482–4 (at p. 484).
[26] See above, pp. 122–3.

he consistently maintained the position that the cathedral should be retained in its reformed, secular state.[27] Moreover, he was willing to state this position publicly, albeit in a restrained and circumspect manner. When the viceroy went back to the Irish council in the early autumn of 1543 to put together the detailed extent of the cathedral's income required by the king, Browne advised them against proceeding with the conversion, on the pragmatic grounds that the revenue of Christ Church was insufficient to fund the project for which it was being expropriated; and because the disappearance of the cathedral – the metropolitan church 'in whose name or title much of the . . . archbishop's lands is annexed to his . . . see' – might bring into question his own entitlement to the patrimony of the see of Dublin.[28]

It is doubtful, however, that the archbishop's arguments made much of an impression on the viceroy, as he was aware, before he launched his scheme to convert Christ Church into a permanent residence for the council, that Browne harboured an attachment for the cathedral, and that the funds that would accrue to the Irish exchequer by downgrading it would not be extensive. Nevertheless, by the time the archbishop had aired his careful defence of the cathedral at the council board, the debate on the future of Christ Church was beginning to take what for St Leger was an undesirable, and ultimately decisive, turn. At some point in September or October, an unidentified source – or so St Leger and the council later claimed, though Archbishop Browne and the dean of Christ Church stand out as the most likely candidates – alerted the mayor and citizens of Dublin to the existence of the viceroy's scheme. Immediately, they entered the fray on the cathedral's behalf, lobbying St Leger and the council to preserve Christ Church 'in the estate it is now in'; for, despite all the measures the viceroy had put in place to assure them to the contrary, they still believed that the downgrading of the cathedral would cause 'their city to be totally defaced and disparaged'. In the face of such agitated opposition from the loyal citizens of Dublin, the viceroy came to the conclusion that his scheme for Christ

---

[27] It may also be significant that in the years following the vicegerential visitation of the church, Dean Castle and his clergy had endeavoured to cultivate Browne's support, and to establish a more personal and permanent connection between the archbishop and his cathedral. One interesting example of this, which is documented in the account of John Moss, the cathedral proctor, relates to the Christmas festivities of 1542. Browne and his suffragans attended Christ Church during the festivities as guests of the dean and chapter, and were the recipients of lavish hospitality, including four sumptuous meals, on the 'first night' of Christmas and throughout the course of the following day (Proctor Moss's account, copy in Registrum Novum of Christ Church, RCB, C6/1/6, no. 3, pp. 1147–8, under the heading 'The expenses on the Bishops at Christmas').

[28] Reported in a letter from the deputy and council to the king of 20 January 1544 (*SP* III, pp. 489–90).

Church had become more trouble than it was worth, and that it was time to cut his losses and abandon it. This decision – which was initially taken around November or in the first week of December 1543, when the viceroy elected to proceed with the appointment of a new dean following the death of Dean Castle – was formally communicated to the king in a letter of 20 January 1544, wherein St Leger was 'moved' to be a humble petitioner to the king that 'the said Christ's Church may stand as it now is', as a secular cathedral of the 'new erection'.[29]

On the face of it, the abandonment of St Leger's scheme for the downgrading of Christ Church was a significant political reversal for the viceroy. It seemed to signify that his capacity to manage and direct religious and ecclesiastical affairs in a manner that would serve his own political ends, was not as great as it appeared when he had cleverly averted, and exploited, the crisis surrounding the king's demand for the enactment of legislation against clerical concubinage three years earlier. Yet, while the collapse of the scheme was undoubtedly frustrating for the viceroy, the damage done to his political standing was more apparent than real. It was the viceroy himself who had called time on the Christ Church scheme, and he had done so not because he believed there was no chance of seeing it through to completion, but because he estimated that the political cost of pursuing it to the bitter end – in effect, it would mean alienating the mayor, citizens and archbishop of the chief city of the realm – would far outweigh the benefits to be gained. Moreover, he did not abandon it without first seeking to put in place an alternative and compensatory scheme that would allow him and his administration to tap the wealth of the institutional church. And he was determined that those ecclesiastics who had stood in the way of his scheme for Christ Church, especially Archbishop Browne, would facilitate the implementation of his new plans. What he had in mind, and what he forced the archbishop and his clergy to accede to before he brought the final curtain down on the Christ Church scheme at the end of January 1544, was that the provisions that were then being made for the upkeep of Browne's children, and which involved the alienation of property belonging to the archbishopric of Dublin, would be extended to include himself or designated clients within the 'king's party'.

---

[29] Ibid. The letters patent confirming Christ Church's alteration into a secular cathedral, which St Leger had withheld in 1541, vested the appointment of the dean in the crown (RCB, C6/2/32, nos. 3–5). A new dean, Thomas Lockwood, was in place by 6 December 1543. Castle's death, which had been predicted by St Leger in the previous June, occurred at some point between 17 October and 6 December 1543 (*CCD*, nos. 1190, 1192; *SP* III, pp. 465–9, at p. 468).

II

The initial arrangements for the care and upkeep of Archbishop Browne's three sons were made in the summer or autumn of 1541, soon after it had emerged that the king was intent on pursuing a campaign against clerical concubinage in the Irish Church. To protect the archbishop's position, it was decided that the boys should be separated from their family, and thus, with the knowledge of the viceroy, they were put into fosterage with an Irish clan who had been at peace with the Englishry since the mid-1530s, and who resided in the southern part of Browne's diocese, the Críoch Branach O'Byrnes. The O'Byrnes inhabited largely hilly and mountainous terrain which, although becoming increasingly accessible to the Dublin government, especially after they formally submitted to the crown in July 1542, provided a relatively secure refuge to keep the boys out of general view.[30] As well as these fosterage arrangements, the archbishop also put in place an additional measure to maintain contact with the clan. In 1541, he appointed the priest, Nicholas Miagh, who was a kinsman of the boys' mother, to a living in the heart of the O'Byrnes' country, the rectory of Ennisboyne. From here, Miagh had easy access to the clan and was able to watch over the boys' interests.[31]

These fosterage arrangements provided for the basic care of Browne's sons during their early boyhood. However, as the 1540s wore on, additional arrangements were required to provide for their education and their future livelihood. To address these particular needs, the archbishop set up a series of trust funds for his three sons, involving the alienation of a variety of different properties belonging to his see.[32] The best documented example of such a trust, which was established in the late 1540s on foot of the alienation of the mensal rectories of Ballybaught, Boystown and Usk, reveals that the cathedral clergy worked in tandem with Lord Deputy St Leger and his affiliates, as per the agreement of 1542, to assist the

---

[30] 'Matters' against St Leger (TNA: PRO SP 61/2, no. 53), printed in Maginn, 'A window on mid-Tudor Ireland', pp. 470–82, at p. 480; on the Gaelic custom of fosterage generally see Nicholls, *Gaelic and Gaelicised Ireland*, pp. 90–1; on the O'Byrnes' relationship with the crown during the 1530s and 40s see Maginn, '*Civilizing*' *Gaelic Leinster*, pp. 33–62, 76–98.

[31] Vice-Treasurer Brabazon's account 26–29 Henry VIII: TNA: PRO SP65/1/2 (f 25v). It is possible that some contact between the boys and their mother may also have been permitted, as she too is known, from a later documentary source, to have possessed property in Ennisboyne (NAI, Salved Chancery Pleadings, N/147).

[32] Amongst the ecclesiastical properties that are known to have come into the possession of the boys, or their guardians, during the 1540s and 1550s are the tithes of St Kevin's parish, Dublin, some enclosures in the suburban lordship of St Sepulchre, the mills of Dunlavin and Ballymore, and port corn from the watermill of Clondalkin (NAI, RC 6/1, pp. 43, 50; Will of Alexander Browne, 1578, Fisher Abstracts: Dublin Consistorial Wills, GO MS 290, pp. 18–19).

archbishop. In this particular instance, Browne began on 20 September 1547 by alienating the property to a government-sponsored syndicate, which comprised eleven gentlemen from the Pale, including the eldest sons and heirs of three senior crown officials: Sir Thomas Luttrell, chief justice of the Common Pleas, James Bathe, the chief baron of the Exchequer, and Patrick Barnewall, the king's prime sergeant-at-law and solicitor general.[33] By 1 December following, the Pale gentlemen had assigned their interest to the dean and chapter of Christ Church who, on that date, alienated it to William Mowseherst, the registrar of the archbishop's court.[34] The trail of assignments finally ended on 6 September 1548 when Mowseherst conveyed the property in trust to yet another syndicate. On this occasion, it was made up of five clergymen, including three members of the chapter of St Patrick's that had helped Archbishop Browne secure his divorce in 1542 – James Humphrey, Nicholas Miagh and Robert Eustace – and one layman, Robert Bathe, the husband of Browne's former wife, Katherine Miagh. Together they undertook to dispose of the revenues of the rectories to maintain Browne's sons in 'good houses, meat, drink, clothes and lodging' and to educate them in 'reading, writing, singing and grammar'.[35]

It was Browne's willingness to dispose of see property in this manner – on give-away terms that consciously overlooked and neglected the future well-being of his archbishopric – that presented St Leger with the opportunity to advance a number of his key political objectives. The viceroy knew that if the archbishop could be prevailed upon to extend his largesse beyond his family circle to include designated clients of his administration, he would obtain access to a new and valuable ecclesiastical resource that could be made to contribute – just as the crown's monastic properties had done before it – to the maintenance and expansion of his political support base. Indeed, the potential benefits of such a strategy extended further for, as well as providing for the material interests of his supporters, it also held out the prospect of establishing new or deeper ties between his administration and the ecclesiastical establishment in Dublin. That such a possibility was also on offer was due to the fact that St Leger would only gain access to the archiepiscopal estates if he managed to secure the buy-in not just of Archbishop Browne, but also of the deans and chapters of Christ Church and St Patrick, as both bodies had to sign off and append their seals to any deed of alienation, lease or other form of conveyance involving that

---

[33] RCB, C.6.1.6, no. 3, pp. 1173–5 (*CCD*, nos. 441–2).   [34] *CCD*, no. 1214.

[35] *CCD*, no. 1220. These provisions were to be maintained until one of the brothers, Anthony, reached the age of eighteen. Their guardians were also instructed to give their mother Katherine Miagh 'such portion, if any, as shall remain after rent and maintenance . . . until the said Anthony reaches 18 years of age'.

property.[36] The bargaining process required to strike such a deal would provide him with an opportunity, if it was handled astutely, to build upon the earlier, positive engagement of his regime with Dublin's senior clergymen – on the matter of Browne's marital settlement – and complete their assimilation into the 'king's party'. In the winter of 1543–4, then, St Leger quickly overcame his frustration at having to abandon the scheme to convert Christ Church into a permanent residence for the council. Instead, he entered into immediate discussions with the ecclesiastical authorities in Dublin to put in place a compensatory scheme which would allow for the distribution of a more abundant ecclesiastical resource, the estates of the archbishopric of Dublin, to new or existing supporters of his regime.

Of the three parties, Archbishop Browne was the most easily persuaded to accede to St Leger's wishes, as he was already dependent on the viceroy's co-operation to enable him to exploit his benefice on behalf of his family. The archbishop held all of his manorial properties as a tenant-in-chief of the king, and was required by common law to obtain a licence from the crown, and pay a fee, any time he wished to alienate any portion of them. More-over, where such a licence was requested, it was also normal practice to hold an inquisition *ad quod damnum* before a jury to determine whether the prospective grant would be prejudicial to the interests of the crown or of any other party.[37] As viceroy, St Leger was ultimately in control of these legal and administrative processes in Ireland, and could elect to make them run smoothly for the archbishop, or use them to obstruct his property dealings. In these circumstances, it was in the mutual interest of both parties to reach an accommodation. Thus, when St Leger came calling in the winter of 1543–4 with his proposal that he and his affiliates be included in the archbishop's property dealings, Browne was quick to accept it for, not only was he indebted to the viceroy for the protection and assistance he had received during the crisis over his marriage, but he also knew that, if he refused, St Leger had it within his power to impede his efforts to provide for his young sons.

The clergy of Christ Church Cathedral, like their archbishop, also had little room for manoeuvre in their dealings with the viceroy. Although St Leger had had to abandon his scheme to convert their church into a permanent residence for the council, he remained determined that, as a condition of the cathedral's reprieve, he would receive their future

---

[36] See Appendix 1.

[37] On the origins of the crown's claim that church lands should not be alienated without royal permission see J. Hudson, *Land, law and lordship in Anglo-Norman England* (Oxford, 1994), pp. 230–51; on inquisitions *ad quod damnum* generally, see *Guide to the contents of the Public Record Office*, i, p. 28.

co-operation in all matters touching upon the interests of his administration. Characteristically, the viceroy's expectations were communicated to the cathedral clergy in a discreet and informal fashion, but they did leave one significant mark in the historical record. Having already encountered their independent spirit in the summer of 1541, when they tried to pressurise him into issuing a patent confirming their new secular constitution, St Leger needed more than words to convince him that the clergy of Christ Church would behave in a suitably compliant manner thereafter. As a form of insurance, therefore, the viceroy decided to appoint one of his own clerical protégés, Thomas Lockwood, to head the institution as successor to Dean Castle in late 1543.[38]

The appointment had the desired effect. From the outset, the new dean was unambiguous as to where his primary loyalties lay. In April 1544, and as a token of his friendship to the viceroy, Lockwood and his chapter granted St Leger's private secretary and political confidante, John Parker, a sixty-one-year lease of the lordship of Cabragh.[39] As well as giving Parker a lengthy interest in the lordship, the dean and chapter's lease also included a series of unusually generous provisions that would enable him *inter alia* to hunt hawk, fish and fowl – presumably with the viceroy and other members of the St Leger circle – throughout all of the cathedral's estates.[40] This desire to please such an intimate affiliate of the viceroy and, by extension, St Leger himself, was easily transferable to other business matters. It was inevitable, therefore, that from 1544 on St Leger would encounter no difficulty in securing Lockwood's signature, or the seal of his chapter, upon each and every grant of episcopal property that he and his circle sought from Archbishop Browne.

The dean and chapter of St Patrick's, in contrast to their colleagues in Christ Church, appeared to occupy a more independent position in relation to the viceroy. However, St Leger did have one key adherent in the

---

[38] Prior to the Reformation, Lockwood had been a nondescript, though noticeably worldly, absentee benefice holder in the diocese of Meath. His rise to prominence is entirely attributable to St Leger. As well as appointing him to the deanery of Christ Church, it appears that the viceroy was also responsible for preferring him to the prebend of Yago in St Patrick's Cathedral *c*.1541 – the living was in the gift of the crown at this time following the Earl of Kildare's attainder. Lockwood's elevation under St Leger culminated in his admission, in the summer of 1545, to the Irish council. He held on to the deanery of Christ Church and remained a councillor until his death in 1565: Griffith, *Exchequer inquisitions*, pp. 69, 87; *LP* XIX, i, no. 840; Morrin, *Patent rolls*, i, pp. 112–13. On his career generally see R. Gillespie, 'The coming of reform, 1500–58', in Milne, ed., *Christ Church Cathedral*, pp. 169–73.

[39] *CCD*, no. 1120. On Parker, generally, and his place in the St Leger circle see Brady, *Chief Governors*, pp. 31–2.

[40] *CCD*, no. 1120. It also appears that Lockwood went to law on behalf of Parker to end the interest that Walter Kerdiff of Shallon had in Cabragh (*CCD*, no. 436).

cathedral who was honour bound to support his demands for a share of the coveted estates of the archbishop of Dublin. This was Edward Basnet, the dean of St Patrick's who, like Archbishop Browne, had taken a wife in the late 1530s and had benefited from the viceroy's protection when the king attempted to institute a statutory prohibition on clerical marriage in 1541.[41] Nevertheless, the events surrounding the abandonment of his scheme for Christ Church and, particularly, the part played in it by Browne, served to warn St Leger that the assistance he had given the married clergy in 1541 did not, in itself, guarantee unqualified loyalty from that quarter. He took the precaution, therefore, of putting in place some additional measures to bolster Basnet's support, and to ensure that the rest of the chapter would be equally biddable. The issuing of two twenty-one-year leases to Basnet – one on the old royal outpost of Newcastle MacKinegan in the Dublin marches in December 1543, the other on the former monastic estate of Ballydowd in Co. Dublin in June 1544 – were sufficient to win the dean's compliance.[42] With regard to the rest of the chapter, St Leger employed a more subtle, though no lest effective, inducement. On 20 August 1544, and on foot of a royal warrant which he himself procured while he was in England conferring with the king 'upon the state and affairs' of the realm, the viceroy granted a licence to the canons of St Patrick's that exempted them from personal attendance at the benefices they held in other dioceses.[43]

The licence granted to the cathedral canons in 1544 was, like so many of St Leger's actions, finely calculated to win their support, as it addressed a longstanding difficulty for them that stemmed from their practice of pluralism. As the absentee holders of additional benefices in other dioceses, they were regularly investigated by the barons of the exchequer for transgressions against the two medieval statutes on clerical absenteeism in Ireland

---

[41] Above, p. 141.

[42] *Fiants, Henry VIII*, nos. 389, 418. The Newcastle MacKinegan lease contained a stipulation that it would be voided if the king decided to place a garrison there in the future. This may indicate that, like Archbishop Browne's sons, the children of Basnet's marriage were also put into the fosterage with the O'Byrnes and that the castle was a temporary base for maintaining contact with them. Basnet appears to have had four sons – Richard, William, John and George – and a daughter Katherine (Will of Edward Basnet, 15 May 1553, *Pembroke deeds*, pp. 77–8). Archbishop Browne's youngest son, Alexander, later married a Katherine Basnet, who may have been the dean's daughter (Fisher Abstracts: Dublin Consistorial Wills, GO MS 290, pp. 18–19). S.T.B. Percival conjectured, however, that the Katherine Basnet mentioned in the dean's will was his wife ('The Basnetts during the 16th and 17th centuries', pp. 32–3). Dean Basnet added to his property portfolio in February 1545, when he purchased the castle and lands of Kiltiernan, again on favourable terms from the viceroy (*Fiants, Henry VIII*, no. 449).

[43] *LM* V, pt. 2, p. 1; *Fiants, Henry VIII*, no. 432; *Dignitas decani*, pp. 128–32; Morrin, *Patent rolls*, i, p. 109.

and, when found guilty, were liable to pay fines of up to two-thirds of the value of the livings concerned.[44] St Leger's licence of exemption was designed to protect the canons from such scrutiny, and to ensure that they did not lose any of the income from their supernumerary livings in punitive fines payable to the crown. Not surprisingly, those who gained most from the licence included influential figures like Precentor Humphrey, whose support would be needed if the viceroy and his clients were to secure a share of Archbishop Browne's impending property giveaway. Before the licence was issued, Humphrey had been the subject of the barons' inquiries on at least three separate occasions between November 1538 and June 1543 for his failure to attend at the two benefices he held in the diocese of Meath, the rectory of Painestown and the vicarage of Culmullin. After August 1544, in contrast, he was left undisturbed by the barons, which enabled him to pocket an annual net income of IR£60 from the two livings, and which ensured that he was favourably disposed to respond positively to all future requests for see property that emanated from the viceroy and his clients.[45]

By the late summer of 1544, then, the viceroy and his administration had completed the groundwork to enable them to partake, along with Archbishop Browne's family, in a new property bonanza centred on the estates of the see of Dublin. One of the first beneficiaries of this windfall was the ubiquitous John Parker who, under St Leger's tutelage, had become a leading player in a small group of property speculators that the viceroy had established to build and maintain support for his regime in Ireland.[46] On 6 December 1544, Archbishop Browne, with the consent of his two chapters, granted the viceroy's secretary – for 'good services rendered' – various unspecified lands and tenements in the towns of Dunboyke, Kilbride and Mowlaght in the manor of Ballymore in perpetuity, reserving only a modest annual rent of 13s. 4d. per annum.[47] Although rent rolls and other estate

---

[44] The acts in question dated from 1380 (3 Richard II) and 1458 (36 Henry VI, c. 8), for which see *Statutes Ireland, John to Henry V*, pp. 476–7; *Statutes Ireland, Henry VI*, pp. 504–5.
[45] Griffith, *Exchequer inquisitions*, pp. 69–70, 87, 102–3.
[46] On Parker's property speculation generally see Brady, *Chief Governors*, pp. 37–9.
[47] NLI, Ainsworth's reports on private papers, vol. VII, p. 1582. It is unlikely, as Ciaran Brady has shown in relation to his acquisition of crown properties, that Parker held on to the interests in the property that he acquired from Archbishop Browne and the dean and chapter of Christ Church in the 1540s. As with the monastic and other properties he secured, these interests would have been resold or sublet to others at a considerable profit. The Dunboyke property alone was three carucates in extent (very roughly 360 medieval acres) and had yielded an income of 5 marks per annum to the archbishops of Dublin before being overrun by the Irishry in the Middle Ages (*Alen's register*, pp. 58, 191). The submission of the Wicklow Irish to St Leger in the 1540s, and the increased prospect for peace and prosperity in the Ballymore region that this entailed, made Parker's investment in the property potentially very lucrative, especially given the low rent he was paying to Archbishop Browne.

and financial records are generally lacking for the diocese of Dublin in the sixteenth century, we know from contemporary testimonies – including, especially, the testimony of Browne's successor as archbishop, Hugh Curwen – that the Parker grant was typical of many of Browne's property dealings at this time. Curwen asserted that his predecessor had 'without any reasonable consideration, alienated, discontinued, granted and made away to sundry persons in fee simple, fee tail and fee farm a great part of the best possessions' of the see of Dublin. Indeed, Browne's activities had 'reduced' the archbishopric 'to such poverty', contended Curwen, that he was unable 'to maintain *mensam episcopalem* in the estate of an archbishop' and was thus compelled to seek redress in parliament in 1557, in the form of a comprehensive act of resumption. Significantly, the act identified two categories of transaction which Curwen wanted voided. First, there were those grants and leases that Browne made to 'any person or persons by covin [collusion], or whereupon the old accustomed rent and more is not reserved' – these were the grants that benefited clients of the viceroy, such as Parker. The second category consisted of those 'leases or demises . . . of the possessions of the . . . archbishopric' that were made 'to the use of the said George, of any bastard of his or of any person reputed for his child or bastard'.[48]

Yet while Browne's property dealings were distinguished and categorised by Archbishop Curwen in terms of those who benefited from them, it is also the case that they shared one common feature which gave them an underlying unity: namely, that many of them were executed in a fraudulent manner, and that this was done with the full co-operation of the viceroy's administration. Curwen's act of resumption of 1557, for example, relates that the formalities of the crown's licensing system were almost entirely dispensed with during the 1540s and 1550s when it came to the disposal of the see of Dublin's property. The property 'was alienated . . . and put away without any licence of your majesties, or of any of your progenitors, or without any ad quod dampnum sued forth upon the same'. This, of course, was to cover up the fact that, in the majority of cases, it was being granted away forever to the archbishop's sons or to the viceroy's clients, without, as the act stated, 'any reservation of any yearly rents, profits, commodities or other casualties rising, or in any wise growing of and upon the said premises'.[49] As a result, it was not only Archbishop Curwen who lost out on real or potential income from his archbishopric. The actions of the archbishop and viceroy also affected the revenue streams of the crown in

---

[48] Transcript of a statute of 3 and 4 Philip and Mary in favour of Hugh Curwen, archbishop of Dublin, voiding all of Browne's alienations of see property: TCD, MS 578, f. 22v.
[49] Ibid.

Ireland, for during the Browne episcopacy few licences of alienation were either sought or paid for by the archbishop, while the potential overall value to the crown of having the custody of the 'temporalties' of the see during periods of vacancy was also considerably reduced.[50]

The avoidance of the formal licensing system was one of a number of sharp practices employed by Browne in his property dealings in the 1540s and 1550s. It was also alleged – by an anonymous observer, writing in the late 1540s – that he made alienations and reversionary leases 'of the most of his bishopric to his children, Robert Bathe and other[s]', including a series of transactions that were falsely dated.[51] Further, the act of resumption of 1557 indicated that through secret, collusive actions, devices like corrodies, pensions, annuities and appointments to diocesan offices were also exploited to hide the fraudulent disposal of property. One beneficiary of such a device was Patrick Barnewall of Grace Dieu, the king's prime sergeant-at-law and solicitor general, who in November 1546 was granted the constableship of the manor of Swords forever. As part of this grant, that is, in satisfaction of the £5 annuity associated with the office, Barnewall got his hands on some very desirable properties in the manors of Swords and Clonmethan at a knockdown rent of 39s. per annum.[52]

Intricate transactions of this sort, and with the same underlying intent to serve the needs of the viceroy and the archbishop's family, continued apace throughout the 1540s. Indeed, by the end of the decade, Browne's position had become so compromised that the viceroy, at least, was prepared to act as if there were no restrictions upon the schemes that might be conceived to wrest his remaining properties from him. Thus, for example, in the early months of 1548, and in association with a syndicate of senior clergymen from Browne's diocese, including James Humphrey, St Leger hatched a plan

---

[50] Ibid. St Leger granted Browne a general pardon on the eve of his replacement as viceroy in May 1548 (*Fiants, Edward VI*, no. 207). This was one of a spate of pardons that he issued in the last weeks of his first viceroyalty (*Fiants, Edward VI*, nos. 161–212 *passim*), and may have been intended to cover all the alienations of see property which the archbishop had made to his sons and the viceroy's clients since the mid-1540s.

[51] TNA: PRO SP 61/1, no. 141, printed in Shirley, *Church in Ireland 1547–1567*, pp. 18–20, at p. 18. Christopher Maginn has suggested that the author of this document may have been William Brabazon (Maginn, 'A window on mid-Tudor Ireland', pp. 465–70). However, as Brabazon himself was a major beneficiary of the archbishop's property dealings, this seems unlikely. For Brabazon's grants see RCB, D6/113, no. 3 ('Inquisitions in Edward VI's and Queen Mary's reigns, relating to the archbishopric of Dublin'); Griffith, *Exchequer inquisitions*, pp. 133–5.

[52] Statute 3 and 4 Philip and Mary in favour of Hugh Curwen, archbishop of Dublin, voiding all of Browne's alienations of see property (TCD, MS 578, f. 22v); *Fiants, Henry VIII*, no. 510. In this instance, Browne did obtain a licence from the crown. Barnewall was also a significant beneficiary of St Leger's distribution of the crown's monastic property for which see *Fiants, Henry VIII*, no. 335.

to trade in some of the rectories he had acquired from the crown from the dissolved priory of Graney, in exchange for temporal lands worth £50 per annum. The manorial properties of the see of Dublin were, inevitably, a prime target for this exchange, and the first step in the process, involving the alienation of the rectories to the holding syndicate, was completed in April 1548. However, the second step in the process, the transfer of see property, was still outstanding when St Leger was replaced as viceroy and returned to England, in the following month. Nonetheless, he remained undaunted and confident that Browne would play his expected part. In the following July, therefore, he was still petitioning Sir William Cecil, the master of requests, to give him licence to effect the transfer from his London base at Southwark.[53]

It is not known now whether this particular transaction was ever brought to a satisfactory conclusion for St Leger. What is certain, however, is that from the mid-1540s many comparable transactions were completed, by means of which substantial tracts of the archiepiscopal patrimony of the see of Dublin were frittered away by Archbishop Browne, in order to support his own family or to provide a supplementary resource to maintain St Leger's client base.[54] It is also the case that this asset-stripping process could not have been executed without the active support and collaboration of Dublin's two cathedral chapters. The historical significance of the ecclesiastical establishment's complicity in Archbishop Browne's property give-away of the 1540s cannot be overestimated. Through and by means of their participation in the archbishop's property dealings, the leading clergy were drawn inexorably into the heart of the 'king's party', and gently induced into accepting the viceroy's political ideology, which comprehended not only the notion of Henry VIII's kingly rule in Ireland, but also the doctrine of the royal supremacy that many of the same clergy had had such difficulty with in the late 1530s. An easy familiarity with the deputy and his circle, and a willingness to engage in a variety of business transactions with the regime, were the most visible signs of the clerical elite's assimilation, features that were particularly marked amongst those clergymen who had played a part in establishing and maintaining Archbishop Browne's marriage settlement after 1542.

One of the most prominent of these figures was Robert Eustace, the prebendary of Rathmichael who, at the time Archbishop Browne's marital difficulties emerged in the summer of 1541, had been a member of the

---

[53] *CSPD Edward VI*, p. 52; *Fiants, Edward VI*, no. 162.

[54] For some examples of Archbishop Curwen's efforts to resume properties alienated by Browne see NAI, RC6/1, p. 60 (Dunlavin and other townlands in the manor of Ballymore) and Morrin, *Patent rolls*, i, p. 494 (the manor of Tallaght).

chapter of St Patrick's for close to twenty years.[55] Throughout this time, the Oxford-educated Eustace had displayed a decidedly worldly streak and had built up strong connections, on foot of his own gentry family background, with some of the most prominent families in Co. Dublin, including the Trimblestone Barnewalls and the St Lawrences, lords of Howth, for whom he had acted as a trustee in a variety of property and other legal transactions.[56] Significantly, Eustace continued to perform this function even after the families began to speculate in the booming market in monastic properties that Lord Deputy St Leger engineered in the early 1540s. Thus, for example, in the summer of 1542 he was separately engaged both by Patrick Barnewall of Grace Dieu, the king's prime sergeant-at-law and solicitor general, and Sir Thomas Luttrell of Luttrellstown, the chief justice of Common Pleas, to act as an agent in their purchasing of the sites of three friaries in Cos. Kilkenny and Kildare.[57] Eustace's connections and experience in dealing with conveyancing matters drew him, inevitably, to the attention of Archbishop Browne, who saw in the prebendary of Rathmichael a figure who could assist him in executing the property trusts that he intended to put in place for his sons. It was not long, therefore, before Eustace was appointed as one of the guardians of the three boys and, in reward for his efforts, the archbishop promoted him to the valuable prebend of Mulhuddart around 1545.[58] By the mid-1540s, then, it was clear that Eustace had forged very strong links with a number of the key constituencies of the 'king's party', including Archbishop Browne's family circle. However, his acceptance of the new orthodoxy, and his absorption into the 'king's party', was finally sealed in February 1546 when, taking his cue from many of the figures on whose behalf he acted over the years, he acquired his own ambitions to become a property speculator, and used his connections to secure a twenty-one-year leasehold interest in three chapels that had once belonged to the priory of St Peter's, Trim.[59]

Not all of the interactions that took place between the Dublin ecclesiastical establishment and Lord Deputy St Leger's regime at this time led

---

[55] The earliest notice dates from 1523, when he was one of the prebendaries of Tipperkevin (*Alen's register*, p. 269). The earliest notice of him as prebendary of Rathmichael dates from 1528 (*Pembroke deeds*, p. 69).

[56] *BRUO 1501–40*, p. 195; Griffith, *Exchequer inquisitions*, pp. 26, 50–1, 123–5, 136–8, 168–70, 298–9; Morrin, *Patent rolls*, i, pp. 30, 83, 131, 193–4, *Fiants, Henry VIII*, nos. 270, 473, 510; *Ormond deeds 1509–47*, p. 193; *Pembroke deeds*, p. 64. Robert was a younger brother of John Eustace, a member of the Kildare gentry, resident in Confy (Griffith, *Exchequer inquisitions*, pp. 130–3).

[57] *Carew MSS, 1515–74*, pp. 199–200; Morrin *Patent rolls*, i, p. 190.

[58] *CCD*, no. 1220; Lawlor, *Fasti of St Patrick's*, p. 138. The earliest surviving notice of Eustace as prebendary of Mulhuddart dates from February 1546 (*Fiants, Henry VIII*, no. 473)

[59] *Fiants, Henry VIII*, no. 473.

necessarily to the enrichment of individual clerics. Some members of the chapter of St Patrick's, for example, were prepared to give back a part of what they had gained, in order to display their allegiance to, and cement their relationship with the 'king's party'. James Humphrey, the precentor of St Patrick's, was a case in point. In April 1546, he decided that he would distribute a share of the proceeds he had gained – as a result of the licence granted by the viceroy to the canons of St Patrick's in August 1544 – to another staunch St Leger ally, Bishop Edward Staples of Meath, in the form of an annual pension of £20, to be taken out of his supernumerary living of Painestown.[60] In one respect, this gesture was unremarkable, for it is known that Humphrey had enjoyed close relations with Bishop Staples as far back as the late 1530s, when the two men had come together in their opposition to Archbishop Browne's aggressive reformist activities.[61] However, the gesture can also be seen as part of a broader development in which the old religious conservative established ties with a wider circle in the 'king's party', including, most notably, his former enemy Archbishop Browne and the two families, the Miaghs and the Bathes, that looked after the interests of Browne's children. Indeed, after his death in 1555, the strength of the ties that had developed between Humphrey and Browne's extended family – ties which had their roots in the viceroy's intervention in the crisis surrounding the archbishop's marriage in 1541–2 – was revealed by his appointment of Robert Bathe, the man who had taken Katherine Miagh as his wife in 1542 after the precentor and his colleagues had processed her divorce from Browne, as executor of his will.[62]

There is considerable evidence, then, that Lord Deputy St Leger lured many of Dublin's most senior clergymen into the web of economic and social relationships that he had spun in the 1540s; and that, as a result, they were assimilated, almost imperceptibly, into the 'king's party'. Yet, although this represented a considerable political achievement in its own right, and ensured that the English Pale enjoyed an exceptional period of religious consensus and tranquillity in the 1540s, which contrasted markedly with the religious division prevailing in England at this time,[63] it did not affect greatly the viceroy's broader political agenda of securing the incorporation of the independent Gaelic lordships into the kingdom of Ireland. In terms of maintaining the security and prosperity of the English Pale, one of the biggest challenges facing St Leger was the reform of Gaelic

---

[60] Morrin, *Patent rolls*, i, pp. 116, 123. [61] See above, pp. 109–10.
[62] NAI, RC 6/1, p. 62. Bathe is known to have had at least one child, a daughter, Alison, with Browne's ex-wife (Fisher Abstracts: Dublin Consistorial Wills, GO MS 290, pp. 18–19; NAI, Salved Chancery Pleadings, N/147).
[63] On the division in England see Ryrie, *Gospel and Henry VIII*, *passim*; MacCulloch, *Thomas Cranmer*, pp. 275–348.

Ulster, and the need to identify a mechanism to bring about the submission of Ulster's most powerful lord, Con Bacagh O'Neill, and the integration of his lordship into the English polity in Ireland. Traditionally, the crown's engagement with the O'Neills had been channelled through the house of Kildare, as the clan had been among the most prominent members of the vast network of clients the Fitzgeralds had maintained in Ireland in the late medieval period. However, following the Geraldines' disastrous rebellion in the mid-1530s, this conduit to the O'Neills had been closed off, and neither of the other two great English Irish houses, Ormond and Desmond, had sufficient influence in Ulster to provide an alternative.

In these unpromising circumstances, the viceroy had to look elsewhere for support for his reform project and turned to the only other English institution in Ireland with which the O'Neills had had a consistent historical engagement: the Church of Armagh *inter Anglicos*. Specifically, in collaboration with the former prior of Ardee, and veteran canon lawyer, George Dowdall, who he advanced to the archbishopric of Armagh in 1542–3, the viceroy sanctioned the utilisation of the canon law as a means of enforcing the treaties that had been established between the crown and independent lords of Gaelic Ulster in the early 1540s. Whether it was part of his calculations or not, the pursuit of this course did more than simply address an immediate political need. The formal adoption of Armagh's canonical processes into his reform project gave recognition to and validated the traditional canonical culture of the archdiocese and that of the English Pale more generally. More than anything that St Leger did during his viceroyalty, it was this recognition of the Pale clergy's cherished canonical culture, and his willingness to embed it within his own political reform project, that convinced his new clients in the ecclesiastical administration in Dublin that their acceptance of Henry VIII's Reformation was, after all, a legitimate and orthodox undertaking.

III

That St Leger would form such a partnership with George Dowdall in the 1540s could not have been easily predicted at the outset of his viceroyalty. On assuming office, the viceroy's primary concern was to consolidate his support amongst the anti-Grey and pro-reformist faction on the Irish council and, initially at least, he tended to accept its analysis that the leading conservative clergymen in the English Pale were not to be trusted or patronised. Dowdall stood out amongst this group of untrustworthy clerics. Not only had he been a political ally of St Leger's much despised predecessor, Lord Leonard Grey,[64] but his religious conservatism was deemed by

---

[64] See above, p. 111.

the viceroy's closest political advisors to be so intractable – as late as 1538, for example, Sir Thomas Cusack had described Dowdall as 'such a papistical fellow' that he was able 'to corrupt a whole country'[65] – that there seemed to be little prospect that he would assume high office under the new viceroy. Certainly, when St Leger's regime looked at drawing up a short list of candidates to replace the sickly and moribund George Cromer as archbishop of Armagh in the opening months of 1541, Dowdall's name did not feature very prominently. Instead, the viceroy opted for a more compliant figure and recommended the appointment to Henry VIII of an unnamed son of Richard Nugent, the late baron of Delvin.[66]

Within weeks of this recommendation having being made, however, the situation changed dramatically. Not only did the king greet Nugent's candidacy with little enthusiasm, which effectively quashed it, but he also announced his intention – in the same communication of 26 March 1541 – to put in place new legislation to rid the Irish church of incontinent clergy.[67] This announcement, of course, set in motion a series of events that culminated in the viceroy putting in place a new religious settlement in 1542, which reaffirmed the crown's support for traditional forms of religious practice and clerical behaviour, and which altered the political landscape in Ireland in a number of fundamental ways. Ultimately, it had the effects of lessening the viceroy's dependency on the pro-reformist clerics in his administration and of creating the necessary conditions for a rapprochement with those religious conservatives, like George Dowdall, who had been alienated by the crown's radical religious policies in the 1530s.

The viceroy effected his reconciliation with Dowdall at some point in the autumn/winter of 1541–2. St Leger spent much of this period in the Louth–Armagh region, during which time he led a series of hostings against Con Bacagh O'Neill in a bid to force his submission to the crown, and almost certainly encountered Dowdall, who was then official principal of the archdiocese of Armagh and based at Termonfeckin in Co. Louth.[68] The encounter was to prove significant. The viceroy found in Dowdall a man

---

[65] 'The extent of all the abbeys within the English Pale', TNA: PRO, SP 60/3, no. 87 (*LP* XI, no. 1416); Bradshaw, *Dissolution of the religious orders*, p. 126.

[66] The dispatch in which the deputy and council made this nomination is lost, but is referred to in the king's response of 26 March 1541 (*SP* III, pp. 292–300, at p. 299).

[67] *SP* III, pp. 293–4, 299. The king informed the viceroy and council that he considered Armagh to be 'a great and principal dignity' and commanded that the party be 'sent hither, that we might both see him, and further know how he is qualified for such an office'. Whether or not this visit ever took place is not now on record, but Nugent's candidacy was never subsequently mentioned.

[68] *SP* III, pp. 318–21, 336–8, 350–3; Bradshaw, *Irish constitutional revolution*, pp. 208–12; PRONI, MS DIO/4/2/13 (Archbishop Dowdall's register), pp. 1, 4, 13–4, 37–9, ('Dowdall's register', nos. 1, 4, 12, 32).

who possessed many of the skills and attributes that would be needed by his regime if it was to press ahead with the implementation of his reform project in Ulster, including an in-depth knowledge of the political and social affairs of the province, gleaned from over twenty years' service as a canon lawyer in the diocesan administration in Armagh;[69] an ability to speak and write in the Irish language; and prior experience of working as a crown envoy amongst the Irishry.[70] These were qualities that St Leger could ill afford to do without and he moved quickly in early 1542 to persuade the official principal of Armagh to enter his service. Dowdall responded positively to the viceroy's entreaties and worked assiduously, thereafter, to secure the full incorporation of the O'Neill lordship into the kingdom of Ireland, including accompanying Con Bacagh O'Neill to court for his investiture as the first earl of Tyrone in October 1542.[71]

But St Leger expected Dowdall to contribute more to the reform of Gaelic Ulster than merely act as his envoy with O'Neill. He was also required to help the viceroy solve a very substantial legal difficulty that had beset the viceroy's reform project from its inception. Collectively, the treaties and submissions which St Leger had negotiated between the crown and the Gaelic lords were envisaged as the first steps in introducing the common law into Gaelic Ireland.[72] However, the introduction and enforcement of English law in the Irish lordships was not something that could be achieved quickly.[73] It was a long-term aim which would only be realised on an incremental basis, especially in relation to matters such as homicide or the inheritance of property, where the indigenous customs and laws were so different to those prevailing in the English legal tradition, that any attempt

---

[69] Dowdall's career as a diocesan administrator and canon lawyer is traceable in PRONI, MS DIO/4/2/11 (Archbishop Cromer's register), Book I, ff. 3r, 5–10v, 31, 49–51, 53, 60, 109r–110r, 111 and Book II, ff. 13v, 29v-30, 62v, 64v ('Cromer's register', Book I, nos. 9, 19, 47, 64, 68, 77, 146, 149 and Book II, nos. 30, 70, 153, 158); PRONI, MS DIO/4/2/13 (Archbishop Dowdall's register), pp. 1, 4, 13–4, 37–9, ('Dowdall's register', nos. 1, 4, 12, 32); see also Gwynn, *Medieval province of Armagh*, pp. 261–2; Murray, 'Tudor diocese of Dublin', pp. 160–1.

[70] Depositions of the Baron of Slane and Sir George Dowdall, late prior of Ardee, concerning the treasons and misdemeanours of Lord Leonard Grey, 23 October 1540: TNA: PRO, SP 60/9, no. 62; for evidence of Dowdall's linguistic abilities see the agreement between himself and O'Neill from 16 December 1555, which is written in Irish and preserved in the Armagh Breviary: M.V. Ronan, 'Some Medieval Documents', *JRSAI* 7 (1937), pp. 239–41; and T. Gogarty (ed.), 'The Archbishop of Armachane's opinion touching Ireland', *LASJ* 2, no. 2 (1909), p. 153, where Dowdall explains the ancient division of Ireland into five parts 'as they did, and doth yet in their language call it, *Cuig cuigid i ne hernon*'.

[71] *Carew MSS 1515–74*, pp. 188 (no. 166), 190–3 (no. 169); Bradshaw, *Dissolution of the religious orders*, pp. 126–7; *LP* XVII, nos. 890, 924; *APC 1542–47*, pp. 36, 37.

[72] See, for example, the various agreements reached with O'Neill in 1542 (*Carew MSS 1515–74*, pp. 188–93, 198–9).

[73] The point was acknowledged in a letter from the Irish council and peers to Henry VIII on 20 March 1546 (*SP* III, pp. 560–1).

to impose common-law rulings would, at best, have been disregarded or, at worst, violently opposed. Political reality, then, dictated that caution and gradualism would be the bywords of St Leger's reform project.[74] Yet, in the meantime, there still remained the very substantial problem of finding alternative and effective sanctions to ensure that basic law and order would prevail while the common law took root, or to ensure that the basic terms of the treaties themselves would be upheld. It was in respect of this legal conundrum that the viceroy envisaged Dowdall making his most telling contribution to the reform project. As an experienced canon lawyer and diocesan administrator, the viceroy looked to him to provide a ready-made solution in the form of the customary canonical procedures that the ecclesiastical authorities in Armagh had developed to curb their age-old 'O'Neill problem'.

The 'O'Neill problem' traditionally manifested itself in the clan's encroachment upon episcopal property, and in its imposition of 'coign and livery' upon the archbishop of Armagh's tenants. Generally speaking, the church authorities would counter these offences by activating an elaborately choreographed ritual, which began with the reprehension of the O'Neills and their followers with formal canonical censures. The purpose of these censures was to bring them to the negotiating table to resolve the issues in dispute. Once there, formal concords would be established between the parties in which the O'Neills would solemnly undertake, usually upon the Gospels and upon Armagh's sacred relics, to respect and uphold the rights of the church in the future.[75] While it was true that most of these agreements only lasted as long as the O'Neills believed they would derive some political benefit from them, and that they had to be renegotiated time and time again, the process was significant in three respects. First, it ensured that the church was allowed to function properly, albeit in a fitful manner, in what was a generally inhospitable environment. Second, it provided the English Irish officials in Armagh *inter Anglicos* with a very practical means of realising in the present the reforming, canonical imperative that had underpinned the original English conquest of Ireland, and which lay at the heart of the canonical ethos that they shared with their peers among the Pale's clerical elite. Third, it ensured that canon law was the normal legal medium for settling civil disputes between the Church authorities and the 'wild Irish'.

It was the latter feature, in particular, that attracted the viceroy. If the Armagh canonical process could be utilised not just in cases pertaining to

---

[74] On the differences between Irish and English law as perceived by the political community of English Ireland see the observations in Sir Thomas Cusack's 'Device' (*SP* III, pp. 326–8). See also Bradshaw, *Irish constitutional revolution*, pp. 205–6.

[75] On the procedures generally see Watt, 'Confrontation and coexistence in Armagh', pp. 51–3.

the see of Armagh's property rights, but in respect of temporal causes more generally, and as a means of buttressing the treaties between the crown and the Gaelic Irish lords in Ulster, then the viceroy would have at his disposal a workable legal system with which to maintain basic law and order while he waited for the common law to become effective in the region. The necessity of putting such a system in place became a political imperative as soon as O'Neill made his submission to the crown. Thus, even as Con Bacagh was being invested with the title of earl of Tyrone in October 1542, the viceroy's regime took the first step in establishing the Armagh canonical system as the basic medium for maintaining law and order in the newly incorporated Gaelic lordships. At the instance of St Leger and the Irish council, Henry VIII was prevailed upon to grant Dowdall a reversionary interest in the archbishopric of Armagh – the office that would give him the fullest possible authority to control and direct Armagh's canonical procedures in support of St Leger's political objectives – which he took full possession of towards the close of 1543, in the wake of Archbishop Cromer's long anticipated death.[76]

With his ally Dowdall installed as the new primate, the viceroy's next step was to make provision for the formal establishment of canon law as the transitional legal medium through which he would proceed with the peaceful and gradual assimilation of Gaelic Ulster into a fully anglicised Irish kingdom. This was achieved through two agreements – one dated 14 July 1543, the other dated 24 August 1545 – which St Leger brokered between the two most powerful Ulster lords, Con O'Neill and Manus O'Donnell, the chief of Tirconnell. Together, these agreements were intended by the viceroy to bring to a final conclusion all controversies pending between the parties, including disputes over the lordship of Inishowen and the castle of Lifford, and formed a central plank of his overall reform strategy in Ulster. Yet, notwithstanding the facts that O'Neill and O'Donnell had already made formal submissions to the crown and had undertaken to live under the king's laws,[77] it is evident from the terms of both concords that the viceroy elected to look beyond the common law to the canon law to find effective sanctions to enforce them.

In the first of the two agreements, which was signed around four months before Dowdall's consecration, the viceroy took the opportunity to

---

[76] Cromer died in March 1543 – the royal mandate for Dowdall's investiture and consecration was issued on 28 November 1543: *SP* III, p. 429; Gwynn, *Medieval province of Armagh*, pp. 260–1; *Fiants, Henry VIII*, no. 380; Morrin, *Patent rolls*, i, p. 103. On Dowdall's sense of custodianship of this canonical process, and his willingness to use it a device for maintaining civil order see Shirley, *Church in Ireland 1547–1567*, pp. 82–3; Queen Mary to Sussex, 4 August 1558 (TNA: PRO, SP62/2, no. 64).

[77] *SP* III, p. 217; *Carew MSS 1515–74*, pp. 188–90, 198–9.

announce that his regime was fully supportive of traditional canonical structures, and that, in particular, it recognised the canonical authority of the new archbishop of Armagh. To this end, O'Neill, O'Donnell and the other inferior captains of Ulster were ordered by the viceroy to permit the new primate, the other bishops and the rest of the clergy to exercise their jurisdictions without any hindrance, and to have their ecclesiastical patrimonies free from all exactions and bonnaughts. However, the viceroy was equally determined to establish the parameters against which canon law would be utilised to support the achievement of his political objectives. Thus, as a reminder to the former papist Dowdall, and as a reassurance to the pro-reformist witnesses of the agreement, which included Archbishop Browne and Dean Basnet of St Patrick's Cathedral, he also ordered that the two lords should never accept the authority of the pope within their domains. In effect, the viceroy wanted to ensure that the endorsement he was giving to the canon law would not be seen to be providing a back door for the return of popery or to prejudice in any way Henry VIII's ecclesiastical prerogatives.[78]

The establishment of these principles enabled Archbishop Dowdall to become, in effect, the viceroy's chief magistrate in Ulster, and to use, as he himself would later express it, 'the censures of the church' in those causes 'where there is no remedy against the Irishry, that doth not answer writ or bill for any hurts that they do either to bishop, or any other inferior place'. These censures, which included interdict and excommunication, had long been respected by the Irishry, and provided a basis for settling civil disputes, where no other remedy could be had.[79] The advantage of proceeding with this approach was that it would enable the incorporation of the Gaelic lordships to advance within a reassuringly familiar legal environment, and allow for a necessarily long lead-in period before the potentially alienating introduction of the full system of common law.

The viceroy's commitment to this legal process, and his determination to see it implemented, was made explicit in the second of the two O'Neill–O'Donnell concords. As set out in clause four of the 1545 agreement, it was decided that the sanctions to be imposed for failure to comply with the terms of this agreement and, indeed, the earlier agreement, would be canonical in nature. Thus, the archbishops of Armagh and all other prelates and spiritual pastors were deemed to be 'intercessors upon the premises . . . so that they can fulminate censures and ecclesiastical penalties against the . . . violators of this peace'. Further, St Leger also made it clear that Dowdall's use of canon law as the transitional legal system of his reform

---

[78] *Carew MSS 1515–74*, pp. 205–7 (clause 7).
[79] Shirley, *Church in Ireland 1547–1567*, pp. 82–3.

project in Ulster represented the agreed approach of his entire administration, including the reformist clerics on the Irish council. Thus, in a move that would not have gone unnoticed by the conservative clerical elite in Dublin, Archbishop Browne was named explicitly as one of the prelates who was authorised to impose canonical sanctions on those who would break any of the terms of the 1543 or 1545 concords between O'Neill and O'Donnell.[80]

By the summer of 1545, then, the viceroy was exploiting canon law in a secular manner, according to the rules developed by the medieval ecclesiastical authorities in Armagh *inter Anglicos*, to advance his reform project in Gaelic Ulster. Moreover, in doing so, he gave the Armagh canonical custom a contemporary seal of approval, and provided it with a new rationale. Where in the recent past the custom would have been perceived as an expression of the traditional, pre-Reformation mode of English reform in Ireland, as enshrined in old papal grants like *Laudabiliter*, it could now be reasonably argued that it was an expression of the new English drive to reform Gaelic Ireland, as proclaimed in the act for the kingly title. For conservative clergymen like Archbishop Dowdall, and his peers amongst the clerical elite in the English Pale, the viceroy's utilisation of canon law acted as a bridgehead between the old and the new modes of reform, and demonstrated that the two were broadly consonant with each other. This development had important historical consequences, which extended beyond the secular into the religious domain. Its overall effect was to allay many of the fears and anxieties that the English Irish clergy and community had felt about state-sponsored religious reform in the 1530s, and to move them to a position where they were able to accept a Reformation, as mediated by the viceroy's religious settlement, that at one and the same time upheld Henry VIII's supremacy, maintained traditional doctrine and worship, permitted the depredation of ecclesiastical property and upheld the legitimacy of canon law as a tool for reforming the Irishry.

Thus the years 1542 to 1546 represented the high watermark of the Reformation in the English Pale. It was a period in which the eclectic makeup of the viceroy's religious settlement, and his unique style of government, combined to neutralise the discontent of English Ireland's clerical elite, and to unite them with their former enemies amongst the reform-minded clergy, in a common cause to reform and anglicise Ireland in a manner that was recognisably in line with the medieval efforts of the Englishry to achieve the same end. Yet if all this can be termed a success, it was a success which was

---

[80] 'et Archiepiscopi Armachensis et Dublinensis, ac ceteri omnes prelati et pastores spirituales, sunt super premissis intercessores . . . ita quod illi fulminare possint censuras et penas ecclesiasticas contra violatorem et violatores huius pacis', *SP* III, p. 507.

built upon uncertain foundations. In reality, the attachment to the Reformation that St Leger cultivated in the 1540s was created out of the rough and tumble of contemporary politics and was entirely dependent upon the continuance of a stable political environment, the endurance of a doctrinally conservative religious settlement and the prolongation of St Leger's own viceroyalty. Unfortunately, these conditions were well beyond the capacity of the viceroy to control or deliver, as he would soon discover. One by one, in fact, in an eventful period between 1546 and 1551, they were swept away, with the result that he quickly lost the early successes he had gained through his flexible approach to the implementation of religious change. The first sign of the emerging crisis occurred towards the end of 1545 and arose directly from a breakdown in his political relations with James Butler, the tenth earl of Ormond.

I V

Initially, at least, St Leger had enjoyed a positive relationship with the earl of Ormond. Not only had the earl and his supporters been adherents of 'the king's true subjects', the broad political alliance that had helped St Leger secure his accession to the viceregal office in 1540; but they had also been among the most vocal proponents of the group's political ideology – which was grounded upon firm monarchical, anti-Geraldine and anti-papist principles – and had exercised, as a consequence, some influence in the conception and elaboration of St Leger's early policies, including the decision to proceed with the enactment of the act for the kingly title in June 1541.[81] Yet, despite this early political understanding, and the fact that Ormond was a significant beneficiary of St Leger's distribution of monastic property in the opening phase of his viceroyalty,[82] the earl's support for the viceroy did not continue long after the passage of the act for the kingly title. Within months of the act having been proclaimed, it became evident that St Leger intended to establish a system of supra-factional politics in Ireland, which was purposely designed to limit the power of the great Irish lords, and which would necessarily place restraints on the Butlers' ambitions to replace the Fitzgeralds as the dominant political force on the island. Once they realised that the Irish political system was moving in this direction, Butler disenchantment with the new viceroy quickly set in.

The first sign of Butler unease appeared in the autumn of 1541, when Robert Cowley, the master of the rolls and an Ormond acolyte, attempted to undermine the viceroy's position at court by accusing him of adopting a pro-Geraldine stance in the conduct of government, and of using fraudulent

---

[81] See Chapter 4.   [82] *Fiants, Henry VIII*, nos. 161, 308.

practices in his stewardship of the crown's Irish possessions. St Leger saw off this particular challenge easily enough, largely because the Butlers failed to garner support for the attack from outside their immediate circle.[83] But the episode was instructive. It highlighted the fact that Ormond would pose a pervasive and potentially acute threat to the viceroy's position, and that, if left unchecked, would have the capacity to impede his plans to establish the kingdom of Ireland on a sound political footing. To address these problems, the viceroy instituted a series of measures against the earl in the ensuing years – including encouraging anti-Butler interests in the frontiers of the Ormond lordship, investigating the earl's conduct of government in his territories, and challenging a number of his feudal rights – which, collectively, were designed to bring him to heel. In practice, however, they served only to further alienate Ormond who, in contrast to the majority of the political community in Ireland, developed a deep mistrust of the viceroy in the course of the 1540s. The full extent of this mistrust, and the degree to which relations between the earl and viceroy had soured in the period, emerged in November 1545 when Ormond made public – in a letter to the lord privy seal in England – his belief that St Leger was intent not only on undermining his political reputation, but also on organising his assassination. This revelation, together with the general disquiet that the Ormond–St Leger dispute was now generating on both sides of the Irish Sea, moved the king to intervene and to attempt to bring the feud to an end. Thus, on 29 December 1545, Ormond was given permission to repair to England to present his case in person. In the following February, the viceroy was ordered to do likewise.[84]

On the surface, Henry VIII's intervention in 1545–6 seemed to herald nothing more than an exercise in dispute resolution, the ultimate aim of which was to restore amity between the king's deputy in Ireland and the premier peer of the realm. However, by the time St Leger reached England in April 1546, it was clear that Ormond and his supporters were intent on exploiting it to achieve more sinister ends: they were attempting to use their appearances at court to secure St Leger's removal from power altogether. In particular, through the earl's factotum, Walter Cowley, the solicitor general of Ireland, the Butler party had prepared and presented a book of articles against the viceroy, which criticised his conduct of government along familiarly Ormondist lines, and which the viceroy was forced to rebut point

---

[83] Brady, *Chief Governors*, pp. 41–2.
[84] Ibid., pp. 42–3; Edwards, *Ormond lordship*, pp. 169–73; Ormond to Lord Russell, 15 November 1545 (*SP* III, pp. 538–40) and Ormond to the English privy council, 20 February 1546 (*SP* III, pp. 550–1); Irish council to the English privy council, 5 January 1546, 26 February 1546 (*SP* III, pp. 545, 553–4); *APC 1542–1547*, p. 302; Morrin, *Patent rolls*, i, p. 125.

by point before the English privy council. St Leger defended himself against this opening salvo with some success. Cowley was adjudged by the council to have 'proceeded by malice' and was sent to the Tower of London on 28 April, while his master, Ormond, was bound over to attend daily before the privy council, and to submit himself to the king's judgement regarding the 'offences, enormities and misdemeanours' that St Leger had accused him of during his rebuttal of Cowley's accusations.[85]

Yet this successful strike against Ormond can only have been of cold comfort to St Leger, for in the hearing before the council, and in the subsequent interrogation of Cowley in the Tower, it had become evident that the plot to overthrow him extended beyond the Butler circle to include the more substantial figure of Lord Chancellor Alen. The endorsement of Ormond's complaints by the Irish chancellor, and his willingness to support the intended coup against him, raised the stakes for St Leger immeasurably. Unlike the Butler spokesmen, Alen was capable of framing a more persuasive and penetrating critique of his government, the main lines of which he had already hinted at in a letter to the king that he and the chief justice, Gerald Aylmer, had drafted at the end of February. Set out in a series of questions, which Alen and Aylmer suggested should be the basis of an independent inquiry on the state of the realm to take place during the viceroy's absence, the lord chancellor intimated that the much vaunted efforts of St Leger to assimilate the Gaelic Irish lordships into the kingdom of Ireland represented nothing more than an illusory achievement, given that very little of the country was truly reformed; that the Irishry remained impervious to English law and custom; and that the Irish revenues remained disappointingly low.[86] The chancellor's disgruntlement with the viceroy was not something that could easily be overlooked by the English authorities. Thus, on 5 May 1546, the privy council sanctioned his call for an inquiry, though not in the manner he had hoped for. As part of the inquiry, Alen was himself summoned to appear before the council to explain his objections to the viceroy's rule. In addition, a set of sixteen interrogatories was also issued to each member of the Irish council, which they were ordered to respond to independently of each other in writing, and which, taken together, endeavoured to ascertain the truth regarding 'certain matters touching the state, policy and government of . . . his majesty's realm' of Ireland.[87]

By the early summer of 1546, then, St Leger was facing into the greatest political crisis of his career in Ireland to date. The re-emergence of what

---

[85] *APC 1542–1547*, p. 396; *SP* III, pp. 578–80.

[86] For the original questions, and their subsequent development into a more explicit critique of St Leger's government, see *SP* III, pp. 555–6, 564–5.

[87] *LP* XXI.i, nos. 920–4; *APC 1542–1547*, pp. 396, 403–4; *SP* III, pp. 566–7, 577–80.

was, in effect, the old anti-Grey alliance, which he had successfully exploited in 1540 to engineer his own ascent to power, now threatened to take that power away from him, and bring what had generally been deemed to be a successful viceroyalty to a sudden and unanticipated end. St Leger was determined, however, that he would not depart the Irish political scene in the same ignominious manner as his predecessor, and from the moment he set foot in England in April 1546 he used all his political skills and know-how to protect his position. For a start, he made sure that he arrived at court accompanied by a series of glowing testimonials from the great Irish lords, the Palesmen and the Irish council, which attested to his achievements in Ireland since 1540.[88] He was also careful to ensure that he gained access to the king, and that his personal ties with his monarch were reaffirmed. Thus, while Ormond lodged in London, and awaited the arrival of the lord chancellor, St Leger attended in person on the sickly king at Greenwich and acted as one of his deputies in the Garter ceremonies that took place in the early summer.[89] The final and most adroit political move which St Leger made at this time, however, was to secure administrative control over the English privy council's questioning of the Irish council. Not only did he ensure that one of his own confidantes, John Goldsmith, the Irish clerk of the council, was given the responsibility for administering the inter-rogatories to each of the Irish councillors, but he also succeeded in con-vincing the English privy council that the list of questions should not be released to any Irish councillor until Lord Chancellor Alen had boarded his ship, and was prevented thus from influencing their answers.[90]

These manoeuvres served the viceroy well. Although he would still have to endure a tense and uncertain few weeks immediately after the chancellor's arrival in England in July – during which time he participated in an inconclusive altercation with Alen before the privy council, and took part in what he considered to be the tedious activity of preparing written statements in support of his position – the appearance in mid-August of the Irish councillors' answers to the privy council's articles tilted matters decisively in his favour. Abbreviated versions of the councillors' answers, along with the written statements of the two adversaries, were read before the privy council in the presence of both men on 17 August 1546.[91] Not surprisingly, given that the process had been controlled by John Goldsmith, the councillors' answers backed St Leger's version of events and suggested that there was little of substance in the Alen–Ormond critique of his

---

[88] Brady, *Chief Governors*, pp. 40–1. [89] *LP* XXI.i, no. 736.
[90] *APC 1542–1547*, pp. 403–4. On Goldsmith see Brady, *Chief Governors*, pp. 31–2.
[91] *APC 1542–1547*, pp. 497, 517. For the statements of Alen and St Leger see *SP* III, pp. 564–5, 569–78.

government. The privy council concluded that what stood out from the evidence 'for the most part' was the chancellor's 'malice' against the viceroy. Alen was adjudged to have used 'all naughty means to set the earl of Ormond against the deputy to the subversion of the quiet state of that realm'.[92]

In August 1546, then, the viceroy had met and faced down the very substantial challenge mounted against him by the earl of Ormond and Lord Chancellor Alen, the 'subverter of deputies'. Yet, although it again demonstrated his formidable political skills, the victory achieved was not an unmitigated triumph. The events of the summer of 1546 had shown that the viceroy occupied a far from unassailable position and that he would have to take further steps both to buttress his authority and to invest his viceroyalty with a renewed political vigour. His most immediate concern was to weed out and crush all remaining traces of opposition to his rule. In particular, he resolved to end once and for all the influence of that meddlesome political grouping that had come together in the 1530s, and that had once supported him, 'the king's true subjects'. Lord Chancellor Alen, the longstanding ringleader of the group, was the first to feel the heat of the viceroy's anger. At the end of August, he was stripped of his office, committed to the Fleet prison in London and ordered not to interfere any further, either 'by act, writing or any other his means ... with the state of that realm or any manner [or] thing touching the government, order or policy of the same'.[93]

The removal of the residual threat posed by the Butlers and their allies soon followed. At St Leger's instigation, the king agreed to replace Walter Cowley as his solicitor general in Ireland. Further, in a more sinister development, the viceroy's principal political enemy, the earl of Ormond, met his end in suspicious circumstances in October 1546, having contracted food poisoning, along with a number of his servants, at a banquet hosted by Sir John Dudley, Lord Lisle. Whether Ormond's death was directly attributable to the viceroy's actions, or simply a remarkable coincidence, is now impossible to determine.[94] What is certain, however, is that the earl's death did not quell St Leger's determination to subdue all political opposition to his regime. With the Ormond and Alen threat nullified, the viceroy turned his attention to one of the last remaining figures associated with 'the king's true subjects', and one who, thus far, had barely featured in the high political drama of the summer, Archbishop Browne of Dublin.

---

[92] *APC 1542–1547*, p. 517.   [93] *APC 1542–1547*, pp. 523–4.
[94] *SP* III, p. 584; Morrin, *Patent rolls*, i, p. 140; for discussions of the circumstances, and evaluations of the evidence surrounding Ormond's death see D. Edwards, 'Malice aforethought? The death of the 9th earl of Ormond, 1546', *BSJ* 3/1, (1987), pp. 30–41 and 'Further comments on the strange death of the 9th earl of Ormond', *BSJ* 4/1 (1997), pp. 61–3.

On first sight, St Leger's pursuit of the archbishop seems odd for, up to the point of his departure for England in March 1546, Browne had continued to support the viceroy and had actively endeavoured to maintain the ties that had developed between the pair, in the wake of St Leger's career-saving intervention on his behalf in the crisis surrounding his illegal marriage in 1541–2. One example of this occurred around 1545 in the aftermath of Browne's promotion of Robert Eustace to the prebend of Mulhuddart. Eustace's promotion created a vacancy in the prebend of Rathmichael, which Browne duly filled by appointing the viceroy's brother, Arthur.[95] More significantly, and despite his former attachment to the Butler circle, the surviving evidence also demonstrates that the archbishop agreed with and supported the viceroy in his estimation of the earl of Ormond, and the negative impact he had on Irish affairs. In a letter written to Henry VIII in February 1546, in which he petitioned the king to settle the quarrel between St Leger and Ormond, Browne accused the earl of being 'more like a prince than a subject, more like a governor than an obedient servant'. He also criticised Ormond's use of coign and livery, because it was a form of 'extortion' which affected not only the earl's tenants, but also his own tenants on those occasions when the earl visited Dublin with his 'company of galloglass'. And he concluded this damning critique of Ormond by intimating that he had failed to defend the crown lands he had been granted 'on this side the water of the Barrow', and that there was 'more Irish order, more Irish rule, and more stealth' in these lands 'then was before a great while'.[96]

Yet, despite all this, St Leger was given reason in the summer of 1546 to question the archbishop's loyalty to him. As had been the case with Lord Chancellor Alen, one of Walter Cowley's written statements implicated the archbishop in the plot to overthrow the viceroy. According to Cowley, Browne had sent information to him in London, via one Walter Howth, an uncle of the lord of Howth, which resulted in him putting 'three notable articles' against St Leger in the book he had presented to the privy council in the preceding spring.[97] This hearsay evidence was not damning in itself. But in the highly pressurised situation in which St Leger found himself in the summer of 1546, Cowley's testimony would have quickly brought to mind

---

[95] Lawlor, *Fasti of St Patrick's*, pp. 138, 144; *Fiants, Edward VI*, no. 66. Arthur St Leger was a prebendary of Canterbury Cathedral. Of pronounced conservative religious tendencies, he was one of the leaders of the so-called 'Prebendaries Plot', in which opponents of the Reformation attempted to unseat Archbishop Cranmer in 1543. His appointment to a Dublin prebend would have given him the option of moving to Ireland if his position in Canterbury had became untenable in the wake of the failure of the plot (MacCulloch, *Thomas Cranmer*, pp. 285, 297–322; P. Marshall, 'Mumpsimus and sumpsimus: the intellectual origins of a Henrician bon mot', *JEH* 52 (2001), p. 581).
[96] *SP* III, pp. 555–6. [97] *SP* III, pp. 578–80, at p. 579.

the fact that the archbishop's attachment to Ormond and Alen predated, and possibly ran deeper, than his attachment to the viceroy. Moreover, it would also have reminded him that Browne himself had already raised doubts – in opposing St Leger's scheme to convert Christ Church Cathedral into a residence for the Irish council in 1543 – about the depth of his commitment to the viceroy's cause. Thus, having just survived a plot to topple him, St Leger was in no mood to conduct a lengthy or forensic examination of the evidence for or against Browne's involvement in the Ormond–Alen conspiracy. Although the case against him was slim, St Leger elected to reassert his authority over the archbishop and to punish him for the suspected contribution he had made to the attempted coup. Specifically, he chose to strike on the very matter on which Browne had stood against him in 1543. In October 1546, the viceroy secured the king's agreement to dissolve one of the archbishop's two cathedrals. This time, however, it was not Christ Church that the viceroy targeted. Rather, he proceeded against the once favoured secular cathedral of St Patrick.

The viceroy had other reasons, of course, for seeking the suppression of St Patrick's at this time: with an annual income of nearly IR£1,400 to its name, it was inevitable that he would consider dissolving the cathedral as he searched for untapped sources of revenue to re-launch his viceroyalty through a new wave of property distribution.[98] Yet, notwithstanding this, it is evident from the manner in which he approached the dissolution – at no point in the process was the archbishop consulted by the viceroy, nor was he allowed to participate in any aspect of it – and the fact that he possessed full knowledge of the damaging effects that the cathedral's disappearance would have for Browne in terms of the loss of patronage, and the disruption to his administration, that it was deliberately intended to undermine the latter's authority, and to send out a clear message to him that any act of disloyalty to the viceroy would not be tolerated.[99]

The process of dissolution itself began in early October 1546, when St Leger secured Henry VIII's support for the plan, and spoke with the chancellor of the court of augmentations about current administrative practices for the swift and efficient suppression of a religious corporation and the distribution of pensions to its members. All of this was done without Browne's knowledge. On 8 November, again without forewarning, letters subscribed by the English privy council were issued under the king's secret stamp to Browne and the dean and chapter of St Patrick's informing

---

[98] J. Murray, 'St Patrick's cathedral and the university question in Ireland, c. 1547–1585', in H. Robinson-Hammerstein (ed.), *European universities in the age of Reformation and Counter Reformation* (Dublin, 1998), pp. 3–7; Brady, *Chief governors*, p. 43.

[99] On the implications of the dissolution for the administration of the diocese see Murray 'St Patrick's cathedral and the university question in Ireland', pp. 8–9.

them of the cathedral's imminent suppression. This was the first notice that the archbishop was given that the dissolution was to proceed, and he was not requested at this or any subsequent point to give his assent to it.[100] The viceroy's determination to exclude Browne from the dissolution process went further however. On the same day that the letters announcing the cathedral's suppression were issued, St Leger and six other officials in his administration, including Bishop Staples of Meath but not, pointedly, the archbishop of Dublin, were appointed to receive its surrender. This was the first time that Browne had been excluded from a major royal commission concerning ecclesiastical matters since his arrival in Ireland in 1536.[101] Although the king commanded that the 'thing' was to 'pass immediately without delay', the dissolution of St Patrick's was not completed until early January 1547, because Precentor Humphrey and eighteen members of the chapter withheld their consent. Again, pointedly, St Leger looked to the dean of St Patrick's, Edward Basnet, and not their now out of favour archbishop, to break the canons' resistance and secure a voluntary surrender. This was achieved on 8 January 1547 after Basnet had subjected his clergy to the humiliating experience of forcible imprisonment.[102]

Overall, then, it is clear that the political convulsions of 1546, although entirely secular in nature, had a very significant impact on religious and ecclesiastical affairs in Ireland. In a bid to re-establish his political authority in the aftermath of the failed Ormond–Alen coup, St Leger had taken the unparalleled step of dissolving the see of Dublin's secular cathedral, and of putting his carefully constructed religious settlement, and the religious consensus that it had sustained in the 1540s, at considerable risk. As always, however, the risk taken by the viceroy was calculated. He pressed ahead with his plans in the belief that, with the right political handling, he could ride out this latest storm, and that his religious settlement could absorb the shock of the cathedral's demise. Thus, although the events of the autumn of 1546 undoubtedly reawakened many of the suspicions and fears that the clergy had previously held about state-sponsored religious reform,

---

[100] TNA: PRO, SP 1/225, f. 125r (*LP* XXI. ii, no. 212); TNA: PRO, SP 4/1 (*LP* XXI. ii, no. 475). For evidence that Browne never assented to the dissolution see the opinion of the English judges in 1569 concerning the legality of a lease he made after the dissolution: Sir James Dyer, *Les reports des divers select matters et resolutions . . . en le several reignes de . . . Hen. 8 et Edw. 6 et . . . Mar. et Eliz.* (London, 1688), f 282v; *Dignitas decani*, pp. 147–80. According to the judges, 'one [of two] churches, namely St Patrick's, with the consent of the dean and the most part of the chapter of the same . . . did yield and give up *without the assent of the bishop* into the king's possession the said church with all thereto belonging . . . [author's italics]'.

[101] *Dignitas decani*, pp. 141–3; Morrin, *Patent rolls*, i, p. 132.

[102] TNA: PRO, SP 1/225, f 125r (*LP* XXI. ii, no. 212); Mason, *History of St Patrick's*, p. 150; *Dignitas decani*, pp. 143–4; Morrin, *Patent rolls*, i, p. 132.

the viceroy endeavoured to cushion the blow by granting the canons of St Patrick's state pensions, which not only reflected the real value of their livings but, in the majority of cases, were also well above the valuations at which those livings had been rated by the exchequer in 1538–9 for the purposes of collecting the first fruits and twentieth taxes.[103] Two stalwarts of the 'king's party', James Humphrey and Robert Eustace, were amongst the beneficiaries of these pension arrangements. The ex-precentor was granted a pension of IR£60, even though his living was rated by the exchequer at IR£51 12s. 8d. The prebendary of Mulhuddart did even better – he received a pension of IR£33 6s. 8d. though the first fruits valuation on the benefice was just IR£18.[104] For men such as these who, in 1546, were reaching middle or old age, the viceroy's generous settlement probably did enough to secure, at the very least, a resigned acceptance of the fate that had befallen them.

Initially, at least, St Leger exhibited no similar inclination to lessen the blow that the dissolution of St Patrick's had entailed for Archbishop Browne. On the contrary, in the months that followed the suppression of the cathedral he continued to signal his displeasure towards the archbishop for his perceived complicity in the Ormond–Alen conspiracy. In March 1547, for example, he left Browne out of yet another major ecclesiastical commission which, on this occasion, related to the granting of faculties and dispensations pertaining to marital matters and clerical pluralism. The snub was compounded, once again, by the appointment of Bishop Staples to the commission.[105] In the same period, and echoing his earlier scheme to convert Christ Church into a permanent residence for the Irish council, the viceroy also obtained permission from the crown to 'treat' with the archbishop with a view to him surrendering his palace of St Sepulchre – in exchange for the house of the late dean of St Patrick's – so that he would be 'well lodged for the repair of our noble men and councillors at all times'.[106] But the viceroy did not execute this plan. Having decided, finally, that enough exemplary punishment had been meted out to him, he elected to call a halt to his proceedings against the archbishop and to endeavour to

---

[103] The cathedral's property was surveyed on 27 January 1547 by the suppression commissioners, the day before Henry VIII died, and again on 13 May 1547, after the accession of Edward VI and the granting of a new commission (Mason, *History of St Patrick's*, pp. 28–99 *passim*, 151–4, lxv; Griffith, *Exchequer inquisitions*, pp. 113–17). The Henrician survey survives in a seventeenth century copy in the cathedral's archive – RCB, C.2.1.27, no. 2; for a useful comparison of the first fruits valuations, the suppression valuations and the pensions granted to the cathedral clergy see Ronan, *Reformation in Dublin*, p. 316.

[104] *Fiants, Edward VI*, nos. 43, 46; *Valor beneficiorum*, p. 9.

[105] *SP* III, p. 582; Morrin, *Patent rolls*, i, p. 150; *Patent rolls 1547–1548*, p. 136.

[106] Morrin, *Patent rolls*, i, p. 151; Mason, *History of St Patrick's*, pp. 152–3.

normalise relations between them. Thus, in the ensuing months, not only did he not effect the exchange of Browne's palace for the late dean's house,[107] but when he set about disposing of the cathedral's property to his clients in the summer of 1547, he signalled a willingness to bring Browne back into the fold by granting him – in conjunction with his own brother, Arthur – a lease of the tithes of the archbishop's demesne lands in Ballymore.[108]

It seemed possible, then, that in the months which followed the collapse of the Ormond–Alen conspiracy, not only would the viceroy re-establish his political authority, but also that the religious settlement he had put in place in 1542, and the broad religious consensus which had been established on foot of it, would survive intact. The supposition, however, was to prove unfounded for, before the dust had settled on the events of the summer and autumn of 1546, the viceroy was presented with a new challenge that put his religious settlement at even greater risk than the fallout from the recent political crisis. On 28 January 1547, less than a month after the clergy of St Patrick's Cathedral surrendered their church to him, Henry VIII died and was succeeded by his young son, Edward. The accession of Edward VI inaugurated a more radical and now identifiably Protestant programme of religious reform in the Tudor dominions, which St Leger, as the new king's viceroy, had the task of administering and enforcing.

v

The Edwardian Reformation in Ireland was a curiously muted and, to modern eyes at least, a somewhat impenetrable affair. Indeed, despite the best efforts of its historians, it stubbornly refuses to submit itself to coherent interpretation. Among the difficulties that its historians face is the task of explaining why the godly regimes of Protector Somerset and the Duke of Northumberland spearheaded a Protestant religious revolution in England with such fervour, while at the same time exhibiting a startling level of detachment and remoteness – evinced in their failures to call a parliament to enact the new religious decrees, or to proceed with the suppression of the chantries – in relation to the religious affairs of Edward VI's other realm.[109]

---

[107] The ex-dean, Edward Basnet, was granted a life interest in his former residence in September 1547 (*Fiants, Edward VI*, no. 104).

[108] *Fiants, Edward VI*, no. 50; the bulk of the cathedral property was distributed to the viceroy's supporters on 21-year leasehold terms throughout the summer and autumn of 1547 (*Fiants, Edward VI*, nos. 32–111 *passim*). The tithes of Ballymore had belonged to the treasurer of St Patrick's.

[109] The definitive treatment of the campaign to enforce the Edwardian Reformation in Ireland is Bradshaw, 'Edwardian Reformation', pp. 83–99; for other useful accounts see Ellis, *Ireland in the age of the Tudors*, pp. 219–23; Heal, *Reformation in Britain and Ireland*,

The same contradictions abound even when the Irish version of Edwardian religious change is considered in isolation from what happened in England. Most historians agree that Lord Deputy St Leger remained the dominant political force on the island during the reign, and that he continued to play the leading role in the crown's efforts to enforce religious change. Yet they find it less easy to explain why the conciliatory and gradualist approach to reform that he employed with such success in Henry VIII's reign, did not yield similar results under his son, and are compelled to deliver the somewhat unsatisfactory verdict that the Irish were not enthused by the new Protestant doctrines.[110] The contradictions do not end here. They even extend to the leading ecclesiastical personalities of the period, including, most notably, Archbishop Browne of Dublin. Depending on the historical sources selected, it is possible to portray the archbishop of the late 1540s and early 1550s either as a papist, or as someone who was in the vanguard of Edwardian religious change.[111]

The existence of such contradictions in the sources, and in the treatment afforded to the Edwardian period by historians, are not accidental matters, or a reflection of the practitioners' inability to master the material. On the contrary, they reflect the real religious contradictions that existed on the ground in Ireland during this time. Yet, while it is not possible or, indeed, historically accurate, to explain these contradictions away, it is certainly possible to contextualise them and to come to a fuller understanding of what they mean and signify. The key to developing such an understanding of the Edwardian contradictions is to consider them in relation to what came before them: specifically, the religious settlement constructed by Lord Deputy St Leger in 1542. Much of what transpired in Ireland in the late 1540s and early 1550s resulted from the encounter between the viceroy's religious settlement and Edward VI's Protestant settlement, and from the viceroy's ultimately unsuccessful attempt to absorb Edwardian Protestantism into the same construct.

Characteristically, St Leger endeavoured to subordinate the religious demands of the new king's regime to his own political objectives, and to ensure that they did not disrupt or stand in the way of the implementation of his reform project. Thus, he sought to avoid or minimise religious contention, and consistently maintained the view that any attempt to convert

pp. 166–9. The Edwardian Reformation in England is best approached through D. MacCulloch, *Tudor church militant. Edward VI and the Protestant Reformation* (London, 1999).

[110] Bradshaw, 'Edwardian Reformation', pp. 83–99; Ellis, *Ireland in the age of the Tudors*, pp. 219–23; Heal, *Reformation in Britain and Ireland*, pp. 166–9; Scott, *Tudor diocese of Meath*, pp. 47–51; Lennon, 'The chantries in the Irish Reformation', pp. 6–25.

[111] Murray, 'Ecclesiastical justice and the enforcement of the Reformation', pp. 50–1.

the indigenous population to Protestantism – much like the state's effort to incorporate the Gaelic Irish lordships – should be undertaken by means of persuasion, and in a gradualist manner. Yet, notwithstanding the fact the St Leger followed this conciliatory course during his two spells as viceroy under Edward VI, his underlying aims of avoiding religious contention, and of maintaining the same kind of consensus on religion that had existed in the 1540s, became increasingly difficult to sustain. In part, this was attributable to the fact that his viceroyalties in the Edwardian period were short lived. Moreover, they were also punctuated by the deputyship of the committed Protestant, Sir Edward Bellingham (April 1548–December 1549). Although the latter's viceroyalty was equally short lived, his attempt to force the pace of religious change with regard to the proscription of 'superstitious' ceremonies and customs, and the uncompromising attitude he displayed in his dealings with individual clergymen, began to erode the trust and allegiance of the religious conservatives that St Leger had won over to the Reformation in the preceding reign.[112]

The disruptive impact of the Bellingham viceroyalty was exacerbated by St Leger's inability to reconstruct a working political relationship with Archbishop Browne in the aftermath of the Ormond–Alen conspiracy. The viceroy had attempted to build bridges with Browne from the late spring of 1547. However, the archbishop was unwilling to reciprocate, because he considered St Leger's judgement on the part he had played in that conspiracy, and the retribution which followed, to be unjust and unwarranted. The first indication that their fractured relationship would not be healed emerged in the winter of 1547–8 when, under the guise of a proposal to the new king for the foundation of a university out of the revenues of the dissolved cathedral of St Patrick, Browne launched a thinly veiled critique of St Leger's role in the dissolution and the nakedly materialist motives which had underpinned it.[113] Thereafter, especially during St Leger's second spell as lord deputy in 1550–1, Browne openly distanced himself from his former ally, and endeavoured to undermine his standing before the Edwardian regime in England, largely on religious grounds. As part of this campaign against St Leger, the archbishop began to assert a new-found enthusiasm for the Protestant religion in his correspondence with leading English politicians, like the earl of Warwick, and to associate with overtly Protestant figures in the Irish administration, such as Sir Ralph Bagenal. His

---

[112] Bradshaw, 'Edwardian Reformation', pp. 83–7; Bellingham to Archbishop Dowdall, c. December, 1548 (TNA: PRO SP 61/1, no. 162); Bellingham to Nicholas Fitzwilliam, late treasurer of St Patrick's, c. 1548 (TNA: PRO, SP 61/1, no. 171, printed in Shirley, *Church in Ireland 1547–1567*, p. 30)

[113] On Browne's university proposal generally see Murray, 'St Patrick's cathedral and the university question in Ireland', pp. 3–11.

main concern, however, was to bring to the attention of the English authorities particular instances of what he now adjudged to be St Leger's toleration of papist practices, and his sympathetic handling of errant religious conservatives. Thus, for example, in the spring of 1551, he tried to impute that the viceroy was allied to an indigenous clerical network that was circulating tracts in defence of the doctrine of transubstantiation. Later in the same year, he also brought to their attention the fact that the viceroy had taken no action when, following the promulgation of the Book of Common Prayer, Archbishop Dowdall had refused to abandon the mass and the use of Catholic sacramentals in his diocese. So complete, in fact, was Browne's alienation from St Leger by this time that, even after the viceroy's recall in the spring of 1551, the archbishop followed him to court where he laid charges of treason against him which, for a brief period in the spring of 1552, led to him being excluded from Edward VI's privy chamber.[114]

Thus, as St Leger stumbled through his second short viceroyalty between September 1550 and his final recall under Edward in the following spring, all that he had achieved in the 1540s, in establishing a religious settlement that brought the religious conservatives and religious reformers together, disintegrated before his eyes. Archbishop Browne was the first to leave the community of ecclesiastics that had formed around the viceroy in the 1540s: he repudiated the settlement explicitly when, with the backing of a new English statute that legalised clerical marriage in the Edwardian Church, he abandoned the marriage settlement St Leger had brokered for him in 1541–2, by resuming his relationship with Katherine Miagh; and when he began to alienate episcopal property, on the same favourable terms that had once been the preserve of the viceroy's designated clients, to new Protestant allies like Sir Ralph Bagenal.[115]

Browne was not alone, however, in abandoning St Leger. Despite his most patient and conciliatory efforts, the viceroy fared little better in retaining support for his tattered settlement from amongst the conservative clergy. Although it had survived many shocks, and had been modified continuously since its inception in 1541–2, the challenge of accommodating

---

[114] Browne to the earl of Warwick, 6 August 1551 (TNA: PRO, SP 61/3, no. 45, Shirley, *Church in Ireland 1547–1567*, pp. 54–60); Morrin, *Patent rolls*, i, p. 494 ; W.K. Jordan (ed.), *The chronicle and political papers of King Edward VI* (London, 1966), pp. 102, 119; *CSPD Edward VI*, nos. 594, 609; *APC 1550–2*, pp. 456, 466. There is a useful if somewhat jaundiced discussion of the transubstantiation tracts, including an edited version of the text in M.V. Ronan, ' "Booke oute of Ireland in Latten", fresh light on the "Reformation" in Dublin', *IER* 25, nos. 33, 39 (1925), pp. 501–13, 606–22.

[115] *Vocacyon of Johan Bale*, ed. Happé and King, p. 68; Morrin, *Patent rolls*, i, p. 494. On the Edwardian legislation on clerical marriage in England see Parish, *Clerical marriage and the Reformation*, pp. 180–6.

and absorbing the radical doctrinal, and innovatory liturgical content of the first Book of Common Prayer, which St Leger himself was obliged to introduce during his second spell as King Edward's deputy in 1550–1, stretched it past the point at which it retained any meaningful continuity with its antecedents, and past the point where that other major clerical associate of the viceroy, Archbishop Dowdall of Armagh, could give his allegiance to it. Nothing demonstrated the viceroy's failure, and the collapse of the settlement he had framed in 1542, more graphically, than the resolute refusal of Dowdall, the viceroy's 'sage senator', to contemplate the abolition of the mass in 1550–1. The viceroy's recall in the spring of 1551, and Dowdall's subsequent defection and flight to the continent in the following summer, set the final seal on this failure.[116]

Yet while the collapse of the viceroy's settlement, and of the religious consensus which it supported, represented a significant political failure on St Leger's part, it did not lead to any dramatic polarisation of religious attitudes in Ireland. Overall, the Edwardian period was characterised by religious confusion and ambivalence, because the dominating figure of St Leger, and to a lesser extent, the other Edwardian viceroys, Bellingham and Sir James Croft (May 1551–December 1552), proceeded slowly and cautiously with the implementation of the new liturgical and doctrinal changes; and because the changes themselves, given the shortness of the reign, made little more than a superficial impact. No one embodied the religious ambivalence of the period more than Archbishop Browne of Dublin. Although Browne was thought by some contemporary Protestant observers to have fully embraced the Edwardian Reformation after 1550,[117] the surviving evidence suggests that he did not make any significant effort to enforce Protestantism on the ground throughout his diocese and province in the succeeding years. On the contrary, observers who were close to the scene, like the dedicated reformer, Bishop Bale of Ossory, remained unconvinced by the archbishop's rhetoric, and sceptical that he had resumed his role as a radical, reforming activist. Bale contended that one of the reasons his own clergy disobeyed his command that they follow the Book of Common Prayer was 'the lewd example of the archbishop of Dublin, which was always slack in things pertaining to God's glory'. Indeed, he went so far as to describe Browne as 'a dissembling proselyte' and 'a very pernicious papist ' who, in the past, had prayed for Ireland's Reformation, but now 'commandeth her to go a whoring again, and to follow the same devil that she followed before'.[118]

---

[116] Browne to the earl of Warwick, 6 August 1551 (TNA: PRO, SP 61/3, no. 45, Shirley, *Church in Ireland 1547–1567*, pp. 54–60).

[117] John ab Ulmis to Heinrich Bullinger, 31 December 1550, printed in *Zurich letters*, ii, pp. 425–8.

[118] *Vocacyon of Johan Bale*, ed. Happé and King, pp. 55–6, 67–8.

Browne's public adoption of a Protestant religious position in the Edwardian period, then, was more a reflection of the breakdown in his relations with St Leger than the adoption of a radical ideological stance. All of the archbishop's pronouncements and actions in support of Protestantism in the period represented, first and foremost, political arrows aimed against his former ally. Indeed, despite his public avowal of support for the new religious dispensation, and in an irony that would not have been lost on the viceroy, he also strove to maintain the good relations that he had established with the conservative clergy of his diocese in the 1540s. One example of this relates to his acquisition of the title of primate of all Ireland from Edward VI following Archbishop Dowdall's departure into exile in 1551. The essential arguments that Browne advanced in support of his petition for the primacy were deeply traditional in nature, and would have appealed to the archbishop's senior clergy, including the ex-prebendaries of St Patrick's Cathedral. Thus, like many a medieval archbishop of Dublin before him, Browne contended that the title should come to his see because of its inherently English character and because the archbishops of Dublin had 'since the conquest . . . been chief stays under the king in these parts of the realm and ever true to the crown'.[119]

As well as underlining his support for the cultural traditions of the see of Dublin, Browne was also careful not to alienate his clergy by promulgating and enforcing advanced doctrine in relation to the sacrament of the altar. And it appears he was successful in this aim. Notwithstanding his attacks against Dowdall at the council board for the latter's support of the mass, Browne was heavily criticised by radical reformers like the Scotsman, Walter Spalding (in the late 1540s) and John Bale (in the early 1550s), for his cautious approach to liturgical and doctrinal reform. Indeed, in the reign of Mary Tudor, while seeking a dispensation for his marriage from Cardinal Pole, he was able to call upon 'the testimony of trustworthy persons' – doubtless his own clergy – that, during the Edwardian period, he was 'a champion and defender of the truth of the most holy sacrament of the Eucharist'.[120]

---

[119] Browne to the earl of Warwick, 6 August 1551 (TNA: PRO, SP 61/3, no. 45, Shirley, *Church in Ireland 1547–1567*, pp. 58–9); above, pp. 41–5. Edward VI granted the title to Browne on 20 October 1551 (Morrin, *Patent rolls*, i, p. 250).

[120] 'et quod ut fidedignorum testimonio informati fuimus, tu veritatis sacratissimi Eucharistie sacramenti accerrimus assertor et defensor fuisti': Cardinal Pole's absolution of Browne 12 March 1555, BMD, MS 922, II, ff. 4v-6r, printed in M.V. Ronan, 'Cardinal Pole's absolution of George Browne', *IER* 5th series, 72 (1949), p. 195 and see also T.F. Mayer (ed.), *The correspondence of Reginald Pole* (3 vols., Aldershot, 2002–4), iii, p. 60; J. Durkan, 'Heresy in Scotland: the second phase, 1546–58', *RSCHS* 24 (1992), pp. 347–9; *Vocacyon of Johan Bale*, ed. Happé and King, pp. 55–6.

By the time Edward VI died in July 1553, then, the legacy of St Leger's viceroyalties on the religious condition of Ireland remained uncertain. No clerical grouping in Ireland, whether supportive of religious change or against it, had remained untouched by the viceroy and the eclectic religious settlement he had introduced in 1542. And no grouping had remained uncompromised by that settlement. Thus, in religious terms, the St Leger era in Ireland is best summed up as being a series of unresolved contradictions, which were embodied in the clerical circle that had gathered around the viceroy in the 1540s. At the centre of this circle were two archbishops: Archbishop Browne, who rejected the viceroy on a personal level, but who continued to operate in the pragmatic manner that he had become accustomed to under the tutelage of his former patron; and Archbishop Dowdall, who remained personally loyal to the viceroy, but who ultimately rejected St Leger's pragmatism in favour of principle. It remained to be seen, therefore, whether, and in what manner, these contradictions would be resolved, following the accession of the staunchly Catholic Queen Mary in the late summer of 1553.

6

Archbishop Dowdall and the restoration of Catholicism in Dublin, 1553–5

When Mary Tudor was proclaimed queen few of her subjects were in any doubt about the religious significance of her accession. The prospect that the old religion would receive official sanction once again was generally welcomed in Ireland.[1] However, while there is no doubting the existence of this residual affection, the common assumption that it led to a relatively smooth and trouble-free process of Catholic restoration is more questionable.[2] Certainly, this was not the case in the diocese of Dublin. Here, the restoration of Catholicism was neither carried forward upon a groundswell of popular affection for traditional religion nor relief that Edwardian Protestantism was about to be abolished. Nor was it even driven primarily by a determined queen through her officials in the Irish administration. Rather, the impetus for restoration came from a group of senior diocesan clergy whose actions on behalf of the old religion would provoke opposition at the highest level of the Irish administration. It was an unusual feature of the Marian restoration, which gives the lie to the belief that it, alone of all the religious settlements promoted in sixteenth-century Ireland, failed to engender any controversy.

I

That the senior clergy of Dublin would play such a prominent role in restoring the old religion in their diocese could not have been easily predicted at the outset of Mary's reign, for one simple reason. Clerical

---

[1] Edwards, *Church and state*, pp. 158–9; G.A. Hayes-McCoy, 'Conciliation, coercion, and the Protestant Reformation, 1547–71', *NHI* III, pp. 75–6; Lennon, *Sixteenth century Ireland*, p. 306.

[2] See for example Edwards, *Church and state*, pp. 158–9 and *Ireland in the age of the Tudors*, p. 78; M. MacCurtain, *Tudor and Stuart Ireland* (Dublin, 1972), pp. 65–6; Lennon, *Lords of Dublin*, pp. 130–2 and 'The Counter-Reformation in Ireland, 1542–1641', in Brady and Gillespie (eds.), *Natives and newcomers*, pp. 79–80; P. Williams, *The later Tudors. England 1547–1603* (Oxford, 1995), p. 111.

leadership in the diocese had been dealt an apparently fatal blow at the end of Henry VIII's reign because of the dissolution of St Patrick's Cathedral. Where, in the past, the dean and chapter of St Patrick's had provided the essential core of clerical leadership in the diocese, they had now been out of existence as a body corporate for six years and, like the monastic chapters before them, were in danger of becoming a dim and increasingly irrelevant memory.[3] Nothing demonstrated this more graphically than the spectacle of life in the cathedral close. The manses of the former canons, which had once symbolised their status, power and corporate existence, were now in the hands of officials from the Dublin administration, local gentry or out of town ecclesiastics. Deprived of their dwellings and ecclesiastical livings, albeit with pensions, the ex-prebendaries of St Patrick's had become a scattered, disembodied group. Notable conservatives from among their number, men like Thomas Creef and Bartholomew Fitzsimon, were beneficed and based outside the diocese. Others of a similar bent like James Humphrey, the late precentor, Simon Jeffrey, the former prebendary of Howth, and John Wogan, one of the ex-prebendaries of Donaghmore in Imaal, were either dead or approaching the end of their lives.[4] In fine, the memory and traditions of St Patrick's, and the clerical leadership that had once emanated from it, were becoming attenuated, and dying a slow but inevitable death. The former canons were adrift and, without some external push, they were quite incapable of influencing the direction of religious policy in the diocese of Dublin.

The succession of a new avowedly Catholic queen would appear to have been just the kind of stimulant that was needed to stiffen the resolve of the old clerical elite. But, initially, this proved not to be the case. Paradoxically, the effect of the new queen's actions in the first year of her reign actually inhibited their active participation in the first phase of the reintroduction of Catholicism, and dampened any ambitions they may have harboured for

---

[3] The devastation inflicted by the Henrician dissolution campaigns on late medieval monasticism is reflected in the small number of religious houses restored in England and English Ireland during the Marian period: D. Loades, *Mary Tudor. A life* (Oxford, 1989), pp. 246–7; Ellis, *Ireland in the age of the Tudors*, p. 225; Lennon, *Sixteenth century Ireland*, p. 306.

[4] Fitzsimon, the former prebendary of Tipper, was rector of Clongill in Co. Meath (*Patent rolls 1553–54*, p. 302); Creef, the former prebendary of Saggart, was prebendary of Tascoffin in Ossory Cathedral (Leslie, *Ossory clergy*, p. 144); Humphrey died on 29 March 1550, Jeffrey on 28 March 1555 (Refaussé with Lennon, *Registers of Christ Church*, p. 51; Mason, *History of St. Patrick's*, p. 156, nt. e); Wogan died *c.*1556 ('Index to the act . . . books and . . . original wills of . . . Dublin', p. 930); Fitzsimon, Humphrey, Jeffrey and Wogan were signatories to the letter of protest against Thomas Cromwell's attempt to curtail their cathedral's liberties in 1537, Creef had been sacked from his post as an archiepiscopal steward by Archbishop Browne for his 'popishness' (TNA : PRO, SP 60/4, no. 10, TNA: SP 60/7, no. 27). For the distribution of the prebendaries' manses see *Fiants, Edward VI*, nos. 32, 36, 50, 61, 69, 78–9, 88, 91–2, 101–2, 104, 113–14, 648, 762, 955, 1109.

resuming their position at the apex of the local clerical hierarchy in a fully restored and functioning secular cathedral. The main reason for this was the queen's reappointment of Sir Anthony St Leger as her viceroy in the autumn of 1553. St Leger had not stood out as a religious radical in Edward VI's reign. Indeed, Archbishop Browne had accused him of worshipping 'after the old sort' as late as 1551. Thus the queen had sufficient confidence in his orthodoxy to give him a leading role in the restoration of the old religion. Soon after his appointment, he and the Irish council were urged 'by their own doings and example' to encourage the celebration of mass and the divine service 'among our loving subjects . . . as near as they may that hath been of old time used'.[5] The fact remained, however, that St Leger had also been the architect of the dissolution of St Patrick's Cathedral and was thus responsible for destroying the old clerical elite's pre-eminent position in the local church. Moreover, as his reaction to the eventual re-establishment of the cathedral would demonstrate, he was still convinced that the dissolution should stand, as one of those reasons which had led him to this course of action in the first place – his need for a ready supply of crown property to dispense in patronage and to sustain a vibrant and politically popular market in real property, the chief means of retaining his party support – was still applicable.[6]

The inhibiting effect of St Leger's reappointment on the old prebendaries was exacerbated by the problems then plaguing their ordinary, Archbishop George Browne. Browne's initial disagreement with the dissolution of St Patrick's in Henry VIII's reign, his dislike of St Leger and the fact that he later took a prebend in the restored cathedral indicate very strongly that he would have supported its re-establishment at this juncture. Indeed, his claim that he had defended the Eucharist in the previous reign suggests that he would have even been quite willing to continue as archbishop of Dublin under a fully Catholic religious settlement.[7] In reality, however, there was no real likelihood that he would be allowed to do so, mainly because of his earlier marriage to, and continuing relationship with, Katherine Miagh, and especially after the queen appointed a clerical commission in April 1554 to deprive married, schismatic and heretical clergy in Ireland.[8] Browne, in effect, was a totally emasculated figure waiting for his inevitable demise. His most immediate concern was not to lock horns again with the viceroy on the matter of St Patrick's – an issue upon which he had already taken a battering at the hands of the same adversary at the end of Henry VIII's

[5] Shirley, *Church in Ireland 1547–1567*, pp. 54–60, 65–72, 75–6.
[6] Above, pp. 194–7.
[7] Ronan, 'Cardinal Pole's absolution of George Browne', p. 195.
[8] *Patent rolls, 1553–4*, pp. 302–3.

reign – but to negotiate a personal settlement in which his own future would be provided for. The combination of St Leger's return to Ireland and Browne's impending dismissal, then, served as a very strong deterrent to those amongst the former prebendaries who might have supposed that the reintroduction of Catholic doctrine and practice afforded an opportunity to seek again the past glories of their medieval history. The fact was that if the cathedral prebendaries were ever to see these days again, they would need to overcome the legacy of the immediate past and to find a mechanism to achieve this end. Above all, they would need the support of a very strong advocate, armed with very powerful arguments, to plead their case. Fortunately for the cathedral prebendaries, all of these requirements would be met in the person of George Dowdall, the recently reinstated archbishop of Armagh.

George Dowdall had risen to a position of national prominence in the early 1540s when, under Lord Deputy St Leger's patronage, he was appointed to the archbishopric of Armagh and took a leading role in the viceroy's great project to reform Gaelic Ulster.[9] Yet, despite his commitment to this project, and his broad acceptance of the Henrician Reformation – as mediated through the religious settlement that the viceroy had brokered in 1542 – Dowdall felt unable to comply with the basic tenets of Edwardian Protestantism that were established in Ireland in the early 1550s, and he went into self-imposed exile on the continent rather than abandon the mass.[10] Little is known about this period of exile save that, according to Ware, he 'lived . . . with the Abbot of Centre in Brabant' and that, following the death in November 1551 of his former rival, Robert Wauchop, the papally appointed archbishop of Armagh, he effected a reconciliation with the papacy. This led ultimately to him being provided by Pope Julius III to the archbishopric as successor to Wauchop on 1 March 1553.[11] Dowdall's principled rejection of the Edwardian settlement also brought him to the notice of Mary Tudor. Returning to Ireland via England, it is likely that he met the queen in the late summer or early autumn of 1553 – Dowdall later recalled that he was in England at the time of Queen Mary's coronation and that he returned to Ireland in Lord Deputy St Leger's company – during which visit he obtained confirmation of his

[9] Above, Chapter 5.

[10] Edwards, *Church and state*, pp. 138–141; Shirley, *Church in Ireland 1547–1567*, pp. 54–60; above Chapter 5. On Dowdall's first period as archbishop of Armagh see Gwynn, *Medieval province of Armagh*, pp. 264–74 and Jefferies, *Priests and prelates of Armagh*, ch. 7 *passim*.

[11] Gwynn, *Medieval province of Armagh*, p. 275; Sir James Ware, *The history and antiquities of Ireland* (Dublin, 1705), p. 146; P.F. Moran, *History of the Catholic archbishops of Dublin since the Reformation* (2 vols., Dublin, 1864), i, pp. 32–3; Brady, *Episcopal succession*, i, pp. 217–18.

papal provision and several other marks of royal favour.[12] These included
the restoration of the title of primate of all Ireland, which had been
transferred to George Browne and the see of Dublin by the late king after
Dowdall had gone into exile. They also included, in consideration of the
loss of his goods and his estate, and the spoil of his archbishopric during his
exile, a life term free of rent in the priory of the Crutched Friars of Ardee, an
establishment which he himself had ruled as the last prior before its dissolution in 1539.[13]

It was through yet another mark of royal favour, however, that Dowdall
first revealed his intention of involving himself in the affairs of the diocese
of Dublin. This was his placement at the head of the commission, appointed
by Queen Mary in April 1554, to deprive married, heretical and schismatic
clergymen in the Irish Church. The real significance of this commission lay
not so much in the task which it was originally appointed to fulfil, but in the
use that Archbishop Dowdall made of it as a vehicle for communicating and
realising his own particular vision about how the restoration of Catholicism
should proceed in the English Pale. The archbishop, in fact, had already
conceived a fully worked out programme of restoration, which he had
instituted in his own diocese and province. Built upon the traditional values
of the clergy of the English Pale – it encompassed the revival of independent
ecclesiastical jurisdiction, the unencumbered practice of the medieval canon
law and the renewal of the clergy's traditional role of reforming the Irishry
along conventional canonical lines – Dowdall had sought to revive Catholicism both by the enactment and enforcement of local synodal legislation,
and through the recreation of the politico-cultural setting in which it had
existed prior to the Edwardian Reformation. Given its politico-cultural and
canonical foundations, Dowdall's programme was profoundly attractive to
the former canons of St Patrick's. Ultimately, it instilled in them the conviction and confidence to argue that a full and proper restoration of
Catholicism in the heart of English Ireland would be wholly dependent
upon the re-establishment of their cathedral.

II

Dowdall's decision that canon law should reoccupy a central place in the
life of the local church was not simply an attempt at reviving one of
the many Catholic traditions that were abandoned or marred during the

---

[12] Dowdall and St Leger landed at Dalkey on 3 November 1553: Gogarty (ed.), 'Archbishop
of Armachane's opinion', p. 163; Chronicle of Dublin, TCD, MS 591, f. 17v.
[13] Morrin, *Patent rolls*, i, pp. 250, 301–2, 315; A. Gwynn and R.N. Hadcock, *Medieval
religious houses in Ireland* (London, 1970), p. 210. The grants to Dowdall were given under
the queen's signet at Westminster on 23 October 1553.

previous two reigns. Rather, its rehabilitation was conceived as the means and engine of reintroducing and enforcing all of them. For the archbishop, there were compelling tactical reasons for adopting such a strategy, the first of which stemmed from the disposition of the new queen. She was personally committed to restoring respect for the canon law and, in the opening months of her reign, made it abundantly clear in her correspondence and instructions to Cardinal Pole and the English bishops that the re-establishment of the old religion would, in the first instance, be an authoritative legal process, involving not only the repeal of all Edwardian legislation, but also the 'execution' of 'all such canons and ecclesiastical laws heretofore in the time (of Henry VIII) used within this realm'[14] If for no other reason, then, than to reaffirm his loyalty and orthodoxy before the new monarch, the archbishop had good cause to follow her lead and proceed with a canonically driven programme of Catholic restoration.

But it was not the only consideration. Dowdall was also aware – as an experienced legal mind who had served as archbishop of Armagh during the reigns of Henry VIII and Edward VI, and who was fully conversant with the theoretical and practical changes wrought by their regimes upon the ecclesiastical law[15] – that such a programme offered the clearest and speediest means of restoring the old religion within the Irish context. This was so because the Edwardian settlement had never been enacted by parliamentary statute in Ireland. Instead, it had been enjoined upon the crown's subjects through royal injunctions and through the proclamations of the crown's viceroys.[16] These injunctions and proclamations were effectively additions to the corpus of Irish ecclesiastical law, and could therefore be overturned, now that the Supreme Head was so inclined, simply by establishing alternative ecclesiastical ordinances that she would find agreeable. For Dowdall, this could mean only one thing: the enactment of new canons upholding the rites and traditions of the late medieval church, and he acted quickly and decisively to put them in place. Thus, sometimes towards the close of 1553 or in the early months of 1554, he convened the traditional

---

[14] R.H. Pogson, 'Cardinal Pole – papal legate to England in Mary Tudor's reign' (Ph.D. thesis, Cambridge University, 1972), p. 199. The meeting of minds established at this time between the queen and Dowdall goes a long way towards explaining the degree of political influence he exerted in Irish affairs for the duration of the reign.

[15] This is nicely illustrated by Dowdall's inclusion of some of the key Reformation legislation from Henry VIII's reign in his register, namely the acts of appeals and first fruits, and the acts for the twentieth part, for regularising the law of matrimony and for the payment of probate fees in the church courts (PRONI, MS DIO/4/2/13, pp. 153–67, 187–209, 212–13). For a general account of the changes wrought by the Reformation on ecclesiastical law see W.N. Osborough, 'Ecclesiastical law and the Reformation in Ireland', in R. Hemholz (ed.), *Canon law in Protestant lands* (Berlin, 1992), pp. 223–52.

[16] Bradshaw, 'Edwardian Reformation', *passim*.

canon law-making body of the province of Armagh, the provincial council, to a meeting in St Peter's Church in Drogheda. The council enacted eighteen canons or 'reformanda'. These included measures for the deprivation of married clergy, for the absolution of bishops and priests who had taken part in heretical rites, for the restoration of the 'ancient rites and ceremonies' of the church, for the rooting out of heretics by specially appointed diocesan and metropolitan inquisitors and for the burning of heretical books. Collectively, they restored the religious and ecclesiastical life of Armagh to the state it had been in at the death of Henry VIII.[17]

Dowdall's action, however, extended far beyond its tactical significance as a means of formally restoring Catholic practice, and of publicly demonstrating his orthodoxy. More than any other consideration, the enactment of the new canons was motivated by the archbishop's own ideological imperative. Dowdall perceived canon law as an embodiment of the value system of the community from which he had emerged and its rehabilitation was intended as a reassertion and reinforcement of those values. An ultra-loyal Palesman, he saw it as his essential duty to uphold and defend the English political and socio-cultural order in Ireland. Like so many of his community, the archbishop perceived the contrasting socio-cultural order of the 'wild Irish' as a lawless and barbarous threat to this system, and as something which he and his community were historically bound to reform. In particular, the community believed that the original English conquest of Ireland had been papally sanctioned in Adrian IV's bull *Laudabiliter*, because the Gaelic Irish were adjudged to be uncivilised and required reformation, especially in religious matters, where the survival of many of their pre-Christian social codes were deemed to be in direct contravention of the canon law. Although the first conquest had failed, and successive generations of the Englishry had gone native outside the English Pale, the historical imperative to reform the Irish along the lines envisaged in the first conquest – in particular, through the enforcement of the canon law – retained a powerful hold on the imagination of the Pale community, especially upon clergymen with a corporatist and canonical background like George Dowdall.[18]

---

[17] 'Reformanda in concilio provinciali Reverendissimi in Christo Patris ac Domini Domini Georgii Dowdall Archiepiscopi Armachani totius Hibernie Primatis celebrato in Ecclesia Sancti Petri de Drogheda Anno Domini 1553': PRONI, MS DIO/4/2/13, pp. 101–5 ('Dowdall's register', no. 85). The council took place sometime between Dowdall's arrival in Ireland on 3 November 1553 and the end of 1553 as it was then reckoned i.e. 24 March 1554.

[18] See Chapter 2. For a different view of Dowdall and his role in the Marian restoration of Catholicism see H. Jefferies, 'Primate George Dowdall and the Marian Restoration', pp. 1–18.

Dowdall's attitudes towards the Irishry are evident in a written submission he made to the English privy council on the eve of his death in 1558, in which he endeavoured to provide 'advice of some kind of reformation' to be applied in Ireland to eradicate the political and social disorder that had long bedevilled the country.[19] He affirmed in this text that he believed that the Irishry had remained in the unreformed condition they had been in at the time of the first conquest – the 'pride and ravenous behaviour' of their ancestors was 'printed' in their hearts – and that nothing, 'neither ... preaching, good counsel, good example or yet any good mean' that he knew of, could get them to change their ways. He therefore considered it 'the most godly way of reformation' to subdue and banish them and to plant the country anew with civil English settlers because they were 'always disposed to all naughtiness as murder, robbery, stealth and deceit and do not obey god or man's laws'. It was this disposition, he contended, that had 'moved the pope's holiness to give the king licence at the time of the first conquest to take their lands from them as the chronicles doth declare'.[20]

Despite this allusion to *Laudabiliter* and the original conquest, and his underlying belief that a new conquest and plantation were worthy of serious consideration, Dowdall was too much of a political realist to recommend the undertaking of a violent and expropriatory policy to the English privy council. Past experience had shown that a new and expensive reconquest of the island would not be seriously countenanced by the crown. The only realistic option available, therefore, was to continue with the conciliatory and gradualist approach to political reform that Lord Deputy St Leger had inaugurated in the early 1540s, and which sought to bring the Irishry under control and to assimilate them into the English way of life by peaceful and persuasive means. Yet, while Dowdall had and continued to be supportive of this approach, his passionate and trenchantly critical views on the Irishry should not be discounted as hyperbolic polemic. They were serious and heartfelt and provide, in effect, the context in which we must estimate the full significance of the canon law enacted by the 1553/4 provincial council.

[19] 'The Archbishop of Armagh's opinion touching Ireland delivered in 1558', BL, Harleian MS 35, ff. 195r-204v; Gogarty (ed.), 'Archbishop of Armachane's opinion', pp. 153–64. Dowdall's memorandum was specifically requested from him by the English privy council following an earlier submission in which he outlined these political and social ills (TNA: PRO, SP 62/2, no. 44).

[20] BL, Harleian MS 35, f. 197rv; Gogarty (ed.), 'Archbishop of Armachane's opinion', pp. 156–7. It is significant that Dowdall's notion of instituting a new conquest and plantation was, like so much of his thought, influenced by his legal background in the romano-canonical tradition: he justified it by quoting the civil law maxim, adapted from the Digest of Justinian, 'Quod princeps debet purgare provinciam suam malis hominibus'. For the original source see T. Mommsen, P. Kreuger and A. Watson (eds.), *The Digest of Justinian* (4 vols., Philadelphia, 1985), i, D.I.18.3.

For Dowdall, canon law was one of those very codes of law and civility which the Irishry and their clergy traditionally flouted, both through their general lawlessness and through a specific and aberrant set of ecclesiastical practices, which ranged from tolerance for the practice of clerical concubinage to the usurpation by the laity of clerical functions. By the same token, canon law also represented a code of ethics or behavioural standards, which his own community, especially its clergy, subscribed to, and which he believed set them apart from their Gaelic counterparts. More than that, it was a system of law which, at the time of the first conquest, had been designated as the standard of English civility to which the Gaelic Irish should aspire. In Dowdall's eyes, therefore, the English Irish clergy had a particular and historical responsibility to enforce the canon law amongst the Irishry, which he personally, at every stage of his career as a canon lawyer and archbishop, had endeavoured to discharge.

Nowhere was this more apparent than in the decision he took in the early 1540s to put, at the service of Lord Deputy St Leger's reform project in Ulster, the canonical practices that the diocesan authorities in Armagh *inter Anglicos* had developed to curb the O'Neills' depredation of the church. At base, the adoption of Armagh's canonical practices provided the viceroy's regime with a workable legal system to maintain basic law and order, and to buttress the treaties that he had negotiated between the crown and the Gaelic Irish lords, until such time as the common law took root in the newly incorporated Gaelic lordships.[21] For Dowdall, however, this approach had an additional and deeper significance. The recognition of the Armagh practices in the crown's treaties with the great Irish lords validated the canon law at a time when its legitimacy had been brought into question elsewhere in the Tudor dominions. Moreover, the treaties also strengthened his own personal canonical authority as archbishop of Armagh and gave him effective sanction to pursue, in the present, the reforming canonical imperative that had underpinned the original English conquest of Ireland, and which lay at the heart of the canonical ethos that he shared with his peers among the Pale's clerical elite. Thus, with the backing of the treaties, Archbishop Dowdall had been able to call upon O'Neill, as earl of Tyrone, to secure for him the obedience of the Gaelic Irish clergy of his diocese during the 1540s and early 1550s. Such obedience, although it was achieved more out of fear of O'Neill than out of respect for Dowdall's own office,[22] provided him with a solid base upon which to proceed with anglicising measures such as the ecclesiastical clauses in the act for the English Order,

---

[21] See Chapter 5 above.
[22] For Dowdall's own admission of this point see his letter to Lord Chancellor Alen, 22 March 1550, TNA: PRO, SP 61/2, no. 51.

Habit and Language.[23] It also enabled him to enforce the unmistakeably conservative canonical legislation that his diocesan synods and provincial councils enacted throughout the 1540s.[24] This is evident, for example, in the surviving record of the diocesan visitation of Armagh of 1546, which shows that the archbishop, both personally and through his commissaries, made very real efforts to enforce conventional canonical standards amongst the Gaelic clergy of the Irish deaneries of Orior and Tullaghogue, including the strict enforcement of celibacy.[25]

It is evident, then, that the theory and practice of canon law had exercised a great influence on Dowdall's thinking and actions, from the moment he began his career as a professional legist in 1518 through to his enforced exile in 1551. It is also clear that he would have considered the formal revival and rejuvenation of the canon law, through the provincial council he held in 1553/4, to be a matter of great cultural significance for himself and the wider English Irish community. In particular, coming so soon after the shock of the Edwardian attack on their traditional and canonically orthodox Catholic values, the revival of the canon law would have given them a renewed sense of their *raison d'être* in Ireland. This kind of thinking was implicit in two distinct aspects of Dowdall's programme for Catholic restoration. The first of these concerned the constitutional basis of the settlement, which was realised on 7 June 1555 when Pope Paul IV granted Queen Mary and King Philip a bull erecting Ireland into a kingdom, following a request made by Cardinal Pole on their behalf.[26]

---

[23] The act was transcribed into Dowdall's register under the title 'An act of presentation of benefices', which is indicative of a very pragmatic determination to enforce it (PRONI, MS DIO/4/2/13, pp. 174–82). It is printed in *Statutes at large*, i, pp. 119–27. The ecclesiastical clauses in the act reflected the traditional thinking of the English Irish clergy on cultural matters, and bound Dowdall and other prelates to confer spiritual promotions only upon those who spoke English, if such could be found, and to administer an oath to all others that they would endeavour to learn and teach English in their cures.

[24] On the Armagh synodal tradition, and Dowdall's contribution to it during the Henrician Reformation, see Jefferies, *Priests and prelates of Armagh*, pp. 96–102, 149–50.

[25] The record of the visitation is printed in A. Gwynn (ed.), 'Documents relating to the medieval diocese of Armagh', *AH* 13 (1947), pp. 24–6. For commentary and analysis see Gwynn, *Medieval province of Armagh*, pp. 272–4; Jefferies, *Priests and prelates of Armagh*, pp. 77–82, 102–5, 151.

[26] The bull was obtained during the embassy of Thomas Thirlby, bishop of Ely, Sir Edward Carne and Viscount Montague who were in Rome to make solemn obedience to the Holy See in the wake of England's return to the papal fold: L. Von Pastor, *The history of the Popes from the close of the Middle Ages*, translated by F.I. Antrobus and R.F. Kerr (24 vols., London, 1891–1933), xiv, p. 360; A. Bellesheim, *Geschichte der katholischen Kirche in Irland* (vol. 2, Mainz, 1890), pp. 107–8; Cardinal Pole to Pope Julius III, 10 March 1555 (*EPR*, v, pp. 4–7; *CSP Venice 1555–6*, pp. 16–17). The Latin text of the bull is printed in J. Hogan (ed.), 'Miscellanea Vaticano-Hibernica, 1420–1631', *AH* 4 (1915), p. 217.

III

The granting of this bull has traditionally been seen as a matter strictly between the English crown and the papacy, though there has been no consensus as to which of the parties was the most desirous to see it effected, nor why they felt so. In the mid-1570s, for example, Nicholas Ormanetto, the bishop of Padua and a former servant of Cardinal Pole at the time he requested the papacy to grant Ireland kingly status, was of the view that the initiative originated solely with the queen, being an attempt to overcome her scruple about using a title which had been assumed by her father during the time of the schism.[27] In contrast, Paolo Sarpi, in his early seventeenth-century history of the Council of Trent, saw it as a typically aggressive gesture by Paul IV to reassert the uniquely papal prerogative, arising from the 'Donation of Constantine', of bestowing the title of kingship over all islands; a view which was later echoed by the nineteenth-century papal historian, Ludwig Von Pastor, and more recently by Enrique Garcia Hernán, though in much less emphatic forms.[28] The explanations for the bull offered by twentieth-century Irish historians have been a lot more prosaic, the general view being that it resulted from a concerted action by both parties to regularise Anglo-papal relations vis-à-vis Ireland.[29]

There are problems with all of these assessments. Mary's alleged scrupulousness cannot have been too acute, given that she waited for nearly two years after her accession to relieve it.[30] Similarly, Paul IV's aggressive and jealous guardianship of papal prerogatives was well known, but, as regards the power to bestow the title of king on princes, he was noticeably silent on the matter at the time of the issue of the bull to Mary and Philip, while the bull itself originated in a request from the king and queen to his predecessor which had nothing to do with him.[31] More importantly, the belief that the bull regularised the position between England and Rome as far as Ireland was concerned is open to question. At the time the bull was granted in June 1555 the more controversial and overtly anti-papal legislation of Henry VIII's 1536-7 parliament was as yet unrepealed. Although this legislation

---

[27] Nicholas Ormanetto, bishop of Padua, to the Cardinal of Como, 19 December 1575 (*CSP Rome*, ii, pp. 240–1).

[28] Pietro Soave Polano (Paolo Sarpi), *The Historie of the Councel of Trent*, trans. Nathaniel Brent (London, 1629), pp. 391–2; *Carew MSS 1515–74*, pp. 251–2; Pastor, *History of the Popes*, xiv, p. 360; E. Garcia Hernán, *Irlanda y el rey prudente* (Madrid, 2000), pp. 37–8.

[29] Ellis, *Ireland in the age of the Tudors*, p. 224; Lennon, *Sixteenth century Ireland*, p. 306; Jefferies, 'Primate George Dowdall', p. 12. R.D. Edwards described the bull as 'a gracious acknowledgement of an unalterable fact' (Edwards, *Church and state*, p. 166).

[30] Pole stated that the king and queen sought the papal confirmation 'out of their piety' (*ERP*, v, p. 5).

[31] Cardinal Pole to Pope Julius III, 10 March 1555 (*ERP*, v, pp. 4–7; *CSP Venice 1555–6*, pp. 16–17).

had fallen into abeyance, Ireland had not been formally reconciled to the Holy See in the same way that England had been, which strongly suggests that the bull was never envisaged as a means of normalising Anglo-papal relations on the question of Ireland. The major difficulty with the existing explanations, then, is that the alleged intentions and motivations, which underscored the parties' effort to acquire and promulgate the bull, do not fit easily with the timing of the grant. An alternative and more cogent explanation, which is borne out by some very strong circumstantial evidence, is that the papal grant was sought at the instigation of Archbishop Dowdall, and conceived as an integral part of his strategy of Catholic restoration in the English Pale. The main evidence for Dowdall's involvement in the acquisition of the papal grant lies in the content of the bull itself, and in the circumstances surrounding the initial request for papal confirmation of the crown's title to kingship over Ireland.[32]

It is evident from the terms of the bull of 1555 that it was prepared with a view to reconciling the two conflicting views of Ireland's constitutional status that had existed throughout the period of the schism. On the one hand, the bull expressly re-established the legitimacy of the papacy's original grant of the lordship of Ireland to the English crown, which had been unilaterally abolished when Henry VIII abandoned the old style of lord and assumed the kingly title without papal approval, through an act of the Irish parliament in 1541. At the same time, by erecting Ireland into a kingdom, the bull recognised implicitly the political utility of the kingly title, but treated it as an extension of the original papal grant of lordship, in effect, as an addendum to *Laudabiliter*:

We raise in perpetuity the island of Ireland into a kingdom, in the pattern of other islands resplendent with royal title, dignity and honour, of which the kings of England, who were at the time accustomed to be called lords only, from the time they received lordship over her from the aforesaid See, and of which first the late Henry VIII after he had seceded from the unity of the Catholic church and from obedience to the Roman pontiff on the pretext of a certain law passed, so it is claimed, by the parliament of that same island, then his son Edward, the sixth of that name . . . usurped *de facto* the title of king.[33]

The intended effects of this exercise in constitutional reconciliation were twofold. In the first instance, it ensured that the defiant anti-papal implications of the 1541 act were negated. Yet it also determined that the

---

[32] The negotiations which led to Cardinal Pole's request for papal confirmation of the 'kingly' title are discussed below pp. 224–30.

[33] Hogan (ed.), 'Miscellanea Vaticano-Hibernica', p. 217. I would like to thank Dr Stephen O'Connor, formerly of the Medieval Latin Dictionary and now of the National Archives in London, for his help with the translation of the bull.

programme of political reform which the 1541 act initiated was absorbed into or harmonised with the Catholic reforming mission that lay at the heart of the original papal grant of lordship, the new grant being made 'to the praise and glory of almighty God ... the Virgin Mary, and the honour of the whole court of heaven and the exaltation of the Catholic faith'.[34]

The first person to have perceived a need for the formal harmonisation of the historical and contemporary modes of English reform in Ireland was George Dowdall, who moved to this position during the crisis surrounding the enforcement of the Edwardian Reformation in 1551. In truth, however, his espousal of this viewpoint did not mark a particularly radical departure in his thinking for, throughout the 1540s, he had been a very enthusiastic supporter of the reform project on the grounds that he already considered it to be virtually indistinguishable from the reforming mission that had been instituted at the time of the first conquest. For Dowdall, such a viewpoint had been possible because his patron, Lord Deputy St Leger, had sanctioned the utilisation of canon law as a supportive tool in the enforcement of the contemporary reform project, and had allowed him to use his position as a leader of the reform party to promote religious measures which were distinctly conservative in nature. Thus, although Dowdall had to reject the pope's authority in favour of the royal supremacy, he could content himself in the knowledge that his involvement in the renewed English drive to reform Gaelic Ireland, was contributing to the protection and preservation of the Catholic spirit and thinking that had infused the original reforming mission.

These easy assumptions were shattered, however, by the accession of Edward VI and the promulgation of a radical and innovatory liturgy in 1551, which was enshrined in the first Book of Common Prayer. The deep misgivings that the archbishop had about this turn of events are well known, being evinced in his decision to flee the country in the summer of 1551 because 'he would never be bishop, where the holy mass ... was abolished'.[35] Yet what is not generally appreciated is the extent to which Dowdall fought at this time to preserve the status quo of the 1540s, and how his engagement in this process forced him to reappraise and, ultimately, to alter his thinking on the constitutional settlement that underpinned St Leger's reform project. This reappraisal was provoked by the theological controversy that surrounded the introduction of the Prayer Book. While the campaign to enforce the new liturgy was at its height, in the spring of 1551, Dowdall steadfastly continued to maintain 'the old rites of the bishop of Rome's service' in his own diocese. He also came before the Irish council where he 'disputed plainly the massing and other things, contrary the king's

---

[34] Ibid.   [35] Shirley, *Church in Ireland 1547–1567*, p. 58.

proceedings'. Indeed, as the undisputed leader of the conservative cause, and its official disputant, he was doubtless the mastermind behind a series of anonymous manuscript tracts which appeared at this time, and which defended the doctrine of transubstantiation. In all of these activities, the archbishop was afforded the protection of his political ally, Lord Deputy St Leger, who, according to Archbishop Browne, had neither 'caused punishment ne redress to be executed in this behalf' nor condemned Dowdall at the council board. Significantly, St Leger was also the original recipient of the tracts defending transubstantiation, which were most probably prepared as briefing documents ahead of Dowdall's disputation before the council. Certainly, this is the way St Leger treated them for he immediately passed them on to Archbishop Browne, the most qualified theologian on the Irish council, for consideration around Candlemas 1551.[36]

It was in this highly charged atmosphere of theological disputation that Dowdall's constitutional thinking developed, the crucial first step being his rejection of the royal supremacy. The archbishop's support for the royal supremacy had always been conditional, being permissible only so long as the crown was willing to preserve essential Catholic doctrine intact. The abolition of the mass in the early 1550s was clearly an infringement of this condition, however, and fatally undermined the claim that the royal supremacy was in anyway congruent with the authority and traditions of the Western Church. For Dowdall, the crown's wilful and erroneous decision to pit itself against the authority of the patristic writers that he had cited in support of traditional eucharistic doctrine – such luminaries as Cyprian, Ambrose, Augustine, Anselm, Bernard, Gerson, Bede, John Chrysostom and Eusebius – meant that it had necessarily relinquished any call that it had on him and the inhabitants of Ireland to accept the supremacy.[37] The papacy, it had now transpired, was the true guardian and upholder of the authority and traditions of the church, while the crown, through the supreme headship, was a promoter of fundamental doctrinal innovation.

Yet Dowdall's abandonment of support for the royal supremacy in 1550–1, and his rediscovery of the papal supremacy, posed for him an acute political problem. During the breach with Rome, the English crown had begun a process of political reform in Ireland which the archbishop had personally supported and which he wished to continue, because he believed that it provided the best means of securing the long sought after

---

[36] Shirley, *Church in Ireland 1547–1567*, pp. 54–8; 'Fides priscorum de veritate carnis et sanguinis Christi in sacramento Altaris, quam ab ipsa Assensione dominica semper tenuit universalis Christi ecclesia, à vetustissimis auctoribus in suis scriptis nobis relicta' (TNA: PRO, SP 62/2, no. 78); Ronan, 'Booke oute of Ireland in Latten', pp. 501–13, 606–22.

[37] TNA: PRO, SP 62/2, no. 78 *passim.*

acculturation of the Irishry. However, this reform project was constitu-
tionally grounded upon a parliamentary statute – the act for the kingly title
of 1541 – which had been enacted not only to create a unified polity in
Ireland, but also to side step or counteract all claims that the English crown
had forfeited its right to rule in Ireland, because it had rejected the papal
authority upon which its sovereignty was traditionally deemed to rest. In
short, the political settlement that Dowdall, St Leger and their fellow
reformers had worked so hard to establish in the previous decade was as
much a slight to the papacy as it was the basis upon which the anglicisation
of Ireland was now proceeding.[38] Thus, any call for the re-establishment of
papal supremacy, while entirely necessary to protect Catholic doctrine and
the interests of the church, could also serve to undermine the reform project,
should the now necessary reconciliation between England and Rome ever
occur. For Dowdall, there was only one way to overcome this dilemma.
This was to sever all links between the kingly title and the royal supremacy,
and to seek the formal harmonisation of the contemporary mode of English
reform in Ireland with its medieval antecedent, by securing a formal papal
sanction for it.

On the eve of or soon after his departure for the continent in the summer
of 1551, then, George Dowdall had already accepted the need for papal
confirmation of the kingly title on religious grounds. The timing of this
development in Dowdall's thinking is hugely significant. It suggests very
strongly that he was not only the originator of the idea to seek papal
confirmation for the kingly title but that, in pursuing his suit at the Roman
Curia to succeed Robert Wauchop as the papal archbishop of Armagh, he
was also the man who made the principle figures in the later granting of the
bull, Cardinal Pole and Cardinal Carafa (later Paul IV), aware of the issues
surrounding it. Both of these men, in fact, were present at the sessions of the
consistory which led to Dowdall's appointment to Armagh in March 1553,
and took a personal interest in his case. Although the evidence is sketchy, it
appears that Pole supported Dowdall's provision from the outset, but
Carafa, as a direct snub to his fellow cardinal, objected to it. While the
substantive issue in this dispute is not now known, and was most likely
rooted in the well known enmity that existed between the pair, the fact that
it took place at all suggests that Dowdall would have had to make some
kind of submission, most likely via Pole, to justify his appointment, given
his longstanding record as an undispensed religious and schismatic
archbishop. In this context, his unique vision of the compatibility of the
kingly title and papal supremacy must certainly have been raised during the
deliberations on his appointment, and may well have played a decisive part

---

[38] See Chapter 4 above; Bradshaw, *Irish constitutional revolution*, pp. 193–4, 231–3.

in the final decision to provide him to Armagh. At the very least it would have prepared the way for the granting of the bull in 1555.[39]

IV

There is strong circumstantial evidence, then, that George Dowdall was the pivotal figure, both intellectually and politically, in the process that led to the papal confirmation of the kingly title, and that he did so out of a deeply held conviction that English political reform in Ireland was synonymous with Catholic religious orthodoxy and traditional canonical rectitude. Dowdall's determination both to give formal expression to the link which he perceived between Catholicism and English reform in Ireland, and to preserve the role of the clergy in that reform process, lay at the heart of the legislative output of his provincial council of 1553/4. The legislation enacted by the council was not confined solely to anti-Reformation measures. Only five canons, in fact, dealt specifically with Reformation matters at all. The remainder ranged far and wide over the spectrum of ecclesiastical and religious matters normally legislated for by synodal bodies in the pre-Reformation Irish Church, and included canons, the first four in fact, which proscribed practices traditionally associated with the Gaelic Irish, such as the conferral of benefices on laymen and boys, and the acquisition by laymen, through deception, of the power to confer benefices from the papacy. Other canons included measures for the reconciliation of divorcees, for the repair of ruined churches and for the institution of a fast for the vigil of St Brigid. Viewed as a whole, the legislation shows that Dowdall was not only attempting to restore the externals of the old religion but to recreate the full historical and avowedly English Irish cultural context in which that religion had traditionally existed and from which it had derived its full meaning.[40]

In this context, the reformist practices introduced during the schism, no more than a host of other canonical offences, were deemed to be anathema because they had undermined a code of ethics and behavioural standards which were perceived as being uniquely English. In other words, Dowdall's 'reformanda' defined the English Irish clergy's rejection of the Reformation in a manner that was directly comparable to their traditional rejection of the uncanonical practices of the Gaelic Irish. Indeed in one important respect these two preferences were inextricably linked, a feature evident in

---

[39] On the dispute between Carafa and Pole and its general context see T.F. Mayer, *Reginald Pole. Prince and Prophet* (Cambridge, 2000), pp. 175–202.

[40] PRONI, MS DIO/4/2/13, pp. 101–6 ('Dowdall's register', no. 85); on such legislation generally see M.A.J. Burrows, 'Fifteenth century Irish provincial legislation and pastoral care', in Sheils and Wood (eds.), *The churches, Ireland and the Irish*, pp. 55–67; Jeffries, *Priests and prelates of Armagh*, pp. 96–102.

the provincial council's opening canon, which legislated against clerical marriage. Here, a practice specific to the reformers was given a particularly derogatory slant by linking it to the traditionally Gaelic, pre-Reformation practice of clerical concubinage. The new canon stated that all priests, not only those who had 'presumed' to contract marriage at the time of the schism, but also those 'notorious fornicators who, despite many warnings, publicly detained their whores as wives in their own homes', should be declared deprived of their livings and unfit to administer the sacraments until they received proper canonical dispensations.[41] The implication here was that the Protestant reformers' rejection of the canonical bans on clerical marriage and incontinence were exactly akin to the Irishry's traditional rejection of the same laws, offences which Dowdall had long endeavoured to correct. In English Irish eyes, therefore, the reformers' cause was particularly discredited in that it seemed to justify Irish, non-English, behaviour.

Clearly, then, Dowdall's strategy for the restoration of Catholicism in the province of Armagh had a very marked English politico-cultural agenda attached to it, an agenda that was clearly adumbrated in canon fifteen of the 1553/4 provincial council, which commanded the clergy to make in their masses a procession twice weekly, and one collect or prayer, for the state or well-being of the 'royal majesty'. Here was the old order of the English Pale in all its ancient fullness: old religion, old politics, and old loyalties.[42] The existence of this politico-cultural agenda is particularly significant because it strongly suggests that the archbishop, perhaps mindful of his primatial responsibilities, framed it with the English Pale in view, and not just in terms of his own predominantly Gaelic province. Although theoretically the eighteen 'reformanda' of the provincial council of 1553/4 were legally binding only in Armagh and its suffragan sees of Ardagh, Clogher, Clonmacnoise, Derry, Down, Dromore, Kilmore, Meath and Raphoe, their relevance extended beyond these boundaries to the church in English Ireland as a whole, including the diocese of Dublin and its suffragan sees.

---

[41] 'Imprimis ut declarentur omnes sacerdotes non modo qui hac in tempestate matrimonium contrahere presumpserunt verum et notarii fornicatores tam pluries moniti [?qui] ut scorta sua non secus quam uxores in domibus suis publice detinuerunt suis beneficiis privatos [?privati] et inhabiles ad regimen vel ad sacramentorum administrationem donec cum eis super his sufficienter erit dispensatos et aliis fornicatores privandi sicut per superiorem': PRONI, MS DIO/4/2/13, pp. 101–2; Gwynn, *Medieval province of Armagh*, pp. 272–4. The text of Dowdall's register, which has come down to us in a late seventeenth or early eighteenth century transcript, is corrupt in several places including this section (see also Gwynn, *Medieval province of Armagh*, p. 265, nt. 2), but its meaning is clear. I would like to thank Dr Stephen O'Connor for his help in reading the text.

[42] 'Item quod processio bis hebdomade fiat pro statu regie majestatis et una collecta in missis': PRONI, MS DIO/4/2/13, p. 106 ('Dowdall's register', no. 85).

It is very likely, then, that Dowdall's strategy was designed to appeal to the clergy of the English Pale as a whole, including the ex-prebendaries of St Patrick's Cathedral. They, no less than Dowdall, would have appreciated the legal ingenuity of restoring Catholicism by amending local ecclesiastical law. They too would have appreciated that the revival of medieval canon law was of profound historical and cultural significance for the English Irish community as a whole and, for themselves in particular, the living embodiment of English Irish canonical correctness. Above all, however, they would have appreciated the potential significance of what Dowdall was doing for their suppressed cathedral.

Dowdall's strategy provided, in effect, the strongest possible reason for seeking the re-establishment of St Patrick's Cathedral because his aim of restoring the old religion by canonical means throughout the English Pale could not have been seriously countenanced without it. If the requisite synodal legislation was to be enacted in Dublin, and it had to be as the Armagh legislation was not binding outside the boundaries of that province, it would require proper monitoring and enforcement by a fully functional diocesan administration. Such an administration did not exist in the see of Dublin at this juncture. The suppression of St Patrick's had severely disrupted the workings of the pre-Reformation administrative structure, and it badly needed reconstruction before it would be in a fit state to support the implementation of new provincial legislation. Similarly, if any such canon law was to take proper effect in Dublin's suffragan sees, then the full apparatus of provincial ecclesiastical government would also have to be revived. Here the main administrative organ was the archbishop's metropolitan or consistory court. Although the consistory did not cease to operate during the period of the cathedral's suppression, its standing had been greatly diminished. Instead of occupying its traditional and unique position as the supreme court of appeal for ecclesiastical causes in the province of Dublin, an eminence that in the past had been reflected in its association with the visible wealth and splendour of the old cathedral, the consistory had been reduced in status to that of a junior partner in a larger judicial complex, following the crown's decision in March 1547 to remove the four courts of judicature to a portion of the skeletal church.[43] The logic of Archbishop Dowdall's strategy, then, demanded not only that it should be implemented throughout Dublin and the English Pale, but that as a precondition for this the cathedral church of St Patrick should also be restored

The implementation of Dowdall's strategy in Dublin began in the spring and early summer of 1554, through the operation of a commission, issued

---

[43] For a discussion of the administrative disruption caused by the dissolution of St Patrick's see Murray 'St Patrick's cathedral and the university question in Ireland', pp. 8–9.

by the queen on 14 April, to deprive married clergy of their benefices. Dowdall headed this commission and was joined on it by Patrick Walshe, bishop of Waterford, Alexander Devereux, bishop of Ferns, Terence Donnelly, dean of Armagh, Robert Luttrell, archdeacon of Meath, William Walshe, S.T.P. (later appointed bishop of Meath), and Bartholomew Fitzsimon, rector of Clongill, Co. Meath. According to the terms of the commission many clerks, priests and religious in Ireland, including benefice holders, had committed 'grave enormities' by unlawfully cohabiting with women 'under the colour and veil of matrimony' and had sown heresies and schisms away from the true Catholic faith. The commissioners were ordered to summon all such clergy to appear before them and if, after summary examination they were found guilty, to deprive them of their benefices, to enjoin upon them salutary penance and to divorce them from their wives or concubines.[44]

The royal commission made an impact on the diocese of Dublin in two related ways. First, it provided a vehicle or forum for Dowdall to communicate his strategy to the clergy of Dublin; either directly, through a personal visit to the diocese at the head of the commission or, more likely, through associates and intermediaries who were well connected with himself and the old ecclesiastical establishment in Dublin, and fully supportive of the notion of reintroducing pre-Reformation canonical norms. Such figures would have included his fellow commissioners, Bartholomew Fitzsimon, a cleric who had himself been a notably conservative member of the chapter of St Patrick's Cathedral at the time of its suppression; and Robert Luttrell, a qualified canonist and the archdeacon of Meath, who had served as Dowdall's official principal during his first period as archbishop of Armagh, and who had held the rectory of Hollywood in the diocese of Dublin during Henry VIII's reign.[45] It is likely that the archbishop mobilised support for his strategy outside the province of Armagh through clerics such as these.

The commission did more, however, than provide an excuse for old clerical friends to gather, learn about and discuss the implications of Dowdall's strategy of Catholic restoration. In a very practical way, it was also a necessary step in the implementation of the strategy itself, although this is not readily apparent when the terms of the commission are considered in isolation. On first sight, in fact, the commission seems at odds with the strategy Dowdall had instituted in Armagh. Dowdall's plan aimed at re-establishing the autonomy of the local ordinary on matters pertaining

---

[44] TNA: PRO, C 66/874, mm. 39–40d (*Patent rolls 1553–4*, pp. 302–3).
[45] Above p. 39; *BRUO 1501–40*, p. 367; 'Dowdall's register', no. 76; *Statutes at large*, i, pp. 131–2.

to ecclesiastical jurisdiction and discipline. The queen's commission, by contrast, could be interpreted as a statement that she retained the ultimate authority to pronounce on all local ecclesiastical disciplinary matters, given that the Henrician act of supremacy, passed by the Irish parliament in 1536, was still on the statute books. There are, however, a number of factors that indicate strongly that Dowdall and the queen viewed the commission in a quite different way. First there was the attitude of Queen Mary herself. It has long been recognised that, from the outset of her reign, Mary was anxious to shed the supremacy from her list of royal prerogatives and that she only ever exercised authority on ecclesiastical matters to further the cause of Catholicism. Given this, and her known predilection for restoring the traditional disciplinary machinery of the medieval church,[46] there can be little doubt that she approved of Dowdall's strategy of reviving Catholicism through the enactment and enforcement of local canon law, a fact borne out by her appointment of the archbishop at the head of a commission which was dominated by like-minded, clerical associates from his own province. As well as Robert Luttrell and Bartholomew Fitzsimon, these included Terence Donnelly, the dean of Armagh, whose subscription to the Dowdall programme in its anglocentric entirety is evident from his acquisition of a grant of English liberty less than three weeks after the archbishop's return to Ireland in November 1553.[47]

That the royal commission was instituted not to undermine, but to advance Dowdall's strategy is confirmed both by the circumstances in which it was issued and by the manner in which it was executed. In reality, Dowdall faced a problem with his programme of restoration in that the majority of Pale sees were held by bishops who, of their own accord, were unlikely or incapable of initiating it effectively, either because they were still supporters of the Reformation, or because they were compromised in canonical terms by their marriages or their past behaviour as reformers. In this sense Thomas Lancaster of Kildare, Robert Travers of Leighlin, Edward Staples of Meath and George Browne of Dublin were all compromised to a greater or lesser degree. The effective implementation of Dowdall's plan was predicated upon the removal of such men and their replacement by unambiguous or untainted Catholics. And it was this crucial need which the commission was appointed to serve, because at this juncture the only authority on the island which could lawfully deprive all of these bishops, or which would be accepted by those bishops about to be deprived, was the

---

[46] On Mary's attitude to the supremacy and her revival of the traditional disciplinary machinery of the church see C. Cross, 'Churchmen and the royal supremacy', in F. Heal and R. O'Day (eds.), *Church and society in England Henry VIII to James I* (London, 1977), pp. 20–1.
[47] Morrin, *Patent rolls*, i, p. 307. Donnelly was generally known as Terence Daniel thereafter.

monarch. Thus, once in operation, the first victims of the commission were not surprisingly the bishops named above. Significantly, only a handful of lesser clergy were deprived as a result of its activities, the commissioners being content to leave this work to local diocesan administrations once they were happy that they were headed by trustworthy ordinaries.[48]

Archbishop George Browne was deprived sometime during the summer of 1554, an act which drew a very firm line under the see of Dublin's recently schismatic and heretical past. Browne's deprivation enabled Dowdall to move to the second vital step in the implementation of his counter-reformation. This was his campaign to secure the queen's agreement to three related measures: the appointment of a suitable successor to Browne, the re-establishment of St Patrick's Cathedral, and the regularisation of Ireland's constitutional status. The thinking behind these measures was clear. The first was designed to reconstruct the Dublin diocesan administration from top to bottom according to the model of its pre-Reformation structure. The second would qualify it to take over all further responsibility for the revival of canon law and the restoration of the old religion. And the third sought to re-establish – following the innovations of Henry VIII and Edward VI – an orthodox constitutional setting in which to undertake these essentially English Irish politico-cultural activities, through the harmonisation of the act for the kingly title and old papal grants like *Laudabiliter*. Given these objectives, the timing of their execution was all-important. In order that the Dowdall programme could be implemented without delay, it was required that all three measures should be realised quickly and simultaneously. Thus they were dealt with as a unit, a feature evident in the fact that final decisions on all were resolved and announced within weeks of each other in the spring of 1555. On 18 February, Queen Mary issued two letters missive under her signet from Westminster. One of them commanded the dean and chapter of Christ Church Cathedral to elect Dr Hugh Curwen, dean of Hereford Cathedral, as archbishop of Dublin. The other signified to the lord deputy, lord chancellor and council of Ireland her intent, to restore 'our metropolitan and prebendary church and chapter of St Patrick ... unto her pristine honourable state' from Lady Day following. On 10 March, Cardinal Pole wrote to Pope Julius III requesting that he confirm the kingly title over Ireland to Queen Mary and King Philip.[49]

The securing of these measures was the culmination of weeks, or perhaps months of negotiations, conducted between the crown and a delegation of

---

[48] For the Dublin deprivations which resulted from the commission see Ronan, *Reformation in Dublin*, pp. 428–9; Morrin, *Patent rolls*, i, p. 325.

[49] RCB, C6/1/6, no. 3 (Registrum Novum of Christ Church), p. 1190 (*CCD*, no. 447); Mason, *History of St Patrick's*, pp. 155–6 (Morrin, *Patent rolls*, i, pp. 328–9); Cardinal Pole to Pope Julius III, 10 March 1555 (*ERP*, v, pp. 4–7; *CSP Venice 1555–6*, pp. 16–17).

former prebendaries, 'them of St Patrick's', who attended upon the queen sometime in the latter half of 1554 or in the opening months of 1555. The crown appears to have been represented by a sub-committee of the privy council, consisting of William Paulet, marquis of Winchester and lord treasurer of England, Bishop Thomas Thirlby of Ely, Sir Francis Englefield and Sir Edmund Peckham, who, on 10 August 1554, had been given responsibility for the 'stay and good order' of the realm of Ireland.[50] The identities of the members of the St Patrick's delegation are not now on record, but it is certainly known that they conducted their business under the aegis and direction of Archbishop Dowdall. His involvement in and all-pervasive influence on the process is clearly revealed in his domination of the new cathedral chapter appointed by Queen Mary. Dowdall himself received the prebend of Saggart. More importantly, the two most senior positions, the deanery and precentorship, went to two close associates, Thomas Leverous and Thomas Creef. Leverous, the former tutor of Gerald Fitzgerald, eleventh earl of Kildare, was appointed archdeacon of Armagh by Dowdall following his return to the diocese in late 1553.[51] This suggests very strongly that they had become acquainted before the Marian restoration, perhaps as early as the Henrician period, but more likely in the early years of Edward VI's short reign, when Leverous returned to Ireland from continental exile prior to the restoration of the earl of Kildare, and received a pardon from the crown in October 1549 for his part in the earlier escape of the young earl.[52] Dowdall's relationship with Creef, the religiously conservative ex-prebendary of Saggart, is also dateable to this period.

---

[50] Signet letter from the queen to the lord deputy, lord chancellor and council of Ireland, 23 February 1555, printed in Mason, *History of St Patrick's*, pp. 156–8 (Morrin, *Patent rolls*, i, pp. 327–8); *APC 1554–6*, p. 59.

[51] It is recorded in Dowdall's register that the synod of the clergy of Armagh *inter Anglicos* of 3 July 1554 was adjourned until the bell was rung after nones on the same day, high mass having been celebrated previously by Archbishop Dowdall in St Peter's, Drogheda, the accustomed procession having taken place through the town to the high cross and back to the church again, 'and a sermon having been made at the church in the pulpit by the reverend lord bishop Thomas Leverous archdeacon of Armagh for the instruction of both the clergy and the people (ad ecclesiam factaque ceremonia in pulpido per reverendum dominum Thomam Leverus episcopum archidiaconum [abbreviated as 'archum' in the original] Armachanum ad informationem tam cleri quam populi . . . '): PRONI, MS DIO/4/2/13, pp. 96–7; see also 'Dowdall's register', no. 82.

[52] *CSPD Edward VI*, nos. 79, 549; *Fiants, Edward VI*, no. 379; Shirley, *Church in Ireland 1547–1567*, pp. 61–2. It has been suggested that Leverous and Dowdall may have met in Cardinal Pole's household in the Papal states after Dowdall went into exile in 1551 (Jefferies, 'Primate Dowdall', p. 10). This is unlikely as Leverous had left Rome and was back in Ireland at least two years before Dowdall departed for the continent. Having obtained his pardon from the crown, Leverous was considered for promotion to the see of Cashel or Ossory by the Edwardian regime in the autumn of 1551.

Before the archbishop departed for the continent in the summer of 1551, Creef had served in his household as one of his chaplains.[53]

Of the matters under discussion, the finding of a successor to George Browne was perhaps the easiest to accomplish. Fully briefed about and fully sympathetic to the requirements of Dowdall's strategy of restoration, the delegation of ex-prebendaries would have been able to provide a full specification to the privy councillors of the kind of person that was needed to fill the position: a professional legist with extensive experience of diocesan administration. It seems clear too that their arguments were listened to, for, in the person of Hugh Curwen, this is precisely what they got. A native of Cumberland, Curwen's career as a legist commenced in the 1520s when he undertook studies for a baccalaureate in canon law in one of the halls or inns of Oxford. After acquiring his degree in 1528, he supplicated to lecture on the books of the Institutes, and five years later he obtained a doctorate in laws. Like any well-educated clergyman of his day, he went on to secure a host of benefices and ecclesiastical offices. These included, during the period 1535 to 1540, appointments as vicar general and official principal to two successive bishops of Hereford, Edward Foxe and Edmund Bonner, appointments which were punctuated by a spell as keeper of the spiritualities *sede vacante* between May 1538 and March 1539. His ascent to the upper echelons of the Hereford clerical hierarchy was completed in 1541, after his appointment by Henry VIII to the deanery of the cathedral.[54]

Curwen, then, was ideally suited for the job of archbishop as specified by Dowdall and the ex-prebendaries. A proven ecclesiastical lawyer and bureaucrat, he had the qualifications and experience necessary to enact and enforce the synodal legislation required by Dowdall's strategy for restoring the old religion. Curwen's appointment was also facilitated by the presence of Bishop Thomas Thirlby on the crown's negotiating team. Thirlby, best known as a royal servant and diplomat, was himself a highly qualified legist who throughout an episcopal career spanning three reigns and three dioceses – Westminster, Norwich and Ely – had become well versed in the

[53] Memoranda Roll 1 & 2 Edward VI, m. 164 (NAI, Ferguson MS, v, p. 69). Patrick Dowdall, a nephew of the archbishop, was also appointed beadle and registrar of the cathedral on its re-establishment: 'Account of the proctor of the economy of St Patrick's, c. June 1555 – c. June 1556', printed in Mason, *History of St Patrick's*, p. xxxii. This account, of which only the expenses section survived, is undated. However, as Mason surmised, it is clearly related to the period of the re-establishment and probably spans the traditional accounting period used by the proctors of St Patrick's, i.e. mid-summer to mid-summer (cf. the accounts of John Andowe, June 1509 to June 1510, RCB, C2, no. 106, and James Ussher, June 1606 to June 1607, TCD, MS 788, ff. 87r-91r). On Patrick Dowdall's relationship with the archbishop see K.W. Nicholls, 'A calendar of salved chancery pleadings concerning County Louth', *LASJ* 17/4 (1972), pp. 251–2.

[54] *BRUO 1501–40*, pp. 137–8.

task of finding dependable ecclesiastical administrators to fill his absentee shoes. Thus he would have been both attuned to the needs of Dowdall and the clergy of St Patrick's, and possessed of the information and connection to find them the man that they wanted. It is almost certain too that he was acquainted with Hugh Curwen before the Dublin vacancy arose, if not directly, then at least indirectly through Curwen's brother Richard. Before his death in 1543, Richard Curwen had worked very closely with Thirlby, sharing membership of Doctors Commons and, more significantly, the Council of the North, where they participated in the suppression of the Pilgrimage of Grace under the Duke of Norfolk.[55] Thirlby's promotion of the candidacy of his former colleague's brother may well have been crucial given that the queen herself, and Cardinal Pole, the recently arrived papal legate to England, preferred to appoint clerics with a theological and pastoral background to the episcopate, rather than the 'worldly' legists and administrators who had dominated the bench in Henry VIII's reign, and who had conspicuously failed to defend the old religion in its hour of need.[56]

Reassurance on the advisability of appointing Hugh Curwen was available from another reliable source. Archbishop Dowdall's plans for the restoration of St Patrick's Cathedral also made careful provision for keeping a watchful eye on future proceedings in the diocese, and for ensuring that the new archbishop's administration would be irreproachably orthodox and unrelenting in its efforts to fulfil its appointed task. Both of these objectives were realised in the nature of the personnel selected by the archbishop and his cohorts to staff the new chapter of St Patrick's. Including his own inner circle, consisting of himself, Dean Leverous and Precentor Creef, a group who could be counted on to keep the programme of reviving canon law on track, it purposely comprised a coalition of clergymen from the English Pale which represented in miniature the main clerical power bases and groupings of the pre-Edwardian church, with particular emphasis on those corporate clergy whose existence and values had been attacked, or who had shown markedly conservative religious leanings during the previous two reigns. Moreover, in recognition of what Dowdall would have considered to be the essential orthodoxy of Lord Deputy St Leger's religious settlement of the

[55] T.F. Shirley, *Thomas Thirlby Tudor bishop* (London 1964), pp. 3–17, 34–9, 104–8, 134.

[56] P. Hughes, *The Reformation in England* (revised edn, 3 vols. in one, London, 1963), ii, pp. 231–2; R. Pogson, 'The legacy of the schism: confusion, continuity and change in the Marian clergy', in J. Loach and R. Tittler (eds.), *The mid-Tudor polity, c. 1540–1560* (Basingstoke, 1980), pp. 123–7; MacCulloch, *Later Reformation*, p. 24. Pole arrived in England in November 1554. Significantly, he dispensed Curwen for being schismatic and heretical in the previous reigns on 6 March 1555: Mayer (ed.), *Correspondence of Pole*, iii, p. 50.

1540s, it also included a number of clergymen who, like himself, had been prominent supporters of that settlement within the context of the 'king's party'.[57]

Thus, apart from Thomas Creef, the group included another ten clergymen who had served in the pre-suppression cathedral (seven ex-canons, two ex-vicars choral and one petty canon), amongst whom were the former prebendaries, Simon Jeffrey and Henry Parker, original signatories to the letter of protest against Thomas Cromwell's attempt to curtail the cathedral's liberties nearly two decades earlier.[58] It also included a number of former monastic heads from the Pale: Robert Wellesley, late prior of Greatconnell in Co. Kildare; John Galbally, the former abbot of the Cistercian Abbey of Baltinglass; and John Willey, a former neighbour of Dowdall's as pre-dissolution prior of the Augustinian priory of the Blessed Virgin Mary at Louth. And, in recognition of the progress that had been made in the previous fifteen years in incorporating the Irishry into the kingdom of Ireland, a man of Gaelic background, Patrick Byrne, was also admitted to the chapter for the first time in its history. Lastly, it included two prominent Dublin ecclesiastics who had maintained, albeit in a highly ambivalent manner, the doctrinally conservative religious positions they had acquired in the 1540s throughout the reign of Edward VI. These were Thomas Lockwood, the dean of Christ Church Cathedral, a cleric who had earned the opprobrium of the ardent Protestant reformer, Bishop Bale of Ossory, for resisting his attempt to introduce the second Edwardian Prayer Book in 1552; and George Browne, the ex-archbishop of Dublin, who was equally disliked by Bale and who, following his attainment of a dispensation from Cardinal Pole for his ill-fated marriage in March 1555, completed his abandonment of the reformist cause and his integration into the fold of the old clerical guard by accepting the prebend of Clonmethan. In the process he also provided a major propagandist coup for the adherents of the old religion.[59] Taken together, these clergymen formed a group who

---

[57] For a complete list of the clergy appointed to the new chapter see the documents printed in Mason, *History of St Patrick's*, pp. 156, 160, xxi–xxvi (Morrin, *Patent rolls*, i, pp. 329, 332–3).

[58] The other canons were Richard Ellercar, Nicholas Miagh, John Sonnyng, Richard Johnson and Henry Dancy; James Sarsfield and John Cane or Come were the ex-vicars; and Patrick Fynne, the ex-petty canon; Simon Jeffrey died before the restoration was completed (Mason, *History of St Patrick's*, pp. 156, 160, xxi–xxvi).

[59] Morrin, *Patent rolls*, i, pp. 57–8 [as a former religious, Robert Wellesley subsequently had to obtain a dispensation from Cardinal Pole (27 April 1557) because he had taken his cathedral living without papal sanction, and while technically still an Augustinian canon and in a state of schism (Mayer (ed.), *Correspondence of Pole*, iii, p. 411)]; White, *Monastic extents*, p. 133; Mason, *History of St Patrick's*, pp. 156, 160, xxi–xxvi; *Vocacyon of Johan Bale*, ed. Happé and King, pp. 52–3, 55–6, 67–8; BMD, MS 922, II, ff. 4v-6r, (Ronan, 'Cardinal Pole's absolution of George Browne', p. 195). We may assume at this point that

through their differing experiences were living symbols of the old order's triumphant restoration and its reconciliation with St Leger's vice-regal reform programme. They also supplied a pool of almost exclusively conservative clerical talent from which Archbishop Curwen would select his administrative officers.

The reconstruction of the chapter along these conservative lines was achieved with relative ease. Dowdall's negotiators provided the names of the clergy, the queen duly approved them and, in her missive of 18 February, reiterated again on 23 February, she ordered Lord Deputy St Leger, Lord Chancellor Cusack, and the Irish council 'to make out in our name . . . unto every of the said persons several grants, gifts, presentations and letters patents of the said dignities, offices and prebends' bearing the date 26 March 1555. The deputy and chancellor responded promptly to her command. On the required date letters of appointment for Dean Leverous and his colleagues, as well as letters patent of admission and installation into the chapter, were issued out of the Irish chancery at a total cost of £1 17s. 10d. to the recipients.[60]

Details of how Dowdall and his cohorts proceeded with the procurement of the constitutional requirements of their reform programme are relatively sparse. Nevertheless, there is enough circumstantial evidence – in the events surrounding Cardinal Pole's solicitation of the grant of the kingly title to Queen Mary and King Philip – to link all three events. Significantly, the resumption of Thirlby's ambassadorial role was announced on 18 February 1555, the same day that Curwen's appointment and the restoration of St Patrick's were announced.[61] This suggests that Thirlby played a crucial role in the episode. It is likely that he and Dowdall's negotiating team pressed the idea of seeking papal confirmation for the kingly title in their discussions of late 1554 or early 1555, once it became known that Thirlby would be undertaking the embassy to the Vatican. In truth, they were probably knocking on an open door. Cardinal Pole, who was then finalising the arrangements for the mission of Thirlby, Sir Edward Carne and Viscount Montague, the ambassadors being sent to Rome to make solemn obedience to the Holy See in the wake of England's return to the papal fold, was probably well briefed on the issues surrounding the need for papal confirmation of the kingly title, following his encounter with Dowdall in Rome

---

Browne's relationship with Katherine Miagh finally ended. Katherine lived on until the early 1590s and, apart from Browne and Robert Bathe, she also entered into marriages with three other men: John Ball, John Crompton and James Barry, a merchant and alderman of Dublin ('Index to the Act . . . Books and . . . Original Wills of . . . Dublin', p. 591; NAI, Salved Chancery Pleadings, N/147; Lennon, *Lords of Dublin*, p. 230).

[60] Mason, *History of St Patrick's*, pp. 155–8, xxxiii; Morrin, *Patent rolls*, i, pp. 328–9.
[61] Pastor, *History of the popes*, xiii, p. 288; Shirley, *Thomas Thirlby*, p. 142.

two years earlier. His support for Dowdall's provision to the see of Armagh at this time also indicates that he agreed with the archbishop's arguments for the papal confirmation even at this point. It is little surprise, then, that he now agreed to append a request for the papal confirmation of the crown's title in his letter to Pope Julius, introducing the newly appointed ambassadors.[62] Nevertheless, it is clear that the pursuit of the bull was and remained a local and clerically based initiative. Significantly, on Thirlby's return from the continent in August 1555, he and the privy council chose Archbishop-elect Hugh Curwen, and not the lord deputy or council of Ireland, to bring the bull to Ireland and to publish it throughout the kingdom. Thus, although the bull was a matter of state, it would appear that it was considered to be of primary interest to the clergy involved in restoring the old religion in the English Pale, for no other reason, as Thomas Thirlby well knew, than that it was they who had sought it in the first place.[63]

V

The decision of Archbishop Dowdall and the clergy of St Patrick's to proceed with their restoration strategy in an independent manner, and the support which the crown evinced for their actions, were not accidental. From the outset, the clergy knew that their plans for the restoration of St Patrick's Cathedral were unlikely to gain the support of Lord Deputy St Leger and his supporters in the Irish administration, as it was the viceroy who had orchestrated the original dissolution of the cathedral in the dying days of Henry VIII's reign. Indeed, their worst fears about St Leger's intentions were soon confirmed. Apart from granting the patents of appointment to the cathedral clergy in March 1555, and a formal charter of restoration in the following June,[64] the viceroy's administration refused to co-operate further in the process of the cathedral's re-establishment. Moreover, in regard to the most substantive element of this process, the restitution of the cathedral's goods and property, St Leger resisted all attempts throughout the spring and summer of 1555 to prise them away from the state, and return them to their former owners. It was a course of

---

[62] Above, pp. 218–19; Cardinal Pole to Pope Julius III, 10 March 1555 (*ERP*, v, pp. 4–7; *CSP Venice 1555–6*, pp. 16–17).

[63] Edwards, *Church and state*, p. 164; *APC 1554–6*, p. 179.

[64] The text of the charter is printed in *Dignitas decani*, pp. 149–63 (calendered in Morrin, *Patent rolls*, i, pp. 329–35). The charter, which recapitulates the earlier foundation charters and property grants to St Patrick's, as well as reaffirming the queen's decision to revive it, was solicited by the cathedral clergy. Patrick Dowdall, the cathedral registrar and Archbishop Dowdall's nephew, drafted the text. It was issued by the Irish chancery, dated at Dublin 15 June 1555 ('Account of the proctor of the economy of St Patrick's, c. June 1555 – c. June 1556', Mason, *History of St Patrick's*, p. xxxiii).

action that would greatly anger the queen and undermine the credibility of an already unravelling administration.

The queen and her advisers were fully aware that the restitution of the property of St Patrick's was likely to cause some problems. At the very time that they began discussing its mechanics, in the latter half of 1554, England's long-awaited return to the papal fold was effected, but only after Cardinal Pole, bowing to the concerted political pressure of the queen's 'possessioner' subjects, relinquished the church's claim over the monastic and other ecclesiastical lands that had been secularised during the reigns of Henry VIII and Edward VI. The lesson from this was obvious. Secular opposition, rooted in a similar economic self-interest, could be expected in Ireland, once it became generally known that it was the queen's intention to restore the lucrative prebends of St Patrick's to their original owners.[65]

The task of overcoming this prospective opposition was complicated by the legal position of the dissolved cathedral. As the dissolution of St Patrick's had been effected by 'voluntary surrender', it was the dean and chapter themselves who had voted it out of existence and who, in their final corporate act, had voluntarily given up all its property to the crown, including the property of the subordinate corporations of vicars choral and petty canons.[66] Thus the simplest and least controversial way of undoing the dissolution would have been for the crown to found the cathedral anew and, as the legal proprietor, to endow it afresh with its old property in a staged manner. In this scenario, the crown lessees could have held on to their interests in the property but paid their rents to the clergy instead of the crown, thus avoiding any contention over the re-establishment. Thereafter, the property would have reverted to the clergy on the expiration of the existing twenty-one-year leases.[67] For Dowdall and the cathedral clergy, however, the adoption of such an arrangement was not a serious option. By pursuing a settlement based on the premises of refoundation and re-endowment, they would have been acknowledging implicitly the moral validity of the Henrician dissolution of St Patrick's and, most embarrass-ingly, the clergy's reluctant complicity in the matter. In turn, such acknowledgements would have compromised and undermined Dowdall's strategy of Catholic restoration because it was based on a claim to con-tinuity with, and loyalty to, the ecclesiastical and canonical past. What Dowdall and the clergy wanted was not a new St Patrick's Cathedral, however much it may have resembled the old one, but the revival of the

---

[65] On the manoeuvres and discussions, in and out of parliament, which led to the English possessioners retaining their ecclesiasical property see J. Loach, *Parliament and the crown in the reign of Mary Tudor* (Oxford, 1986), chs. 6, 7.

[66] *Dignitas decani*, pp. 143–4; Morrin, *Patent rolls*, i, p. 132.

[67] Most of the existing crown leases were due to expire in 1568 or 1569.

same institution which had been established over 300 years previously.[68] Thus they had to ensure that the Henrician dissolution, the act which had broken the continuity with the medieval past, would not merely be over-turned but wholly negated.

Queen Mary and her advisers supported this position. By placing the restoration of St Patrick's at the very heart of his strategy for restoring the old religion in English Ireland, Archbishop Dowdall had appealed directly to the queen's high moral sense, and provided her in the process with a ready-made policy which sat well with her own brand of conviction politics. She had already forsaken her desire to return the bulk of the expropriated English ecclesiastical property to its original owners, in order to achieve the greater good of bringing the realm back into the papal fold. The re-establishment of a fully endowed St Patrick's thus offered an alternative and consoling means of making amends to the church, particularly as it would play such a crucial role in the general restoration and strengthening of the old religion in English Ireland. In short, the re-establishment of St Patrick's was a matter of fundamental principle. All that had to be done was to find the legal and administrative means to make this principle a reality.

To achieve this, the queen called upon her 'learned counsel' to furnish the requisite legal formula. Instead of attacking the Henrician dissolution outright, the counsellors found a solution to the problem by highlighting the legal validity of the original foundation of St Patrick's, which they con-cluded was 'godly and right honourable'. It was this finding, rather than any inadequacies in the process per se, which raised serious questions about the legitimacy of the Henrician dissolution of St Patrick's. Seen in this light, it was difficult to find a moral or legal justification for the act and, not sur-prisingly, when the counsellors went looking for one, their search was unsuccessful. St Patrick's Cathedral, they advised the queen, had been 'at no time by the order of our laws of that our realm [of Ireland] dissolved'. In short, what had transpired in January 1547 was a 'pretensed dissolution'.[69]

This finding had two important implications. The first was that the new dean and chapter of St Patrick's, and the new colleges of vicars choral and petty canons, would from the moment they received their patents of appointment be legally entitled to enter into the property of the cathedral. The second was that the state, which had engineered the original dissol-ution, would also be duty bound to place at the clergy's disposal its full legal and administrative apparatus to enable them to regain possession of the

---

[68] This desire for continuity is evident in the restoration charter of 15 June 1555.
[69] The queen to the lord deputy, lord chancellor and Irish council, 23 February 1555 (Mason, *History of St Patrick's*, pp. 156–8); the queen to the lord deputy, the keeper of the great seal and the attorney general, 10 September 1555, Memoranda Roll 2 & 3 Philip and Mary, m. 2 (NAI, Ferguson MS, v, pp. 21–4).

property which had been wrongly detained from them. On 23 February 1555 the queen spelt this out in no uncertain terms to Lord Deputy St Leger, Lord Chancellor Cusack and the Irish council, commanding them to suffer the new dean and chapter 'without contradiction to enter the said church, and all the lands, possessions and goods thereto belonging, and all the rents and profits thereof to take ... in like sort as the late dean and chapter did ... before the pretensed dissolution'. She also ordered them to deliver unto the dean and chapter 'such writings and processes, under our great seal out of our chancery and other courts there, as be necessary for the accomplishment of our said pleasure, and the sure and lawful assurance of the said dean and chapter in this behalf'.[70]

Despite the explicit nature of the queen's commands, however, it is apparent that – in his decision to challenge them – Lord Deputy St Leger greatly underestimated the seriousness with which the combined forces of the crown and the local clergy were pursuing the full restoration of St Patrick's. Yet, in some ways, it is also explicable. At this juncture, the viceroy was beset by a series of problems which threatened to engulf him and his administration, and which created the pressurised context that moved him to put his political future on the line by subverting the queen's wishes. Amongst an ever-growing list of troubles was the imminent destruction, at the hands of the resurgent O'Mores and O'Connors, of his plantation scheme in Laois and Offaly. It also included, in the work of an ongoing royal commission investigating corruption at the heart of the Irish government, the threatened exposure of his longstanding financial mal-practices. And as if these troubles were not bad enough, St Leger's trad-itional method of papering over cracks in his administration – his use of crown property as a source of patronage – was becoming increasingly dif-ficult to sustain. Alienations and long leases had diminished the politico-economic value of the monastic lands. The restoration in May 1554 of Gerald, eleventh earl of Kildare, had taken away the possibility of exploiting further the valuable Fitzgerald estates. And now he was faced with the prospective loss of the lucrative parsonages of St Patrick's Cath-edral, property which through his own machinations had only relatively recently come on to the market.[71] Nevertheless, it is doubtful that St Leger would have challenged the queen had he not sensed in her settlement of the property of St Patrick's a genuine opportunity to salvage something from the wreckage. This opportunity presented itself in the one concession that Queen Mary made to a beneficiary of the dissolution of St Patrick's

---

[70] Mason, *History of St Patrick's*, pp. 156–8

[71] For a general account of the difficulties experienced by St Leger during his last spell as viceroy see Brady, *Chief Governors*, pp. 66–71.

Cathedral. The beneficiary in question was Matthew King, the English-born clerk of the check in Ireland.

Prior to Mary's accession in 1553, King had bought a lease of the prebends of Kilmactalway, Mulhuddart and Newcastle Lyons, from the original crown lessee, James Walshe, 'to his great charges'. The lease had cost him £300, which was two-and-a-half times the value of the annual rent of £118 13s. 8d., and he stood to make a very significant loss from the transaction now that the parsonages were to be returned to their former owners, respectively the prebendaries of Mulhuddart and Kilmactalway and the archdeacon of Glendalough. He therefore petitioned the queen for some redress, counting on his long service to the crown in Ireland to win him a sympathetic hearing, a ploy which had already yielded substantial dividends in a series of unrelated suits made in the opening months of Mary's reign. King's unerring ability to tap the queen's largesse did not fail him on this occasion either. Having discussed his predicament with the delegation from St Patrick's, and bearing in mind how he 'had served us and our dearest father and brother right honestly', the queen once again acted as his good lady and prevailed upon the clergy 'to suffer the same Matthew to enjoy the moiety of the said lease'.[72]

As far as the queen was concerned, this concession to Matthew King was unique and, even on it own terms, strictly limited in scope. The clerk of the check would only be allowed to retain his interest in half of the leased tithes, for which he would have to pay the reserved rent to the clergy instead of the crown. The clergy themselves would repossess the remainder of the tithes with immediate effect, and would be free to demise them to whoever they wished at whatever price the market would bear. Furthermore, on the expiry of King's existing lease in 1569, they would also regain full possession of his moiety.[73] Overall, then, it is clear that the cathedral clergy had entered into a bargain that was designed not to disadvantage them unduly. Nor was the arrangement indicative of any general concern on the part of the queen to mollify prospective lay discontent over the imminent

---

[72] *LM* I, pt. 2, p. 99; Mason, *History of St Patrick's*, pp. 48 (note f), 158; *Fiants, Edward VI*, no. 87; Matthew King to Sir William Cecil, 9 August 1565 (TNA: PRO, SP 63/14, no. 43). For King's earlier and successful petitions at the Marian court see the grants of (i) a discharge of a debt of £234 16s. 4d. and an instruction to the lord deputy to take order with the Irish rebels to undo the despoliation of his goods in Kilkenny and Upper Ossory, he being 'a man of long service', dated at Westminister 31 October 1553; and (ii) of leases of the manors of Lucan and Moyclare, 'in consideration of his long and honest service', given under letters dated at Westminster 13 and 19 December 1553 (Morrin, *Patent rolls*, i, pp. 317–18). King had originally come over to Ireland in the 1530s as a servant of Lord Deputy Grey (*SP* II, pp. 314, 530). His repeated success at court suggests that he may have had a patron close to the queen, perhaps related in some way to his earlier association with Grey.

[73] Mason, *History of St Patrick's*, p. 158; *Fiants, Edward VI*, no. 87.

restitution of the lands, tithes, buildings and valuables of St Patrick's. In reality, it was an attempt, exceptional at that, to accommodate the conflicting wishes of a favoured royal servitor and three members of the newly appointed, and equally favoured, chapter of St Patrick's.

It is doubtful, however, that many of the cathedral property holders saw King's concession in these terms. In theory, it held out the possibility that others in a similar position to him might be able to negotiate personal settlements which would allow them to retain some or all of their cathedral holdings; an inference which the queen and her counsellors inadvertently led others to draw by including the announcement of the concession in the same letter in which the general settlement of the cathedral's property was disclosed.[74] For Lord Deputy St Leger, in particular, already aware of the queen's capitulation over the expropriated monastic lands, this contradictory juxtaposition of uncompromising royal resolve and apparent liberality served to highlight one possible way in which his mounting problems might be eased. And it was on this basis – the hope of extending King's concession to the other holders of cathedral property – that he mounted his campaign of opposition.

St Leger's immediate objective, then, was strictly delimited. There is no real evidence to suggest that he wished to obstruct the restoration of St Patrick's in general terms, a conclusion evident from his compliant participation in the early formalities of re-establishment, such as the granting of the clergy's patents and their charter of restoration. Nor, in accepting the principle of re-establishment, could he have hoped to prevent outright the restitution of the cathedral's goods and property, given that the full resumption of its old endowments would have been both a necessary and inevitable part of its revival. Rather, St Leger's aim in challenging the queen's will was to bring the clergy to the negotiating table so that he and his supporters might salvage some as yet indeterminate portion of their cathedral holdings, in the same way that Matthew King had done. Once at the table, St Leger could be quietly confident that he would wring worthwhile concessions from a queen who had already shown a willingness to abandon high principle when faced with the unpalatable reality of well-organised political opposition, and from a clergy who only eight years previously had submitted to him on the matter of the dissolution. Such concessions, once achieved, would ultimately help preserve the reputation of his increasingly tarnished style of viceregal government.

The limited purview of St Leger's campaign of resistance was otherwise evident in the dilatory and secretive tactics that comprised it, which reveal that he was determined to avoid gestures or utterances that might be

74 Mason, *History of St Patrick's*, p. 158.

construed as an open, outright rejection of the cathedral's re-establishment and the restitution of its property. Such manoeuvres began almost as soon as he received the queen's letter of 23 February 1555, which commanded him to put the clergy into possession of their property by the feast of the Annunciation (26 March) following. It appears that St Leger and his officials responded by seeking the postponement of the restitution until Easter (14 April), probably on the grounds that they would have had insufficient time to effect it in the short interval between the receipt of the queen's letter and the designated date for restitution. On this occasion, at least, the argument was plausible and the request was upheld by the queen and the dean and chapter.[75]

Easter 1555 came and went, however, and still St Leger and his officials made no move to put the clergy in possession of their goods and property.[76] On the contrary, the dean and chapter were of the view, later accepted by the queen, that St Leger had not only encouraged the cathedral property holders to withstand her pleasure, 'refusing or delaying to make restitution according our said desire', but was actually holding in his own custody a 'great part' of the plate and ornaments. In the spring or early summer of 1555, therefore, the dean and chapter, who had retained Richard Netterville[77] as their legal adviser, served a writ of *sub poena* upon the 'farmers' of the cathedral property – amongst whom was St Leger's stalwart supporter, John Parker, the master of the rolls, and such local luminaries as John Plunket of Dunsoghly and Richard St Laurence, lord of Howth – in the hope that the issue would be finally resolved in their favour in the court of chancery. Yet even in this, the court of equity and conscience, the clergy found that they faced not only the occupiers of their property, but the political muscle of the viceroy. Sir Thomas Cusack, the lord chancellor, who sat in judgement on the case, was one of St Leger's closest and

---

[75] That official sanction was given for this later date is confirmed by the queen's letter to the lord deputy, the keeper of the great seal and the attorney general of 10 September 1555, Memoranda Roll 2 & 3 Philip and Mary, m. 2 (NAI, Ferguson MS, v, p. 21). The queen stated that St Leger had been instructed 'to restore or see full restitution made unto the . . . dean, prebendaries, chapter and company from Easter last of all their lands, tenements and whole possessions and of all jewels, ornaments, books, plate and moveables'. The queen also mentioned that St Leger had not 'since Easter last signified any cause or good matter' why he had failed to effect the restitution, which clearly implies that he had done so prior to Easter.

[76] The reconstruction of events in this paragraph is based on information contained in the following sources: the queen to the lord deputy, the keeper of the great seal and the attorney general, 10 September 1555, Memoranda Roll 2 & 3 Philip and Mary, m. 2 (NAI, Ferguson MS, v, pp. 21–4); 'Account of the proctor of the economy of St Patrick's, c. June 1555 – c. June 1556' (Mason, *History of St Patrick's*, pp. xxxii–xxxiii); NAI, RC 6/1, p. 47.

[77] Netterville later emerged as one of the leading spokesmen of the Pale community's protests against the viceregal imposition of the cess (Brady, *Chief Governors*, pp. 149, 153, 236–7).

longstanding allies in Ireland. The viceroy had procured his advancement to the chancellorship, and he was now in a position to reciprocate. To the frustration of the dean and chapter and, later, the great annoyance of the queen, it appears that Cusack, at St Leger's bidding, found 'an office' or title in the property for the crown.[78]

The lord chancellor's judgement that the crown was the lawful owner of the cathedral's property, a judgement made on the grounds that the extant documentation on the Henrician dissolution in the Irish chancery was sound in law and witnessed the irrefutable fact that the dean and chapter had surrendered voluntarily, marked the high point of St Leger's campaign of opposition. For the viceroy, this was the ultimate delaying tactic, a clever stroke that denied and overrode the dean and chapter's contention that the Henrician dissolution was illegitimate; a move which would finally convince them that their interests would best be served by reaching an accommodation with him. The clergy, however, were to prove more resilient than St Leger had bargained for. Encouraged by their conviction in the righteousness of their cause, a conviction that Dowdall's strategy had instilled in them, and the confidence that the crown's recently professed support engendered, they were prepared to carry the fight beyond the Irish chancery, all the way back to the court of Queen Mary. Thus, at some point in the early summer of 1555, the dean and chapter wrote to the queen informing her of the judgement the lord chancellor had made. The queen and her counsel responded in kind, advising the dean and chapter to enter a 'traverse' or a formal denial against the unwanted office. She also wrote to St Leger and the attorney general, Barnaby Scurlock, ordering them to 'confess' or admit the traverse as soon as the dean and chapter entered it in court.[79]

The queen's decision that the dean and chapter should formally contest her 'office' or title to their lands was an admission of sorts that the viceroy's tactics, no matter how unscrupulous, were technically valid. St Leger's 'victory', however, was very hollow. In reality, all that the queen had done was acknowledge that the deputy's campaign of resistance had remained within strictly legal limits. A more sober analysis, an analysis that was becoming increasingly apparent to the viceroy himself, was that he had

---

[78] On the relationship of Cusack and Parker with St Leger see Brady, *Chief Governors*, pp. 31–2.

[79] None of these letters are now extant but their existence is either implied or referred to explicitly in the queen's letter to the lord deputy, the keeper of the great seal and the attorney general of 10 September 1555, Memoranda Roll 2 & 3 Philip and Mary, m. 2 (NAI, Ferguson MS, v, pp. 21–4). A 'traverse of office' was a mode of disputing an office or inquisition which found the crown entitled to property obtained by or belonging to the party traversing: D.M. Walker, *The Oxford companion to law* (Oxford, 1980), p. 1231.

made a major miscalculation in his estimation of the resolve of the queen and the cathedral clergy. Their response to his machinations during the summer of 1555 clearly showed that they had no intention of submitting to him, and that they were quite content to play and were confident of beating him at his own game. Indeed they were even prepared to apply the kind of political pressure which he himself was used to dispensing, but which he had rarely been forced to endure, a pressure which was applied to the deputy most vigorously, and to its greatest effect, in the late summer of 1555.

In late June or early July, Sir Thomas Cusack was summoned to London to appear before the lords of the English privy council. The precise reasons for this summons are unknown. It is possible that Cusack's involvement in finding the queen's unwanted office in the cathedral property lay behind it, although this cannot now be proved. More likely, it was part of a general investigation into St Leger's government, which was being conducted at this time following recent revelations of the deputy's financial misconduct produced by the royal commissioner, Sir William Fitzwilliam.[80] What is certain, however, is that Cusack's summons demonstrated the increasing vulnerability of St Leger and his regime. And it was a vulnerability which the dean and chapter of St Patrick's were quick to recognise and turn to their advantage. At some point in July or in the opening weeks of August, Dean Leverous and the chapter appointed John Sonnyng, the prebendary of Wicklow, and Richard Johnson, the prebendary of Maynooth, as their agents to attend upon the queen to seek her further support in their efforts to resume the cathedral's property. It was a mission that was designed to coincide with Cusack's stay in England and to cause the maximum discomfiture to the chancellor, the viceroy, and the latter's tottering administration.[81]

Sonnyng and Johnson appeared before the queen sometime in late August or early September and made 'lamentable complaint' against the viceroy and his officials for their conduct in resisting the restitution of their property. In truth, it is unlikely that the queen was made aware of anything substantially new by the prebendaries. Nevertheless, their first-hand

---

[80] *Patent rolls, 1554–5*, p. 344; Brady, *Chief Governors*, pp. 66–7. Ralph Cockerill, St Leger's private secretary, was also subjected to questioning by the privy council at the same time as Cusack (*APC 1554–6*, p. 158).

[81] The queen to the lord deputy, the keeper of the great seal and the attorney general, 10 September 1555, Memoranda Roll 2 & 3 Philip and Mary, m. 2 (NAI, Ferguson MS, v, p. 21). The precise date of Sonnyng and Johnson's appointment cannot now be ascertained. However, we can assume that it pre-dated the dean and chapter's discovery, made in August 1555, that Johnson was a married priest. Formal proceedings against Johnson commenced in the consistory court in Dublin on 31 August 1555 while he was in England (*RDD*, pp. 77–8).

testimony was still significant. It threw the deputy's evasive and secretive disobedience and, more particularly, its consequences, into sharper focus. Johnson and Sonnyng painted a vivid picture of the suffering which they and their colleagues had endured as a result of the deputy's proceedings, recounting how they had been 'oppressed and driven to their shifts without house or any provision towards household, in such wise as they be fain to seek their dinners in the city, and there to hostry undecently'. Their testimony had the desired effect. The pious queen was both scandalised and infuriated by these revelations. On 10 September she voiced her anger in a stinging letter to St Leger in which she castigated him for actions that had not only caused the clerical suffering reported by Sonnyng and Johnson, but which had also hindered 'the service of God' and caused great offence 'amongst our subjects'. She therefore demanded in uncompromising terms that he and his officials do 'all that by order of law and justice is necessary to be done' to bring about the long-delayed restitution, including the complete abrogation of the crown's 'pretensed office' in the property, and the immediate restoration to the dean and chapter of those parcels of the premises which were held by the deputy and his supporters.[82] And in case they were in any doubt about the seriousness with which she viewed this matter, the queen demonstrated in the most graphic of terms what the consequences would be for anyone in the Irish administration still contemplating further disobedience. Three days after writing to St Leger, on 13 September 1555, the queen removed Sir Thomas Cusack, the man who had marshalled opposition to the restitution of the cathedral's property in the court of chancery, from his office. The timing of his removal, and the fact that he was replaced as chancellor by the incoming archbishop of Dublin, Hugh Curwen, an appointee who had a vested interest in looking after the cathedral's interests, suggests very strongly that Cusack's recalcitrance featured very prominently among the queen's reasons for instituting the change in personnel.[83]

Cusack's removal from office marked the effective end of Lord Deputy St Leger's campaign of resistance. Bereft of a supportive lord chancellor, he had neither the capacity nor the will to sustain an outwardly lawful challenge against the queen's order to restore the cathedral's property. Thus,

---

[82] NAI, Ferguson MS, v, pp. 21–4.

[83] *Patent rolls 1555–7*, p. 33. Lascelles, without citing any source, stated that Cusack resigned from office on 3 July 1555 (*LM* I, pt. 2, p. 4). An entry on the Irish patent rolls refutes this, however, confirming that he was still chancellor on 10 July (Morrin, *Patent rolls*, i, pp. 340–2). The most likely explanation for his departure is that he was forced out of office after the investigation of his conduct, including his contribution to St Leger's campaign of resistance against the restitution of the cathedral's property, was concluded by the English privy council.

within the year and following their procurement of a judgement of *Amoveas manus* in the Irish exchequer in Michaelmas term 1555,[84] the dean and chapter obtained decrees in chancery, and at least one judgement in a common law court, which finally quashed the opposition to the restitution.[85] Cusack's departure from office also had much wider ramifications however. More than anything, it signified the declining powers of Lord Deputy St Leger and the ailing condition of his regime. He too was dismissed from office within the year, having failed to rebut the many charges of corruption and incompetence levelled against him by the queen's commissioner, Sir William Fitzwilliam. Amongst this catalogue of perceived failings, St Leger's defiance of the queen on the matter of St Patrick's must have loomed very large.[86]

There was a certain irony in this denouement. When Archbishop Dowdall conceived and commenced the implementation of his strategy of Catholic restoration at the beginning of Mary's reign, he could not have foreseen, and certainly did not intend, that it should have had such ultimately negative consequences for St Leger and Cusack. Dowdall had been a close ally of St Leger in the halcyon days of his government during Henry VIII's reign. Sir Thomas Cusack was his kinsman. Both men had defended him when his religious conservatism came under fire at the council board in Edward VI's reign.[87] Despite these old friendships, however, it was inevitable that the implementation of Dowdall's strategy would lead to this undesired outcome. Based, as it was, on a rejuvenated, independent and assertive clericalism, there was no place for the Dowdall strategy in the St Leger mode of government, which had been created in the era of, and which had come to depend upon, clerical submissiveness and the despoliation of the church. It was St Leger's misfortune that at a time when most other aspects of his government were beset by crippling problems, Mary Tudor

---

[84] Mason, *History of St Patrick's*, pp. 150 (note k), 162, xxxii: the sealing of the writ of *Amoveas manus* cost the cathedral three shillings. The writ of *Amoveas manus* commanded the return to a person or institution of property belonging to him, which was in the possession of the crown (Walker, *Oxford companion to law*, p. 53).

[85] Surviving notices of chancery decrees in the dean and chapter's favour, dating from the spring and summer of 1556, were against Richard St Lawrence, lord of Howth, William Basnet and Robert Bathe (NAI, RC 6/1, pp. 47–8, 50); the common law ruling, dating from the same period, was against George Carey (*Patent rolls 1560–3*, p. 113). St Laurence, Basnet and Bathe were probably the last to hold out against the restoration of the cathedral's property. It is likely that most of the crown lessees submitted after the judgement of *Amoveas manus* was given in the exchequer.

[86] For a general account of the circumstances and significance of St Leger's fall see Brady, *Chief Governors*, pp. 66–71.

[87] Shirley, *Church in Ireland 1547–1567*, pp. 54–60. Cusack's sister, Thomasine, was married to Christopher Dowdall, the archbishop of Armagh's brother: Gallwey, 'The Cusack family of Counties Meath and Dublin', *IG* 5/3 (1976), pp. 311–13; Nicholls, 'Calendar of chancery pleadings concerning County Louth', p. 251.

cut off one of the main avenues of escape by turning back the clock and allowing the revival of an independent, richly endowed and newly reinvigorated church in the English Pale. Faced with the loss of existing ecclesiastical resources, and no prospect of acquiring others, St Leger's ability to buy himself out of trouble was fatally undermined. His departure from Ireland, and the fall of his ally Thomas Cusack, symbolised nothing less than the victory of medieval clerical corporatism over the secular forces that were so integral a part of the Henrician Reformation. The defeat of these forces provided Archbishop Curwen with the most favourable of circumstances in which to implement Archbishop Dowdall's strategy in the diocese of Dublin.

7

Rejuvenation and survival: the old religion during the episcopacy of Hugh Curwen, 1555–67

Hugh Curwen, archbishop of Dublin and lord chancellor of Ireland (1555–67), is one of the more obscure figures to have featured in Ireland's Reformation story. Unlike the other men who occupied the archbishopric after Henry VIII's break with Rome, Curwen's career is poorly documented in the sources through which the history of sixteenth-century Ireland is normally studied, in particular, the records of the English secretaries of state, which are held in the National Archives of the United Kingdom (formerly the Public Record Office). Thus there are no readily accessible insights into the character, motives and actions of a man who, in a tumultuous period in the late 1550s and early 1560s, presided over the successive restoration of Catholic and Protestant religious settlements in the heart of English Ireland.[1]

Curwen's inconspicuousness in the historical record has had a negative effect on the way historians have treated him hitherto. In the nineteenth and early twentieth centuries, for example, when much of the historiography was infused with religious polemic, it led to a very crude concentration on the best-known fact about his career: his apparent willingness to accept whatever creed was promoted by the Tudor monarchs. In this connection, Curwen was perceived as something of an embarrassment by Catholic and Church of Ireland writers alike; a figure unworthy of approbation, yet one who could not be disowned entirely. To Catholics, he personified the happy but all too brief reconciliation of the see of Dublin with Rome in the mid-1550s, a man who then ruined it all by becoming an 'even more abandoned character than Brown[e], his heterodox predecessor', when he accepted

---

[1] Most of the surviving Curwen correspondence is printed in Shirley, *Church in Ireland 1547–1567*, pp. 142–8, 151–3, 240–1, 248–9, 253–4, 304–5. The majority of these letters date from the latter end of his career in Ireland and are mainly concerned with his attempt to secure a translation to an English bishopric, on account of age and mounting health problems.

Queen Elizabeth's call to acknowledge her supremacy.[2] Similarly, for supporters of the established church, the fact of Curwen's compliance, although welcome – it legitimated the claim that the Church of Ireland alone maintained the apostolic succession on the island[3] – could not disguise the reality that the most devoutly Protestant of his episcopal colleagues castigated him as a crypto-Catholic, who did nothing to further the cause of godly reform.[4] Thus, in an effort to reconcile these opposites, historians on both sides of the religious divide treated the archbishop contemptuously and dismissively. Following the lead of the English historian, John Strype, they judged him to be a temporising product of an amoral age, 'a complier in all reigns'.[5]

The emergence of a more objective school of historical writing in the twentieth century has created one of the essential preconditions for a much needed re-evaluation of Curwen's role in the religious upheavals of his time. Yet it has proved difficult to reconstruct an alternative picture to the caricature of Curwen as a religious trimmer. Instead, lacking the controversial convictions which informed previous estimations of the archbishop, and beset by the same problems with the sources that past historians experienced, modern writers have allowed Curwen to assume an increasingly bland historical persona, a feature typified by the treatment afforded him in Robin Dudley Edwards's standard account of the Irish Reformation, *Church and State in Tudor Ireland*. Here, Curwen is the subject of a mere handful of incidental references which do little more than depict him as a shadowy, almost anonymous, figure, a depiction that has remained in being to the present day.[6]

The existing portrayals of Curwen, then, are deeply unsatisfactory. Yet, paradoxically, it is Curwen's very inconspicuousness that provides one of the essential keys to opening up our understanding of his role and impact. While we cannot discount the possibility that important records have been

---

[2] M. J. Brennan, *An ecclesiastical history of Ireland, from the introduction of Christianity . . . to the year MDCCCXXIX* (2 vols., Dublin, 1840), ii, p. 104.

[3] R. Mant, *History of the Church of Ireland* (2 vols., London, 1840), i, pp. 269–70; H. J. Lawlor, *The Reformation and the Irish episcopate* (London, 1932).

[4] This was starkly revealed by E.P. Shirley in his edition of letters and papers relating to the history of the Church of Ireland in the mid-Tudor period. Ironically, one of the avowed aims of his book was to show 'that the true succession of Bishops in the Church was ever preserved, and that *solely* in the line of Prelates acknowledged by the State' (Shirley, *Church in Ireland 1547–1567*, p. vii). The damning letters about Curwen were written by Archbishop Loftus of Armagh and Bishop Brady of Meath (ibid., pp. 200–2, 225–7, 274–6).

[5] J. Strype, *Memorials of the most reverend father in God, Thomas Cranmer . . .* (2 vols., Oxford, 1812), i, p. 54; Ronan, *Reformation in Dublin*, pp. 429–31; P. Wilson, *The beginnings of modern Ireland* (Dublin, 1912), pp. 336–8; Phillips, *History of the Church of Ireland*, ii, pp. 281–2, 298.

[6] Edwards, *Church and state*, pp. 163, 178, 188, 190, 211, 217.

lost in the conventional sources, it is not entirely accidental that they are silent about the archbishop's beliefs and activities. The main reason for this was the nature of Curwen's mission in Ireland. As we saw in the preceding chapter, he was sent to Dublin with the express purpose of implementing the strategy for Catholic restoration that had been conceived and promoted by Archbishop Dowdall of Armagh and the clergy of the English Pale, and which was grounded upon the revival of local ecclesiastical jurisdiction, and the unrestricted practice of medieval canon law. Given this, it was inevitable that Curwen's sphere of activity would be confined largely to local ecclesiastical institutions, whose personnel would also be predisposed towards supporting his endeavours. Thus, certainly in the early years of his episcopate, he had no compelling reasons to write about religious matters to the crown and its advisers on a regular basis. Fully appraised of the requirements of the Dowdall strategy, and fully possessed of the wherewithal to give them effect – both by virtue of his qualifications and the support that he commanded from his clergy – Hugh Curwen needed none of the guidance, nor succour, so frequently sought by the reformist archbishops of Dublin, George Browne and Adam Loftus, from their political masters in London. His story, then, cannot be, nor arguably could ever have been, reconstructed from the cross-channel communications of the Dublin and London governments. Rather, it is to be found in the surviving, albeit sketchy, notices of the activities of the two institutions over which he presided during his stay in Ireland: the Dublin diocesan administration and the court of chancery.

I

Hugh Curwen landed at Ringsend on 22 October 1555[7] and immediately set about implementing the Dowdall strategy for the canonical restoration of Catholicism. His first task was to make known the constitutional basis of the settlement. Thus, as instructed by the crown on the eve of his departure from England, he brought with him the bull of Pope Paul IV erecting Ireland into a kingdom, and published it throughout the realm. This document – which had been sought specifically by the clerical elite of the English Pale and which aimed, in effect, to harmonise the medieval bull *Laudabiliter* and the act for the kingly title of 1541 – re-established in one stroke the Catholic and canonical credentials of the Englishry in Ireland, and renewed the validity of their traditional role of reforming the Irishry along conventional

---

[7] Chronicle of Dublin (TCD, MS 591, f. 18r). The manuscript gives 1557 as the year of Curwen's arrival, but this was clearly an error for 1555. Thomas Rogers, who the chronicler stated was mayor of Dublin at the time Curwen landed, held this position during 1555–6. In addition, Curwen took his oath of office for the chancellorship on 24 October 1555 (*NHI* IX, p. 554; Morrin, *Patent rolls*, i, p. 340).

canonical lines. As such, the bull signified that the return of the country to the Catholic fold would not merely be a religious event, but also a reaffirmation of the political, social and cultural values of the community of the English Pale, in the modernised form into which they had evolved under Lord Deputy St Leger in the 1540s. Whether Hugh Curwen himself shared in these beliefs and aspirations is not now known, but in assuming the role of herald of the pope's grant – by its very nature indicative of a formal acceptance of the message it proclaimed – he quickly established his *bona fides* with those who did uphold them, in particular the senior clergy of his diocese.[8]

Curwen's dedication to supporting the interests and aspirations of his clergy was also apparent in another early activity. Only three days after he arrived in Dublin, the archbishop held his first session in the court of chancery.[9] This was significant on a number of counts. In the first instance, the reappearance of a Catholic, English-born archbishop of Dublin as president of the court of equity and conscience – a throwback to the days before the schism when the office of lord chancellor was regularly held by the archbishop – had great symbolic resonance. Like Pope Paul IV's bull, it too proclaimed that the impending restoration of the old religion would take place in its traditional politico-cultural setting, in which the organs of church and state would work together to promote a mutually held notion of a canonically orthodox, English civility in Ireland. But it also had a more practical ramification. One of the key measures of the Dowdall strategy for restoring Catholicism was the re-establishment of St Patrick's Cathedral, the traditional centre for the administration of canon law in the diocese of Dublin. Despite the queen's support for this measure, however, it had met with considerable resistance from Lord Deputy St Leger and some of his supporters in the months prior to Curwen's arrival in Ireland, a group who hoped to retain some or all of the interests which they had acquired in the cathedral's property following its dissolution in 1547. The appointment of Archbishop Curwen as lord chancellor in September 1555 – an appointment pointedly made at the expense of St Leger's trusted supporter, Sir Thomas Cusack – was intended to bring this resistance to an end, an intention which was quickly realised. Ranged against an institution which commanded such powerful political and judicial backing, much of the

---

[8] *APC 1554–6*, p. 179; Morrin, *Patent rolls*, i, p. 339. Some political reformers in the Pale saw the propaganda potential in the bull and sought to make the most of it. One writer, for example, in proposing 'A present remedy for the reformation of the north and the rest of Ireland', suggested that Queen Mary and King Philip should exploit their position by writing letters to the Irishry declaring that the pope had given them his whole interest in the kingdom (TNA: PRO, SP 62/1, no. 13).

[9] Chronicle of Dublin (TCD, MS 591, f. 18r); Morrin, *Patent rolls*, i, p. 340.

opposition to an unconditional restitution of the cathedral's property col-
lapsed. The few recalcitrant individuals who continued the fight – men like
Richard St Lawrence, lord of Howth, William Basnett and Robert Bathe –
were finally defeated in chancery, where Archbishop Curwen granted
decrees in favour of Dean Leverous, Chancellor Nangle and the cathedral
chapter during his first ten months in office.[10]

Curwen's early appearances in chancery, then, not only helped define the
politico-cultural context in which the old religion was to be restored, but
also established the fact that the local church was a rejuvenated body, an
institution which had rediscovered and repossessed important links to its
past and, as a result, had recovered the moral authority and political
strength that it had lost during the reigns of Henry VIII and Edward VI. All
of these developments were crucial, given that Archbishop Curwen and his
clergy – following the lead and direction of Archbishop Dowdall in Armagh –
were about to restore traditional religion solely by means of their own
clerical and canonical authority. The chosen medium for instituting this
restoration of the old religion was the provincial council, the body traditionally responsible for enacting local canon law for the diocese and its
suffragan sees.

Curwen held his provincial council sometime between his arrival in
Ireland on 22 October 1555 and the close of that year as it was then
reckoned, on 24 March 1556. Few notices of the council's deliberations
have survived, but it is known that careful efforts were made to ensure that
it conformed in every possible way with its medieval predecessors, an
important consideration given the very fundamental appeal to the canonical
past upon which the whole restoration strategy was founded. Thus it was
held in its traditional location, Christ Church Cathedral, in the heart of the
city of Dublin. In addition, apart from the defunct religious houses, its
membership would have been the same as that which had sat in the pre-
Reformation councils, comprising the archbishop of Dublin, his four suffragan bishops of Kildare, Ossory, Ferns and Leighlin, all the archdeacons
of the province, and representatives of the deans and chapters and of the
parochial clergy from each diocese. It also included a representative of the
mayor and commons of Dublin, Alderman Nicholas Bennet, a papal notary
who had once served William Power, the Henrician archdeacon of Dublin,
as registrar of his court. Together, this group met and prayed for a total of
forty-two days, concluding its deliberations by promulgating a set of new

---

[10] NAI, RC 6/1, pp. 47–8, 50. The cathedral's business was expedited in chancery by John
Wicombe who received a fee of 23s. in the year June 1555 to June 1556. The cathedral also
paid 17s. in this year for the drafting of a copy of one of the decrees granted by Curwen
('Account of the proctor of the economy of St Patrick's, c. 1555 – c. 1556', printed in
Mason, *History of St Patrick's*, p. xxxiii).

canons that restored the religious and ecclesiastical life of the province to something closely akin to its late medieval condition.[11]

It is reasonable to assume that one of the key objectives of Curwen's legislation – given the fact that the entire restoration settlement was predicated upon the notion of traditional canonical authority – was the reaffirmation of conventional standards of clerical behaviour and deportment, especially priestly celibacy, the litmus test of canonical rectitude for the English Irish clerical elite. This assumption is corroborated by the fact that similar measures had already featured prominently in Archbishop Dowdall's canons of 1553/4, the paradigm upon which the new Dublin legislation would have been based; and, more importantly, by the fact that it was known to the new diocesan administration in St Patrick's Cathedral that there were still a number of married priests operating within the boundaries of the diocese and province. Any doubts that may have persisted on this score were resolved in the late summer of 1555, when it was discovered that one of their own number, Richard Johnson, a cathedral prebendary, was himself a married priest.[12]

Johnson's case was a source of some embarrassment to the local church. An Englishman by birth, he originally came to Ireland in the mid-1530s in the retinue of Lord Deputy Skeffington, from whom he acquired a number of livings, including the rectory of Delgany, and the prebend of Maynooth in St Patrick's, which he held until the cathedral's suppression in 1547.[13] Johnson was regarded by his peers as sufficiently orthodox to receive their nomination for his old prebend on the cathedral's restoration in the spring of 1555. Indeed, in July or August of that year, he was actually at court campaigning on the cathedral's behalf to secure the crown's help in the battle against Lord Deputy St Leger and his supporters over the restitution of its property.[14] Yet it was while he was on this mission in England that a scandalous and apparently hidden part of his past was brought to the notice of Robert Wellesley, archdeacon of Dublin, and official principal of the see *sede vacante*. One of Johnson's parishioners from Delgany, James

---

[11] Marsh's Library, MS Z4.2.7 (Loftus Annals), f. 431; *RDD*, pp 28–35; Book of accounts of the corporation of the city of Dublin, 1541–1613 (DCA, MR/35, p. 140); Registrum Novum of Christ Church (RCB, C.6.1.6, no. 3), pp. 1084–5. Bennet sought an allowance of 2*s.* per day in expenses from the Trinity Guild for attendance at the council.

[12] PRONI, MS DIO/4/2/13, pp. 101–5 ('Dowdall's register', no. 85); *RDD*, pp. 77–8.

[13] *LP* VIII, no. 729; D.S. Chambers (ed.), *Faculty office registers 1534–1549. A calendar of the first two registers of the Archbishop of Canterbury's faculty office* (Oxford, 1966), p. 221; Morrin, *Patent rolls*, i, pp. 1, 142. Johnson's livings were in the gift of the crown *sede vacante* and because of the earl of Kildare's attainder.

[14] Mason, *History of St Patrick's*, pp. 155–6; the queen to the lord deputy, the keeper of the great seal and the attorney general, 10 September 1555, Memoranda Roll 2 & 3 Philip and Mary, m. 2 (NAI, Ferguson MS, v, p. 21); above pp. 238–9.

Archebold, appeared in the consistory court at the head of a delegation from the parish, and gave evidence that Johnson had solemnly contracted matrimony with one Margery Sutton in the late 1530s, and that they had lived together for years as man and wife. Moreover, 'heedless of his salvation', he had continued to celebrate masses and other divine services without obtaining any absolution or dispensation 'to the great denigration of honest clerics established in sacred orders', the damage of his 'humble flock' and 'the most pernicious example of other christians not immediately entrusted to himself'. Thus, notwithstanding the fact that he had played an important role in the re-establishment of St Patrick's, and particularly because he had failed to come forward to confess his past indiscretion, Johnson was deprived of his livings and removed from the cathedral body shortly after returning from England in September 1555.[15]

The condemnatory tone of the language used in the official record of the proceedings against Johnson clearly reveals how strongly the new diocesan administration felt about the issue of clerical celibacy. Thus, on Curwen's arrival, it was inevitable that the traditional bans on clerical marriage and clerical concubinage would be re-enacted by the provincial council and rigorously enforced by the various diocesan administrations thereafter. In the diocese of Dublin proper Johnson's is the last recorded prosecution for clerical marriage during Mary's reign, but it is possible that there may have been more, just as there were elsewhere in the province. In the suffragan see of Kildare, for example, Bishop Leverous, who was also dean of St Patrick's Cathedral, deprived at least one married clerk, James White, vicar of Moynam, during an episcopal visitation in November 1557. This was probably done on the back of Archbishop Curwen's provincial legislation of 1555–6.[16]

The pursuit of such offenders was undertaken for a number of reasons, all of which would have been understood and accepted by the provincial council. Not only did it confirm the clergy's own commitment to the traditional discipline of celibacy, a discipline which they believed defined their canonical rectitude vis-à-vis the Irish clergy; but, more importantly, it also provided the essential, legitimating context for the introduction of the second major element in Dowdall's strategy for restoring Catholicism. As the parishioners of Delgany had expressed it, the ministration of the

---

[15] 'necnon missas et alia divina officia atque sacramenta et sacramentalia sine aliquibus absolucione et dispensacione per eum in hac parte obtentis immemor sue salutis adhuc celebrare et ministrare non erubescit in magnam denigracionem honestatis clericorum in sacris ordinibus constitutorum dampnumque non modicum gregis sibi immediate commissi et aliorum Christifidelium perniciosissimum exemplum': *RDD*, pp. 77–8; Lawlor, *Fasti of St Patrick's*, p. 129.

[16] *RDD*, pp. 61–4

sacraments and other observances by priests with serious canonical impediments denigrated the work of the clergy as a whole and was a pernicious example to all Christians. The regularisation of their position, therefore, whether through dispensation or deprivation, would be necessary to clear the way for the formal reintroduction of the mass and other proscribed Catholic services and devotions.[17]

The provincial council's laws for restoring the mass and other observances, like its measures for reinstituting traditional clerical discipline, are not now extant, but they were certainly passed and enforced with genuine energy and commitment, as is evident from surviving documentation relating to Dublin's two cathedrals. In St Patrick's, for example, the restoration of the old liturgy coincided with the cathedral's re-establishment, and followed an eight-year hiatus in which the building had been used to house the four courts of judicature. As a result, much work had to be done, and a good deal of money spent, to refit the building to make it a suitable place for traditional worship. The most pressing need was for the re-erection of the altars. David Walsh, a local stonemason, was entrusted with the task and paid IR40s. for his labour. Additional work was required to beautify them, especially the high altar. Here, IR£11 1s. 8d. was spent on the wages and refreshment of carpenters, two labourers, and a painter and his boy, a group whose tasks included the erection of an image of St Peter, which had been brought over especially from Chester at a cost of IR18s. 9d., and a picture of the resurrection which was purchased for IR20s. Apart from the renovatory work done to the altars and their surrounds, extensive repairs were also undertaken on the windows, especially on the north window, and on the 'great' and 'second' bells in the cathedral belfries.[18]

The repair and adornment of the fabric and fittings of St Patrick's was only one element of the preparations necessary for the restoration of the mass and other Catholic services. The losses incurred by the cathedral during the period of its suppression also necessitated the purchase of new, and costly, liturgical accoutrements. In the year June 1555 to June 1556, for example, almost IR£180 was spent on a rich and ornate collection of vestments and altar cloths. These included vestments made from cloth of gold, damask, baudkyn and red velvet. In addition, three new crucifixes were purchased at a cost of IR£6, as well as two new thuribles for IR£1 10s., and a silver gilt staff for IR£19 8s. 2d. Lost or destroyed service books also had to be replaced. In the year in which the provincial council sat, the

---

[17] Ibid., pp. 77–8.
[18] 'Account of the proctor of the economy of St Patrick's, c. 1555 – c. 1556', Mason, *History of St Patrick's*, pp. xxxii–xxxiii.

cathedral purchased four new antiphonaries at a total cost of *IR£15*. This process of refitting and replenishing St Patrick's was substantially completed by Easter 1556 when, with the full authority of local canon law behind them, the cathedral clergy and choristers enacted the elaborate ritual, drama and music of the Sarum Easter services for the first time in a decade. Something of the richness and complexity of these services is hinted at in the facts that additional singers were hired on Palm Sunday to supplement the resident choir, and a special incense angel was made for the feast of Pentecost.[19]

In Christ Church Cathedral, the impact of Tudor religious reform had been less dramatic than in St Patrick's but, in terms of the restoration of a traditional liturgy, it still presented a challenge to Archbishop Curwen. The Reformation years constituted a period of confusion in the cathedral's history, which saw it undergo a change from a monastic to a secular constitution under Henry VIII, and the adoption of a vernacular, Protestant liturgy under Edward VI. As a result, the clergy of Christ Church were not fully apprised of the roles and standards which were expected of them now that a Catholic liturgical round had been re-introduced following the enactment of the provincial council's legislation of 1555–6. To clarify these matters, therefore, Archbishop Curwen drew up a set of acts or articles on liturgical observance which the cathedral clergy subscribed to, and which were probably intended to supplement the general legislation passed by the provincial council.[20]

One of the main objectives of Curwen's acts was to identify which of the various groups of cathedral clergy were responsible for particular aspects of the liturgy and to institute a series of punitive measures to ensure that they would be fulfilled. Thus, for example, the six vicars choral were held responsible for celebrating in turn the weekly 'Rood' mass, the Jesus mass in Lent and the daily Lady mass, as well as reading the Martyrology, assisting at the high altar during high mass and, again in turn, leading the choir during the canonical hours. Failure to do so was punishable by a 12*d*. fine

---

[19] Ibid.

[20] The articles, a later copy of which has survived in the Chapter Act Book of Christ Church 1574–1634 (RCB, C.6.1.7 no. 1, ff. 1r–2r) are undated, but can be assigned to the period 13 February 1557 to 18 February 1560, the dates at which John Cardiff, treasurer of the cathedral and one of the signatories of the document, was presented to and deprived of this living (Morrin, *Patent rolls*, i, pp. 353, 440; *Fiants, Elizabeth*, nos. 225–6). They were probably drawn up after an episcopal visitation of the cathedral and, given their content, and the concern that they show about maintaining proper standards for the newly restored Catholic liturgy, they probably date to the beginning of this period, *c*.1557. The articles appear to have been copied into the Elizabethan chapter act book for use as a general guide to the drafting of disciplinary articles for the clergy, even though they were of Catholic origin. They are now printed: Gillespie (ed.), *First chapter act book of Christ Church*.

payable to the vicars' board, which was to be split amongst the remaining vicars who attended the services. Similarly, the three prebendaries had to sing high mass in turn, all masses of the time and the second daily mass, as well as attending the daily office on Sundays, ferial days and upon all principal feasts. The fine for neglect of these duties was also 12*d.*, again payable to the vicars' board.[21] In addition to these regulations for the various clerical groupings, rules were also put in place for particular observances, including the canonical hours. Thus, for those ministers who 'without reasonable cause and licence neglecteth his course appointed to matins', there was a fine of 2*d.*; for prime, lauds, terce, sext and none, 3*d.*; and for evensong and compline, 2*d.*[22]

Curwen's acts not only aimed at ordering the liturgical round in Christ Church however. They were also concerned with instilling a genuine sense of decorum, solemnity and beauty into the proceedings, something which would have been deemed necessary after the iconclastic and demyth-ologising attacks to which the traditional forms of worship had been sub-jected during the Henrician and Edwardian reformations. Such concern was particularly evident in the archbishop's injunctions for the cathedral's sextons. The clerk of the choir, for example, was ordered 'to see the altars appertaining to his charge decently arrayed with clean towels and other apparel for the same' and 'to see the ornaments, copes and vestments well folded and set up'. He was also expected to 'help mass to his charge daily', to wear his surplice 'in time of divine service' when he went 'through the chancel or by the high altar', and to 'see the pavement of the chancel and aisles appointed to his charge clean and well broomed and the cobwebs to be done away'.[23] The clergy, of course, were also expected to contribute to the maintenance of a dignified and solemn liturgical round in the cathedral. Thus Archbishop Curwen instituted the general order that no cathedral cleric 'shall walk in the church in time of divine service without their habit'. Other clergymen had more specific duties in this regard. The chanter's vicar, Nicholas Dardis, and the chancellor's vicar, Edward Ellis, were, 'for the more honour of god's divine service', held responsible for appointing

---

[21] RCB, C.6.1.7 no. 1, f. 1r (Gillespie (ed.), *First chapter act book of Christ Church*, p. 23). The acts also laid down the observances to be undertaken by the three dignitaries of precentor, chancellor and treasurer, though they said nothing about the dean's liturgical responsibilities, except that he knew 'his charge'.

[22] RCB, C.6.1.7 no. 1, f. 2r (Gillespie (ed.), *First chapter act book of Christ Church*, p. 24).

[23] RCB, C.6.1.7 no. 1, f. 2r (Gillespie (ed.), *First chapter act book of Christ Church*, pp. 24–5). Similar instructions were also instituted for the Mary clerk. He was expected to maintain the same standards of decorum for the altars over which he was responsible and 'to help the mass appointed to his charge always in his surplice'. His cleaning duties extended to the 'rood loft and body of the church'.

'for Mary mass daily certain of basses and counter tenors, and for the epistle and gospel of high mass, deacon and subdeacon'.[24]

It is clear from the foregoing that the re-establishment of the mass and other Catholic observances was a central part of Curwen's synodal legislation of 1555–6, a series of measures which, like all aspects of the restoration strategy conceived by Archbishop Dowdall, was designed to recapture in all its various facets the religion of the English Pale as it had been practised in the canonically authoritative medieval past. Nowhere was this more clearly illustrated than in the elaborate religious ritual and ceremonial that was enacted to mark the occasion of the swearing-in of Thomas Radcliffe, Viscount Fitzwalter, as lord lieutenant of Ireland in the spring of 1556; ceremonies which spoke eloquently of the local church's attachment to conventional Catholic devotions, the seamless integration of that religion into the political and social fabric of English Ireland, and the local clergy's perception of themselves as the defenders of the old religion and English rule in Ireland. Thus on the day after he took his oath in Christ Church, Fitzwalter returned to the cathedral to hear divine service. Here, at the church door 'under a canopy', and accompanied by noble and civic dignitaries, he was received by Archbishop Curwen and a kneeling clergy, who censed and blessed him while he kissed the cross. He then went to the high altar and, while *Te Deum* was sung, knelt in prayer. Thereafter, he was censed and blessed again, heard divine service in the choir and, finally, proceeded to the altar once more where he offered a piece of gold. Similar ceremonies were subsequently held in St Patrick's Cathedral, presided over by Archbishop Curwen, and in churches in Drogheda and Dundalk, which were led by Archbishop Dowdall. It is difficult not to think of these ceremonies as anything other than a festival of Pale culture, a triumphant celebration held to mark the re-integration of the religious, political and social values that had traditionally defined the identity of the English Irish community of eastern Ireland.[25]

The restoration of the old religion in Mary Tudor's reign, then, was an unqualified success in Dublin. Even before parliament met in 1557 to repeal the anti-papal legislation of Henry VIII's reign,[26] even before Cardinal Pole's papal legateship in Ireland became fully operative,[27] and even before

---

[24] RCB, C.6.1.7 no. 1, f. 1v (Gillespie (ed.), *First chapter act book of Christ Church*, pp. 24–5).
[25] *Carew MSS, 1515–74*, pp. 258–9.
[26] Mayer (ed.), *Correspondence of Pole*, iii, pp. 418–20.
[27] Pole was appointed legate to Ireland on 1 July 1555. He intended to send commissioners and officials to visit the clergy and people of Ireland, but this was not achieved before his legateship was revoked by Pope Paul IV in the summer of 1557. He did, however, make a significant number of *acta* relating to Ireland prior to this, usually in response to petitions that emanated from there. Between 1555 and 1557, he is known to have issued around twelve dispensations relating to the diocese of Dublin. One of these was Curwen's own

royal commissions were issued in December 1557 to enquire into the whereabouts of the plate, ornaments, bells and real property that parish churches had lost during the schism,[28] Archbishop Curwen and the indigenous clergy had done a considerable amount of work to ensure that medieval Catholicism had been brought fully back to life in the heart of English Ireland. The real testimony to this success, however, is not to be found in the small body of evidence that has survived from Mary Tudor's reign concerning the restoration of traditional religious practices. Rather, the strength of this revitalised version of the old religion would only become fully apparent when the state attempted to dismantle it and to impose an alternative Protestant religious settlement following the accession of Queen Elizabeth in November 1558.

II

The deaths of Queen Mary and Cardinal Pole within hours of each other on 17 November 1558, deaths which literally and figuratively heralded the cessation of the Catholic restoration in England, were also paralleled in Ireland. Only three months previously, and while in England campaigning against the ill-effects of the government of Lord Lieutenant Sussex, Archbishop George Dowdall of Armagh also died.[29] The death of Dowdall, as much an architect of Catholic restoration in the English Pale as the queen and the cardinal had been in England, instantaneously changed the nature of Archbishop Hugh Curwen's mission in Ireland. Hitherto he had played the part of the faceless, bureaucrat-legist, a man who implemented in a completely efficient manner the requisite steps in Dowdall's strategy for the restoration of the old religion in Dublin. Now, however, he was unexpectedly thrust into a position of general leadership over the English Irish clergy, a position which, in the wake of Queen Mary's death, would require him to provide direction and guidance in a period fraught with difficult

---

absolution for schism during the Henrician and Edwardian periods; two more were for clerical marriage, i.e. for Archbishop Browne and Walter White, chancellor of Christ Church Cathedral. The majority of the remainder related to ex-religious, including two canons of Christ Church – Christopher Rathe and John Cardiff – and absolved them for leaving their monasteries and taking the secular habit and/or for being schismatic during the preceding reigns: Mayer, *Reginald Pole*, pp. 268–72; Mayer, *Correspondence of Pole*, iii, pp. 50, 60, 100–1, 131–2, 204, 363, 411, 414, 418; Edwards, *Church and state*, p. 164; *Carew MSS, 1515–74*, pp. 252–3; Loades, *Reign of Mary Tudor*, pp. 362–5; Edwards, *Ireland in the age of the Tudors* (London, 1977), pp. 80–1; Ronan, 'Cardinal Pole's absolution of George Browne', pp. 193–205; C.H. Garret, 'The legatine register of Cardinal Pole', in *Journal of Modern History*, xiii (1941), pp. 189–194; Douai Municipal Archives, MS 922 (microfilm in NLI).
[28] *Fiants, Mary*, no. 181.   [29] ODNB; Brady, *Chief governors*, pp. 89–91.

choices, as the ramifications of the accession of the Protestant Queen Elizabeth began to make themselves felt in the Irish Church.

The path which Curwen chose for himself, and the example which he provided for the clergy of the Pale, was almost unique amongst Englishmen on the Marian episcopal bench. Whereas in the English church all of the Marian bishops, saving Kitchin of Llandaff, had opposed the enactment of the Elizabethan religious settlement, Curwen chose to conform to it both by supporting its passage in the Irish parliament in 1560 and by taking the oath of supremacy thereafter. In so doing, the archbishop apparently confirmed the worst suspicions that Mary Tudor and Cardinal Pole had harboured about equivocating and 'worldly' Henrician canonists, a view subsequently adopted by more than one generation of historians.[30] Yet while this evaluation of Curwen's motivation is certainly plausible, it does not accord well with the extant evidence. What we know about the events which occurred in and around the time of the 1560 parliament suggests, rather, that the archbishop's response to the Elizabethan settlement was arrived at after some serious soul-searching on the part of the senior Pale clergy, and for reasons which had more to do with religion and conscience than earlier historians were prepared to admit.

Although poorly documented, it is evident that that the senior Pale clergy held a genuine debate amongst themselves as to what course they should follow once parliament was presented with, or had passed, bills on religion, a feature evinced in the fact that the participants split into distinct, coherent groups once the time for making definitive decisions was reached. One of these groups followed Curwen's lead, and was comprised of the chapter of St Patrick's Cathedral who, with the single exception of their dean, Thomas Leverous, appear to have taken the oath of supremacy in the spring of 1560. The other group, which consisted of former associates of Archbishop Dowdall in the upper echelons of the Armagh provincial administration, was led by William Walshe, the bishop of Meath, who, following the death of the primate, had become the most senior cleric in the province of Armagh *inter Anglicos.* This group rejected Curwen's counsel and withheld its support for the Elizabethan settlement both within and without parliament. In addition to the Armagh constituency, amongst which were numbered Bishop Leverous of Kildare, Dowdall's former archdeacon and the dean of St Patrick's Cathedral, support was also forthcoming from four members of Curwen's cathedral chapter of Christ Church. Amongst the latter were Christopher Rathe, the Marian precentor, and John Cardiff, the Marian

---

[30] MacCulloch, *Later reformation in England*, pp. 24, 29–31; H.A. Jefferies, 'The Irish parliament of 1560: the anglican reforms authorised', in *IHS*, xxvi (1988), pp. 129–30, 137; *Fiants, Elizabeth*, no. 226.

treasurer, whose Catholic resolve may have been stiffened as a result of having recently received dispensations from Cardinal Pole (in May 1557) for taking secular habits without papal dispensations at the time Christ Church was altered into a secular institution.[31]

While no documentary evidence now survives on the substance or course of this clerical debate, there are still a number of assumptions that we can make about it. The first is that the positions of the leaders of both groups were publicly known as early as the first half of 1559, as the government is known to have considered taking steps at this time to nullify the influence of the anti-conformity party. Thus, in a proposal endorsed by the earl of Sussex, it was suggested that Bishops Walshe and Leverous should be brought over to London to discuss matters of state, and kept there while parliament sat in Dublin. In their absence their proxies would be given to the reliably con-formist Archbishop Curwen.[32] The second assumption we can make about the debate is that its terms of reference would have been exclusively Catholic in nature, given that all of the participants were committed adherents of the old religion and none of them supporters of any form of Protestantism. Thus it follows that the point at issue between the different camps was not the efficacy or otherwise of the Elizabethan settlement. All would have agreed that the Protestant religion which it advanced was heterodox and uncanonical. Rather, what had to be decided was which of the two possible responses to it – outward conformity or principled rejection – would be the most beneficial course of action for the local, recently rejuvenated, Catholic Church. In seeking an answer to this question, the main protagonists of the debate brought their own personal and individual concerns to the table, which were directly attributable to their background formation and training.

Such personal concerns were particularly evident in the leader of the anti-conformity party, Bishop Walshe of Meath. Walshe was the holder of a doctorate in theology and had lived in exile in Rome in the entourage of Cardinal Pole prior to his promotion to Meath in 1554. More than most of the Pale clergy at this time, then, he was both aware and a zealous supporter of Counter-Reformation Catholicism, a stance which had secured him, ahead of the canon lawyers Archbishops Dowdall and Curwen, the position of deputy-legate to Cardinal Pole in Ireland.[33] Thus from a moral

[31] Edwards, *Ireland in the age of the Tudors*, pp. 92–5; idem, *Church and state*, pp. 187–8; *Fiants, Elizabeth*, nos. 198–9, 226, 236; Morrin, *Patent rolls*, i, p. 435; Mayer, *Correspondence of Pole*, iii, p. 414; R. Gillespie, 'The shaping of reform, 1558–1625', in Milne (ed.), *Christ Church Cathedral*, pp. 175–6.

[32] Jefferies, 'Anglican reforms authorised', p. 129; *Calendar of the MSS of the marquis of Salisbury* (23 vols., HMC, London, 1883–1973), iii, no. 968.

[33] TNA: PRO, C 66/874, mm. 39–40d (*Patent rolls, 1553–4*, pp. 302–3); Shirley, *Church in Ireland 1547–1567*, pp. 87–9; J.J. Silke, 'The Irish abroad, 1534–1691', in *NHI* III, p. 592; Edwards, *Ireland in the age of the Tudors*, p. 80.

theological perspective, as well as from his sense of the deepening credal division that was developing between Catholicism and Protestantism on the continent, the royal demand for conformity to the Elizabethan settlement was totally unacceptable. For Walshe, this demand presented a stark moral choice between right and wrong which the informed Catholic conscience could not fudge. Moreover, judging from the vigour with which he maintained this stance in the years following his deprivation,[34] it is likely that he was a very persuasive advocate in convincing others to follow his lead, certainly among those with Armagh ecclesiastical connections, like Bishop Leverous of Kildare and Archdeacon Luttrell of Meath; and perhaps even amongst those outside the province, like the four members of the chapter of Christ Church who refused the oath in 1560.[35]

By way of contrast, it is unlikely that Hugh Curwen saw the choices that confronted him with the same immediacy and in such stark and compelling moral terms. An old Henrician hand who had lived through all the religious changes introduced by the Tudors, he would have been keenly aware of the fact that the mere enactment of a particular religious settlement by parliament would not of itself guarantee it longevity nor ultimate success. Thus, no matter how distasteful the situation in 1560 may have appeared to the archbishop and his St Patrick's-based supporters, their conformity to the Elizabethan settlement would have been informed by a natural predisposition to adopt a wait-and-see approach. Yet it would be wrong to assume that such cautiousness signified a passive disengagement from the religious controversies of the age. While it was certainly true that the archbishop and his supporters would have believed that the best hope for the old religion lay in a future dynastic alteration or some other unpredictable and uncontrollable political change, they were not content to remain inactive in the meantime. On the contrary, as adept canon lawyers and experienced ecclesiastical administrators, they were fully conversant with the fact that the 1560 legislation devolved much of the responsibility for enforcing the new Protestant settlement upon the existing diocesan administrations. Thus, by adopting a position of outward conformity, they knew they would be able to maintain control over one of the key parts of the judicial

---

[34] Walshe was committed to Dublin Castle in the summer of 1565 by the High Commission for refusing to take the oath of supremacy and for refusing to answer a series of articles administered to him by the commissioners. According to the commission's leader, Archbishop Loftus of Armagh, Walshe had, ever since the last parliament, 'condemned and openly showed himself to be a misliker of all the queen's majesty's proceedings; he openly protested before all the people the same day he was before us that he would never communicate or be present (by his will) where the service ahould be ministered, for it was against his conscience, and . . . against god's word' (Shirley, *Church in Ireland 1547–1567*, p. 220).

[35] Morrin, *Patent rolls*, i, p. 435; *Fiants, Elizabeth*, nos. 226, 236.

machinery upon which the overall success of the Elizabethan settlement would ultimately rest. It is extremely likely, then, particularly when we consider their behaviour as diocesan administrators in the early 1560s, that the decision to conform was taken firmly in the knowledge that it would allow them every opportunity to subvert Elizabethan Protestantism from within. Indeed, this feature would also go some way towards explaining why the chapter of St Patrick signed up to the Elizabethan settlement, while the chapter of Christ Church neglected to do so. As a group directly involved in the process of diocesan administration, the chapter of St Patrick's knew they would have a valuable role to play as Catholic subversives under the new dispensation. For the chapter of Christ Church, by contrast, a group whose main function was the daily performance of a liturgy which was about to take on an unmistakably Protestant hue, there was no such consolation.

There is considerable evidence to support the contention that Archbishop Curwen and his diocesan administration consciously set out to subvert the 1560 settlement from day one. One of the earliest signs concerned the passing of two amendments to the English version of the act of uniformity in the Irish parliament of 1560, amendments which permitted the use of a conservative Latin version of the Book of Common Prayer, and the clerical vestments and ornaments that had been allowed at the outset of Edward VI's reign. While there is insufficient evidence to attribute these amendments directly to Archbishop Curwen's machinations in parliament, and although one of them was ostensibly enacted to give non-English speakers access to the godly religion of the Prayer Book, there is little doubt that they were introduced by a predominantly conservative English Irish parliament – prodded no doubt by the conservative clergy – to allow the maintenance of a service which looked and sounded like mass. Certainly, this was the way Curwen's diocesan administration interpreted and exploited them. Under his government, the use of the Latin Prayer Book became the norm throughout much of Dublin and elsewhere in the English Pale, establishing a precedent which would last until well into the 1580s.[36]

There were, however, even more obvious signs of the Curwen regime's subversive intentions. Led by his official principal, Thomas Creef,[37] and the

---

[36] Jefferies, 'Anglican reforms authorised', pp. 133–4; *APC 1587–8*, pp. 410–11. On the 1560 edition of the Latin Prayer Book, the version which was probably in circulation in Elizabethan Ireland, and its use of rubrics and forms from the earlier and more conservative of the two Edwardian Prayer books, see Haugaard, *Elizabeth and the English Reformation*, pp. 112–17.

[37] The earliest notice of Creef acting as official principal that I have found is an unspecified date in 1558, but he was probably appointed as soon as Curwen arrived in Ireland in October 1555. Likewise the last notice I have found of him acting in this capacity is from the winter of 1562–3, but again he probably held the post until at least the time of Curwen's

archdeacon of Dublin, Robert Wellesley, men who had been put in place to supervise the restoration of Catholicism under Mary Tudor, it turned a blind eye to the continued usage of proscribed Catholic practices in the diocese and neglected to enforce some of the most basic requirements of the 1560 settlement; failings which came to light during the summer of 1565, in the wake of a Pale-wide investigation of the state of religion conducted by the newly appointed High Commission. The most disturbing of the commission's findings concerned the fact that the nobility and chief gentlemen of Dublin and other Pale counties were allowed, notwithstanding the existence of the Latin Prayer Book, to frequent mass unhindered, and had done so since the parliament had proscribed it in 1560. Neither were they troubled to attend the prayer book services, with the result that 'very few of them ever received the holy communion, or used such kind of public prayer and service as is presently established by law'.[38]

It was not only the nobility and gentry who were allowed to practise their Catholicism with impunity however. Curwen, Creef and Wellesley permitted the continuance of the old ways in the parishes, and even in Christ Church Cathedral in the heart of the city of Dublin. Thus in 1564–5, for example, the clergy of Christ Church rung the 'mind' of Christopher Rathe. Rathe had been precentor of the cathedral during Mary's reign but had lost his living because he refused to take the oath of supremacy in 1560; a show of conservatism which not only commended itself to his former colleagues, but also to Alderman Richard Fyan of Dublin, who gave half a loaf of bread and half a beef to feed the masons that were currently being employed by the cathedral in return for the five peals rung for Rathe's soul.[39] In a similar vein, Hugh O'Lurchan, the curate of Templeogue in south Dublin, erected two wooden wayside crosses in September 1567 to commemorate 'according to the custom of the district' the deaths of Gilpatrick Roe McShane and Gilpatrick McThomas, two husbandmen from Knocklyon.[40]

It is clear, then, that Archbishop Curwen's decision to conform to the Elizabethan settlement in 1560 was a very significant act indeed. In essence, it threw a protective veil over the community of the diocese of Dublin in the crucial early years of the Elizabethan settlement, which ensured that the local and customary attachment to the old religion – an attachment that had

---

departure in late 1567. It is possible that he also held it during the opening months of Archbishop Loftus's episcopate as the latter is not known to have made an appointment to the post until late 1568 (Act book of the Dublin consistory c. 1596–99, Marsh's Library, MS Z4.2.19, p. 7; Will of Robert Golding, 26 December 1562, TCD, MS 1207, no. 297).

[38] Shirley, *Church in Ireland 1547–1567*, pp. 194–7.

[39] R. Gillespie (ed.), *The proctor's accounts of Peter Lewis 1564–1565* (Dublin, 1996), pp. 28, 109.

[40] TCD, MS 1207, no. 299.

been revived and strengthened in all its shades and forms in the Marian period – would be preserved and consolidated even as the state endeavoured to destroy it. Thus, while the brand of 'compromising' church papism practiced by Curwen, Creef and Wellesley may not have met the strictest standards of post-Tridentine Catholicism, it was still one, if not the most important, of the factors which contributed to the failure of the Reformation in the diocese. Certainly, its potency was recognised by the two men who were charged with the task of promoting godly Protestant religion in the Pale in the 1560s, Bishop Brady of Meath and Archbishop Loftus of Armagh. It was no accident that their major initiative during this period – the attempt to establish a Protestant university out of the revenues of St Patrick's Cathedral – was motivated more by the need to destroy Archbishop Curwen and his diocesan administration, than by the need to create an institution for the training of Protestant clerics.[41]

Although Curwen and his clergy successfully fended off this attempt to bring their regime to an end, it did mark a turning point for the archbishop. The criticism that he received at the hands of dedicated Protestants like Loftus and Brady, and which he knew had been levelled at him because of his staunch defence of the old religion and the institutions which underpinned it, began to take a heavy toll on him. The strain was keenly articulated in a letter to the queen in April 1564 wherein he wrote:

I fear much lest your highness upon sinister information have conceived some misliking towards me and my doings, which grieveth me more than any wordly matter, and therefore I humbly beseech your majesty to will my lord lieutenant or the commissioners [Sir Nicholas Arnold and Sir Thomas Wroth] to enquire and certify my doings to your majesty, wherein I trust your majesty shall understand my duty, doing without corruption, and my travail in furthering all your proceedings belonging to my function.[42]

From this point on, therefore, the archbishop knew that it would be increasingly difficult to sustain his outwardly conformist attitude to the established religion, while at the same time continuing to defend the interests of the old religion and his conservative clergy. Thus, he was eager to secure his release from Ireland on the grounds, ostensibly, of his old age and increasing ill-health. His wish was finally realised in the spring of 1566 when the queen announced his translation to the see of Oxford.[43]

Curwen departed Ireland in the winter of 1567 and was succeeded as archbishop of Dublin by Adam Loftus, the Protestant archbishop of Armagh. He left behind him a major legacy however. Thanks to his efforts,

[41] Murray, 'St Patrick's cathedral and the university question in Ireland', pp. 11–21.
[42] Shirley, *Church in Ireland 1547–1567*, pp. 142–5.
[43] Ibid., pp. 145–8, 240–1, 248–51, 299–303.

or the carefully contrived lack of them, the old religion was in a very healthy state on his departure, while the Reformation, as a report from Lord Deputy Sidney to the English privy council had made clear in April of the previous year, 'goeth slowly forward . . . by reason of the former errors and superstitions inveterated and leavened in the people's hearts'.[44] No one was more responsible for sustaining such errors and superstitions in the people's hearts than Hugh Curwen. It was this legacy that Loftus would have to confront, and somehow overcome, in order that true Protestant religion would gain a foothold in the diocese.

[44] Ibid., p. 234.

8

Archbishop Loftus and the drive to protestantise Dublin, 1567–90

I

The nomination of Adam Loftus to succeed Hugh Curwen as archbishop of Dublin in the spring of 1567 was greeted with great hope and expectancy amongst the reforming circle in the Irish administration. Lord Deputy Sidney gave the clearest expression of this official anticipation, when he heralded the appointment as signalling nothing less than the coming of 'the hour' for the reformation of the church. It is doubtful, however, whether Loftus himself was quite so sanguine about his promotion. While it was certainly true, as Sidney averred, that the see's wealth and English culture offered the most favourable conditions for establishing the reformed religion in Ireland, the new archbishop would have had few illusions that the task was anything other than formidable.[1]

Loftus's appreciation of the difficulties that lay ahead was rooted in an already extensive knowledge of the state of religion in Dublin, which he had acquired from two distinct sources. The first of these was his role as a participant on the commission for ecclesiastical causes appointed in October 1564. By virtue of this commission, which was executed largely through his own lead, Loftus had built up a detailed dossier of 'all manner disorders and offences' committed against the Elizabethan settlement throughout the English Pale. Thus he was fully aware – whether he contemplated the Dublin stonemasons who upheld proscribed holy days, or the nobility and gentry who refused to receive communion according to the Prayer Book rite – that traditional religion still retained a very strong hold on the affections of the inhabitants of most Dublin parishes, and that the officially approved doctrines and practices of the crown's religious dispensation were equally disliked.[2]

---

[1] Shirley, *Church in Ireland 1547–67*, p. 294.
[2] *Patent rolls 1563–66*, pp. 32–3; Morrin, *Patent rolls*, i, p. 490; Shirley, *Church in Ireland 1547–67*, pp. 194–7; Gillespie (ed.), *Proctor's accounts of Peter Lewis*, pp. 86–7; Edwards, *Church and state*, pp. 194–6.

Loftus's knowledge about the ailing condition of 'true religion' in Dublin, however, went beyond the mere cataloguing of these 'disorders and offences'. He also had a deep understanding of why and how they occurred, which was founded upon insights derived from his incumbency of the two livings he held prior to his promotion to Dublin, the archbishopric of Armagh and the deanery of St Patrick's Cathedral.[3] As the successor to George Dowdall in Armagh, and as the head of Dublin's secular cathedral, Loftus saw at close hand the lingering and harmful effects of the canonical restoration of Catholicism which Dowdall, Archbishop Curwen and the prebendaries of St Patrick's had instituted in Queen Mary's reign. This legacy was particularly manifest in the Dublin diocesan administration, which was based in and funded from the cathedral, and which was responsible, in ecclesiastical terms, for policing the statutes of supremacy and uniformity, the bedrock legislation of the Elizabethan religious settlement. Despite the fundamental importance of this task, the administration which Archbishop Curwen maintained to fulfil it was the same one which had been put together in 1555 to oversee the restoration of Catholicism. Still deeply loyal to the old religion, it was this body which had done much to foster and sustain the communal attachment to Catholicism in the aftermath of Queen Elizabeth's accession, through both its covert approval of proscribed Catholic services and practices, and its wilful neglect of those enforcement responsibilities which it had acquired under the Reformation statutes.[4]

By accepting the nomination to the see of Dublin, then, Loftus knew he would have to combat a deeply ingrained communal religious conservatism, which permeated the entire social spectrum, and which had a long-standing intellectual and institutional basis that was sustained by an indigenous coterie of canon lawyers at the heart of his own diocesan administration. Yet this communal conservatism did not mark the full extent of the archbishop's impending difficulties. More troublesome still was the crown's equivocal attitude towards the problem of securing religious uniformity. In theory at least, the queen and her councillors had a clearly defined and uncompromising attitude to the problem. The establishment of the High Commission of 1564 gave the reformers extensive powers to seek out and punish all forms of disobedience to the new religious settlement, and seemed to betoken a real determination to secure universal outward conformity to the new settlement.[5] Similarly, the crown's simultaneous

---

[3] Loftus was appointed to Armagh in October 1562 and to the deanery of St Patrick's in January 1565.

[4] See Chapters 6 and 7.

[5] *Patent rolls 1563–66*, pp. 32–3; Morrin, *Patent rolls*, i, p. 490.

sponsorship of a scheme to dissolve St Patrick's Cathedral, and to establish a university in its place, seemed to show a genuine sensitivity to the particular needs of Irish Protestantism, as articulated by the leading reformers such as Loftus and Bishop Brady of Meath. This was a scheme that sought not only to create a seminary for the education of 'godly' ministers for the Irish Church, but was also intent on destroying the nerve centre of the conservative canonical culture which had hitherto sustained the old religion.[6]

Nevertheless, while the queen and her councillors were quick to encourage the formulation of practical reformist policy, recent experience had shown that they were also extremely tentative about supporting its implementation in Ireland, particularly if it threatened to alienate sections of the loyal community or to disrupt the government of the realm, as, in the secular sphere, the imposition of the cess had so recently done in the Pale. The queen's refusal to endorse, in the summer of 1565, an aggressive suggestion of Loftus to levy upon the Pale nobility and gentry 'a good round fine and sum of money' to observe her 'most godly laws and injunctions' was a clear indication of her circumspection.[7] Again, the abandonment of the university project in 1566 was due, in large part, to the regime's fear that the dissolution of St Patrick's would provoke an adverse local reaction.[8] Thus, as Adam Loftus set out to govern the see of Dublin, it had become painfully obvious to him that the radical Protestant policies which he had advocated since his arrival in Ireland in 1560 – even to the eve of his nomination to the archbishopric[9] – were impracticable, because there would be no guarantee that the crown's ministers in London and Dublin would give them the necessary political support.

Loftus's pragmatic re-assessment of the situation that confronted him soon became apparent in the way he conducted his business in the opening years of his episcopate. Far from delivering anything even remotely

---

[6] For the university project see Murray, 'St Patrick's cathedral and the university question in Ireland', pp. 11–21.

[7] Shirley, *Church in Ireland 1547–67*, pp. 194–7. A few months before Loftus wrote, Sir William Cecil had voiced what was tantamount to being the official view from London about the religious non-conformity of her Irish subjects when he advised Lord Justice Arnold to 'stir no sleeping dogs in Ireland . . . many things in commonweals are suffered that are not liked' (Cecil to Arnold, 28 February 1565, TNA: PRO, SP 63/12, no. 50). On the problem of the cess in the 1560s see Brady, *Chief Governors*, pp. 87–91, ch. 6 *passim*.

[8] On the abandonment of the scheme see Murray 'St Patrick's cathedral and the university question in Ireland', pp. 11–21.

[9] Loftus's continued advocacy of a tough policy on religion is evident from his contributions to the debate on the nomination of Curwen's successor in Dublin. He wrote at least six letters touching on the matter to Secretary Cecil between April 1566 and January 1567, as well as proffering advice to Lord Deputy Sidney on possible candidates (Shirley, *Church in Ireland 1547–67*, pp. 242–3, 255–9, 269–71, 274–6, 289–91).

approaching the radicalism of the once-touted plans to destroy the popish cathedral of St Patrick, and to found a Protestant seminary in its place, this period was notable for the emergence of a new conservatism on Loftus's part, which was particularly noticeable in the efforts that he made to preserve and consolidate the traditional structures and rights of his see. Thus, when Lord Deputy Sidney endeavoured – *à la* St Leger and as part of a national programme of integrated political and religious reformation – to dissolve the cathedral in the late 1560s, and have its chapter house converted to the use of the viceroy and council, and its revenues used to defray some of the costs of maintaining the English garrison in Ireland, Loftus stood against it. This was evident not only from the lobbying he undertook throughout 1567–8 to prevent the proposed enactment in the upcoming parliament of a statute which would have abolished the ancient liberties of St Patrick's Cathedral and those of his own manor of St Sepulchre, but also in the precaution that he and his diocesan administration took to enroll the cathedral's 1555 charter of restoration on the Irish patent rolls, with a view to buttressing its standing as a royal foundation. By so doing, the archbishop signalled his willingness to maintain the conventional feudal attributes associated with the unreformed medieval prelacy. In addition, and, again, in stark contrast to his earlier advocacy of the scheme, he also resisted the viceroy's plans for the establishment of an Irish university in the same parliament. In part, this was due to the fact that Sidney wished to secure funding for his proposed college from the local community, a plan which Loftus and the other bishops were sceptical about on the grounds that it would have entailed the surrender of some ideological control over the new foundation to the donors, many of whom would have been favourers of the old religion. However, it also grew as much from the fear that St Patrick's Cathedral might once again be drawn into the fray, which Loftus, as evinced by his protection of the cathedral's liberties, was now clearly set against.[10]

Yet while the tempering of Loftus's Protestant radicalism was certainly prompted by the crown's reluctance to embark upon a tough, coercive policy of religious enforcement, it was not solely a political, and therefore reversible, response to circumstances beyond his control. In reality, it

---

[10] Brady and Murray, 'Sir Henry Sidney and the Reformation in Ireland', pp. 18–23; Murray, 'St Patrick's Cathedral and the university question in Ireland, c. 1547–1585', pp. 21–5; V. Treadwell, 'The Irish Parliament of 1569–71', *PRIA* 65 C (1966–7), pp. 62–3; Shirley, *Church in Ireland 1547–67*, pp. 308–10; Sidney's instructions, 28 May 1565, TNA: PRO, SP 63/13, no. 46; petitions of Lewis Chalonar, on behalf of Loftus, to Cecil, May 1568 (TNA: PRO, SP 63/24, nos. 39, 40); Loftus to Cecil, 10 June 1568 (TNA: PRO, SP 63/25, no. 4); Morrin, *Patent rolls*, i, pp. 524–6; *LM* II, pt. 5, p. 100; a brief abstract of the bills certified by the viceroy and council to the queen, c. January 1569 (TNA: PRO, SP 63/27, no. 12).

marked the beginning of a much deeper reappraisal of the reform strategy he had employed hitherto, one outcome of which was his firm rejection of the aggressive and ultimately impolitic policies of the recent past. Indeed, in place of the old policies, and here Loftus's new willingness to defend the interests of St Patrick's Cathedral was a sign of things to come, the archbishop chose to govern his see in a conventional manner – through the traditional administrative structures based in the cathedral – and, by this means, to attempt to win the allegiance of the local community to the Reformation through a less coercive approach to enforcement. Loftus did not come to these conclusions alone. In developing an alternative to the tough and thorough strategy of enforcement, the archbishop drew inspiration from the latest recruit to the Dublin Castle administration, the new lord chancellor of Ireland, Sir Robert Weston.

II

The decision to appoint Robert Weston as lord chancellor in 1567 was made by Lord Deputy Sidney and the English privy council as part of a broad policy initiative in which the perceived 'insufficiency' of the Irish bench would be remedied by appointing judges from England; and on the specific grounds that he was an ably qualified and experienced civil lawyer, being the holder of a doctorate in the discipline from Oxford, and a curriculum vitae which listed judgeships in various ecclesiastical courts, most notably, the archbishop of Canterbury's Court of the Arches.[11] Weston's appointment was made without any reference to the needs of the new archbishop of Dublin, and indeed appeared even to undermine them, because the new chancellor, a lay man, was also granted the deanery of St Patrick's as a sinecure, despite the fact that Loftus, the incumbent, had requested that he be allowed to retain the living to augment his archiepiscopal income. Yet, more than any other single event or influence, Weston's arrival in Ireland would help him confront the tasks of episcopal government that lay ahead.[12]

Whatever tensions may have existed between the two men at the outset were quickly assuaged once Loftus had experienced the chancellor's learning and piety. In regard to the latter, Weston exhibited scruples of conscience over holding a spiritual benefice with five appropriated parishes because he was not in orders, and thus attempted to make amends by

[11] Queen Elizabeth to Lord Deputy Sidney, 10, 11 June 1567 (TNA: PRO, SP 63/21, nos. 6, 10); *ODNB sub nomine* 'Weston, Robert'; W.H. Frere (ed.) (transcribed by E. Margaret Thompson), *Registrum Matthei Parker Diocesis Cantuariensis AD 1559–1575* (Canterbury and York Society, 3 vols., Oxford, 1928–32), i, pp. 334–7.

[12] Shirley, *Church in Ireland 1547–67*, pp. 295–7.

endowing new vicarages on the three decanal prebends of Clondalkin, Esker and Rathcoole. Yet not only was Weston a pious and devout layman, he was also a professional ecclesiastical lawyer of a type which Loftus had rarely encountered: 'a notable and singular man, by profession a lawyer, but in life divine'.[13] Loftus's experience of ecclesiastical lawyers had been negative. In Ireland, they were unreformed canonists, men like Thomas Creef, the conservative official principal of his own consistory court.[14] But Weston had actively and consistently used his legal skills in the service of the reformed church in England; initially as an ecclesiastical commissioner during the regal visitation of 1559, subsequently as diocesan chancellor of the see of Coventry and Lichfield and the proctor of its clergy in the convocation of 1563 and, latterly, as the archbishop of Canterbury's dean of the Arches.[15]

This was promising. Weston's coming opened up the possibility of acquiring a moral, intellectual and practical justification for the abandonment of the radical, almost iconoclastic, ideas on church reform that he had once purveyed. With the new dean by his side, Loftus came to appreciate that being a bishop was not just about executing the queen's ecclesiastical commission, a method of church government which he had favoured because of his own inexperience of conventional ecclesiastical administration, his deep suspicion of the canonists that staffed the existing diocesan establishments and, above all, the great difficulty he had experienced in governing the O'Neill-dominated see of Armagh.[16] Rather, this was a church which was held to exist in administrative continuity with its medieval and Marian predecessors; a church which, although ultimately subject to the monarch, was expected to be governed in her name by her bishops, and the ancient judicial and administrative structures over which they presided.[17]

---

[13] Weston to Cecil, 14 September 1569 (TNA: PRO, SP 63/29, no. 62); Lord Deputy Perrot to Lord Treasurer Burghley, May 1585 (Bodleian, Perrot MS 1, f. 104rv); Abstract of the will of Katherine Bulkeley of Balgaddy, 28 November 1574 (GO, MS 290, p. 17); TCD, MS 567, f. 1v; R. Holinshed and J. Hooker, *Holinshed's chronicles of England, Scotland, Ireland* (6 vols., London, 1807–8), vi, p. 336.

[14] There is no record of Loftus having appointed a new official principal until the winter of 1568–9. This suggests that Curwen's official, Creef, remained in the post for a year or so after Loftus's succession. Curwen's last diocesan registrar, James Cuskelly, also continued in office for a number of years after Loftus's succession (*RDD*, pp. 37, 52; NAI, Chancery Bills, D/73).

[15] W.P. Haugard, *Elizabeth and the English Reformation* (Cambridge, 1970), pp. 130–7; O'Day, 'Role of the registrar', pp. 90–1.

[16] Shirley, *Church in Ireland 1547–67*, pp. 278–80.

[17] For a discussion of the institutional continuities that existed between the medieval and post-Reformation churches in England, a discussion which has much relevance for the Irish situation, see R. O'Day and F. Heal's introduction to *Continuity and Change*, pp. 13–29.

At the heart of this system of traditional episcopal government lay the ecclesiastical law, which Loftus well knew was identical in many respects to the popish canon law that Dowdall, Curwen and the prebendaries of St Patrick's had used to restore Catholicism in Mary's reign, and towards which he was naturally antipathetic. Now, however, under the guidance of Robert Weston, he saw the ecclesiastical law and the diocesan structures which administered it in a new light. These relics of the see's popish past not only showed the inherent continuities that existed between the Elizabethan Church of Ireland and its medieval and Marian predecessors, but actually highlighted some of those elements which attracted the local community to the old religion. Armed with such an appreciation, Loftus was able to recast or reformulate the problem of enforcement in a way which took account of and sought to appease indigenous sensitivities. In particular, he came to see enforcement policy as but an aspect of the wider dispensation and administration of ecclesiastical justice and, as a result, a potential medium for addressing one of the new diocesan administration's most fundamental problems, the difficulty of convincing the local community that the state-sponsored reform of the church was a genuinely orthodox undertaking.

The innovatory nature of Elizabethan English Protestantism, and its apparent heterodoxy, was felt acutely amongst the Pale community because the local clergy – for political and cultural, as well as for religious, reasons – had long believed and taught that the authority of canon law was the definitive means of legitimising religious doctrine and practice. In other words, the more Protestantism departed from medieval canonical forms, whether through its legislation on jurisdictional and devotional matters in secular bodies like parliament, or through its government of the church in novel bodies like the High Commission, the more illegitimate it seemed to the Englishry. Two strategic implications were to be drawn from such an analysis. The first was that the Elizabethan settlement would have to be presented with a veneer of canonical legitimacy if it was ever to receive the approbation and loyalty of the see's inhabitants. The second, and related, implication was that the influence of the senior conservative clergy would have to be nullified to allow such a process to proceed, as they were a group who saw themselves as the guardians of the canonical traditions of the English Pale and who would remain fully committed to preserving this role and to subverting the reformers' plans. With these considerations in mind, Loftus and Weston initiated a new and carefully modulated programme of ecclesiastical discipline, which sought both to marginalise the clerical old guard and the value system which they purveyed, and to establish the Loftus–Weston regime and the Elizabethan ecclesiastical settlement as the more legitimate, conservative and therefore attractive alternative. In order to achieve this aim, however, Loftus and Weston knew from the outset that they would have to establish the authority and credibility of their regime fairly quickly. The only way to do so was to confront and face down the conservative clergy resident in St Patrick's Cathedral.

As the new dean of St Patrick's, Weston was well placed for this new offensive. He began by recruiting the assistance of his nephew from England – John Ball, an Oxford MA and bachelor in civil law – whom he had 'bred up of a little one in learning' and was 'of such knowledge and manners that may be in diverse parts of my service a help and comfort unto me, and whom in weighty and secret matters I may boldly repose above any other'. Loftus appointed Ball as his vicar general and the official principal of his consistory court in the place of Thomas Creef, Curwen's appointee from the previous reign. And together with Ball, the archbishop and dean undertook their inaugural visitations of the cathedral, beginning in April 1569.[18]

Ordinary jurisdiction over St Patrick's, according to the cathedral's statutes, was held conjointly by the archbishop and dean; the dean having cognisance of the majority of ecclesiastical causes concerning the cathedral clergy in the first instance, the archbishop having cognisance over those crimes which carried the penalty of deprivation. In addition, the archbishop was also obliged to obtain the assistance of the dean and chapter in cases where he wished to proceed against an individual canon. The implication of these rulings, which were originally drawn up by Archbishop Rokeby and his chapter in 1515, and approved by Pope Leo X,[19] was that the co-operation of Loftus and Weston in their visitations was not only desired by the parties, but legally enshrined in local canonical customs. The irony of this cannot have been lost on the visitors themselves, nor on the cathedral clergy about to be visited, especially when Loftus chose to depute the archiepiscopal visitation to his new vicar general, John Ball. By means of this decision Loftus was effectively invading the canonical citadel of St Patrick's in the cause of reform, not, however, in the manner that would previously have been expected – at the head of a commission to take its surrender – but through a formally trained family of ecclesiastical lawyers who came to administer and apply many of the legal principles and procedures which the cathedral clergy had so recently used on behalf of the old religion.

Weston and Ball did their visitorial work with devastating thoroughness over the course of the ensuing eighteen months. Every member of the

---

[18] Lord Justice Weston to Cecil, 2 August 1568 (TNA: PRO, SP 63/ 25, no. 29); *AO*, i, p. 62. The extant record of the visitation is from a precedent book of the metropolitan court of Dublin, which was compiled in the 1570s (RCB, D6/12, pp. 47–65) and published by the Irish Manuscripts Commission in 1959 (*RDD*, pp. 40–52).

[19] *Alen's register*, pp. 262–3; Mason, *History of St Patrick's*, pp. 143–4; *Dignitus decani*, pp. 56–64.

cathedral body was cited to appear at the visitation, either personally or through their legitimately appointed proctors, whether they were a known Protestant or a known conservative, whether a bishop or a humble vicar choral. And every one of them had to produce before Loftus's vicar general each and every of their letters of ordination, presentation and dispensation, all of which were scrupulously examined and registered in the acts of the court. Furthermore, for those who failed to exhibit the requisite documentation on their first appearance, terms were assigned for one or more additional appearances, all of which were followed up until they proved their eligibility to be a member of the cathedral, resident or otherwise. Meanwhile, Dean Weston probed the morals and character of the cathedral clergy to detect and correct all forms of delinquency.[20]

Although such visitorial rigour had been prefigured in an investigation into the non-residence of two prebendaries in early 1568, it appears that most of the cathedral clergy were neither expecting it, nor were prepared for it, when it arrived.[21] Among the unprepared were men like Robert Daly, the Protestant bishop of Kildare and prebendary of Clonmethan, who, after an initial appearance on 12 December 1569, was forced to travel 'twenty miles and more' to gather his letters of ordination, collation, institution and dispensation, for exhibition on 18 January following; and Walter Busher, a vicar choral, who had to return to Wexford to collect his letters of ordination. Leniency, even where the circumstances seemed to warrant it, was rare in this visitation. Richard Johnson, a pluralist whose livings included the prebend of Tipperkevin, was unable to exhibit his letters of institution to the vicarage of Wicklow on his first appearance on 12 December 1569, because of the wars there and the attendant danger that any journey to retrieve them would entail. Ball still insisted, however, that he should appear with the document on the morrow of the feast of the Purification following or, failing that, on the next judicial day after the feast of the Ascension.[22]

The same visitorial rigour was also extended to the well connected. Robert Comander, a chaplain of Lord Deputy Sidney and the pluralist prebendary of Kilmactalway, was summoned to appear on 19 November and commanded, with six other canons, to exhibit letters of dispensation three weeks hence. Weston and Ball's endeavours over the previous seven months had clearly made a big impression on Comander, however, for, unlike many of his colleagues, he came armed with what were probably

---

[20] *RDD*, pp. 40–52 *passim.*
[21] Ibid., pp. 37–9. The absentee canons were Dr Thomas Ithell, prebendary of Castleknock, and Geoffrey Crosse, one of the prebendaries of Donaghmore in Imaal and a chaplain of Hugh Curwen, who was then bishop of Oxford.
[22] *RDD*, pp. 43, 45, 47, 48.

hastily drafted 'letters of qualification of the worshipful man Sir Henry Sidney, deputy of the kingdom of Ireland, under his seal at arms'. These were accepted and registered in the acts.[23] In contrast, a client of Sidney's predecessor as chief governor, the earl of Sussex, was much less fortunate. This was John Vulp, his Hungarian physician, who, despite being a layman, had acquired the archdeaconry of Glendalough from Archbishop Curwen in 1565. Ball deprived him on 12 December 1569 for non-residence, evinced in his repeated failure to appear at the visitation.[24]

The most striking evidence of Ball's stringency, however, was exhibited in his investigation of Edmund Barnewall, the non-resident treasurer of the cathedral. On 6 March 1570, Robert Wellesley, the archdeacon of Dublin, appeared on behalf of the absent treasurer, and alleged that he was too sick to appear personally, and that he was excused from residence by means of letters of dispensation granted during the reigns of Henry VIII and Edward VI, all of which were in the custody of David Delahide, an Irish scholar at Oxford.[25] Ball would not accept Wellesley's contentions, however, and asked him to take an oath that all the premises were true, and that they were not being put forward to delay proceedings or to prevent a judgement being pronounced against Barnewall. Under this pressure, the archdeacon wilted and refused to take the oath, admitting that he had only learned of the premises from one Thomas Cusake, a lawyer, who had brought Barnewall's letters of procuration to Wellesley. The vicar general, scenting blood, continued his pursuit. Cusake was summoned to the chapter house immediately after the archdeacon, and interrogated as to whether he had seen the letters of dispensation. He too, it transpired, had not seen them, stating that he had only 'heard' that Barnewall held such letters. Ball decreed, therefore, that Barnewall should either produce his letters on the morrow after the feast of St Patrick, or else make personal residence in the cathedral. It seems he failed on both counts and was subsequently deprived.[26]

The purpose behind all of these summonses and such intensely pursued enquiries was manifold. In the first instance, they asserted and demonstrated the authority and professionalism of the newly constituted Loftus regime, and the conventional legal basis upon which it intended to operate. They also demonstrated the seriousness of its reforming intent which, in the case of St Patrick's, meant ridding it of those non-productive members

---

[23] Ibid., p. 43: 'litteras qualificationum honorabilis viri domini Henrici Sydney deputati Regni Hibernie sub sigillo eius ad arma'.

[24] Lambeth, Muniment Book, F1/B, f. 127r; *AC*, iv, p. 306; *RDD*, pp. 40–4.

[25] Ibid., p. 51. Barnewall had already been pronounced contumacious by Ball for failing to answer his initial citation (ibid., pp. 43, 48–9).

[26] Ibid., p. 51. Barnewall was replaced as treasurer in 1570 (Lawlor, *Fasti of St Patrick's*, p. 70).

whose only identifiable activity in connection with the cathedral benefices they held was the collection of the revenues. Above all, however, they were designed to strike a particular blow at the heart of the conservative clerical interest which had played such havoc with the reform of the established church in the early years of Elizabeth's reign; a blow which the conservatives would not be able to gainsay in terms of its legitimacy, as it was prompted by the old canonical rules which they themselves held so dearly. The attack on Edmund Barnewall was a striking case in point. Barnewall, a scion of an illegitimate line of the Barnewall's of Crickstown in Co. Meath, had been appointed treasurer at the restoration of St Patrick's Cathedral, which indicates very strongly that he was of a markedly conservative religious bent, and which was otherwise confirmed by his relationship with David Delahide, an Irish civilian who had been committed to prison in 1560 for refusing to comply with the Elizabethan settlement, following the visitation of Oxford University by royal commissioners.[27] Yet, officially, this had no bearing on the case. Barnewall was deprived for an offence against the cathedral's own time-honoured statutes, prebendal non-residence.

Another case in point was the deprivation of Leonard Fitzsimon. Fitzsimon was a member of one of most eminent families amongst the Dublin city oligarchy, which also had a long-standing association with the local church. Indeed, his own personal embodiment of this association began at a very early age, as a six-year-old choirboy in Christ Church Cathedral, and, in more propitious times, especially with his scholastic abilities – he was an Oxford graduate and a 'deep and pithy clerk, well seen in the Greek and Latin tongue' – he could have expected to enjoy a long and prosperous career in the upper echelons of the Dublin diocesan administration. His conservative religious instincts, however, which were fostered within the social milieu in which he was raised, would eventually lead him to Louvain and ordination as a Catholic priest. Yet, like Barnewall, it was not for his attachment to the old religion that he lost his cathedral prebend in December 1569, but for contumacy in repeatedly failing to leave Oxford to appear at the visitation.[28]

The deprivations of Barnewall and Fitzsimon on points of traditional canon law were of largely symbolic significance, given that they were

[27] S.B. Barnewall, 'The Barnewall family during the 16th and 17th centuries (Part II)', *IG* 3, no. 6 (1961), p. 199; J. Brady, 'Some Irish scholars of the sixteenth century', *Studies* 37 (1948), pp. 227–8.

[28] Morrin, *Patent rolls*, i, p. 143; *RDD*, pp. 40–4; *AO*, ii, p. 504; Stanyhurst, *Holinshed's Irish chronicle*, p. 101; Lennon, *Lords of Dublin*, pp. 154–5, 158; Brady, 'Some Irish scholars', pp. 228–31. It is not known which prebend Fitzsimon held at the time of his deprivation. In the early 1560s he was prebendary of St Audoen, but at the time of the visitation this prebend was held by one John Alen, who had been appointed in 1564 (First Fruits Account Michaelmas 1566–Michaelmas 1568, abstract in TCD, MS 1745, ff. 1–2; *RDD*, p. 46).

inactive members of the chapter at the time of the visitation. Yet Loftus and Weston were also determined to cow into submission those conservative prebendaries who resided within the cathedral and who had actively undermined the reformers' cause during Archbishop Curwen's episcopacy. At the forefront of this group was Thomas Creef, the old precentor of St Patrick's, a man who had lived through all the religious vicissitudes wrought by the Tudors, but who, despite nominal conformity to the Elizabethan settlement, had remained stubbornly loyal to the traditional religion he had upheld since he first entered St Patrick's as a vicar choral in the early 1520s. Creef was regarded as the chief fomenter of papistry in the cathedral and was thus singled out for what was effectively, and intentionally, a ritualistic harassment and humiliation; ritualistic both in the sense that it was conducted on the back of that most damaging of allegations for the English Irish clerical psyche – a charge of sexual impropriety – and in the sense that it was administered to him through canonical procedures which he himself was well versed in, having used them to revive the old religion during his incumbency of the official principalship in the reign of Mary.

Creef's troubles emerged in January 1570, when Ball, the man who had replaced him as vicar general and official principal of Dublin, formally charged him to respond on oath to articles touching a crime of adultery detected by Dean Weston in his visitation of the cathedral. Nothing is known about the background to the alleged crime, but it does seem an unusual allegation, given that the precentor was in or around seventy years of age at the time. Thus, while the charge was probably not wholly manufactured – all the dean needed to bring it forward was a rumour or some gossip – it seems likely that it was politically motivated, being proceeded with to publicly embarrass the leader of the old religion in St Patrick's.[29]

Not surprisingly, when it was put to him under formal examination, Creef denied the allegation and, on 25 February, was ordered to undergo compurgation, a canonical process whereby he would have to produce six 'compurgators' of his own sex and standing, effectively six prebendaries, who would be prepared to swear in the vicar general's court that they believed the charge to be untrue. On 3 March, Creef nominated his compurgators – Robert Nangle, chancellor of St Patrick's, Robert Wellesley,

---

[29] *RDD*, pp. 43, 48, 49. Creef was already a vicar choral of St Patrick's, and thus probably in major orders, in 1523. He would therefore have been at least twenty-four years of age (the minimum for major orders) in 1523, making him at least seventy years of age at the time of the visitation (Memoranda Roll, 15 Henry VIII, Michaelmas term, m. 17, NAI, Ferguson MS, iv, p. 74; Lawlor, *Fasti of St Patrick's*, p. 35). In April 1574 Loftus described Creef as 'well spent in years', Loftus to Burghley, 23 April 1574 (TNA: PRO, SP 63/45, no. 81).

archdeacon of Dublin, Patrick Byrne, prebendary of Swords, Christopher Browne, prebendary of Wicklow, Richard Johnson, prebendary of Tipperkevin, and Ninian Menywell, prebendary of Dunlavin – a group notable for the fact that five of the six were colleagues of Creef from the chapter nominated by Queen Mary in 1555, Menywell being the exception. It is clear from what followed that Weston and Ball recognised Creef's compurgators for what they were – the old clerical guard closing ranks – and determined to derive the maximum effect from the proceedings by turning them into an attack on the group as a whole. Thus, having prepared the case thoroughly in advance with his uncle, Ball decreed four of Creef's nominees to be illegitimate, three of them – Nangle, Browne and Byrne – on the grounds that the dean had also detected unspecified crimes committed by them and they were not as yet purgated; the fourth, the recently arrived Menywell, on the grounds that he had been convicted of usury in the English exchequer. The embarrassed Creef had no other recourse at this juncture but to respond by seeking another term for compurgation.[30]

Unfortunately, no further record of the proceedings against Creef is now extant, but it appears that he restored his good name in a second compurgation, for he is known to have survived as precentor of St Patrick's beyond the visitation.[31] The relief and satisfaction that Creef derived from his survival can only have been short-lived however, for, in the months that followed, a substantial number of his conservative allies were to lose their livings as a result of Weston and Ball's strict application of canonical standards in the cathedral close.[32] These included Patrick Byrne, one of Creef's own compurgators;[33] Richard Betagh, the prebendary of Saggard

---

[30] *RDD*, pp. 49, 50. Creef was allowed another term for compurgation because there was an insufficient number of prebendaries in Dublin on that day to supply the deficiency in his nominees, and because he successfully contended that he had believed his original selection to be irreprehensible. On compurgation generally see Houlbrooke, *Church courts and the people*, pp. 45–6; Ingram, *Church courts, sex and marriage*, pp. 51–2, 331–4.

[31] *Fiants, Elizabeth*, nos. 3014, 3216. This outcome corroborates the view that the proceedings were politically motivated, as the second compurgation would not have been upheld if substantial evidence or witnesses could have been produced to contradict it.

[32] The evidence for these deprivations is circumstantial. Each of the four clergy concerned is known to have vacated his cathedral living c.1570, the year in which the visitation was concluded (Lawlor, *Fasti of St Patrick's*, pp. 129, 159, 164, 185). All had demonstrable links with the conservative clerical interest, or possessed a background typical of the group; and, in three cases out of the four, proceedings for non-residence or delinquency are known to have been initiated by Dean Weston and Vicar General Ball during their visitations. The outcome of these cases is not recorded in the extant record.

[33] Byrne had to undergo compurgation himself for an unspecified offence detected by Dean Weston. It appears that he did not complete it successfully for he was replaced as prebendary of Swords by Edmund Ennos in 1570 (*RDD*, pp. 43–4, 48, 50; Lawlor, *Fasti of St Patrick's*, p. 159).

and, like Creef, a former confidante of Archbishop Curwen;[34] Thomas Fleming, prebendary of Maynooth;[35] and John Dillon, prebendary of Yago.[36] Taken together, such deprivations represented a very considerable dent in the power-base of what Loftus called the 'papist faction' in St Patrick's Cathedral,[37] a purge effected by the archbishop's ecclesiastical lawyers in the name of the reformed religion. For Creef and his allies the visitation and its outcome thus presented a grim warning of the threat which hung over the conservative religious position within St Patrick's Cathedral. For Loftus, Weston and Ball, on the other hand, it marked a satisfying beginning to the task of reforming the church in Dublin, one which was cemented by the conferral of the newly vacated livings on genuinely Protestant clergymen and administrators, including Ball himself, who received the archdeaconry of Glendalough;[38] John Kearney, the Cambridge graduate and Connaught-born author of the first Protestant catechism in the Irish language, who received the treasurership;[39] and Edmund Enos, a Cambridge MA graduate, who received the prebend of Swords.[40]

---

[34] Betagh, a vicar choral at the suppression of St Patrick's in 1547, and nominated to the prebend of Stagonil at the restoration in 1555, was a witness to Curwen's will on 20 November 1564, along with Creef and another known conservative cathedral cleric, Christopher Browne, the prebendary of Wicklow (Morrin, *Patent rolls*, i, pp. 142–3, Mason, *History of St Patrick's*, pp. 155–6; TNA: PRO, PROB 11/50, f. 182v). Betagh was in possession of the prebend at the outset of the visitation and was replaced by one William Prott or Pratt in 1570 (*RDD*, p. 40; Lawlor, *Fasti of St Patrick's*, p. 164).

[35] Fleming was appointed to the prebend of Maynooth in September 1555 in place of Richard Johnson, who had been deprived by Archdeacon Wellesley because he was married. He was still prebendary in 1562 and is undoubtedly the 'Thomas J. prebendary of Maynooth' who was pronounced contumacious for non-residence on 6 March 1570. His punishment, which was reserved to the morrow of the feast of St Patrick but which is not now on record, was probably deprivation, for he was replaced around this time by one John Doyne (*RDD*, pp. 48–9, 51–2, 77–8; RCB, C2/2, no. 11; Lawlor, *Fasti of St Patrick's*, p. 129).

[36] Dillon was cited, but failed to appear, on a number of occasions during Ball's visitation. On 12 December 1569, the same day that Fitzsimon, Vulp and the prebendary of Rathmichael, Edward Croft, were deprived for non-residence, Robert Nangle, the conservative chancellor of St Patrick's, appeared on Dillon's behalf and alleged that he was studying arts at Oxford where he had performed well, and that he was his legitimate proctor but did not have the requisite letters to hand. Had Nangle not intervened, Dillon would have been deprived there and then. His efforts were to no avail, however, because Dillon lost his prebend soon after, possibly on the quindene of Easter 1570, the date on which Nangle was required, but presumably failed, to produce the letters of procuration. It is likely that Dillon was a young protege of Nangle and his fellow conservatives (*RDD*, pp. 40–4).

[37] Loftus to Burghley, 26 September 1571 (TNA: PRO, SP 63/34, no. 13).   [38] *RDD*, p. 80.

[39] *AC*, i, p. 294; *ODNB, sub nomine* 'Kearney, John'; Lawlor, *Fasti of St Patrick's*, p. 70; B. Ó Cuív, 'The Irish language in the early modern period', *NHI* III, pp. 511–12. The catechism was published in 1571 shortly after Kearney received the treasurership: B. Ó Cuív (ed.), *Abidil Gaoidheilge & Caticiosma. Seaán Ó Ceanaigh's Irish primer of religion published in 1571* (Dublin, 1994).

[40] *AC*, i, p. 104; *Calendar of the manuscripts of the . . . marquess of Salisbury* (HMC, London, 1883–1973), xiii, p. 113; Lawlor, *Fasti of St Patrick's*, p. 159.

III

But this was just a beginning. Apart from the fact that Creef and some of his allies had survived the visitations, they now had to face the more daunting prospect of extending the Reformation into the parishes of the diocese. The first requirement of this task was to domesticate the Reformation, by turning its legislative aspects into local canon law. To this end, Loftus called a sitting of the traditional canon law-making body of the diocese, the provincial council, in February 1570.[41] This, as he and Weston were fully aware, was the body which had played such a key part in re-establishing and legitimising Catholicism under the previous diocesan administration. Thus, although no record of its deliberations now survives, it is probable that the council was summoned to invest key reformist decrees such as the royal injunctions of 1559,[42] or the twelve articles of religion which Lord Deputy Sidney and the High Commission had promulgated in January 1567,[43] with the same authoritative canonical standing that Dowdall and Curwen had given their Catholic canons of 1553/4 and 1555.

The provincial council also had another important function. As well as enacting what was effectively reformist canon law, it also provided an initial medium for communicating this law to key clerical personnel in the province of Dublin, and for securing their compliance to it, an important consideration given that some of these clerics would be called upon to communicate or enforce the legislation amongst the laity and their clerical subordinates after the council's business was completed. Those summoned to the council included the other bishops of the province, who appeared personally or by their proctors, representatives of the cathedral chapters, the archdeacons of the province, and the proctors of the parochial clergy of

---

[41] *RDD*, pp. 34–5.

[42] The injunctions were prepared for the royal visitation of the English church in 1559, but remained a permanent part of the Elizabethan settlement on both sides of the Irish Sea. As an expert ecclesiastical lawyer who had participated in the royal visitation, but had subsequently learned about the canonical restoration of Catholicism effected by Dowdall and Curwen in Ireland, Sir Robert Weston would have been particularly attuned to the need of validating the injunctions through a provincial council. On the injunctions generally see Haugaard, *Elizabeth and the English Reformation*, pp. 135–44; for the text see Frere, *Visitation articles*, iii, pp. 17–8.

[43] 'A Brefe Declaration of certeine Pryncipall Articles of Relygion: set out by order & aucthoritie aswel of the ryght Honorable Sir Henry Sidneye Knyght of the most noble order, Lorde president of the Councel in the Principalitie of Wales, & Marches of the same, and generall Deputie of the Realme of Irelande. As by Tharchebyshopes and Byshopes: with the rest of her maiesties Highe Commissioneres for causes Ecclesiasticall in her Realme of Ireland, for the unitie of Doctrine to be holden and taught of all Persons, Vicars, and Curates . . . .', reproduced in full in B. Ó Cuív (ed.), *Abidil Gaoidheilge & Caticiosma*, Appendix II, pp. 185–9. For the context in which they were originally promulgated see Brady and Murray, 'Sir Henry Sidney and the Reformation in Ireland', pp. 17–23.

each diocese.[44] Loftus and Weston made no presumption, however, that the council would be an automatically compliant body. The possibility of dissent was real and was soon confirmed in the non-appearance of representatives of the dean and chapter of Ferns and the parochial clergy of Kildare, as well as the archdeacons of those dioceses.[45] Indeed, it seems that Loftus and Weston may have feared that more serious demonstrations of dissent might occur during the council sessions proper, including overt opposition by disgruntled, conservative clerics to the planned programme of legislation. Such fears probably lay at the root of the archbishop's decision to keep the meeting a purely clerical gathering, and to abandon the customary practice of inviting a representative of the mayor and commons of the city of Dublin.[46] This was a move which clearly served notice that he and Weston were intent on minimising the opportunities for unseemly demonstrations of conservative clerical resistance to the Reformation, especially in the sight of an influential figure from lay society.

Although no trace of the council's legislation now exists, there are good grounds for assuming that Loftus was successful in getting it passed. Apart from the fact that the Weston–Ball visitations of St Patrick's had already contributed to making some of the gathering quite malleable, and thus responsive to the demand to give the Elizabethan settlement local synodal validation,[47] the council was immediately followed by the activation of another traditional structure, the metropolitan visitation. Had the legislation run aground, it is unlikely that Loftus would have set about visiting the parishes of his diocese and his four suffragan sees of Kildare, Ferns, Ossory and Leighlin, as he would have had nothing of substance to lay before his flock to show that his regime, and the religion that it upheld, were the legitimate heirs of the see's medieval past. Armed with the new Protestant canons, this is precisely what he set out to do.

The metropolitan visitation took place in the autumn of 1570, and was conducted by specially appointed commissaries in each diocese, such as Daniel Kavanagh, the bishop of Leighlin, and David Clere, the dean of Holy Trinity Cathedral, Waterford, who were deputed by Loftus to visit the diocese of Leighlin.[48] In the diocese of Dublin proper, the visitation was conducted by Loftus's vicar general, John Ball. What we know about Ball's

---

[44] *RDD*, pp. 34–5.   [45] Ibid.

[46] *RDD*, pp. 31–3, 34–5; Book of accounts of the corporation of the city of Dublin, 1541–1613 (DCA, MR/35, p. 140).

[47] The council included, for example, a representative of the clergy of St Patrick's nominated by Dean Weston and the post visitation chapter. It also included the archdeacon of Dublin, Robert Wellesley, a man whose part in the downfall of Treasurer Barnewall had shown that he had little stomach for overtly heroic stands against the Loftus regime (*RDD*, p. 34).

[48] *RDD*, pp. 35–6.

first reforming foray into the parishes shows that, in line with the regime's avowed objective of avoiding unnecessary antagonism of the leaders of the local community, he was much less rigorous in seeking out and punishing lay delinquency, than he had been in his detection and correction of clerical delinquency in the cathedral. One man who appreciated this difference of approach more than most was Christopher Browne, the conservative prebendary of Wicklow, who had experienced the Weston–Ball onslaught on St Patrick's at close hand. Shortly after the metropolitan visitation was completed, Browne complained bitterly that the vicar general, 'having any rich man of the country in the censures of the church for fornication, adultery or any like offence', would absolve them 'for money . . . with the pope's absolution, Absolvo te . . . and hath been seen and heard of credible persons giving that absolution on horseback in the fields, the penitent kneeling before him'.[49]

Although this witness was hostile, the substance of the complaint rings true. What the regime was endeavouring to do was to win the allegiance of the political community to the new settlement by establishing firm canonical credentials for itself, and by creating a firm sense of continuity with the medieval past, an approach which had already been evinced in such measures as the provincial council's translation of reformist articles and injunctions into local synodal canons, and which was now evident in the liberal and highly visible use of the traditional canonical formula for granting absolution during an episcopal visitation. The same approach is also detectable in other aspects of the visitation. The episcopal commissaries, for example, waged an offensive against clerical concubinage, which was deeply redolent of the canonical past, albeit with a Protestant twist, in that the offending clergy were allowed to legalise their relationships through marriage, rather than end them.[50] Most remarkably of all, however, there is evidence to suggest that the visitors were even willing to countenance the use of the Latin version of the Book of Common Prayer, a practice which had started under Archbishop Curwen's conservative administration.[51] Overall,

---

[49] 'Articles objected against Sir John Bale, clerk, commissary unto the archbishop of Dublin' (TNA: PRO, SP 63/71, no. 10; calendared in Brady, *State papers*, pp. 37–9). For the dating, authorship and significance of these articles see below pp. 287–9.

[50] *RDD*, p. 36.

[51] The evidence for this comes from a letter written by the English privy council to Loftus and Lord Deputy Perrot in March 1588, in which they noted that they 'had been of late advertised of a notable abuse continued in the English Pale, where it was said that in sundry parts thereof the Book of Common Prayer is publicly used in the Latin tongue and contrarywise the Book of Prayer in English . . . almost wholly neglected and but little used' (*APC 1587–8*, pp. 410–11). Although this letter was written many years after the visitation of 1570, it had been solicited by the deputy and his supporters as part of a general campaign and critique of Loftus's government of the church to that point. The complaint about the abuse of the Latin Prayer Book was not therefore a complaint about a recent development,

this approach to reform allowed the Loftus regime to present itself, and thus the Reformation, in terms which were more easily assimilable by the leaders of the community; and which, in the fullness of time, would enable it to replace the old clerical elite as the legitimate voice of clerical authority in the community, and to win a similar place in its affections.

Obviously, at this delicate stage, there had to be some sweeteners to begin the process, a consideration which accounts for the relative leniency exhibited both in relation to the the Latin Prayer Book, and the treatment of lay delicts. The leniency on the Prayer Book, although strictly against the letter of the act of uniformity – the Latin version was only supposed to be used in places where the presiding minister was unable to speak English[52] – was designed as a confidence-building measure, which would avoid alienating adherents of the old religion by negating the most overt sign of the changeover from Catholic mass to Protestant communion service, the use of a different language. A similar intent was evident in the way lay offences were handled. Although offences were detected and money fines levied in return for the vicar general's absolution, it was all done in a casual, almost routine, manner, which was intended to avoid causing embarrassment to particular individuals – and a consequent build-up of resentment against the exponents of godly reform – while at the same time showing that the new regime upheld the same moral and canonical standards, and the same procedures for enforcing them, that all previous diocesan administrations had done.[53] In this way the Loftus regime posed not only as the legitimate upholder of the traditional ecclesiastical law, but as a sensitive and caring administrator of it.

The ultimate success of this strategy, as Loftus and Weston well knew, would be dependent upon their ability to sustain it in an uninterrupted manner over a lengthy period of time. In this scenario, habitual loyalty to the old clergy would gradually be transferred to Loftus's regime, thus rendering it more capable of transforming traditional religion into something akin to the religion officially sanctioned by the Elizabethan settlement. In particular, the acquisition of communal loyalty would ultimately help the regime to improve the pastoral care on offer in the diocese, by enabling it to exert an effective influence over the lay impropriators. This ability to

---

but something which was of long duration and something for which Loftus was considered to be responsible. According to the council, the queen could not 'but impute the fault thereof chiefly to the Lord Archbishop, considering how the care to abolish such kind of superstitious abuses principally appertaineth to him'. This suggests very strongly that Loftus's diocesan administrations, all the way back to the Weston era, allowed the use of the Latin Prayer book to go unpunished as part of their conciliatory reform strategy.

52 *Statutes at large*, i, p. 219.

53 The redemption of penances by monetary payments was a long-standing tradition of the English and Irish churches and was sanctioned by local synodal legislation (*Alen's register*, pp. 92–4).

influence the impropriators was vitally important for, as a group, they controlled the rectorial interest in some 46 per cent of all diocesan parishes, and were thus responsible for finding and funding the bulk of the parochial clergy, and for the upkeep of much of the church fabric. Without their co-operation, therefore, it would be virtually impossible to maintain any form of religion in the parishes, let alone establish reformed standards therein, a consideration which must have weighed heavily with the reformers when they conceived their conciliatory reform strategy.[54]

But this essential premise – that the success of the reformers' strategy would be dependent upon their ability to sustain it in the long term – immediately posed an administrative problem. Outside the periods of the triennial archiepiscopal visitation, the responsibility for detecting and correcting lay and clerical delicts, and thus maintaining the visibility of the regime and its policy of fostering communal loyalty through the dispensation of ecclesiastical justice, would reside with the archdeacon of Dublin in his guise as 'oculus episcopi'. And that official, Robert Wellesley, was a conservative who could not be trusted to support this strategy as whole-heartedly as Vicar General Ball. Worse, unlike other diocesan officials, Wellesley could not be removed from the archdeaconry at Loftus's pleasure, because it was annexed to a cathedral prebend and was thus, effectively, a freehold position. The only way Wellesley could be ejected, in fact, was to find sufficient grounds for his deprivation. Yet, although his standing had been undermined by the events surrounding the deprivation of Treasurer Barnewall and the humiliation of Precentor Creef, no such evidence was uncovered to begin proceedings against him. The reality, therefore, was that his removal would either have to wait until he himself presented such grounds for deprivation or until such time as he died.

Aware of this difficulty Loftus and Weston sought to circumvent it by procuring a new commission for ecclesiastical causes, which was granted on 14 June 1568.[55] The new commission had a broad remit. It was issued to pursue and punish offences throughout the entire realm against the acts of uniformity and supremacy in particular, but also against ecclesiastical law generally. It thus provided Loftus and Weston with a means of maintaining their reform strategy in between episcopal visitations, even allowing for

---

[54] On the role of the impropriators in the pastoral care of the diocese see Murray, 'Tudor diocese of Dublin', ch. 7.

[55] Loftus to Cecil, 2 April 1568 (TNA: PRO, SP 63/24, no. 1); A list of 'the Queen's Majesty's Commissioners nominated in her Highness's ecclesiastical commission heretofore granted for Ireland', a list of proposed new commissioners, endorsed by Lord Deputy Sidney, n.d. (TNA: PRO, SP 63/25, no. 52); *Patent rolls 1566–69*, pp. 173–4. The undated lists obviously comprised the document which Loftus sent to Cecil by his servant, Lewis Challoner, in April 1568.

the fact their archdeacon was untrustworthy, as well as offering a highly visible model of proper ecclesiastical government for other diocesan administrations to imitate. This conception of the new ecclesiastical commission was most apparent in its composition. Apart from Archbishop Loftus and Dean Weston themselves, it also included Weston's brother, James, an experienced diocesan administrator based in England, who, at this point, seemed destined to join him in Ireland to help with the reform of the church. All three were on the commission's quorum.[56] In addition, William Fludde, a notary public and practising proctor in the consistory court of Dublin, was appointed to the key position of registrar and receiver of the fines.[57] Overall, then, the reins of the commission were firmly in the grip of the archbishop and the dean, which empowered them to direct it in whatever way they saw fit.[58]

Once established, Loftus and Weston sought to put the commission on a more permanent and formal footing than it had previously been, a feature evinced both in the yielding of accounts 'to her highness's use' by the registrar and receiver of fines – the first since the erection of that office in 1564 – and in the keeping of a formal register of proceedings.[59] The new

---

[56] *Patent rolls 1566–69*, pp. 173–4. James Weston had partnered his brother as diocesan registrar in the Coventry and Lichfield administration before the latter came over to Ireland. It is likely that Robert had envisaged that James would play a similar partnering role in the Dublin diocesan administration and the High Commission. For some reason, possibly because Robert felt that he would be better served by leaving him behind to look after his property interests in their native Lichfield, James never came to Ireland. When this decision was made, probably in the late summer of 1568, Weston turned to his nephew, John Ball, the son of 'my sister Ball', to help him with the reformation of the Irish church. James remained behind and administered the leases of several parsonages and prebends belonging to Robert, which the latter eventually bequeathed to his wife Alice, his son John and his daughter Audrey (O'Day, 'Role of the registrar', pp. 84, 90–1; Will of Robert Weston, 2 May 1573, TNA: PRO, PROB 11/55, ff. 189v–190r).

[57] Brief declaration of the account of William Fludde, gent, registrar and receiver of the fines imposed by the commissioners for ecclesiastical causes, Michaelmas 1568–Michaelmas 1573 (TNA: PRO, SP 63/94, no. 109); *RDD*, pp. 52–4, 79. Lewis Challoner, Loftus's servant, was originally appointed to the post but never took it up (*Patent rolls 1566–69*, pp. 173–4).

[58] On Loftus and Weston's leadership of the commission see Loftus to Cecil, 2 July 1570 (TNA: PRO, SP 63/30, no. 64), and Loftus to Cecil (then Lord Burghley), 14 November 1573 (TNA: PRO, SP 63/42, no. 76).

[59] Brief declaration of the account of William Fludde (TNA: PRO, SP 63/94, no. 109). The High Commission's register, which covered the period 1570–7, survived until the destruction of the Irish Public Record Office in 1922 (Wood, *Guide to the records deposited in the Public Record Office in Ireland*, p. 223). Some details of its contents can be gleaned from Lawlor's *Fasti of St Patrick's*. The period covered by the register corresponds exactly to the era in which Weston presided over the commission and, following his death in 1573, the registrarship of his nephew John Ball (Brief of the account of John Ball, gent, collector of the fines and amerciaments in causes ecclesiastical in the realm of Ireland, 15 October 1573–31 January 1577, TNA: PRO, SP 63/94, no. 109). It is unlikely that the commission was very active prior to 1570 as Weston was then busy with the visitation of St Patrick's.

formality gave the commission the aura and standing of a conventional church court, rather than the appearance of the ad hoc and innovatory body which it had previously had. This, and the overlap of staff between the commission and the diocesan administration, was important as it genuinely made the commission appear as an extension or relative of the conventional diocesan administration, and as a real substitute for Archdeacon Wellesley's court. The formal structure was important in another way however. It geared the commission towards dealing with the whole panoply of ecclesiastical causes, a feature which again set it in contrast to the previous commission, the latter having dealt almost exclusively with offences against the Reformation statutes.[60] Thus, as in Loftus's metropolitan visitation, the enforcement of the Reformation under the commission would be subsumed under the wider dispensation of ecclesiastical justice, and given the appearance of a traditional, less threatening, quasi-canonical undertaking.

The most convincing evidence of Loftus and Weston's intentions, however, is to be found in the surviving record of the commission's proceedings. Two aspects of its work stand out in this period, which clearly show that it was designed to complement the reform strategy that they had instituted in their ordinary visitations. One of these was the ongoing concern with the reformation of St Patrick's Cathedral. Under Loftus and Weston the commission continued to act with the same exacting rigour to rid the institution of manifestly unsuitable clergy. Among its victims were two well-connected canons, who, ironically, had acquired their livings as a result of the clear-out effected by Weston and Ball in 1569–70. These were Richard Dixon, bishop of Cork, prebendary of Rathmichael, and erstwhile chaplain to Lord Deputy Sidney; and John Doyne, a cleric who had been appointed prebendary of Maynooth by the earl of Kildare. Both men were deprived for sexual incontinence.[61] The deprivation of Dixon for bigamy was particularly significant. Loftus and Weston were unsure whether the ecclesiastical commissioners had sufficient authority to deprive a bishop and wrote to Burghley in April 1571 for advice on the matter. It was clear, however, that they wanted to take responsibility for the deprivation, to maintain the tough offensive against clerical incontinence begun in the metropolitan visitation, and to counteract the scandal and damage that Dixon's case had caused for 'the professors of godly word' and their espousal of clerical marriage. To this end, therefore, Dixon was forced to do a very traditional form of penance in St Patrick's Cathedral. On two Sundays, standing under the

---

[60] Shirley, *Church in Ireland 1547–67*, pp. 194–7.

[61] Lawlor, *Fasti of St Patrick's*, pp. 129, 144; Sidney to Cecil, 26 December 1569 (TNA: PRO, SP 63/29, no. 84); Weston, Loftus and Fitzwilliam to Burghley, 16 April 1571 (TNA: PRO, SP 63/32, nos. 10, 10.1); Loftus to Burghley, 26 November 1571 (TNA: PRO, SP 63/34, no. 30).

pulpit, he very publicly acknowledged his offence in the time of the sermon, an action which displayed once again the reformers' concern to demonstrate their conventional canonical rectitude.[62]

The second aspect of the commission's work which complemented the Loftus–Weston reform strategy was its approach to the laity. Here again, and in contrast to its treatment of clerical delicts, the commission's main concern was to define the standards of the reformed religion, and to establish trust in it, rather than to ruthlessly make an example of all those whose behaviour fell short of 'godly' Protestant ideals. The commission attempted this by expending its efforts on the detection of offences, while at the same time neglecting to exact the full retribution of the law. As in the metropolitan visitation, the main form of punishment for delicts was the monetary fine. Overall, however, the volume of fines imposed by the commissioners in the period was quite small. This feature, and the casual approach that they took to collecting them, suggests very strongly that the efforts of the Loftus–Weston commission were neither intended to be aggressive towards, or were perceived as such by, the local community. Thus, in the period Michaelmas 1568 to Michaelmas 1573, fines totalling IR£442 7s. 4d. were levied throughout Ireland.[63] Of this total, about 37 per cent, or IR£163 13s. 7d., were imposed on inhabitants of the diocese of Dublin, making an average annual total of somewhere in the region of IR£32 14s. 8d. during these years.[64] Of this annual diocesan average, about 65 per cent or IR£21 5s. 6d. would have been imposed on the inhabitants of Dublin city, the remaining 35 per cent or IR£11 9s. 2d. on the inhabitants of the country parishes in Co. Dublin.[65]

Although these estimates are not perfect – they do not, for example, allow for variations in the level of fines from year to year[66] – they still illustrate that the ecclesiastical commission exercised a far from draconian policy of

---

[62] Weston, Loftus and Fitzwilliam to Burghley, 16 April 1571 (TNA: PRO, SP 63/32, no. 10).

[63] Brief declaration of the account of William Fludde (TNA: PRO, SP 63/94, no. 109).

[64] These figures were calculated on the basis of the geographical distribution of the accumulated arrears on High Commission fines, IR£500 10s. 2d., in the years 1568–82. Given that £255 13s. 4d. in arrears were carried over from the Weston period (Fludde's account 1568–73), into the next accounting period (Ball's account 1573–7), we can be confident that they made up a substantial portion of the cumulative arrears between 1568–82 and are thus a reasonably reliable indicator to the general distribution of fines levied (Brief declaration of the account of William Fludde; Brief of the account of John Ball; Brief estimate of the account of John Bird, gent, registrar and receiver of fines in causes ecclesiastical in Ireland, 7 February 1577–7 February 1582, TNA: PRO, SP 63/94, no. 109). For the geographical distribution of arrears see Table 8.1.

[65] The city and county figures were calculated on the same basis as the diocesan figure (Table 8.1).

[66] It is likely that the activity of the High Commission, and the level of fines, would have been higher after the ordinary visitations of St Patrick's Cathedral and the province were completed, i.e. from the winter of 1570–1 until Weston's death in the summer of 1573. This is the period which the High Commission's register covered.

enforcement during the period in which Loftus and Weston led it. If, for example, we take the following case – that all of the fines levied in this period consisted of the minimum statutory penalty of 12d. for non-attendance at the Prayer Book service[67] – then the number of individuals fined each year in the diocese of Dublin would have been approximately 654; 425 in the city of Dublin, and 229 in the country parishes. The reality, however, is that not all of these fines would have been for such offences, nor so lowly valued, with the result that the number of individuals punished in this way would have been very much lower. Some offenders, for example, forfeited recognisances – rated at IR£10 to IR£20 in the early 1590s[68] – for failing to appear before the commission. Although it is unlikely that such recognisances were so highly rated at this juncture, four or five of them each year, even at one-fifth of the cost of the 1590s recognisances, would have reduced these worst case figures for those punished from c.654 to somewhere between 454 and 494 annually.[69]

Yet it is likely that the numbers punished were even lower still. It is known that the commissioners also had the authority to impose higher discretionary fines than the statutory minimum, an authority which they must have exercised on at least some occasions during the period 1568 to 1573, and which would have brought the number of individuals fined down further. Given all these considerations, and the facts that not all the fines levied would have had anything to do with the Reformation statutes; that there is no record of anyone being incarcerated for repeated offending by the commissioners at this time;[70] and, above all, that nearly 58 per cent of the total fines imposed under Weston and Loftus, IR£255 13s. 4d., were not collected in the period of their leadership,[71] and it is evident that their aim was not to coerce the population of Dublin into accepting Elizabethan Protestantism through systematic, punitive taxation. Rather the aim was to buttress the diocesan administration's efforts to establish canonical credentials for the reformers' cause – the commission, for example, conducted its business according to the coventional legal forms used by the courts Christian, including the use of the Latin tongue[72] – and

---

[67] *Statutes at large*, i, p. 287.
[68] DCA, MS C1/J3/1, Recognisance Book, 1589–90, p. 34.
[69] When a new ecclesiastical commission was appointed in May 1577, the 1568 commission was revoked. However, power was reserved to the old commissioners to recover 'forfeited recognisances not yet paid in' (*Fiants, Elizabeth*, no. 3047).
[70] In the 1590s, by contrast, the High Commission would acquire its own gaoler (Morrin, *Patent rolls*, ii, p. 290). No such office existed at this time.
[71] Brief of the account of John Ball (TNA: PRO, SP 63/94, no. 109).
[72] For an example see 'The tenor of Sir Richard Plunkett's sentence of deprivation from his benefices . . . pronounced by due course of her majesty's ecclesiastical laws . . . by the Queen's High Commissioners', 1 July 1581 (TNA: PRO, SP 63/108, no. 50.3).

Table 8.1 *Cumulative arrears of High Commission fines 1568–82*[73]

Diocese	District	Fines	Diocesan Total	% (District)	% (Diocese)
Dublin	Dublin City	£120 10s. 0d.		24	
	Co. Dublin	£64 12s. 4d.	£185 2s. 4d.	13	37
Meath	Co. Meath	£139 16s. 0d.		28	
	Co. Westmeath	£13 2s. 8d.	£152 18s. 8d.	2.75	30.75
Kildare	Co. Kildare	£71 14s. 2d.	£71 14s. 2d.	14	14
Armagh	Drogheda	£25 11s. 8d.		5	
Inter Anglicos	Co. Louth	£29 3s. 4d.	£54 15s. 0d.	6	11
Ferns	Co. Wexford	£17 0s. 0d.	£17 0s. 0d.	3.5	3.5
Ossory	Co. Kilkenny	£11 10s. 0d.	£11 10s. 0d.	2.25	2.25
Waterford	Co. Waterford	£6 0s. 0d.	£6 0s. 0d.	1.25	1.25
Cashel	Co. Tipperary	£1 10s. 0d.	£1 10s. 0d.	0.25	0.25

to continue the policy of marginalising the senior conservative clergy. Over time, it was hoped that this firm but relatively conciliatory and gradualist approach would wear away lay resistance to the Reformation through the establishment of real confidence in the new order, through the nullification of conservative clerical influence, and through sheer force of habit and a growing urge to remove the irritation of being hauled before and fined by the commission.

IV

Initially, at any rate, Loftus and Weston had some real cause for optimism that this strategy might work. Their new regime, for example, appears to have been reasonably popular at this juncture. It was no accident that Lord Deputy Fitzwilliam could report to Burghley in August 1571 that Archbishop Loftus was 'greatly well be liked of all sorts of the English Pale'.[74] More significantly, there were encouraging signs that a younger generation of ecclesiastical lawyers in the Pale were impressed by, and willing to give their allegiance to, the civilian, and Protestant, legal culture which was developing in Dublin under the influence of Weston and his nephew, John Ball. One such figure was Thady Dowling, who later became the chancellor of Leighlin Cathedral, and who is best known for his work as an annalist. In the early 1570s, Dowling was in attendance at the free school of Dublin city, under its master Patrick Cusack, where he remained 'about

[73] Brief estimate of the account of John Bird, 1577–82 (TNA: PRO, SP 63/94, no. 109).
[74] Fitzwilliam to Burghley, 24 August 1571 (TNA: PRO, SP 63/33, no. 43).

four years space', a period during which he determined 'to learn the institutions of both laws'. Thus, as he later recalled, he 'did every term and law days resort to the consistory, legates [delegates] and admiral courts . . . and lay nightly in one bed with Mr Birne, a civilian of commendation, and had the use and revolving of his books with his conferences and resolutions'. He also 'became in acquaintance and great amity with Mr John Bale [Ball], master of art and bachelor in both the laws, vicar general'. The 'Mr Birne' in question was probably John Byrne, a notary public, who had served as registrar of Archdeacon Wellesley's court in the late 1560s, and who had subsequently become a lawyer or proctor in the archbishop's consistory during Ball's presidency. The fact that a young student like Dowling, and an aspiring lawyer like Byrne, were willing to attach themselves to Ball, even though Byrne had links with the conservative archdeacon of Dublin, Robert Wellesley, augured well for the regime's avowed aim of marginalising the clerical old guard and forging its own links with the local community.[75]

Yet, despite such early promise, these objectives were never realised. On the contrary, over the course of the following decade or so, the Loftus–Weston strategy was completely destroyed by a very varied sequence of events and processes, which finally and irrevocably put paid to all hopes that the established church would secure the allegiance of the indigenous population of the diocese of Dublin. What all of these events and processes had in common was the great instability they created both within the Loftus–Weston regime itself, and in the environment within which it operated. Ultimately and fatally, they undermined the regime's carefully modulated and delicately balanced efforts to usurp the old clerical elite's position and status in Pale society. The first and most important of these destabilising factors was the poor health of Robert Weston, which culminated in his untimely death in May 1573.

For much of the five years he resided in Ireland, Weston was an ill man afflicted by intermittent but serious bouts of sickness. One of these occurred during the visitation of St Patrick's in February 1570, and it prevented him from attending one of the hearings in the cause against Thomas Creef. More significantly, Weston's frequent illnesses depressed him and, at times, led

---

[75] Notes by Thady Dowling, chancellor of Leighlin cathedral, on the ecclesiastical establishment of Ireland, 12 March 1602 (TNA: PRO, SP 63/210, no. 62; *CSP Ireland*, 1601–3, p. 333); *RDD*, p. 53; Will and inventory of Hugh Kennedy of Dublin, merchant, 17 July 1567, proven before Archdeacon Wellesley and Byrne on 24 September 1567 (Bodleian, MS Talbot c. 99/3). Dowling's support for Ball's work was also evinced by his part in the compilation of the precedent book of legal forms for the province of Dublin, which dates from this time and which drew extensively on Ball's reign as official principal and vicar general of Dublin for its selection of legal precedents (J. Watt introduction to *RDD*, pp. iii–iv). It is possible, in fact, that Ball may have initiated the project; the paper used has a 1570s watermark.

him to seek his recall to England.[76] In the spring of 1571, most observers, including Adam Loftus, thought that the chancellor's departure was imminent, a belief which stimulated and encouraged a very marked, and ultimately, damaging attempt by the conservative canons in St Patrick's to re-establish their authority in the cathedral close.

The attempted coup revolved around the question of finding a successor to Weston as dean of St Patrick's. Both Loftus and the cathedral chapter, including the 'papist faction', were anxious that the crown would refrain from appointing a lay man to the deanery and, in a rare display of unanimity, they agreed that they should petition the crown to allow the living to be bestowed on an 'ecclesiastical person'. In February 1571, Loftus wrote to Cecil to this effect, while the chapter nominated an emissary, Christopher Browne, the prebendary of Wicklow, to pursue the suit in England before the privy council.[77] Loftus was caught badly offguard by this turn of events. Browne was an arch-conservative and, during a lengthy stay in England throughout much of 1571 and 1572, he worked assiduously to revive the fortunes of the conservatives and to discredit the archbishop's reforming regime.[78] He began this task by seeking to solidify his own position. The Weston–Ball visitations had taught him that the Loftus regime was determined to find every conceivable irregularity in the qualifications of its clerical enemies, in order that it might legally eject them from their cathedral livings. Thus, although he already possessed a dispensation out of the Irish chancery dating from January 1567, Browne sought and acquired an additional dispensation from the archbishop of Canterbury's Faculty Office

---

[76] Weston to Cecil, 2 August 1568 (TNA: PRO, SP 63/25, no. 59); Weston to Cecil, 14 September 1569 (TNA: PRO, SP 63/29, no. 62); *RDD*, p. 49; Weston to Cecil, 7 August 1570 (TNA: PRO, SP 63/30, no. 78); Weston to the earl of Leicester, 11 April 1571 (TNA: PRO, SP 63/32, no. 8); Weston to Burghley, 20 October 1572 (TNA: PRO, SP 63/38, no. 16); Weston to Queen Elizabeth, 31 March 1573 (TNA: PRO, SP 63/39, no. 56); Weston to Burghley, 31 March 1573 (TNA: PRO, SP 63/39, no. 57).

[77] Loftus to Cecil, 16 February 1571 (TNA: PRO, SP 63/31, no. 11); Loftus to Burghley, 26 September 1571 (TNA: PRO, SP 63/34, no. 13); privy council to Lord Deputy Fitzwilliam, 9 July 1572 (Bodleian, Carte MS, vol. 57, ff. 389r–390r, 398r).

[78] Browne began his career as chaplain in his native parish of Clondalkin. In this capacity, he first became associated with the conservative cause when, along with James Humphrey, the leader of clerical opposition to the Henrician Reformation in Dublin, and four others, he was entrusted with the task of bringing up Archbishop Browne's sons, as part of the religious settlement that St Leger had instituted, and which re-established the conservatives' position, in the 1540s. Browne maintained his relationship with at least one of the archbishop's sons until the 1570s (see Chapter 4; *CCD*, no. 1220; Morrin, *Patent rolls*, ii, p. 640). His conservatism is also attested to by his subsequent nomination to the Marian chapter of 1555, his witnessing of Archbishop Curwen's will in 1564 and his nomination as a compurgator of Thomas Creef in 1570 (Morrin, *Patent rolls*, i, pp. 142–3, Mason, *History of St Patrick's*, pp. 155–6; TNA: PRO, PROB 11/50, f. 182v; *RDD*, p. 50).

on 10 December 1571, which confirmed his right to hold his prebend and the vicarages of Tallaght and Downings in plurality.[79]

Browne's concern to secure added protection is understandable for, at the time, he was engaged in some deeply subversive plotting. Although he had gone to England with the archbishop's blessing to seek a renewal of the cathedral's 1555 charter of restoration, which would have allowed the chapter to elect its dean freely, Browne used this as a cover for a much more ambitious plan. Through contacts at court like Sir Valentine Browne, and in anticipation of the renewal of the charter, he attempted to procure the queen's, or the privy council's, letters to the chapter of St Patrick, recommending that he himself should be elected to the deanery.[80] Furthermore, having successfully marketed himself to Lord Deputy Fitzwilliam as a 'very wise' Irish-speaking man 'of good civil government and judgement and . . . well given to duty and obedience', he also sought to secure the vacant bishopric of Down for himself, a move designed to increase the power of the conservatives in the church generally.[81] Finally, he endeavoured to undermine the reputation, and instigate the removal from office, of the conservatives' *bête noire*, John Ball, by laying a set of ten articles of complaint against him before the privy council.[82]

---

[79] Loftus to Burghley, 26 September 1571 (TNA: PRO, SP 63/34, no. 13); RCB, C2, 'Maguire's Miscellaneous Papers', vol. 2, p. 54; Lambeth, Muniment Book, F1/B, f. 48r; privy council to Lord Deputy Fitzwilliam, 9 July 1572 (Bodleian, Carte MS, vol. 57, ff. 389r–390r, 398r).

[80] Loftus to Burghley, 26 September 1571 (TNA: PRO, SP 63/34, no. 13); privy council to Lord Deputy Fitzwilliam, 9 July 1572 (Bodleian, Carte MS, vol. 57, ff. 389r–390r, 398r). Sir Valentine Browne had played a prominent part with Sir William Fitzwilliam in bringing about Sir Anthony St Leger's downfall in the 1550s by revealing the extent of his financial malfeasance (Brady, *Chief Governors*, pp. 66–7). This, of course, was an enterprise which Christopher Browne and his fellow prebendaries in St Patrick's would have supported, because of the deputy's efforts to impede the restoration of the cathedral's property. His acquaintance with Sir Valentine probably dated to this period and may have been associated with the campaign against St Leger.

[81] Loftus, Brady and Fitzwilliam to Burghley, 1 October 1572 (TNA: PRO, SP 63/38, no. 2); Lord Deputy Fitzwilliam to the Queen, 19 February 1573 (TNA: PRO, SP 63/39, no. 30). Fitzwilliam's estimation of Browne's qualities suggests that he was reasonably well acquainted with him. As with Sir Valentine Browne, this acquaintance probably dated back to the Marian period and may have been associated with the campaign against St Leger.

[82] 'Articles objected against Sir John Bale, clerk, commissary unto the archbishop of Dublin' (TNA: PRO, SP 63/71, no. 10; calendared in Brady, *State papers*, pp. 37–9). These articles, which are undated and unsigned, but endorsed in a contemporary hand 'p.b. is notes', were incorrectly placed in 1580 by the archivists in the State Paper Office (*CSP Ireland, 1574– 1585*, p. 205). The references in the present tense to Lord Chancellor Weston (articles 2, 9), and to Ball's visitation of Dublin diocese 'giving that absolution on horseback in the fields . . . as he visits in the country' (article 3), date the composition of the document to c.1571–3. In addition, their author's knowledge of the goings on in St Patrick's Cathedral, and the diocese of Dublin generally, clearly identifies him as a member of the chapter of St Patrick's (articles 2, 8). Thus it is virtually certain that the 'p.b.' was Christopher Browne, or 'Parson Browne' as the privy council referred to him (Bodleian, Carte MS, vol. 57,

There is little doubt that Browne's efforts were part of a carefully orchestrated plan on the part of the conservatives, to regain their pre-eminence in the Dublin diocesan administration and in the church generally. The articles against the vicar general in particular – a very heterogeneous and sometimes contradictory series of complaints – bear all the hallmarks of a document which originated in committee. Indeed, a number of the articles can actually be attributed with some confidence to particular individuals in the chapter. The resentful voice of Thomas Creef, for example, the old celibate canonist who had been forced to undergo the humiliation of compurgation by Ball on a charge of adultery, probably lay behind two articles which accused the vicar general of being an adulterer himself; and in the complaint that Ball

challenging a greater pre-eminence than others, is not contented to possess his own stall in the choir next the chanter [Creef], but hath installed his wife in the seat next unto him ... which unseemly seat for a woman is some deal marked, not for any cause of religion, but for some spark of disorder to see a father's wife of the church gibbishly apparalled with ruffled and curled hair ... usurp a father's seat.[83]

In a similarly bitter vein, the voice of Patrick Byrne, a casualty of the Weston–Ball visitation, a known Creef ally, and a man of Gaelic Irish descent, is detectable in the complaint that Ball, having cited 'great flocks of the rudest and miserablest poor people Irish to appear in his consistory at Dublin', would leave them begging in the streets for days 'without further process or indictment', until at last he committed them to prison for failure to pay certain fees, saying that 'when the prison hath consumed them they shall go home like naked Irish slaves'. Byrne prayed that God would 'convert' this 'plague and calamity ... from our poor Irish nation'.[84]

The bitter hatred that the conservative prebendaries felt for the vicar general – a testimony, no doubt, to the early success of the Loftus–Weston reform strategy – and their absolute determination to bring him down, unified these disparate complaints. This determination was evinced in their tactical appeal to every conceivable interest group or shade of opinion capable of furthering this cause, even those which opposed their own traditional values. Hence they could characterise Ball as a papist because of his lecherous instincts, 'lechery being incident to popery'; a 'dissembler in religion' because of his allegedly amoral behaviour; and even an inspiration to puritans, because he refused to wear the surplice, a stand which the

---

ff. 389r–390r, 398r); and that the articles were presented to the council during Browne's visit to England in 1571–2.
[83] 'Articles objected against Sir John Bale', nos. 2, 5, 8 (TNA: PRO, SP 63/71, no. 10).
[84] Ibid., no. 4 (TNA: PRO, SP 63/71, no. 10).

prebendaries claimed bred contempt for 'the injunctions for the decent apparel for ministers in the church'.[85]

Their appeals were not confined to the religious sphere however. They also sought support from political thinkers and reformers. To this end, they carefully highlighted the damage Ball had done, and was doing, to the Irish commonwealth, through his favourable treatment of the rich and his oppression of the poor, and his ill-treatment of the Irishry.[86] The tone and contents of these latter articles, in particular, suggest that the prebendaries may have been influenced by the 'commonwealth men' of the Pale and their campaign against the cess. It is no surprise to find that Browne resided at the London Inns of Court during his sojourn in England, a centre from which some of the earliest opposition to the cess had emerged during the viceroyalty of Lord Lieutenant Sussex.[87] Yet amidst all these calculated, exaggerated and, in some cases, fabricated allegations, the authentic, medieval voice of the prebendaries of St Patrick's was still audible. In particular, their concern to bring John Ball to book over his alleged lechery, and the manner in which they expressed it – they believed it a source of 'great grief' to 'true hearted subjects to see such apparent vices unpunished in their commonwealth' – was a very traditional evocation of the identity and value system of the English Irish clerical caste. Similarly, the complaint about Ball's liberal usage of the 'Pope's absolution' in his visitation, while presented for political purposes in a conformist Protestant light, was really a reflection of conservative disgust at the fact that a reformer should use a technique that was traditionally a Catholic preserve.[88]

The results of Browne's campaign were mixed. The attempt to acquire the deanery failed outright. Not only did Loftus get wind of his plotting, and petition Burghley to stop it in its tracks, but Weston recovered his health and the ensuing vacancy in the deanery thus evaporated. Moreover, the conservatives also discovered that when indeed the next vacancy would arise, they were unlikely to get their man placed as the privy council 'did not think it convenient ... that her majesty should be restrained from the nomination of the dean', as it was a living 'fit to be bestowed upon some chosen personage meet otherwise for her majesty's service in that realm'.[89] Browne's hopes of getting the bishopric of Down were also stymied. The influential courtier, Sir Thomas Smith, who was about to launch a colony

[85] Ibid., nos. 2, 7 (TNA: PRO, SP 63/71, no. 10).
[86] Ibid., nos. 3, 4, 10 (TNA: PRO, SP 63/71, no. 10).
[87] Sir Thomas Smith to Lord Deputy Fitzwilliam, 12 April 1573 (Bodleian, Carte MS 56, ff. 123–8); Brady, *Chief Governors*, pp. 102–3.
[88] 'Articles objected against Sir John Bale', nos. 2, 3 (TNA: PRO, SP 63/71, no. 10).
[89] Loftus to Burghley, 26 September 1571 (TNA: PRO, SP 63/34, no. 13); privy council to Lord Deputy Fitzwilliam, 9 July 1572 (Bodleian, Carte MS, vol. 57, ff. 389r–390r, 398r).

in the area, thought that he lacked the necessary discretion for such a promotion.[90] He thus advised the queen against promoting him, which, to the chagrin of Lord Deputy Fitzwilliam, was heeded. The bishopric was finally given to Smith's own nominee, the English Protestant preacher, Hugh Allen.[91]

The final element in Browne's campaign – the attack on John Ball – did bear some fruit however. Although poorly documented, it appears that the privy council thought that the vicar general had a case to answer, for, during the second round of visitations of the cathedral conducted by the Loftus–Weston regime in the summer of 1572, Ball's authority was briefly suspended. Moreover, he was also compelled to answer an unspecified charge 'detected' by his uncle, Dean Weston. It is likely that this charge related to the accusations of fornication made by Browne before the privy council, in particular to an alleged incident with one Cicelie Fletcher. According to Browne, the same charge had also been raised with Dean Weston on a prior occasion, probably during the visitation of 1569–70, but had been dismissed 'by the sufferance of the dean, being his uncle'. The fact that it was now under investigation suggests very strongly that Loftus was

---

[90] This evaluation was based on an encounter he had with Browne in his home in Mounthawle in Essex during the prebendary's sojourn in England. On the night of 11 or 12 July 1572, Browne and an unnamed companion were brought before Smith, the local JP, by the High Constable, on suspicion of stealing horses and 'because they were so late at night out of all highways and axing their way to Abridge or Romford'. Smith examined them and 'perceived them handsome gentlemen both, Browne the perter, the fuller of words', and conceded that 'he had a very pretty wit, and . . . some knowledge both in logic and the civil law, wherefore I had the more delight to common with him'. Through such banter he also discovered that they had come to Mounthawle 'to make merry' and 'not to steal an horse, but . . . it was a mare with two legs only, the parson's daughter of the town, a pretty handsome wench . . . lately married at London . . . who had been seen very suspiciously and wantonly with them . . . in the fields'. In the end, Smith released Browne and his companion into the custody of the High Constable, who put them up for the night in his own home, and warned them 'not to come again into Essex, except they could show a better errand'. Yet, although the encounter was good natured, it effectively put paid to the prebendary's chances of getting the bishopric of Down. In time, Smith soberly concluded, Browne might make a good bishop 'but a bishopric would not be conferred for hope, but upon trial of gravity, discretion and ability to teach both in doctrine and example' (Smith to Lord Deputy Fitzwilliam, 12 April 1573, Bodleian, Carte MS 56, ff. 123–8).

[91] Smith to Lord Deputy Fitzwilliam, 12 April 1573 (Bodleian, Carte MS 56, ff. 123–8); Morrin, *Patent rolls*, i, pp. 553–4; Lord Deputy Fitzwilliam to the Queen, 19 February 1573 (TNA: PRO, SP 63/39, no. 30). Fitzwilliam openly expressed his disagreement with the queen's decision to appoint Allen ahead of Browne: 'It was not so much for preaching as for your majesty's service that we desired to have those places [the bishoprics of Ardagh and Down] occupied by fit men. The use of a learned English preacher is not so needful in those parts, as the use of a discreet wise and dutifully affected man, having the language to be employed in dealings with the Irishry. Such a one is Browne and of the English race'. Fitzwilliam's evaluation of Browne is an interesting commentary on the perceived value of the political loyalty of the papistically inclined English Irish clergy.

ordered by the privy council to attend to the matter, if for no other reason than to clear Ball's name.[92]

Not surprisingly, Ball did clear his name and was soon back at the helm of the administration.[93] Yet the incident was significant. For the prebendaries, it recalled some of their previous triumphs against their enemies, such as their humbling of Archbishop Browne over his marriage in Henry VIII's reign, and their role in the collapse of Lord Deputy St Leger's administration during the events surrounding the restoration of their cathedral in the mid-1550s. As such, it renewed their self-belief because it showed that, despite the efforts of Loftus and Weston to marginalise them, they were still a real force to be reckoned with in the diocese. Of this, Archbishop Loftus in particular was in no doubt. Hence his response to Browne's machinations. Loftus backed his efforts to gain promotion to the bishopric of Down, no doubt thinking that Browne would cause less harm in the far-away north 'under the elbows of the rebellious Irishry'.[94]

Loftus's failure to get Browne removed to Down was frustrating, because it left *in situ* one of the leading conservatives in St Patrick's, a man who was clearly emerging as the most likely successor to Thomas Creef as the leader of the group, and whose native intelligence and local connections revealed just how formidable an opposition the clergy provided to the archbishop's plans. This became particularly apparent in the following years when, aided by the death of Robert Weston, the conservative prebendaries once again secured a prominent place in the diocesan administration and helped bring the Loftus–Weston reform strategy to a virtual standstill.

Although long expected, Weston's death was a devastating blow for Loftus and his reform strategy on the ground. The first problem which emerged concerned the ecclesiastical commission. Without Weston's leadership and support, Loftus found that he was unable to keep the ecclesiastical commission going on the permanent footing upon which it had been established during the previous five years. Few of the existing commissioners had Weston's enthusiasm for the work and were soon unwilling

---

[92] *RDD*, pp. 79–80; 'Articles objected against Sir John Bale', no. 2 (TNA: PRO, SP 63/71, no. 10).

[93] *Fiants, Elizabeth*, nos. 2124, 2219.

[94] Loftus, Brady and Fitzwilliam to Burghley, 1 October 1572 (TNA: PRO, SP 63/38, no. 2). Loftus's determination to send Browne into exile is reflected in the disparate estimations he made of his abilities as a prospective dean of St Patrick's and as a prospective bishop of Down. When blocking Browne's efforts to become dean, Loftus described him as 'a man without all sense and feeling of true religion . . . ignorant and altogether void of any learning' (Loftus to Burghley, 26 September 1571, TNA: PRO, SP 63/34, no. 13). In contrast, in supporting his candidature for the bishopric 'far in the north', Loftus subscribed to the view that he was 'a very wise man', 'not unlearned' and 'such a one . . . to prefer true religion (whereunto he is well addicted)'.

to assist the archbishop.[95] Thus, despite a genuine attempt to regain the momentum by appointing John Ball to the office of registrar and receiver of the fines, the 1568 commission reverted to type and became an ad hoc body which sat irregularly. The fall off in activity was reflected in a drop in the total of fines imposed, from an annual average of IR£88 9s. 5d. during the period of Weston's leadership (Michaelmas 1568–Michaelamas 1573), to *c.* IR£65 in the three-and-a-quarter years which followed his death (October 1573–February 1577).[96] This decline in the ecclesiastical commission's activity seriously undermined one of the key elements in the Loftus–Weston reform strategy. Devoid of its regular sittings, the archbishop found it increasingly difficult to maintain the visibility of his Protestant, ecclesiastical establishment, an essential prerequisite of a strategy which sought to install this group in the place of the old Catholic clerical elite. Instead, it was Robert Wellesley, the conservative archdeacon of Dublin, who increasingly found himself as the main dispenser of ecclesiastical justice, and the main representative of the diocesan administration, in the intervening periods between Loftus's archiepiscopal visitations.

The conservative revival was even more marked in St Patrick's Cathedral, a development which was accentuated by the privy council's delay in appointing a successor dean to Weston. Archbishop Loftus had been understandably eager that the deanery should go to one of the godly ministers whom he had brought into the chapter since his accession to the see in 1567. But the privy council insisted that it be used again as a sinecure for a new lord chancellor. The council's determination was not matched by a similar decisiveness, however, with the result that the deanery remained vacant between May 1573 and the nomination of a new chancellor, Sir William Gerrard, in the spring of 1576.[97] The main beneficiaries of this hiatus were the 'papist faction' in St Patrick's. It provided them with a pretext to embarrass their archbishop publicly, through the staging of a traditional election, in which one of their number, most probably Christopher Browne, was canonically elected to the deanery in the spring of 1574.[98]

---

[95] Loftus to Burghley, 14 November 1573 (TNA: PRO, SP 63/42, no. 76).

[96] Brief declaration of the account of William Fludde; Brief of the account of John Ball (TNA: PRO, SP 63/94, no. 109).

[97] Loftus to Burghley, 26 September 1571 (TNA: PRO, SP 63/34, no. 13); privy council to Lord Deputy Fitzwilliam, 9 July 1572 (Bodleian, Carte MS, vol. 57, ff. 389r–390r, 398r); Lawlor, *Fasti of St Patrick's*, p. 46.

[98] Loftus to Burghley, 23 April 1574 (TNA: PRO, SP 63/45, no. 81 and enclosure). According to Loftus, the election was organised by Creef and 'their dean elect' a 'man of this country birth'. Loftus clearly disapproved of the candidate and advised Burghley 'that there should be placed someone of our own country birth so qualified with wit, sobriety and learning as might stand her majesty instead to be employed to other services'. All of this, in particular the fact that Loftus was now willing to countenance the use of the deanery as a sinecure for a royal servant, rather than confirm the election, suggests that the dean elect was a conservative. Christopher

More significantly, even after the archbishop had refused to confirm this election, the continuing vacancy gave them a de facto leadership of the cathedral. In the absence of a dean, and to the obvious disgruntlement of Loftus, the headship of St Patrick's passed to Precentor Creef as president of the chapter, 'a man of this country birth, well spent in years and corrupt in religion'.[99] Little is known about Creef's stewardship of the cathedral in these years, apart from the fact that he was the moving force behind the 'election' of Browne to the deanery. However, it is reasonable to assume that the anti-conservative visitations carried out by Robert Weston during his incumbency of the deanery came to an end. With the High Commission languishing, and Creef ruling the cathedral, the early momentum gained by the Loftus–Weston reform strategy ground to a very decisive halt.

These difficulties were also compounded by the contemporaneous failure of the Dublin government to secure a successful prosecution against Richard Creagh, the Catholic primate of Armagh, on treason charges. As Creagh's recent biographer has shown, this committed counter-reformation prelate emerged from the trial as a 'Catholic folk-hero' and a focus for religious resistance in the heart of the English Pale. Through word and deed, and the seditious activities he organised during his lengthy incarcerations in prison during the late 1560s and early 1570s, Creagh affirmed the Catholic thinking that had emerged from the Council of Trent, and criticised the church-papism practised by so many of the inhabitants of Loftus's diocese. All of this struck a further blow at Loftus's now ailing efforts to turn that same church-papism into a fuller commitment to the state church, to such an extent, in fact, that Lord Deputy Fitzwilliam was moved to request permission that Creagh be transferred to custody in London because he 'wonderfully inciteth this people and hindereth the archbishop of Dublin's godly endeavours to promote religion'.[100]

And as if these problems were not onerous enough, Loftus had to contend with one final legacy of Weston's untimely death: his appointment as keeper of the great seal in May 1573. As acting lord chancellor until May 1576, Loftus was called upon to undertake burdensome and time-consuming administrative tasks for the Dublin Castle administration, including a spell 'holding the government of the English Pale' while Lord Deputy Fitzwilliam was on progress in Munster in the late summer of 1574.[101] Demands like

Browne, a Creef ally, and someone who had already attempted to secure the deanery for himself, and who had already received the chapter's approbation in his nomination as their emissary on the 1571 mission, seems the most probable candidate.

[99] Loftus to Burghley, 23 April 1574 (TNA: PRO, SP 63/45, no. 81 and enclosure).
[100] Lennon, *Archbishop Richard Creagh*, ch. 6.
[101] *Fiants, Elizabeth*, nos. 2280, 2444, 2445; Account of Sir Edward Fitton, knight, treasurer at wars in Ireland, 1 April 1573–30 September 1575 (TNA: PRO, SP 65/8, f. 27). Loftus

these deflected his attention away from local ecclesiastical affairs. Indeed, as a result, he was even forced into utilising the legal experience and services of Thomas Creef in the spring of 1574 when faced with the task of appointing judges-delegates out of chancery to hear appeals from Irish ecclesiastical courts. Although, rather pointedly, Creef was only appointed as a judge-delegate to hear appeals from ecclesiastical courts outside the diocese of Dublin, the very fact that he was being brought in from the cold at this juncture – in the immediate aftermath, moreover, of his insubordinate action in organising the 'election' of Browne to the deanery – is indicative of the difficulties that the Loftus–Weston strategy had run into. Such a compromise would have been inconceivable only a few years earlier, when the reformers were fully engaged with the task of humiliating and subjugating the conservative clergy, especially Precentor Creef.[102]

V

Loftus's involvement in secular government, however, was to have even more damaging repercussions for his reform strategy than the dilution of his own energies. His association with Lord Deputy Fitzwilliam's regime laid all his endeavours, ecclesiastical or otherwise, open to the negative effects of the political competition that was so characteristic of the viceregal mode of government in Elizabethan Ireland. Fitzwilliam's regime came to an end in the summer of 1575 after his predecessor Sir Henry Sidney successfully campaigned at court to discredit it, and after Sidney himself had convinced the crown that he would be able, through the newly conceived 'composition' strategy, to make the government of Ireland self-sufficient within three years at a low cost to the crown.[103] The reappointment of Sidney as viceroy at this particular time was singularly unfortunate for Loftus. Unlike Fitzwilliam, who had left the direction of religious reform in the hands of the archbishop, and had supported his endeavours unquestioningly, Sidney had a personal and abiding interest in the progress of the Reformation, which had been demonstrated in his attempt in the mid-1560s to institute a radical, national programme of religious reform.[104] Given

---

was paid IR£246 13s. 4d. for his costs and expenses incurred in the government of the Pale. For other secular tasks undertaken by Loftus in this period see *Fiants, Elizabeth*, nos. 2575, 2623, 2764.

[102] *Fiants, Elizabeth*, nos. 2375, 2377, 2384. Creef had never received such a commission before nor would he do so again until Loftus ended his spell as lord keeper.

[103] On the circumstances surrounding Sidney's reappointment as lord deputy in 1575 and the origins of the 'composition' strategy see Brady, *Chief Governors*, pp. 136–46.

[104] Fitzwilliam's support for Loftus and Weston was no doubt helped by the part they played in securing him a long and favourable lease of the Court of Lessinhall, the prebendary of Sword's large glebe estate, in north Co. Dublin (Murray, 'Sources of clerical income',

this interest, and the part that both Loftus and Weston had played in undermining the implementation of various elements of Sidney's programme, it was inevitable that the archbishop's efforts would be subjected to a rigorous appraisal by the incoming viceroy. Moreover, given Loftus's recent difficulties in maintaining the early momentum of his own reform strategy, it was inevitable that they would be found wanting.

Sidney's judgement on the Loftus years appeared in April 1576 in a damning and oft-quoted memorandum to the queen on the 'lamentable estate' of the Irish Church. The viceroy described in graphic detail an institution which was in such a confused state that no one was prepared to pay for the upkeep of the 'very temples themselves', an institution which was ministered to by poorly paid, unlearned curates who lived 'upon the gain of masses, dirges, shrivings and such like trumpery, godly abolished by your majesty'. Although this description was based primarily on information provided by Bishop Brady of Meath on the state of his own diocese, Sidney was at pains to emphasise that such conditions were typical of the church as a whole, including the diocese of Dublin. More importantly, implicit in his analysis of the causes of the church's problems, and in the most radical of his proposals for solving them, was the view that the blame for this sorry state of affairs lay firmly with the Irish episcopal bench. Whether through inaction or incompetence, the viceroy contended that Loftus and his colleagues had failed to provide for some of the church's most basic needs, in particular the maintenance of a competent, reformed ministry, and the reparation of its decrepit fabric. Thus he recommended that the queen should bypass them altogether and send over 'three or four grave, learned and venerable personages' from England, an 'apostleship' to be supported by the English bishops, 'who in short space, being here, would sensibly perceive the enormities of this overthrown church and easily prescribe orders for the repair and upholding of the same'.[105]

Sidney's critique was a devastating indictment of the bishops and of Loftus in particular. Moreover, with his carefully constructed reform strategy in abeyance, and the conservative prebendaries once again a seemingly immovable object in the cathedral, the archbishop was in no position to rebut it. In this context, talk of gradualist, conciliatory reform, talk of supplanting the old clerical guard at some future indeterminate date, would have seemed facile. The archbishop, as the queen and her advisers now knew, presided over a crumbling institution, and had signally failed to

p. 155). On Sidney's earlier programme of religious reform see Brady and Murray, 'Sir Henry Sidney and the Reformation in Ireland', pp. 18–23.

[105] Sidney to the queen, 28 April 1576 (TNA: PRO, SP 63/55, no. 38). Other copies of the letter are printed in A. Collins, *Letters and memorials of state – from the De Lisle and Dudley papers* (2 vols, London, 1746), i, pp. 112–14 and Brady, *State papers*, pp. 14–19.

fulfil the early prediction that his promotion to Dublin would hasten its regeneration and reformation. His position, therefore, was quite untenable and, with Sidney's eager support, he attempted to secure an honourable discharge from Irish ecclesiastical service after sixteen years' 'pilgrimage', by seeking preferment to an English bishopric.[106]

Loftus's request for a translation to an English bishopric was not granted. Although the precise reasons for this are unknown, it is likely that the queen's secretary, Sir Francis Walsingham, and others on the privy council, like Lord Burghley, regarded Loftus's experience of Irish affairs, both secular and ecclesiastical, as a valuable commodity in its own right, and as a source of stability in the midst of the great administrative fluctuations that accompanied viceregal government. Thus in July 1576 Burghley and the privy council responded to Sidney's memo on the state of the church by informing him that he should discuss the matter further with the Irish council, reduce his opinion into a number of specific action points, and send over some officials for further consultation with the English council. In such a cautious atmosphere, the council's desire to keep Loftus on in Dublin is easily explained.[107]

Yet, if the rejection of Loftus's request for a translation can be construed as a vote of confidence in his ministry in Ireland, it was at best a tentative one, and certainly did nothing to regain him the leadership of the Protestant reform party, nor indeed any significant influence on the origination and implementation of policy. On the contrary, the reforming initiative had now passed firmly into the grip of the viceroy, a fact that would become painfully apparent to Loftus throughout the year 1577. As instructed, Sidney did indeed talk to his conciliar colleagues about the state of religion in Ireland, but what he presented to them, and to the archbishop of Dublin in particular, was not so much a series of points for discussion, as a series of measures and initiatives which he expected them to accept, and for which he was already well advanced in securing the privy council's support. Like his cess policy, these ecclesiastical initiatives were grounded upon his own highly personal conception and utilisation of the royal prerogative; while their intended end was nothing less than the deconstruction of Loftus's discredited reform strategy and its replacement by a more forward religious policy which would seek to reform the parochial clergy, to repair church fabric and to enforce all the religious and ecclesiastical legislation passed since the accession of Elizabeth.

---

[106] Sidney to Walsingham, 15 June 1576 (TNA: PRO, SP 63/55, no. 59); Loftus to Walsingham, 14 September 1576 (TNA: PRO, SP 63/56, no. 27); Sidney to Walsingham, 20 September 1576 (TNA: PRO, SP 63/56, no. 33).

[107] Brady, *State papers*, pp. 20–1. On Sidney's political difficulties at this time see Brady, *Chief Governors*, pp. 146–58.

The first of Sidney's measures was the recruitment of Dr George Acworth, a noted intellectual, civil lawyer, and apologist for English Protestantism, whom the deputy had long admired, and who was now in a position to join his staff as his chief ecclesiastical official following the death in 1575 of his erstwhile patron, Matthew Parker, the archbishop of Canterbury.[108] In February or early March 1577, the deputy forced Loftus to appoint Acworth as official principal and vicar general of Dublin at the expense of John Ball.[109] Thus, with Sir William Gerrard, his colleague from the Council of Wales, already ensconced as dean of St Patrick's, it became apparent that Sidney was fully intent on establishing a controlling influence over the Dublin diocesan administration, which was extended even further when Acworth himself, in a remarkable display of independence from his archbishop, oversaw the judicial sacking of Loftus's favoured diocesan registrar, John Bird, and his replacement by one Nicholas Cuskelly.[110]

[108] Acworth was a graduate of the universities of Padua and Cambridge. He came to prominence in the latter institution when, as public orator, a position to which he was presented by the future archbishop of Canterbury, Matthew Parker, he delivered a famous speech in 1560 in memory of the reformers Martin Bucer and Paul Fagius. After taking his LL.D. at Cambridge in 1561 he served the zealous Protestant Bishop Horne of Winchester as his diocesan chancellor, before resuming his relationship with Parker, from whom he received various preferments, including an advocateship in the Court of Arches and a spell as an episcopal commissary in Canterbury. Side by side with this diocesan work, he also acted as a visitor of various Oxford colleges throughout the 1560s. In the 1570s he retired to Parker's household where he helped the archbishop compile his famous *De Antiquitate Brittanicae Ecclesiae* (published in 1572) and where he wrote a response to Sanders's catholic treatise *De Visibili Monarchia Ecclesiae* (Louvain, 1571) entitled *De Visibili Rom'anarchia* (London, 1573). Acworth's career is conveniently and accurately summarised in L. Graham Horton-Smith, *George Acworth. A full account of his life together with a translation of his letters written in Latin and a complete refutation of all aspersions* (St Alban's, 1953). According to Campion, a 'Mr Acworth' was lined up to become the first provost of Sidney's projected university of 1569–70 (Campion, *History of Ireland*, pp. 17–18, 94; Hammerstein-Robinson, 'Erzchbischof Adam Loftus', pp. 208–9).

[109] According to Loftus, Ball was removed from the registrarship of the High Commission at the same time as he lost the official principalship of Dublin. His tenure of the registrarship ended on 31 January 1577. Thus Acworth's appointment dates to February or early March 1577. He was certainly in place by the 24 March 1577 when he proved the will of Laurence Casse (Loftus to Sussex, 20 November 1577, BL, Cotton MS, Vespasian F XII, ff. 149r-150v; Brief of the account of John Ball, TNA: PRO, SP 63/94, no. 109; NLI, D. 2891). The evidence for Loftus being forced into making the appointment is circumstantial. Acworth's appointment to the vicar generalship and official principalship coincided with a number of other measures instituted by Sidney, and involving Acworth, which sought to undermine and usurp Loftus's authority. In addition, there is no evidence to suggest that Loftus was dissatisfied with Ball's performance at this point. Finally, it is corroborated by the fact that Loftus sacked Acworth in the winter of 1578, soon after Sidney's tour of duty in Ireland ended (*Fiants, Elizabeth*, nos 3510, 3512).

[110] *APC 1592*, pp. 85–7: the editor incorrectly rendered 'Cosley' in the original (TNA: PRO, PC 2/19, p. 519) – itself a scribal error for Coskelly or Cuskelly – as 'Oosley'; NAI, Chancery Bills, D/73. For a later commendation of Bird by Loftus see Loftus to Walsingham, 25 March 1584 (TNA: PRO, SP 63/108, no. 52). Cuskelly had received a

Sidney was not content, however, with subverting Loftus's authority from the inside. He also sought to override it externally through two spectacular viceregal executions of the royal prerogative. On 18 March 1577 he erected a new court of faculties in Ireland, to which he appointed Acworth and the Irish civilian, Robert Garvey, as judges. The new court, an amalgamated imitation of the archbishop of Canterbury's Faculty Office and Prerogative Court, was ceded substantial parts of the bishops' ordinary jurisdiction, including the right to visit all clergy and search for defects in their titles; the right to prove and insinuate wills and testaments, and to hear all testamentary causes; and the right to give dispensations for a wide variety of defects and ecclesiastical offences. With the creation of the court of faculties, and the appointment of Acworth as one of its judges, Loftus found himself in the unprecedented situation that his vicar general super-seded his own ordinary jurisdictional authority in a number of vital areas.[111] Yet the erection of the court of faculties did not mark the end of his discomfiture. In May, Sidney disbanded the Loftus–Weston ecclesiastical commission of 1568, on the grounds significantly 'that her majesty had not been anything answered of the fines assessed by those commissioners'. Furthermore, under his own fiat, he established a new High Commission, and made sure that he was the dominant influence on it by packing it with supporters like Gerrard, Acworth, Jacques Wingfield, President Malby of Connaught and Sir Edward Fitton.[112] Finally, in November 1577, Sidney graphically demonstrated his newly acquired mastery over Loftus by extracting from the archbishop a favourable lease upon one of his chief country residences, the manor of Tallaght, to last as long as his tour of duty in Ireland.[113]

There is little doubt, then, that Sidney deliberately set out to under-mine the Loftus–Weston reform strategy, and the personal authority and

reversionary life term in the office from Archbishop Curwen as long ago as October 1566, but had subsequently lost it when Loftus appointed Bird. Bird, an English born notary who acquired his notarial faculties from the archbishop of Canterbury in 1570, probably joined the Dublin diocesan administration soon after, possibly at the behest of Robert Weston (Morrin, *Patent rolls*, ii, p. 68).

[111] *Fiants, Elizabeth*, no. 2996; 'The contents of certain letters patent granted to George Acworth, doctor of the civil law, and Robert Garvey, for ecclesiastical jurisdiction, by them, and the survivor of them for the term of life to be exercised in Ireland', c. December 1578 (TNA: PRO, SP 63/63, nos. 49, 50).

[112] *Fiants, Elizabeth*, no. 3047; 'The opinion of her majesty's learned council in the laws touching the validity of the ecclesiastical commission in Ireland', n.d., c. winter 1579–80 (TNA: PRO, SP 63/71, no. 12).

[113] 'Certain articles and covenants between Sir Henry Sidney, knight of the most noble order, lord deputy of Ireland, and the lord archbishop of Dublin, being fully agreed upon between them, touching the manor of Tallaght, the xviiith of November 1577', Kent Record Office (Maidstone), De L'Isle and Dudley MSS, U1475, 015/5. I would like to thank Dr David Edwards of University College Cork for this reference.

jurisdiction of the archbishop upon which it rested. Not only did his initiatives bring to an end the gradualist, conciliatory approach to reform
favoured by Loftus and Weston – a development which would soon become
apparent in an upsurge in the coercive activity of the High Commission – but
they also cut across their carefully modulated efforts to present the Reformation in non-innovatory, traditionalist, canonical terms. The fact that a
viceroy – a man who, as Loftus argued, only exercised his office during the
queen's pleasure – could create such august bodies as a High Commission
and a court of faculties, gave the lie to the essential Loftus–Weston contention that the Reformation was built upon the same ancient and authentic
ground that the conservatives claimed for the old religion.[114] The archbishop himself recognised this danger from an early stage and made one bold
attempt, prior to the passing of the patents for Sidney's commissions, to
stave it off. Sometime prior to March 1577, he petitioned the archbishop of
Canterbury to grant him and 'certain others' a new ecclesiastical commission
covering 'only . . . my own diocese and province'. Had he secured this
commission, it would have made him virtually an independent ecclesiastical
authority in Ireland, as well as enabling him to attempt the reconstruction of
his reform strategy untroubled by Sidney's designs and depredations.[115] The
archbishop's plea fell on deaf ears however. By the time it was dispatched, it
was already superfluous as the viceroy's supporters had revealed to the
queen and the council the extent to which the Loftus–Weston commission of
1568 had failed to collect the fines it imposed. Their horrified reaction to this
precluded any possibility that they would make Loftus the master of his own
personal ecclesiastical fiefdom.[116]

Yet Sidney's actions in 1576–7 did more than just deconstruct the
machinery and mechanisms through which Loftus and Weston had
attempted to reform the church. They also established a set of conditions
which, even after Sidney's final departure from Ireland in 1578, were so far
reaching and so damaging psychologically, that they destroyed any possibility that the archbishop would ever again be able to institute such a
progressive reform policy. The psychological damage done to Loftus
stemmed not only from the humiliations that he suffered directly at the
hands of the viceroy, but from the manner in which others – especially the

---

[114] Loftus later voiced his concern about the novelty of Sidney's commissions and challenged
their legality ('The contents of certain letters patent . . .', 20 December 1578, TNA: PRO,
SP 63/63, nos. 49, 50; Loftus to the privy council, 20 February 1579, PRO, SP 63/65,
no. 342).

[115] Loftus to Walsingham, 16 March 1577 (TNA: PRO, SP 63/57, no. 36).

[116] *Carew MSS 1575–88*, p. 58. Substantial progress had also been made toward securing
conciliar approval for the court of faculties, see, for example, the privy council's own
instructions and working papers on the court, dateable to the summer of 1576 (TNA:
PRO, SP 63/55, nos. 63, 64).

conservative clergy of his diocese – exploited his discomfiture to settle old scores. It was no accident that at this very time the archbishop had to answer accusations that he was a puritan, accusations which were based on his early association with Thomas Cartwright, and which to his 'great anxiety' had been brought to the notice of the queen. While the source of these charges is not now documented, it is likely that they were forwarded by the 'papist faction' in St Patrick's – a group who were always alive to the possibility of turning a changing political climate to their advantage – in an effort to topple the archbishop. On this particular occasion, however, Loftus successfully evaded their challenge by playing down the significance of his earlier friendship with Cartwight, by stressing the fact that he had not met with him since the controversies over his doctrine and beliefs had erupted, by expressing sorrow that Cartwright had 'offended the state' and by pleading 'ignorance of what the term and accusation of a puritan meaneth'.[117]

But so complete was Loftus's discomfiture at this juncture that the conservatives were determined not to let it pass without gaining some advantage from it. In the summer of 1577, only a few months after the Cartwright accusations were made, an event occurred which suggests very strongly that they finally exacted their long-awaited revenge. This was the ejection of the hated John Ball from St Patrick's Cathedral. In the end, the plot to remove Ball was deceptively simple. It would appear that the machinations of 1571–2 were replayed, but with one subtle twist. Instead of launching a generalised attack on him across many fronts, some conservative prebendaries, it may be conjectured, fanned the interest of one of Ball's first victims, Dr John Vulp, and his patron, the earl of Sussex, in restaking the physician's claim to the archdeaconry of Glendalough. In this, of course, they were aided by the fact that Ball, following his enforced sacking from the diocesan administration by Lord Deputy Sidney, was a much more expendable figure than he had been in the early 1570s. Appraised of this development, and of the cloud of suspicion which was then hanging over Loftus because of his association with Cartwright, the former lieutenant of Ireland went to the queen and acquired letters from her ordering the archbishop to restore Dr Vulp to the archdeaconry, on the grounds, it seems, that Ball was 'a meer lay man, and for his incapacity can lay no claim or make himself a party for an archdeaconry or any spiritual promotion'. For Thomas Creef, Christopher Browne, and the other surviving conservatives in St Patrick's, a group who would have retained bitter memories of how Ball had effected a purge of their fellow conservatives in the 1569–70 visitations by exploiting analogous canonical irregularities, the irony must

[117] Loftus to Walsingham, 16 March 1577 (TNA: PRO, SP 63/57, no. 36).

have been deliciously sweet. For Loftus, on the other hand, it must have seemed that all of his worst nightmares had come true. Following so soon after the Cartwright scare, the sight of the queen's signature on the letters acquired by Sussex sent the archbishop into a panic. He called Ball in, summarily deprived him of his archdeaconry, restored Vulp and forced Ball to take an oath renouncing 'all appeals and quarrels from anything that in the . . . restitution I should arbitrate or decree'.[118]

1577, then, was truly Loftus's *annus horribilis*. The deprivation of Ball, in particular, marked the lowest point of his career in Ireland and, in a very profound way, was a reluctant acknowledgement that his reformist endeavours of the late 1560s and 1570s had finally come to an end. The death knell of the Loftus–Weston strategy resounded particularly in the way that the archbishop was forced to deny all that had gone before, and the part that he had played in it. He cynically contended, in private correspondence with Sussex, that Ball had 'subtly . . . procured the deprivation of Doctor Vulp by his uncle Doctor Weston . . . for his own private gain, to intrude himself into another man's living'. Ball, for his part, was understandably furious at Loftus's apparent betrayal. Despite his oath, he attempted to appeal his deprivation in the Irish and English chanceries, both of which attempts Loftus had to make strenuous efforts to block; while, to sting the conscience of the archbishop even further, he claimed that he would go to England and seek the revocation of the new ecclesiastical commission, and have it 'committed to such as he will name, and him to be assumed register therein'. Ball, at least, did not wish to abandon the work that he and his uncle had commenced in the late 1560s, not even if it meant having to compete against some of the most powerful interests in the land to rescue it.[119]

In reality, however, and as Loftus grimly realised, Ball was naive. It was precisely because of their inability to compete with such interests – indeed they had not even successfully competed against the 'papist faction' in St Patrick's Cathedral – that their carefully constructed reform strategy lay

---

[118] Loftus to Sussex, 20 November 1577 (BL, Cotton MS, Vespasian F XII, ff. 149r–150v); Lambeth, Muniment Book F1/B, ff. 127r–128r. Loftus's reason for sacking Ball, that he was a lay man, was also applicable to Dr Vulp. Evidence for the involvement of the conservative prebendaries is circumstantial. As a group, they probably knew Sussex from his earlier viceroyalty in Ireland (Sussex was received, blessed by and dined with Archbishop Curwen in St Patrick's Cathedral on 3 July 1556, two days after he was sworn in as lord lieutenant of Ireland, *Carew MSS 1515–1574*, p. 258). Sussex was also a member of the privy council when they attempted to unseat Ball in 1571–2. They more, than any other party or interest group, had the motivation to seek Ball's deprivation and would have appreciated more than most that Archbishop Loftus's difficulties with Sidney provided an ideal opportunity to effect it. Above all, however, they had already tried to secure Ball's deprivation on at least two previous occasions.

[119] Loftus to Sussex, 20 November 1577 (BL, Cotton MS, Vespasian F XII, ff. 149r–150v).

in tatters. The salutary lesson to be drawn from the shambles of 1577, then, was that to survive in Elizabethan public life, let alone achieve anything, it was not enough to rely on one's religious principles, no matter how godly and true they were. Rather, one needed connections, connections built upon connections and connections within connections. Without them, power and authority were illusory. Thus as Loftus contemplated the wreckage of a near decade's work, he resolved that he would never be held hostage again to the workings and intrigues of the personal connections and factional groupings of others, whether they were headed by a great aristocrat like Sussex or a professional politician like Sidney, or manipulated by a group such as the conservative prebendaries of St Patrick's Cathedral. It was from this point on, therefore, that he set about creating – both through the marriage of his children to new English Protestant settlers in Ireland,[120] and through the bestowal of the lucrative prebends of St Patrick's on anybody capable of furthering his interests – his own, soon to be notorious, personal affinity. In this way he built up a connection with foundations in his cathedral, but which reached out into the countryside and ultimately to the court of Queen Elizabeth. This process was neatly illustrated in the action he took on the death of his longstanding adversary, Thomas Creef, the precentor of St Patrick's, in the summer of 1579. Had this death occurred in the early 1570s at the height of the implementation of the Loftus–Weston reform strategy, there is little doubt that the archbishop would have bestowed the precentorship on a godly minister of the word. Post-1577, however, Loftus's concerns were different. In September 1579 he gave the advowson of the precentorship to the earl of Leicester *pro hac vice*. Leicester in turn appointed his personal secretary, Arthur Atye, to the living, a man who would inevitably be a non-resident absentee and who would later convey the living to his master. It was clear from this, an action which had no pretensions to any godly ends, that Loftus was now in the business of unadulterated networking.[121]

The creation of this battle-hardened, more cynical personality, however, was not the only legacy left to Loftus by Sidney's unwelcome intervention in Irish ecclesiastical affairs. More profound still, both for the archbishop and the country, was the deputy's re-establishment of a tough, coercive alternative to the Loftus–Weston strategy for enforcing the Reformation. It was

---

[120] *Carew MSS, 1575–88*, p. 197; D. Jackson, *Intermarriage in Ireland, 1550–1650* (Montreal, 1970), pp. 20–8; Andrew Trollop to Walsingham, 12 September 1581 (TNA: PRO, SP 63/85, no. 39); *CSP Ireland, 1586–88*, pp. 252–3.

[121] Morrin, *Patent rolls*, ii, pp. 17, 31; J. Bruce (ed.), *Correspondence of Robert Dudley, earl of Leycester, during his government of the Low Countries, in the years 1585 and 1586* (London, 1844), pp. 50, 261, 289, 313–14.

this re-emergence of religious coercion, which had not been seen in Ireland for over a decade, that would finally and irrevocably crystallise the Pale community's rejection of the Reformation in the late 1570s and early 1580s. Yet, ironically, following the revocation of the deputyship from Sidney in the summer of 1578, and despite the fact that his strategy had been consciously put in place as an alternative to the archbishop's discredited efforts, the responsibility for its implementation would ultimately fall on Adam Loftus.

VI

Initially, at any rate, it appeared that Sidney's fall from power offered a genuine opportunity to dismantle his ecclesiastical settlement in all its various aspects. It was arguable that this settlement – whether in its attack on episcopal jurisdiction, or in its rigorous application of the Reformation statutes – was both similarly conceived, and likely to arouse the same negative reaction, as the overly ambitious and uncompromising secular policies which had led to his recall.[122] No sooner, then, had Sidney set sail for England, towards the end of September 1578, than Loftus and the other bishops sought a conference with the English privy council to discuss 'certain causes concerning the state of religion' in Ireland. These causes, of course, were Sidney's religious initiatives, and what the bishops wanted to achieve was their wholesale destruction. Thus, when the council responded by requesting that they send over just one of their number to put forward their case, it was Adam Loftus, the man who had suffered most from the deputy's depredations, who was chosen to be their spokesman.[123]

Loftus arrived in England in December 1578 and immediately set to work to overturn the outgoing viceroy's ecclesiastical settlement. One of his main targets was the hated court of faculties, which Sidney had instituted with the express purpose of overriding the bishops' jurisdiction. Over the course of a ten- to twelve-week stay in England, he presented a battery of legal arguments, interspersed with charges of corruption directed against Sidney's commissioners, George Acworth and Robert Garvey, in a bid to impress upon the council the flawed legal basis of the commission, and the necessity of restraining it for the moral and spiritual welfare of the church. The commissioners, however, did not let the archbishop take the field alone. Garvey followed Loftus to England, and he presented an equally voluminous collection of arguments to the councillors, which contended

---

[122] On the circumstances surrounding Sidney's revocation in 1578 see Brady, *Chief Governors*, pp. 148–58.
[123] *APC 1577–78*, p. 420.

that the commission was both legitimate, and successfully engaged in the task of reforming the ministry of the Church of Ireland.[124]

The privy council gave a full hearing to the two protagonists and, in the end, concluded that there was some merit to be found in both cases. While they had no doubts that the bishops suffered great 'inconveniences' as a result of the commission's usurpation of episcopal jurisdiction, they also believed that the commission was legally valid, a view which was corroborated by the queen's own learned counsel. They thus proposed compromise. The first significant step along these lines was taken on 25 February 1579, when the council commanded the new lord justice of Ireland, Sir William Drury, to take order with Acworth and Garvey to forbear the exercise of their commission until further notice. Thereafter they entered into negotiations with the parties towards renewing it. However, there was to be one major difference in the commission proposed by the councillors and that passed by Sidney two years previously. Garvey's partner would not be Sidney's old favourite, George Acworth, but the archbishop of Dublin, Adam Loftus. Agreement on this was reached towards the end of March or early April, and the commission was issued on 25 May. By the time Loftus returned to Dublin, then, in March or early April 1579, he had become the leader designate of a body which he had originally set out to destroy.[125]

Yet, as disappointing as this outcome was, it did not mark the full extent of the failure of his mission. On his return from England, Loftus also found himself taking up an almost identical position in relation to Sidney's High Commission. From the moment Sidney sent his critique on the state of the church to the queen in April 1576, he had envisaged establishing a

---

[124] See inter alia 'The contents of certain letters patent . . .' (TNA: PRO, SP 63/63, nos. 49, 50); 'A note delivered by Robert Garvey of such part of the statutes of Ireland as giveth the governor of that realm authority to pass commission to grant dispensations and faculties within the said realm, with an answer to such objections as are made by certain bishops of that land against that commission, and the exercise thereof', 2 January 1579 (TNA: PRO, SP 63/65, no. 2); 'The answer of Adam, archbishop of Dublin, to Mr Garvey's justification of the commission for faculties and other jurisdiction granted to him and to Dr Acworth', 6 January 1579 (TNA: PRO, SP 63/65, no. 8); Garvey to Burghley, 7 January 1579 (TNA: PRO, SP 63/65, no. 9).

[125] *APC 1578–80*, pp. 16, 58; learned counsel to privy council, n.d., c. end of January 1579 (TNA: PRO, SP 63/63, no. 53); privy council to Drury, 25 February 1579 (TNA: PRO, SP 63/65, no. 48); Queen Elizabeth to Drury, 14 March 1579 (TNA: PRO, SP 63/66, no. 7); 'The special points contained in the commission to be granted by her majesty to the most reverend father Adam, archbishop of Dublin and Mr Garvey, for passing of faculties within her highness's realm of Ireland', n.d., c. March/April 1579 (TNA: PRO, SP 63/63, no. 56); 'Instructions given by her majesty xiiith day of April 1579 to the right reverend father in god Adam, archbishop of Dublin, and Robert Garvey, bachelor of civil law, her highness's commissioners for faculties within her realm of Ireland . . .' (TNA: PRO, SP 63/66, no. 35); TNA: PRO, C 82/1243 (includes signed bill by the queen for granting of commission to Loftus and Garvey, 25 May 1579).

commission which would rigorously enforce all the Elizabethan legislation pertaining to religion, from the act of uniformity to the dashed bill for the reparation of churches. Unlike Loftus, who had come to believe that an over zealous enforcement of such legislation would alienate even further an already estranged community, the viceroy held the view that it was the lax enforcement of the same which had created the conditions in which the nobility, gentry and commons of the Pale felt no compunction to attend the services of the state church, to provide decent salaries for its ministers, or to keep its fabric in order. Thus, even in the short period between the establishment of his ecclesiastical commission in the summer of 1577 and his recall one year later, Sidney had pushed Loftus hard, as a member of the commission, to toughen up his approach to enforcement, especially against openly aberrant Pale gentlemen like James Eustace, the son of Viscount Baltinglass, who was suspected of hearing mass publicly. Throughout June and July 1578, therefore, even as he prepared to leave Ireland for the last time, Sidney gave his constant attention to the commission's process against Eustace, frequently urging Loftus to secure his conformity by threatening him with the full statutory penalty of a hundred mark fine. After many years of promoting the Reformation in a conciliatory manner, however, such intimidatory tactics sat uneasily on Loftus's shoulders, and, despite Sidney's attentions, he tried desperately to win Eustace's heart 'by persuasion' and 'dealing in truth with over much lenity towards him'.[126]

Sidney's removal from Ireland, then, presented Loftus with an opportunity of securing the reversal of his hard-line policy on enforcement. While in England, therefore, and, as in his attack on the court of faculties, he questioned the legal validity of Sidney's ecclesiastical commission before the privy council, a challenge conducted on the particular grounds that the earlier commission of 1568 had been personally sanctioned by the queen, and had not been specifically revoked, and that it was doubtful whether an officer of the crown appointed during the monarch's pleasure had the requisite authority to establish a new commission in its place. At first, it appeared that Loftus had made his case persuasively, for, once again, the council showed some sympathy towards his position. On 22 February 1579 they wrote to Lord Justice Drury, decreeing that the Loftus–Weston commission of 1568 'should be duly executed, and none other until her majesty should expressly revoke the same'.[127] Yet what seemed like a victory for the

[126] Loftus to Walsingham, 11 September 1580 (TNA: PRO, SP 63/76, no. 26 and enclosures).
[127] 'The contents of certain letters . . .', 20 December 1578 (TNA: PRO, SP 63/63, nos. 49, 50); Loftus to privy council, 22 February 1579 (TNA: PRO, SP 63/65, no. 42); *APC 1578–80*, p. 56; 'A minute to the lord justice of Ireland for some order to be taken in matters touching the pastoral charge of that realm', 22 February 1579 (TNA: PRO, SP 63/65, no. 43).

archbishop was in reality a move to help him save face. On his arrival in England, Loftus soon discovered that Sidney's ecclesiastical measures, and, in particular, his underlying belief in the necessity of enforcing existing religious legislation, was the one part of his programme for government which the privy council, and former supporters, like Lord Chancellor Gerrard, wished to retain. Such a policy actually conformed to the modest, post-Sidney aims of English government in Ireland, which sought to reform the country not by the grandiose, expansionist schemes of the programmatic governors, but through the regeneration of the Pale and the gradual extension of the common law throughout the country.[128] There would be no better way of achieving this regeneration than by ensuring that the legislation of the Irish parliament on religious matters was respected and obeyed by the queen's most loyal subjects, or than by furthering the cause of true Protestant religion in English Ireland.

A strong hint that the council was already thinking along these lines had been given in the instructions to the new lord justice of Ireland, Sir William Drury, in the previous May. He was commanded to enforce two measures which Sidney had previously identified as essential to the reform of the church: the re-edification of church fabric and the compulsion of impropriators to maintain proper curates. Now, however, the council's wish to implement the Sidney strategy, and their desire that Loftus should do so too, was made explicit. On 22 February the archbishop was forced to put his name to a petition requesting the lord justice and council of Ireland to take order for the reparation of decayed churches and chancels, to compel the farmers of impropriate benefices 'to find sufficient and able curates' and to execute the statute for the erection of schools. Although this petition had all the appearances of being spontaneous, the fact that it was comprised of staple Sidney reforms, that Loftus combined it with his request to allow the continuance of the 1568 ecclesiastical commission, and that the council drafted its own identical instructions to the lord justice on the very same day, clearly shows that a deal had been struck between Loftus and the queen's advisers. In short, the archbishop had signed up to what was effectively Sidney's programme of ecclesiastical reform in return for the concession on the High Commission.[129]

Yet even this, by now rather meaningless, concession would be denied to him. The impracticality of enforcing Sidney's programme through a

---

[128] For the conception and development of these aims, and Gerrard's role in this process, see Brady, *Chief Governors*, pp. 155–8.

[129] 'Instructions' for Drury, 29 May 1578 (TNA: PRO, SP 12/134 p. 610, another copy calendared in *Carew MSS 1575–88*, pp. 130–3); Loftus to privy council, 22 February 1579 (TNA: PRO, SP 63/65, no. 42); 'A minute to the lord justice of Ireland for some order to be taken in matters touching the pastoral charge of that realm', 22 February 1579 (TNA: PRO, SP 63/65, no. 43).

commission in which much of the membership was dead, soon had Lord Chancellor Gerrard on the case, the man who had become the effective leader of the government's religious reform programme after the deputy's revocation. Gerrard visited England in the autumn and winter of 1579. While there he secured the opinion of the queen's learned counsel that Sidney's 1577 commission was legally valid. Thus there soon followed a memo from the privy council to the Irish council commanding them to give the Sidney commission full effect and affirming 'that execution of the commission granted in the tenth year of her majesty's reign [1568] is taken away by the grant of the latter'. Loftus had no choice but to accept this final confirmation of a reality which he had already conceded in principle.[130]

Loftus's recognition of the Sidney programme of church reform was not merely theoretical however. Even before the 1577 commission received its final validation, the archbishop was perceived by old Sidney hands like Sir Edward Waterhouse to have joined in spirit with Lord Chancellor Gerrard in seeking to enforce the Reformation with the required rigour. Waterhouse put this down to the fact that both men 'held their places with no less authority than now', a happy occurrence due in no small part – and here the contrast with Sidney was marked – to the disposition of Lord Justice Drury. Thus, under the supportive gaze of Drury, and secure in the knowledge that Archbishop Loftus was on the verge of giving his full support to the government's reform programme, Gerrard ensured that Sidney's commission worked assiduously during the summer of 1579 to enforce outward conformity to the Reformation throughout the English Pale. Indeed, according to Waterhouse, the chancellor-dean did it so effectively that in Dublin he found

that which I never hoped of, namely, that the whole inhabitants being in effect all noted to be obstinate papists in times past do now all repair to the church and show themselves obedient in the substance of religion. Most of the nobility (amongst which one who hath been noted to be a Jesuit) cometh to sermons and show themselves examples to others.

In addition, Gerrard also had pews made, presumably in his own cathedral of St Patrick, 'for the nobility, for lawyers, for captains, and all of the better sort, so as the citizens and all being under his eye never dare be absent'.[131]

Loftus joined this crusade formally towards the close of 1579 or in early 1580 after Gerrard confirmed the legality of Sidney's High Commission.

---

[130] 'The opinion of her majesty's learned council in the laws touching the validity of the ecclesiastical commission in Ireland', n.d., c. November–January 1579–80 (TNA: PRO, SP 63/71, no. 12); 'The draft of the letters to the lords of the council in Ireland', n.d., c. November–January 1579–80 (TNA: PRO, SP 63/60, no. 71). Gerrard arrived in England in October 1579 (TNA: PRO, SP 63/69, nos. 29, 73).

[131] Waterhouse to Walsingham, 31 May 1579 (TNA: PRO, SP 63/66, no. 66).

Moreover, he immediately sought to put his own personal stamp on it by securing the appointment, as the commission's registrar, of one of his cadre of Dublin diocesan administrators. According to Loftus, Gerrard had 'placed in that room a man of his own unable to execute it by himself, but by substitutes either of small skill or little credit, whereby almost for two years not only little good was done, but also a greater gap of liberty and courage left open to the enemies of the truth'. Loftus's initial commendation of John Ball as a better alternative appears to have been turned down by the chancellor, presumably on account of Ball's poor record in collecting the fines imposed by the Loftus–Weston commission. Nevertheless, Gerrard did see the value of reconciling the Loftus–Weston regime with Sidney's commission. Thus it appears that he accepted the nomination of a second Loftus associate, John Bird, the former diocesan registrar of Dublin whom George Acworth had sacked shortly after his arrival in Ireland, and who immediately assumed responsibility for the collection of all fines imposed by the High Commission since the removal of Ball in January 1577. With Bird's appointment, Loftus's reconciliation with the official crown-sponsored reform programme was completed.[132]

This reconciliation was hugely significant for the diocese of Dublin and the English Pale generally. What it meant, effectively, was that for virtually the first time since Henry VIII broke with Rome nearly fifty years previously, the agencies of both church and state shared a common commitment and resolve to enforce the Reformation by means of the penal clauses contained in the crown's ecclesiastical legislation. Moreover, there is little doubt that they put this common purpose to real effect. From the spring of 1577 to the spring of 1582, a period which covered the first five years of the Sidney commission's existence, fines totalling £604 17s. 8d. are known to have been levied by the commission throughout the Pale. The annual average was thus c. £121, a figure which represented an 86 per cent increase on the period immediately preceding it (October 1573–January 1577), and a 35 per cent increase on the annual average levied by the Loftus–Weston commission in its heyday (Michaelmas 1568–Michaelmas 1573). There is little doubt that this increase in fines represented a substantial escalation in the level of the commission's activity between the earlier and later periods, which is directly attributable to the divergent concerns of the 1568 and 1577 versions. Loftus and Weston had used the 1568 commission as a support mechanism for a gradualist and conciliatory reform programme which was conducted primarily by the Dublin diocesan administration. The Sidney commission, by contrast, was intent on securing rapid outward

---

[132] Loftus to Burghley, 6 January 1580 (TNA: PRO, SP 63/71, no. 9); Brief estimate of the account of John Bird (TNA: PRO, SP 63/94, no. 109).

conformity to the established church, and the thorough discharge of all attendant communal responsibilities to the institution. This difference in approach would make a major impact on the Pale community's attitude to the Reformation. Despite Gerrard's success in bolstering attendance at the Prayer Book services in the Pale, such coercion – particularly as it came on the back of years of disgruntlement with the cess – was deeply resented by the indigenous population, and hastened its final and irrevocable alienation from the established church and the English government which supported it.[133]

The signs of this growing alienation were everywhere apparent in the early 1580s. One of the most common complaints of the period, which was voiced by those who supported the church, was that the court of faculties under Loftus was overly liberal in its granting of dispensations, allegedly because of the archbishop's desire to share in the profits of the faculties. According to such complainants the court corrupted the clergy, creating a situation where the holding of three or more benefices by individual ministers, and a consequent decline in the quality of pastoral service, was the norm. Yet such complainants neglected to consider one pertinent fact. The increased granting of dispensations was in reality an indicator of a problem in the supply of clergymen. Thus to the extent that it reflected an ongoing reduction in the numbers going forward for ordination, and the need to spread the pastoral burden on a declining pool of ministers, its real significance had less to do with Adam Loftus's alleged cupidity, than the unpalatable reality that indigenous sympathy for the state church was haemorrhaging at an alarming rate. Such reluctance to serve the established church, a longstanding reluctance now exacerbated by its self-consciously coercive policies, was otherwise reflected in the growing numbers of students from the Pale who went to the continent at this time, instead of the Protestant seminaries of Oxford and Cambridge, for a specifically Catholic education.[134]

There were, however, even more direct signs of disenchantment with the government's religious policy, especially in relation to the High Commission's activities. One of the commission's avowed aims from 1577 onwards was to secure the re-edification of decayed churches and chancels. Yet, despite the application of pressure to ensure that impropriators and

---

[133] Brief declaration of the account of William Fludde; Brief of the account of John Ball; Brief estimate of the account of John Bird (TNA: PRO, SP 63/94, no. 109).

[134] Trollope to Walsingham, 12 September 1581 (TNA: PRO, SP 63/85, no. 39); Archbishop Long to Walsingham, 20 January, 4 June 1585 (TNA: PRO, SP 63/114, no. 39, SP 63/117, no. 39); H. Hammerstein, 'Aspects of the continental education of Irish students in the reign of Queen Elizabeth I', in T.D. Williams (ed.), *Historical studies VIII. Papers read before the Irish Conference of Historians May 1969* (Dublin, 1971), pp. 137–54.

churchwardens fulfilled their responsibilities in this regard, little progress was made. Nearly eight years after the Sidney commission commenced its campaign to rebuild the Church of Ireland's decrepit ecclesiastical fabric, the lord deputy of Ireland, Sir John Perrot, concluded that it was generally in 'pitiful decay' virtually all the way to the gates of Dublin. So 'ruinated and broken down' were the churches, in fact, and so little had the commission achieved in its attempt to have them re-edified, that the viceroy rejected the commission as an agency of change and commenced his own alternative initiative to try and rescue the situation. There is little doubt that the commission's failure in this matter signified nothing less than a communal rejection of its authority and aims, and a genuine distaste for the personnel charged with implementing them. Such distaste was otherwise evident in the growth of 'malicious reports' and plots which sought to blacken the character of its registrar, John Bird. For Adam Loftus, the hatching of such plots against the godly were all too familiar, and he defended Bird on the grounds that the office of registrar was 'subject greatly to envy'. The reality, as he saw it, was that Bird had done much valuable service 'to her highness in discovering many wicked practises and treasons of the papists here'.[135]

Yet the most disturbing sign of the Pale community's alienation was not its refusal to repair parish churches, or the plotting of the papists against commission officials, but the outbreak of rebellion in the heart of loyalist English Ireland. The Baltinglass revolt, led by James Eustace, third viscount Baltinglass, was one of a number of rebellions which broke out in Ireland at this time, and which reflected a wider disenchantment with English government in Ireland. Unlike the other rebellions, however, all of which had some religious dimension to them, the Baltinglass conspiracy was motivated almost exclusively by religious concerns. Baltinglass and his small band of supporters rose up in the summer of 1580 in radical defiance of the state religion and in an attempt to assert a new, militant brand of Catholicism imported from the continent.[136] However, while its motives were apparent, its full significance is less easily appreciated, especially as militarily it carried very little threat to Tudor rule in Ireland; and politically it commanded

---

[135] *CSP Ireland 1588–92*, p. 82; 'A copy of such commissions as were sent to every county and country for enquiry of decayed churches, chancels, bridges and schools', 4 March 1585 (TNA: PRO, SP 63/115, no. 11); certificate of the High Commissioners to Lord Grey, testifying the upright conduct of John Bird, their registrar, 29 August 1582 (TNA: PRO, SP 63/94, no. 107); 'An abstract of certain private letters touching John Bird' (TNA: PRO, SP 63/94, no. 108); Loftus to Walsingham, 25 March 1584 (TNA: PRO, SP 63/108, no. 52).

[136] On the revolt generally see Brady, *Chief governors*, pp. 204–7, 209–13; Edwards, *Church and state*, pp. 256–60; H. Coburn Walshe, 'The rebellion of William Nugent, 1581', in Comerford, Cullen, Hill and Lennon (eds.), *Religion, conflict and co-existence*, pp. 26–52; Lennon, *Lords of Dublin*, pp. 150–5; Scott, *Tudor diocese of Meath*, pp. 129–33.

relatively little support amongst the wider Pale community. Nevertheless, despite its limited appeal, the revolt was still a barometer of the declining relationship between the established church and the Englishry, a decline directly attributable to the ecclesiastical programme introduced by Lord Deputy Sidney in the late 1570s.

There are good grounds for arguing that Baltinglass entered on his fateful course in direct response to the upsurge in religious coercion that accompanied the erection of Sidney's High Commission. Baltinglass, while still the heir to the family title, had been hauled before the commission in the summer of 1578 for openly practising Catholicism. And the treatment he received, which was meted out by Archbishop Loftus under direct instruction from Sidney – a day in prison, the threat of a large fine and the possibility of an extended spell of incarceration – forced him into what amounted to a public recantation of his faith. While we can only speculate now on the extent to which this experience affected Baltinglass psychologically, it must have played a formative role in leading him into rebellion two years later. The link between the two events was certainly considered to be important by the government in the aftermath of the revolt, so much so in fact that Adam Loftus went to great lengths to explain that he was not personally responsible for the rough treatment handed out to Baltinglass.[137] A similar link might also be posited between the treatment meted out by the commission to Alderman James Bellew of Dublin and the decision of certain members of two fellow aldermanic families, the Sedgraves and Fitzsimons, to aid Baltinglass in 1580. In 1578, Bellew had been forced by the commissioners to stand barefoot before the altar in Christ Church Cathedral and renounce his many errors, including his denial of the queen's supremacy.[138] The real likelihood that such religious coercion led traditionally loyal and socially important figures like Baltinglass and his cohorts into armed rebellion, strongly suggests that it must also have hardened the religious attitudes of many more in a community already predisposed towards the old religion.

Yet the Baltinglass revolt, and the related Nugent conspiracy, was a watershed in other respects also. One of the main consequences of the revolt was that it created an indelible link in the minds of the officials of church and state between religious dissidence and treason, and thus added a new dimension of fear and suspicion to their perceptions of papistry. In the short term, under the deputyship of Lord Grey de Wilton (1580–2), this had the effect of ushering in a period of ferocious religious repression which both

---

[137] Loftus to Walsingham, 11 September 1580 (TNA: PRO, SP 63/76, no. 26 and enclosures).
[138] On Bellew, and the involvement of the Sedgraves and Fitzsimons in the revolt, see Lennon, *Lords of Dublin*, pp. 118–19, 150–7, 231–2, 250, 267–9.

shook the Pale community to its core and, through its creation of martyrs and heroes for the cause of Catholicism, hardened even further its conservative religious values. The spectacle of witnessing Pale gentlemen like George Netterville, Robert and John Scurlock, and Christopher Eustace, steadfastly processing to the scaffold in unmistakably Catholic prayer, and rejecting the admonitions and taunts of ministers of the established church, must have had a profound effect on the inherently sympathetic populace of Dublin, whether it was witnessed in person or recounted in conversation thereafter.[139]

More importantly, in the longer term, the fear of traitorous papistry convinced many in the officialdom of church and state that severe, coercive policies would need to continue in order to win the conformity of the Irish populace to the Elizabethan settlement. This was certainly the case with Archbishop Loftus. Following the death of Lord Chancellor Gerrard, and his own promotion to the chancellorship in 1581, Loftus willingly assumed Gerrard's mantle as the leader of Sidney's coercive reform programme. Thus, in a few short years, he passed from being an episcopal governor intent on winning adherents to the Reformation through a conciliatory ecclesiastical programme, to being an unwilling and, finally, willing accomplice in a coercive reform strategy that not only failed to win the conformity of the loyal Englishry, but, unwittingly, began to sever whatever tenuous bonds existed between that community and the established church before this time. Loftus's own particular situation was a paradigm for this breakdown in relations. Where in the past, he had sent his officials to give the 'pope's absolution' in the fields, he would now send his minions to extract recantations from Catholics on the scaffold.[140] Where in the past he was willing to argue the case for Protestantism, he would now find himself at the centre of the events surrounding the torture and execution of popular religious dissidents, like the Catholic archbishop of Cashel, Dermot O'Hurley.[141] Where in the past he was once 'greatly well be liked' by the Pale community, he now felt so hated that he feared for his life.[142]

---

[139] Brady, 'Conservative subversives', pp. 26–8; Report of Thomas Jones, preacher, on the deaths of Robert Scurlock, John Scurlock, George Netterville and Christopher Eustace, 18 November 1581 (TNA: PRO, SP 63/86, no. 69, calendared in Brady, *State papers*, pp. 56–7).

[140] Report of Thomas Jones, 18 November 1581 (TNA: PRO, SP 63/86, no. 69). Jones was closely allied to Loftus and eventually became his son-in-law. He was also appointed dean of St Patrick's shortly after penning this report and he eventually succeeded Loftus as archbishop of Dublin on the latter's death in 1605 (*ODNB*; Lawlor, *Fasti of St Patrick's*, p.46).

[141] Brady, *State papers*, pp. 68–80, 83–5.

[142] Lord deputy and council to Walsingham, 3 July 1581 (TNA: PRO, SP 63/84, no. 1); Lords Justices Wallop and Loftus, and Sir Edward Waterhouse to Burghley and Walsingham, 23 August 1583 (TNA: PRO, SP 63/104, no. 38).

In fine, from the early 1580s on, the Pale community's full disengagement from the established church led by Adam Loftus was inevitable. The only uncertainties to be resolved were when the process would be finally completed, and when officials like Loftus would come to admit it.

VII

The resolution of both of these uncertainties came swiftly, hastened by the stormy political events of the viceroyalty of the last of the great programmatic governors in Elizabethan Ireland, Sir John Perrot (1584–8).[143] In terms of religion, Perrot's viceroyalty began conventionally enough. A precisian Protestant by nature,[144] the new viceroy was content to allow the coercive reform strategy which Sidney had originated, and which Loftus had the responsibility of executing, to continue unabated. Indeed, Perrot himself was only too willing to lend this strategy his full support. In October 1584, for example, following the apprehension of three 'notorious massing priests', he reported to the privy council that 'there is a great nest discovered of massmongers, and amongst them diverse gentlemen, whereof some lawyers in places of credit, merchants, ladies and gentlewomen of good sort, with whom I mean to take a fit time, and to deal as shall be meet'. The viceroy's intentions in this regard were soon revealed. Shortly after the discovery of the 'massmongers', he tendered the oath of supremacy to all the justices of the peace and other legal officers, threatening those who refused to subscribe with proceedings in Castle Chamber. Moreover, an obscure entry in the Irish council book from this time suggests that he was even contemplating swearing-in the entire adult populations of Irish counties under English jurisdiction.[145]

Perrot's support of this tough and thorough line in religion made sense in terms of his own ideological preferences. Yet in terms of his own political aims it most certainly did not. From the outset of his viceroyalty, Perrot had preached about the virtues of conciliation, and of bringing about political and social harmony in Ireland. Indeed, his chosen method of implementing his wide-ranging reform programme – through a series of new statutes to be

---

[143] On Perrot's viceroyalty see Brady, *Chief Governors*, pp. 291–300; V. Treadwell, 'Sir John Perrot and the Irish Parliament of 1585–6', *PRIA* 85 C, pp. 259–308.

[144] On Perrot's religious attitudes see Murray, 'St Patrick's cathedral and the university question in Ireland', pp. 25–33.

[145] Perrot to privy council, 25 Oct 1584, and to Burghley, 24 September 1585, Bodleian, Perrot MS 1, f. 42r, 145r, calendared in C. McNeill (ed.), 'The Perrot Papers: the letter-book of Lord Deputy Perrot between 9 July, 1585 and 26 May, 1586', *Analecta* 12 (1943), pp. 23–4; D.B. Quinn (ed.), 'Calendar of the Irish Council Book, 1581–1586', *Analecta* 24 (1967), p. 163; Edwards, *Church and state*, pp. 270–1; Treadwell, 'Irish Parliament of 1585–6', p. 274.

enacted in a specially convened parliament – was actually predicated upon the notion of achieving consensus, especially with the Palesmen.[146] His support for the High Commission's tough line on religion, therefore, which was also evident in his inclusion of a compendious bill to enact English statutes in the proposed legislation of the upcoming parliament – including recent English penal legislation against Catholics – was a profound political misjudgement.[147] Just how misconceived became apparent in May 1585 when, during the opening session of the parliament, and despite advice from the English Irish master of the rolls, Sir Nicholas White – that leniency on the religious question would help secure indigenous support for the viceroy's programme of legislation – he chose to press ahead with the penal laws, thus provoking what would prove to be very a serious and politically damaging opposition against his entire parliamentary programme from the representatives of the Pale community.[148]

This parliamentary opposition was very significant on a number of counts. In the first instance, it provided a clear and unambiguous statement both of the importance of the religious question to the Pale community, and the deep frustration and anger they felt over the government's hard-line enforcement policies of the recent past. In addition, it also provided a rare insight into the kind of Catholicism espoused by the majority of the community. This was not the continental brand of militant, Counter-Reformation Catholicism espoused by the likes of James Fitzmaurice Fitzgerald or Baltinglass, but the old religion of the medieval English Pale, a religion which lay at the heart of the political, social and cultural identity of the Englishry, and which they longed to hold on to for these very reasons. No one articulated this sentiment as clearly, nor as pithily, as the lawyer Edward Nugent who 'said openly in parliament that things prospered in Henry V's and other kings' times when mass was up'. Perrot, Loftus and other committed Protestants, by contrast, were appalled by this 'seditious' behaviour, and, showing a deep lack of understanding of the community's values, withdrew from the house 'thinking we could not but be guilty of a weighty crime if we should afford our presence at the overthrowing of an act that imported her majesty's supremacy and safety of her royal person'.[149] This gesture was compounded

---

[146] Ibid., p. 266.

[147] Ibid., pp. 270–2. Archbishop Loftus headed the committee charged with preparing the bills for the parliament.

[148] *CSP Ireland 1586–8*, pp. 100–1; Brady, *State papers*, p. 125; Treadwell, 'Irish Parliament of 1585–6', pp. 284–6.

[149] Perrot and Irish council to privy council, 12 June 1585 (Bodleian, Perrot MS 1, ff. 100v–101v); Brady, *State papers*, pp. 125–6; Treadwell, 'Irish Parliament of 1585–6', p. 285. Perrot referred dismissively to the dissidents as 'some contentious fellows of the Pale and the English countries adjoining'.

in the following month when the viceroy, exasperated by the opposition he had encountered in parliament, allowed Loftus, Archbishop Long of Armagh and Bishop Jones of Meath to recommence proceedings against the recalcitrant JPs and other legal officers.[150]

Yet if the queen's officials in Ireland were unsympathetic to the strange and archaic values of the Pale community, political developments on the international scene ensured that they got a more favourable hearing in London. England's alliance with the Dutch, sealed in the Treaty of Nonsuch in August 1585, raised the spectre of open war against Catholic Spain, a development which had very profound implications for Irish affairs. In this context, with the threat of a Spanish invasion of Ireland hanging over the queen's and privy council's heads, and the great absorption of English treasure by the Dutch Alliance precluding any possibility of financing any extra Irish defence, the professed political loyalty of the Pale community was perceived as a genuine boon, while Perrot's disruptive and antagonistic methods of government were regarded as harmful and unacceptable. Thus throughout the latter half of 1585, the Queen and privy council directed Perrot to refrain from executing a whole host of measures, including the promotion and execution of any laws against religious dissidents, which might drive loyal English Irishmen into the hands of the Spaniards. As a result, all religious persecution ceased for the remainder of Perrot's viceroyalty.[151]

The Palesmen's constitutional victory against the forces of religious repression, like the Baltinglass rebellion, was an important milestone in Irish religious affairs during the Elizabethan period. It is possible, as Archbishop Loftus later contended, that the 'general defection of this country['s] people in causes of religion', a defection particularly apparent in the general and open recusancy practised by the community in the late 1580s and early 1590s, was due directly to the 'encouragement which they received in Sir John Perrot's government'.[152] Yet Loftus's analysis is not wholly convincing. While it was certainly true that open and general recusancy had not been apparent before the events of the 1585 parliament, there is little doubt that communal anger against the state religion, and the coercive methods used by its agents to win the community's conformity, was running very high at this

---

[150] Quinn (ed.), 'Calendar of the Irish council book', pp. 166, 178; Treadwell, 'Irish parliament of 1585–6', p. 286.

[151] Walsingham to Archbishop Long, December 1585 (TNA: PRO, SP 63/121, no. 50); Treadwell, 'Irish parliament of 1585–6', pp. 291–3; Brady, *State papers*, pp. 101–3; Brady, 'Conservative subversives', p. 29.

[152] Loftus and Bishop Jones of Meath to Archbishop Whitgift of Canterbury, 12 March 1591 (TNA: PRO, SP 63/157, no. 35); see also Loftus to Burgley, 12 September 1590 (Brady, *State papers*, pp. 124–8).

time, finding expression in events like the Baltinglass rebellion or, more importantly, in the parliamentary opposition itself. In reality, therefore, it was this anger and alienation, rather than the muzzling of the High Commissioners, as Loftus liked to believe, which gave rise to the general recusancy of the mid to late 1580s. At best, the curbing of coercion accelerated the defection of the Pale community, which spiritually, if not temporally, was already completed by the time parliament sat.

In conclusion, then, Loftus's argument about the period of Perrot's government was less a description of an objective reality, than a self-justifying explanation of the now, very patent and unpalatable fact that the Reformation had failed in Dublin and the English Pale. In stressing the importance of the reduction of religious coercion, Loftus was in reality seeking to deflect attention away from the equally unpalatable fact that it was religious coercion itself – the government's tough enforcement policies of the late 1570s and early 1580s – which had decisively alienated the Pale community, and which set in motion the process that culminated in the general defection of the late 1580s which he so vividly described in his correspondence.

Afterword

By the early 1590s, it had become an inescapable fact that the Reformation had failed in the diocese of Dublin and, indeed, elsewhere in the English Pale. Writing to the archbishop of Canterbury in March 1591, Archbishop Loftus of Dublin and Bishop Jones of Meath admitted as much, when they acknowledged that the inhabitants of the region had 'grown into such obstinacy and disobedience that we ... find it a matter almost impossible either to reclaim them or to draw them to any good conformity'.[1] This book has contended that the principal cause of this failure was the English Irish community's attachment to a survivalist form of Catholicism. And that this attachment itself had been actively and effectively defended and fostered by the clerical elite of the Pale, especially during the Marian period and the opening decade of Elizabeth's reign.

Yet it is a curiously conservative conclusion. It sits easily, in a number of respects, with some of the main conclusions reached by the two leading writers on Tudor Ireland's religious history in the modern era, Robin Dudley Edwards and Brendan Bradshaw. Edwards's major work *Church and state in Tudor Ireland* was written with the intention of portraying the heroic struggle of a brave Catholic people to defend its religion against a strong and repressive Tudor state, and to show how this struggle – even as early as the sixteenth century – had contributed to the birth of the Irish national tradition. But working under the discipline of a rigorously empirical method, Edwards ended up saying something quite different. The type of Catholicism that he portrays throughout *Church and state* was not weak and heroic, but strong and militant. It won the hearts and minds of the people – both Gaelic and English Irish – from the moment Henry VIII broke with Rome. And it encountered little difficulty in defeating a contrastingly weak and disorganised state church and the latter's tentative sponsor, the Dublin government. Ultimately, it succeeded in establishing the conditions that would allow for the unification of the indigenous peoples of Ireland as a single nation.[2]

---

[1] TNA: PRO, SP 63/157, no. 35.
[2] Murray, 'Historical revisit: R. Dudley Edwards, *Church and state in Tudor Ireland* (1935)', pp. 233–41.

Like *Church and state's* Catholicism, the indigenous Catholicism portrayed in this book also possessed and displayed an impressive strength and
tenacity. It also won the people's hearts. And, as is evident from the internal
battles that were fought out in the Dublin diocesan administration between
the reforming archbishops and the clerical elite from the 1530s through to
the 1570s, it also harboured a similar willingness to pit itself against the
organs of the state and the established church. Yet here the parallel with
Edwards's work begins to break down. The Catholicism of the Pale that
emerges from the pages of this book, and which was embodied by Dublin's
clerical elite, was quintessentially English in its cultural outlook. At the
heart of this outlook was the notion that the Englishry were historically
responsible for civilising the Irishry along conventional canonical lines and
according to the uses and standards of the medieval English Church. This
historical imperative, which was enshrined in papal grants like *Laudabiliter*, was very dear to the clerical elite in the Pale, because it was they
who had maintained – in their most perfect forms and in the face of the
centuries-old threat that the Gaelic Irish posed to their survival – the English
ecclesiological and canonical standards which lay at its heart. The Dublin
clergy's defence of Catholicism, therefore, was not driven by a priori religious impulses that were held in common with the Gaelic Irish, and which
would help to bring the two nations together as they sought to preserve a
common religious heritage against the attack of an external Protestant
threat. Rather, it was informed by a traditional, and deeply conservative,
colonial attitude – a desire to preserve an ethos in which English cultural
values and canonically orthodox Catholicism were inextricably bound
together – which, at heart, was deeply antipathetic to Gaelic Irish culture.
At base, then, this book suggests that the roots of 'Catholic Nationalism', if
that phenomenon existed at all, are not to be found, as Edwards contended,
in Ireland's Reformation experience in the sixteenth century.

The broad conclusions to be drawn from this study resemble more closely
those found in Brendan Bradshaw's substantial oeuvre. Like the latter, this
study is intended to draw the reader's attention to the fact that the Pale
community, including its clergy, conformed in a nominal fashion to the
Reformation during the reign of Henry VIII, and that this conformity was
facilitated and encouraged by the conciliatory approach to government that
was adopted by the viceroy, Sir Anthony St Leger, in the 1540s. However,
the argument is made in a more cautious manner here than in Bradshaw
because, to secure the compliance of the indigenous clergy to the royal
supremacy, the viceroy had to undertake tortuous and time-consuming
negotiations with their leaders throughout 1541–2, and to give his personal
guarantee that the state church was intent on preserving Catholic teaching
and canonical orthodoxy. Moreover, as part of their agreement, and as a

testament to the orthodox nature of the viceroy's settlement, the leaders of the reformist clergy – men like Archbishop Browne and Dean Basnet of St Patrick's – had to abandon their canonically deviant marriages; while the settlement itself was given a further air of canonical credibility when, in the mid-1540s, St Leger sanctioned the utilisation of canon law in support of his political reform project in Ulster. Thus, even as they gave their grudging allegiance to Henry VIII's supremacy in the 1540s, it was also the case – as the viceroy well knew – that the clergy could take some real comfort from the fact that they were doing their best to fulfil the historical imperative of civilising the Irishry along conventional canonical lines.

It is not quite accurate, then, to portray the compliance of the Dublin clergy and their community under Henry VIII as a wholly positive endorsement of the Reformation. It was, instead, a pragmatic stance, which was designed to protect the old religion in the vulnerable circumstances in which the local church found itself after the dissolution of the monasteries. It was also generally consistent with the oppositionist stance that the clergy had maintained during the Kildare rebellion, and during Archbishop Browne's aggressive campaign to enforce religious change in the 1530s. Above all, it was conditional upon the viceroy being able to keep his promise to maintain traditional doctrine and religious practice intact into the future.

The viceroy's ability to keep this promise, and to protect the essentials of traditional religion, disappeared in the late 1540s with the accession of Edward VI and the imposition of a more overtly Protestant religious settlement by his regime. This study concurs with Bradshaw's view that there was no definitive indigenous response to this settlement during Edward's short reign. However, it also suggests that the essential stimuli for the hardening of Catholic attitudes that occurred under Mary Tudor were already in place in the latter half of the reign. One of these, of course, was the abandonment of the mass in favour of a radical and innovatory liturgy, a development which failed to generate any enthusiasm within the Pale. The other was an emerging disenchantment with Lord Deputy St Leger, and his overwhelmingly secular approach to religious matters. The viceroy's unrelenting campaign to expropriate all manner of ecclesiastical property, which reached a new level in 1546–7 with the suppression of St Patrick's Cathedral, caused an increasing number of the indigenous clergy to reappraise their strategy of collaboration with him – including, most notably, his close ally, Archbishop Dowdall of Armagh – ahead of Mary Tudor's accession.

In this connection, the period of the Marian restoration of Catholicism and the episcopacy of Hugh Curwen (1555–67) proved to be a decisive turning point, a view which is also maintained by Bradshaw. However, where Bradshaw saw the Marian restoration of Catholicism as an opening for the Counter-Reformation to gain a foothold in the English Pale, it is argued here that, under the local leadership of Archbishop Dowdall of Armagh, the old, pre-Reformation version of the Catholic religion was revived and revitalised, a process which also encompassed a full and self-conscious revival of traditional English Irish clerical values. Moreover, under the protective eye of Archbishop Curwen, who served as archbishop of Dublin during Mary Tudor's reign and the opening years of the reign of her successor, Queen Elizabeth, the newly reinvigorated spirit of the old religion, and many of its practices, were preserved for a decade or so even after Catholicism was abrogated in 1560.

The revival of the old religion, then, as managed by Archbishops Dowdall and Curwen during the mid-Tudor period, was crucial in determining the ultimate survival of Catholicism, and the ultimate failure of the Reformation, in the diocese of Dublin and elsewhere in the English Pale. But it was not the only factor. At the outset of his episcopacy Archbishop Loftus identified indigenous clerical resistance, and the value system upon which it was built, as the main impediment to the progress of the Reformation and took steps to counteract it. With the help and guidance of Lord Chancellor Weston, the reform-minded dean of St Patrick's, Loftus instituted a carefully modulated programme of ecclesiastical discipline in his diocese which sought to invest the Elizabethan settlement and its advocates with the same kind of legitimating canonical credentials that were possessed, in the eyes of the local community, by the old religion and the conservative clergy. Over time, it was hoped, this strategy would marginalise the old clerical elite and secure the trust and allegiance of their community for his own Protestant ecclesiastical establishment.

Initially, at any rate, there were signs that the Loftus–Weston programme might work, especially in the willingness of a younger generation of aspiring ecclesiastical lawyers to attach themselves to the new regime. However, the gradualist nature of the strategy itself, the loss of momentum that it suffered in the wake of Weston's untimely death in 1573, and, above all, the continuing subversiveness of the indigenous clergy – now realised in a series of overtly political plots designed to destabilise the Loftus–Weston regime – all ensured that more tangible and impressive results were not obtained in the short term. This proved fatal for the archbishop's plans. Other reformers, notably Lord Deputy Sidney, viewed Loftus's plans with impatience or disdain and his strategy was finally dismantled and abandoned at the viceroy's behest in 1577. Thereafter, the archbishop was forced to adopt the more coercive programme of enforcement favoured by Sidney and the government in Whitehall. It was the rigorous implementation of this programme in the late 1570s and early 1580s that finally and irrevocably alienated the Pale community from the established church.

In large measure, then, what is presented here is the story of a generation of clergymen based in St Patrick's Cathedral that set out consciously to subvert the plans of the reforming archbishops, or to negotiate agreements with the secular authorities that would allow them to preserve their religious and cultural values in the most complete form possible at any given time. At the heart of this strategy was their exploitation of their control over the administrative and judicial structures of the diocese of Dublin, a controlling influence which enabled them either to prevent the imposition of reformist measures or to maintain proscribed Catholic practices at the crucial times when new religious settlements were being implemented. In some respects, the conservative clergy held all the trump cards against their rather isolated opponents. However, their ultimate success – measured in their community's continuing attachment to the old religion – was in no way guaranteed as a result, for contingencies such as Lord Deputy St Leger's unexpected dissolution of St Patrick's Cathedral in 1546–7, and the clergy's loss of power over local ecclesiastical structures from the 1570s on, due to natural wastage and their removal from the restored cathedral at the hands of Archbishop Loftus, undermined the traditional basis of their power and influence.

The implications of this study, then, for the key issues raised by the Bradshaw–Canny debate are apparent though hardly conclusive. With regard to the timing of the failure of the Reformation, it is arguable that by the time Adam Loftus – a man who was far more responsive to the religious sensibilities of his flock than he has generally been given credit for – began his episcopate in 1567, the Reformation had failed. The fact that the archbishop identified the basis of conservative religious resistance in his diocese, developed a plausible strategy to nullify its influence but still failed to supplant it, suggests very strongly that the revival of Catholicism in the mid-Tudor period established that religion as a powerful ideological force, that was strong enough to stand up to the theological and liturgical innovations advanced by the Protestant reformers. The origins and potency of this religion resided not in the heroic spirit of the Irish nation, nor in the ideology of the Counter-Reformation, but in the values and reflexes of a clerical elite, which had long sustained the identity of the old colonial community in a hostile world.

Appendix 1
The division of administrative responsibilities between the two Dublin cathedrals

The key document for identifying and delineating the administrative responsibilities of Dublin's two cathedrals is the 'Composicio Pacis'. This ordinance, which was promulgated in 1300 by Archbishop Richard of Ferings (1299–1306) to quell the disputes that had raged between the rival chapters following St Patrick's acquisition of cathedral status, remained in force and regulated relations between the two bodies down to the sixteenth century and beyond.[1]

In general, the 'Composicio' conceded the principle that, in matters of prestige and dignity, Christ Church as the 'older' and 'mother' church would take precedence. Thus all new archbishops were to be consecrated within the cathedral priory, provincial synods were to open and close there, while the ceremonial consecration of the sacred oils on Holy Thursday was to be performed by its clergy. In addition, the prior and convent were to retain custody of the archiepiscopal cross, mitre and ring during episcopal vacancies. They were also to be the first to cast their vote in meetings, such as provincial councils, in which both cathedrals were participating; and they were to take precedence in legal instruments, including documents recording the ratification of episcopal *acta*, in which the two churches appeared as parties.[2]

Yet, despite the proliferation of detail in the document, the 'Composicio' is noticeably silent on the more substantial matters of diocesan administration.

---

[1] The full text is printed in Mason, *History of St Patrick's*, Appendix VI, pp. viii–ix (calendared in *Alen's register*, pp. 155–6). For a discussion of its contents and the context in which it was promulgated see Hand, 'Rivalry of the medieval cathedral chapters', pp. 193–206.

[2] Mason, *History of St Patrick's*, Appendix VI, pp. viii–ix (*Alen's register*, pp. 155–6); H. J. Lawlor (ed.), 'A calendar of the Liber Niger and Liber Albus of Christ Church, Dublin', *PRIA* 27 C (1908–9), pp. 10–11; Morrin, *Patent rolls*, i, pp. 529–30. For some examples of the joint ratification of episcopal leases from Elizabeth's reign see Archbishop Loftus's leases of Cullenswood to Simon Grove, 6 March 1570, and William Ussher, 20 October 1583; and of Lambay Island to William Ussher, 17 February 1594 (NLI, D 9964-D 9966).

There is one simple reason for this. By the time it was drafted, Christ Church had already conceded that these matters would be the preserves of its rival, St Patrick's. Thus there were no instructions in the 'Composicio' regarding the archbishop's consistory court. There were no arrangements for the alternate appointment of vicar generals from each cathedral. Nor were there any moves to restore the archdeacon of Dublin to Christ Church, even though he had had a stall in the priory and a vote at the election of the archbishop before the office was established in St Patrick's.[3] Collectively, these silences spoke of the older cathedral's acceptance that the central organs of episcopal government would continue to function in, and be staffed from St Patrick's, and that its own participation in the daily administration of the diocese would be correspondingly restricted. Indeed, the only aspect of the process in which Christ Church was allowed to play any significant part was in the general guardianship of the archbishop's spiritual jurisdiction and the see's spiritualties during the brief and infrequent periods of episcopal vacancy. The 'Composicio' was unambiguous on this point. When an archbishop died, the exercise of his jurisdiction was expected to devolve upon the two chapters jointly, who would appoint an official to exercise it. Further, the associated revenues or spiritualties – which included probate fees and the monies accruing from the redemption of penances and the collection of visitation procurations – were to be divided between the two chapters according to a pre-agreed scheme. There is little doubt that these arrangements took meaningful effect and that they endured long after. Certainly, all the extant notices of *sede vacante* administration in Dublin from the early sixteenth century – following the deaths of Archbishops Fitzsimon,[4] Rokeby[5] and Alen[6] – show that they were fully operable as the Reformation commenced.[7]

---

[3] *Alen's register*, pp. 155–7.

[4] Lennon and Murray (eds.), *Dublin City franchise roll*, pp. 74–5, granting of probate, June–August 1511, by the custodians Prior Skyrett of Christ Church and Dean Rochford of St Patrick's.

[5] BL, Additional Charters 7043, 7044, confirmations of the elections of the prior of All Hallows Priory, Dublin (5 June 1522), and the abbot of Thomas Court Abbey, Dublin (19 August 1522), by William Hassard, prior of Christ Church and 'one of the (two) custodians of the spiritualities and spiritual jurisdiction of the church of Dublin *sede vacante*', with the assent of his 'colleague' Master John Ricard, dean of St Patrick's.

[6] *LM* II, pt. 5, p. 97, and Morrin, *Patent rolls*, i, p. 14, royal letters of presentation of John Bayley or Bailiff to the vicarage of Narraghmore, directed to Prior Hassard and Dean Fyche, custodians of the see of Dublin *sede vacante* (11 January 1535); RIA, 12.S.28, no. 831, exemplification of the will of Alexander Beswick (1533) made by Robert Fitzsimon, precentor of St Patrick's Cathedral and official of the metropolitan court of Dublin *sede vacante* (dateable to the period August 1534–January/March 1536).

[7] For some fifteenth century examples of the shared custodianship see *CCD*, no. 302; Berry, *Register of wills*, pp. 20, 99.

Appendix 2
The parishes of the diocese of Dublin, 1530–1600

This appendix lists all the parishes that were extant in the diocese of Dublin from 1530 to 1600 and provides details of their pre-dissolution rectors and how the cures were served. It also records changes that were made to the status of individual parishes at different points in the sixteenth century. The main source used as the basis for the compilation is Archbishop John Alen's roll of churches, 'the Reportorium Viride', which is in print: N.B. White (ed.), 'The Reportorium Viride of John Alen, archbishop of Dublin, 1533' in *Analecta* 10 (1941), pp. 173–217. Alen's list of churches was copied from an earlier list compiled for the late thirteenth century register known as the 'Crede Mihi' – printed in J.T. Gilbert (ed.), *Crede mihi: the most ancient register book of the archbishop of Dublin before the Reformation* (Dublin, 1897), pp. 134–49 – and includes a number of churches which had disappeared in the interim and some which disappeared after his own death in 1534. It also designates many churches as chapels of ease which had subsequently become fully parochial. Adjustments to the data in the 'Reportorium Viride' have been made accordingly.

Three early seventeenth-century visitations have also been used extensively for ascertaining which parishes survived throughout the sixteenth century: the metropolitan and prerogative court visitations of the diocese of Dublin in TCD, MS 566; the regal visitation of 1615 in BL, Additional MS 19836; and Archbishop Bulkeley's diocesan visitation of 1630, printed as M.V. Ronan (ed.), 'Archbishop Bulkeley's visitation of Dublin, 1630', *AH* 8 (1941), pp. 56–98.

Deanery of Dublin or Christianity

	Parish	Rector	Service
1.	St Audoen	Prebend, St Patrick's	Curate
2.	St Michael	Christ Church Cathedral/sub-dean of Christ Church[1]	Curate/sub-dean (from 1539)
3.	St Peter	'Entire'	Rector
4.	St Olave[2]	Abbey of St Augustine, Bristol	Curate
5.	St Michan	Christ Church Cathedral/succentor of Christ Church[3]	Curate/succentor (from 1539)
6.	St James[4]	Thomas Court Abbey	Curate
7.	St Catherine[5]	Thomas Court Abbey	Curate/vicar (from 1546)
8.	St Andrew[6]	Precentor, St Patrick's	Curate
9.	St Mary de la Dam[7]	'Entire'	Rector
10.	St Bride	Economy, St Patrick's	Curate
11.	St Nicholas Within	Economy, St Patrick's	Curate
12.	St Nicholas Without	Economy, St Patrick's	Curate
13.	St John	Christ Church Cathedral/ chancellor's vicar of Christ Church[8]	Curate/chancellor's vicar (from 1539)
14.	St Kevin	Economy, St Patrick's	Vicar
15.	St Werburgh	Chancellor, St Patrick's	Curate
16.	St Michael (of the Pool)	'Entire'	Rector
17.	St Stephen[9]	'Entire'	Custos of St Stephen/ chaplain
18.	St George[10]	All Hallows Priory	Curate
19.	St Glannoke[11]	St Mary's Abbey	Curate

[1] As part of the alteration of Christ Church into a secular cathedral in 1539, the church of St Michael was appropriated to the dean's vicar or sub-dean, who was also made president of the vicars choral. He was enjoined to serve the cure and probably did so as the living was too poor to support more than one priest (RCB, C6/1/6, no. 3, pp. 1111–2, Murray, 'Sources of clerical income', p. 151).
[2] The church of St Olave, probably on account of its small value, was united to the parish of St John (Stanyhurst, *Holinshed's Irish chronicle*, p. 45), sometime before November 1553 when it was described as the 'late church of St Tullocks' (*Fiants, Mary*, no. 6). It fell into disuse and was profaned by 1577 (Stanyhurst, op. cit., p. 45).
[3] St Michan 's was appropriated to the precentor's vicar, or succentor, when Christ Church Cathedral's status was altered from regular to secular in 1539. Like the sub-dean he probably served the cure personally (RCB, C6/1/6, no. 3, pp. 1112–13; RCB, C6/1/7, no. 1).

⁴ The church of St James was united to St Catherine's on 18 March 1546 by Archbishop Browne (Morrin, *Patent rolls*, i, p. 122). As part of this process, a new vicarage was erected in the parish. The erection of this vicarage had been planned as early as 1539, as it was then valued by royal commissioners for first fruits and twentieth part taxation (*Valor beneficiorum*, p. 9). The delay in putting it into effect was probably due to the fact that two old monks of Thomas Court, John Brace and John Butler, were then responsible for serving the cures of the two parishes. In the wake of the abbey's dissolution, the Henrician regime may have been reluctant to sever this continuity with the past, preferring to postpone the erection of the new vicarage until the former monks had passed away (*Fiants, Henry VIII*, no. 83; Morrin, *Patent rolls*, i, pp. 56, 60; White, *Monastic extents*, p. 29). Brace died *c*. Michaelmas 1542 (RCB, C6/1/26, no. 3). Butler probably died in 1546.

⁵ As in note 4 above.

⁶ St Andrew's was united to St Werburgh's by Archbishop Browne on account of poverty and paucity of people (*RDD*, pp. 5–6, document undated).

⁷ St Mary's was united to St Werburgh's by Archbishop Browne on account of poverty and paucity of people (*RDD*, pp. 5–6, document undated).

⁸ The chancellor's vicar received the church of St John as part of the alteration of Christ Church in 1539. Like the sub-dean and succentor he probably served his cure (RCB, C6/1/6, no. 3, pp. 1113–4).

⁹ The church of St Stephen was appropriated to the leper hospital of the same name, but appears to have had parochial status. The custos or guardian of the hospital was responsible for serving the cure of souls and was appointed by the mayor and aldermen of Dublin, though in practice it was probably discharged by a chaplain as the custodianship was often given to aspiring Dublin clerics studying at Oxford (*ARD*, i, pp. 399, 439; *ARD*, ii, p. 145; *BRUO, 1501–40*, p. 536).

¹⁰ After the dissolution of the priory of All Hallows, the church of St George continued to function as a guild chapel throughout the reigns of Henry VIII, Edward VI and Mary, under the protection of the citizens of Dublin. Payments were made to the guild priest in 1550 and 1551 (DCA, MR/35, pp. 86, 95) and reparations were made to the church in 1556–7 (ibid., pp. 139, 145). The guild appears to have survived until at least 1563 (ibid., p. 190). It is likely that it was suppressed soon after, which would account for the fact of the church's ruination in the 1570s. Writing in this period, Stanyhurst related that the 'chapel hath been of late razed, and the stones thereof by the consent of the assembly turned a common oven, converting the ancient monument of a doughty, adventurous and holy knight to the coalrake sweeping of a puffloaf baker' (Stanyhurst, op. cit., 49).

¹¹ The parish of 'St Glannoke' extended over St Mary's abbey demesne lands and is mentioned in the extents taken at the time of the dissolution and leases made of the rectory thereafter (White, *Monastic extents*, p. 2; *Fiants, Edward VI*, no. 1083; *Fiants, Elizabeth*, no. 2660). At the dissolution of the monastery the church was occupied by John Travers, master of the ordnance, and used for storing artillery and other munitions. From this time the church fell into disuse and the parish ceased to function.

Deanery of Taney

	Parish	Rector	Service
1.	Taney	Archdeacon of Dublin	Curate
2.	Donnybrook	Archdeacon of Dublin	Curate
3.	Rathfarnham	Archdeacon of Dublin	Curate
4.	Kilgobbin	Archdeacon of Dublin	Curate
5.	Leopardstown	Custos of St Stephen's hospital	Curate
6.	Whitechurch	St Mary's Abbey	Curate
7.	Cruagh	Knights Hospitallers, Kilmainham	Curate
8.	Templeogue	Economy, St Patrick's	Curate
9.	Tallaght	Dean, St Patrick's	Vicar
10.	Crumlin	Economy, St Patrick's	Curate
11.	Saggard	Prebend, St Patrick's	Curate
12.	Clondalkin	Dean, St Patrick's	Curate/vicarage endowed in the early 1570s by Dean Weston[12]
13.	Rathcoole	Dean, St Patrick's	Curate/vicarage endowed in the early 1570s by Dean Weston[13]
14.	Esker	Dean, St Patrick's	Curate/vicarage endowed in the early 1570s by Dean Weston[14]
15.	Calliaghstown	Nunnery of Hogges	Curate
16.	Newcastle	Archdeacon of Glendalough	Curate
17.	Aderrig	Vicars choral, St Patrick's	Curate
18.	Kilmahuddrick[15]	St Mary's Abbey	Curate
19.	Lucan	Thomas Court Abbey	Vicar
20.	Palmerstown	Hospital of St John, Newgate	Curate
21.	Ballyfermot	Knights Hospitallers, Kilmainham	Curate
22.	Kilmainham[16]	Knights Hospitallers, Kilmainham	Curate
23.	Clontarf	Knights Hospitallers, Kilmainham	Curate
24.	Raheny	St Mary's Abbey	Curate
25.	Coolock	Priory of Lanthony	Vicar
26.	Glasnevin	Christ Church Cathedral	Curate
27.	Clonturk	All Hallows Priory	Curate
28.	Finglas	Chancellor of St Patrick's	Curate
29.	St Margaret's, Dunsoghly	Chancellor of St Patrick's	Curate
30.	Ward	Chancellor of St Patrick's	Curate

Deanery of Taney (*cont.*)

	Parish	Rector	Service
31.	Artane	Chancellor of St Patrick's	Curate
32.	Castleknock	Prebend, St Patrick's	Vicar
33.	Mulhuddart	Prebend, St Patrick's	Curate
34.	Clonsilla	St Mary's Abbey	Curate
35.	Cloghran Hiddert	All Hallows Priory	Curate
36.	Chapelizod	Knights Hospitallers, Kilmainham	Curate
37.	Kilmactalway	Prebend, St Patrick's	Curate
38.	Kilmacud[17]	Nunnery of Graney	Curate
	Killester?[18]	Christ Church Cathedral	Curate

[12] Bodleian, Perrot MS 1, f. 104r; GO, MS 290, p. 17; TCD, MS 567, f. 1v.

[13] As in note 12 above.

[14] As in note 12 above.

[15] Kilmahuddrick was united to Clondalkin by Archbishop Browne on 20 March 1541 on account of its poverty and low population (*Dignitas decani*, p. 125).

[16] Kilmainham was united to St Catherine's, Dublin, on 18 March 1540, on account of the poverty and proximity of the parishes (Morrin, *Patent rolls*, i, p. 122).

[17] Kilmacud was united to the church of St Fintan of Clonkeen (Kill of the Grange) by Archbishop Browne, on account of poverty and low population on August 3 1551 (*CCD*, no. 445).

[18] Killester was described as a chapel in the early sixteenth century i.e. in 1505 and c.1530 (*Alen's register*, pp. 256, 258). In the redistribution of Christ Church's endowment, after its alteration into a secular cathedral, Killester was granted to the economy. Here, and thereafter, it was described as a piece of property, i.e. the 'rectory of' or the 'tithes of' Killester, with no reference to it being a chapel. This fact, and the fact that it does not appear in any of the early seventeenth-century visitations, implies that it did not function as a parochial entity, the chapel having decayed and gone out of use in the early sixteenth century. In the mid-seventeenth century this was certainly the case. In the Civil Survey (*CS* VII, p. 173) it was said of Killester that 'there is . . . in the town the walls of a decayed chapel'.

Deanery of Swords

	Parish	Rector	Service
1.	Swords	Prebend, St Patrick's	Vicar
2.	Kinsaley	Vicar of Swords	Curate
3.	Killeek	Economy, St Patrick's	Curate
4.	Killossery	Economy, St Patrick's	Curate
5.	Malahide	Economy, St Patrick's	Curate
6.	Cloghran Swords	'Entire'	Rector
7.	Killsallaghan	Thomas Court Abbey	Vicar
8.	Chapelmidway	Thomas Court Abbey	Curate
9.	Garristown	Knights Hospitallers, Kilmainham	Vicar
10.	Palmerstown	Knights Hospitallers, Kilmainham	Curate
11.	Ballymadun	Nunnery of Grace Dieu	Vicar
12.	Ballyboghill	St Mary's Abbey	Curate
13.	Naul	Priory of Lanthony	Curate
14.	Balscaddan	Christ Church Cathedral	Vicar
15.	Holmpatrick	Priory of Holmpatrick	Curate
16.	Hollywood	Priory of Lanthony	Vicar
17.	Grallagh	Priory of Lanthony	Curate
18.	Balrothery	Priory of Tristernagh	Vicar
19.	Lusk	Treasurer of St Patrick's/ Precentor of St Patrick's	2 vicars (treasurer's part and precentor's part)
20.	Grace Dieu[19]	Nunnery of Grace Dieu	Curate
21.	Donabate	Nunnery of Graney	Vicar
22.	Howth	Prebend, St Patrick's	Curate[20]
23.	Kilbarrack	Prebend, St Patrick's	Curate
24.	Santry	St Mary's Abbey	Curate
25.	St Duileach's, Balgriffin	Christ Church Cathedral	Vicar
26.	Baldongan	'Entire'	Rector
27.	Portrane	Nunnery of Grace Dieu	Curate
28.	Westpalstown	Nunnery of Grace Dieu	Curate
29.	Baldoyle	All Hallows Priory	Curate
30.	Portmarnock	St Mary's Abbey	Curate
31.	Clonmethan	Prebend, St Patrick's	Curate
32.	Fieldstown	Prebend, St Patrick's	Curate

[19] The parish of Grace Dieu seems to have disappeared after the dissolution of the nunnery of Grace Dieu on 28 October 1539. The rectory continued to be leased (*Fiants, Henry VIII*, no. 235; *Fiants, Elizabeth*, no. 3319), but no returns were made for the parish in the early seventeenth-century visitations of the diocese.

[20] There was a vicarage erected in the parish of Howth for a brief period in the 1530s for which see White (ed.), 'Reportorium Viride of John Alen', p. 196.

Deanery of Ballymore

1.	Rathsallagh[21]	Economy, St Patrick's	Curate
2.	Dunlavin	Prebend, St Patrick's	Curate
3.	Tober[22]	Nunnery of Grace Dieu	Curate
4.	Donard	Hospital of St John, Newgate	Vicar
5.	Hollywood	'Entire'	Vicar
6.	Dunboyke[23]	'Entire'	Rector
7.	Yago	Prebend, St Patrick's	Curate
8.	Gilltown	Baltinglass Abbey	Curate
9.	Brannockstown[24]	Economy, St Patrick's	Curate
10.	Coghlanstown (Ballycutland etc.)	Nunnery of Graney	Curate
11.	Ballymore	Treasurer, St Patrick's	Curate
12.	Tipperkevin	Double Prebend, St Patrick's	Curate
13.	Ballybaught	Archbishop	Curate
14.	Tipper	Prebend, St Patrick's	Curate
15.	Rathmore	Knights Hospitallers, Kilmainham	Vicar
16.	Kilteel	Knights Hospitallers, Kilmainham	Curate
17.	Kilbride	Knights Hospitallers, Kilmainham	Curate
18.	Burgage	Precentor, St Patrick's	Curate/Vicar (from c. 1580)[25]
19.	Templebodan (Kilbodan)	Archbishop	Curate
20.	Boystown (Kilpatrick)	Archbishop	Curate

[21] Rathsallagh was functioning *c.*1530 when Archbishop Alen provided Edmond Eustace to the rectory of Usk in the freechapel therein. In the 1547 inquisition concerning the property of St Patrick's Cathedral there is no mention of the church, just a return for 'the tithes of the hamlet of Rathsallowe'. Was the church functioning then? It probably was not as no returns were made for it in the 1610, 1615 and 1630 visitations of the diocese. The cathedral proctor's account of 1606 (TCD, MS 788, f. 87r), reveals that the dean and chapter had let its tithes and the tithes of Moone to Ambrose Forth. It is clear from this entry and a lease from the dean and chapter to Archdeacon Bulkeley in 1645 (RCB, C2/2 no. 47) that Rathsallagh was united to Moone, a unification which may have been instituted in the early days of the Reformation under Archbishop Browne. The lessee in 1645 was only bound to find a curate for Moone.

[22] Does not appear in the 1610, 1615 or 1630 visitations of the diocese, although leases of the rectory from the crown occur in 1541 (*Fiants, Henry VIII*, no. 235), 1562, 1571 and 1575 (*Fiants, Elizabeth*, nos. 398, 1730, 2689). The rectory was granted to Sir Henry Harrington in tail male in 1581 (ibid., no. 3705). The parish, which was situated in the marches, had been devastated in the 1530s (White, *Monastic extents*, p. 77), and probably did not exist as a functioning entity thereafter.

23 An 'entire' rectory was established by Archbishop Alen in the parish of
    Dunboyke after he dissolved the nunnery of Timolin in the early 1530s. The
    archbishop said it was poor however. It appears to have disappeared soon
    after, probably as a result of poverty, as it was not valued by Crown
    commissioners in the late 1530s for first fruits and twentieth part taxation
    (*Valor beneficiorum*, pp. 9–10). It may have been united to Hollywood, of
    which it is now a part.
24 Brannockstown was served jointly with Gilltown by a single curate in the
    early seventeenth century (see 1610, 1615 and 1630 visitations). A lease from
    the dean and chapter, dated 17 March 1630 (RCB, C2/2, no. 36), to one John
    Pue, bound him to find a curate for Brannockstown, which proves that it was
    a functioning parish.
25 A vicarage was established, probably in the early 1580s, following the
    appointment of Arthur Athie, a lay, non-resident absentee to the precentorship
    of St Patrick's Cathedral in 1579 (Murray, 'Tudor diocese of Dublin', p. 319).

Deanery of Bray

	Parish	Rector	Service
1.	Bray	Nunnery of Graney	Vicar
2.	Stagonil	Prebend, St Patrick's	Curate
3.	Delgany	'Entire'	Rector
4.	Kilmacanoge/Glencap	St Mary's Abbey	Curate
5.	Newcastle	Nunnery of Grace Dieu	Vicar
6.	Kilcoole	Archbishop	Curate
7.	Oldconnaught	Archbishop	Curate
8.	Rathmichael	Prebend, St Patrick's	Curate
9.	Kill of the Grange (Clonkeen)	Christ Church Cathedral	Curate
10.	Killiney	Christ Church Cathedral	Curate
11.	Tully	Christ Church Cathedral	Curate
12.	Dalkey	Christ Church Cathedral	Curate
13.	Stillorgan[26]	Christ Church Cathedral	Curate
14.	Monkstown	St Mary's Abbey	Curate
15.	Kiltiernan	St Mary's Abbey	Curate

26 Stillorgan was united to the parish church of St Fintan, Clonkeen (Kill of the
    Grange), by Archbishop Browne on August 3 1551, on account of its low
    population and the exility of its revenues (RCB, C6/16, no. 3, p. 1180).

Deaneries of Wicklow and Arklow

	Parish	Rector	Service
1.	Wicklow	Prebend, St Patrick's	Vicar
2.	Glenealy	Prebend, St Patrick's	Curate
3.	Kilcommon	Prebend, St Patrick's	Curate
4.	Ballydonnell	Prebend, St Patrick's	Curate
5.	Rathnew	Prebend, St Patrick's	Curate
6.	Killiskey	Prebend, St Patrick's	Curate
7.	Ennisboyne	'Entire'	Rector
8.	Derrylossory and Harpstown	Chancellor of St Patrick's	Curate
9.	Glendalough	Archbishop	Curate
10.	Drumkay	'Entire'	Rector
11.	Castlemacadam	'Entire'	Rector
12.	Kilpoole[27]	Knights Hospitallers, Kilmainham	Curate
13.	Arklow	Owney Abbey[28]	Vicar
14.	Killynee	Owney Abbey	Curate
15.	Templerainy	Owney Abbey	Curate
16.	Ballykine	Owney Abbey	Curate
17.	'Kilmagig'	Owney Abbey	Curate
18.	Kilgorman	'Entire'/Archbishop[29]	Rector/vicar
19.	Inch	'Entire'/Archbishop[30]	Rector/vicar
20.	Killahurler	Christ Church Cathedral	Curate
21.	Macreddin[31]	All Hallows Priory	Curate
22.	Rathdrum[32]	All Hallows Priory	Curate
23.	Kilmacoo	Archbishop[33]	Curate
24.	Kilbride	Archbishop[34]	Curate
25.	Templemichael	Archbishop[35]	Curate
26.	Ballintemple	Glasscarig Priory	Curate
27.	Ennereilly	Abbey of St Augustine, Bristol	Curate

[27] In April 1541 it was reported that the rectory of Kilpoole could not be valued as it lay among the Irish from whence information could not be obtained. It was also reported that the late prior of the Knights Hospitallers had not received any profits from the rectory for a long time (White, *Monastic extents*, pp. 90–1).

[28] For the appropriation of Arklow to Owney abbey see *Fiants, Edward VI*, nos. 1020 and 1078, *Fiants, Elizabeth*, no. 463.

[29] Kilgorman's status in our period is somewhat confused. In 1511 the vicarages of Kilgorman and Inch were said to be united to the rectory of Inch: Coleman (ed.), 'Obligationes pro annatis diocesis Dublinensis', p. 25. In the late 1530s it appears to have been regarded as an independent 'entire' rectory: 'Rectoria de Silbernan in patria de O'Birnes' (*Valor beneficiorum*, p. 10). In the 1610 visitation it was listed as a chapel under Arklow, and served by the vicar of

Arklow. In the 1630 visitation it again had its own vicar while the rectory is said to have been appropriated to the archbishop's *mensa*. The dates when these changes in status took place are unknown.

[30] Like the neighbouring parish of Kilgorman, Inch's status in our period is unclear. In 1477 Odo Okirmian bound himself to pay annates to the Roman Curia for the rectory of the parish church of Inch: Coleman (ed.), 'Obligationes pro annatis diocesis Dublinensis', p. 21. In 1511 the vicarages of Inch and Kilgorman were said to be united to the rectory of Inch (ibid., p. 25). In the late 1530s, it was regarded as an independent 'entire' rectory: 'Rectoria de Insula (in patria de O'Birnes)' (*Valor beneficiorum*, p. 10; see also NAI, Ferguson MSS, v, p. 124, a process enrolled on the memoranda rolls of the Exchequer concerning William Tonley, Rector de Insula). In the 1610 visitation it had its own vicarage again (TCD, MS 566, f. 34v). In 1615, however, it was served by a curate. In the 1630 visitation, a vicar was in place again and the rectory was said to be appropriated *ad mensam archiepiscopi*.

[31] Although appropriated to All Hallows priory, the rectory was not accessible to the monks nor their successor rectors, the city of Dublin, during the sixteenth century. Whether it functioned as a parish in any meaningful sense is unknown.

[32] As in note 31 above.

[33] On the appropriation of this rectory to the archbishopric of Dublin see Gillespie (ed.), *First chapter act book of Christ Church, 1574–1634*, pp. 58–9.

[34] As in note 33 above.

[35] As in note 33 above.

Deanery of Omurthy

	Parish	Rector	Service
1.	Castledermot	Nunnery of Graney	Vicar
2.	Graney	Nunnery of Graney	Curate
3.	Kineagh	Nunnery of Graney/Vicars choral, St Patrick's	Vicar
4.	Ballaghmoon and Dunmanoge[36] (Monmehenock)	Thomas Court Abbey/ Prebend, St Patrick's	Curate
5.	Moone	Economy, St Patrick's	Curate
6.	Kilkea	Nunnery of Graney	Vicar
7.	Grangerosnalvan	Baltinglass Abbey	Curate
8.	Timolin	'Entire'/Impropriated post 1549[37]	Rector/Curate
9.	Usk	'Entire'	Rector
10.	Killelan	Nunnery of Graney	Vicar
11.	Belan	Greatconnell Priory	Curate
12.	Donaghmore in Imaal	Double prebend, St Patrick's	Vicar
13.	Freynestown[38]	Economy, St Patrick's	Curate
14.	Kiltegan	Nunnery of Graney	Curate
15.	Ardree	Precentor, St Patrick's.	Curate
16.	St Michael's, Athy	Hospital of St John, Athy	Curate
17.	Churchtown (Fassaghreban)	St Mary's Abbey	Curate
18.	Kilberry	Dean, St Patrick's	Curate
19.	Kilcullen	Christ Church Cathedral	Curate
20.	Narraghmore	'Entire'	Vicar
21.	Tippeenan and Rathsallagh[39]	Knights Hospitallers, Kilmainham	Vicar
22.	'Rathknavys'[40]	Knights Hospitallers, Kilmainham	Curate
23.	Ballycoolan[41]	Knights Hospitallers, Kilmainham	Curate
24.	Fontstown	Knights Hospitallers, Kilmainham	Vicar
25.	Davidstown	Knights Hospitallers, Kilmainham	Vicar
26.	Dollardstown	'Entire'	Curate
27.	Nicholastown	'Entire'	Rector
28.	Dunbrin[42]	Thomas Court Abbey	Curate
29.	Tankardstown	Thomas Court Abbey	Curate

[36] Ballaghmoon and Dunmanoge appear to have been united throughout the sixteenth century (White, *Monastic extents*, p. 37).

[37] After Archbishop Alen's suppression of the convent of Timolin *c*.1530 he reversed the rectory to its pristine state instituting Sir Thomas Festam, prebendary of Dunmanoge, as an 'entire' rector. After the latter's death *c*.1549, it

was changed into an impropriate rectory by the crown (*Fiants, Edward VI*, no. 391).

[38] There is no mention of a chaplain serving in Freynestown in the inquisition taken in 1547 on the dissolution of St Patrick's Cathedral (RCB, C2/1/27, no. 2), nor, indeed, in any sources thereafter. Given this, it probably fell into disuse sometime *c.*1530–47.

[39] The vicarage of Tippeenan and Rathsallagh paid a proxy to Archbishop Alen during his visitation of 1531 (*Alen's register*, p. 277). It was appropriated to the Knight's Hospitallers but was not extended in the 1540s. Presumably, it had disappeared due to the depredation caused by the O'Mores in the Omurthy area (c.f. Ballycoolan). Rathsallagh was part of Fontstown in the seventeenth century. It may have been united to it in the 1530s.

[40] Proxies were paid for the church of 'Rathknavys' during Alen's visitation of 1531 (*Alen's register*, p. 278). It was not returned in the monastic extents of 1540–1, which suggests that it went the way of Tippeenan.

[41] Ballycoolan was said to be 'worth nothing, being adjacent to the marches of the Irish called the Mores' in the early 1540s. It probably ceased to function as a result.

[42] Dunbrin does not appear in any other sources after Alen's 'Repertorium Viride'. This suggests that it ceased to function soon after.

Deanery of Leixlip

	Parish	Rector	Service
1.	St. Catherine's, Leixlip[43]	Thomas Court Abbey	Curate
2.	Leixlip	Thomas Court Abbey	Curate
3.	Confey	Thomas Court Abbey	Curate
4.	Castledillon	Thomas Court Abbey	Curate
5.	Kildrought	Thomas Court Abbey	Vicar
6.	Stacumny[44]	St Wolstan's Priory	Curate
7.	Donaghcumper	St Wolstan's Priory	Curate
8.	Donaghmore[45]	St Wolstan's Priory	Curate
9.	Killadoon	St Wolstan's Priory	Curate
10.	Straffan	Hospital of St. John, Newgate	Vicar
11.	Taghadoe	All Hallows Priory	Vicar
12.	Laraghbryan (Maynooth)	Prebend, St Patrick's	Vicar

[43] St Catherine's, Leixlip, a cell of Thomas Court abbey, appears in Alen's 'Repertorium Viride' and the monastic extents as a separate parish. Its tithes and the lands of St Catherine's continued to be leased by the crown throughout the sixteenth century and were finally granted to Nicholas White to hold forever by the service of a 1/40 part of a knight's fee (*Fiants, Elizabeth*, no. 1369). They remained in the White family until 1640 (*CS* VIII, p. 12), but were then regarded as part of Leixlip parish. The parish, as a separate entity, does not appear in the 1615 or 1630 visitations and may have been formally united to Leixlip parish in the aftermath of the dissolution. By the time of the Civil Survey there was said to be one parish church in Leixlip.

[44] Stacumny does not appear in the 1615 or 1630 visitations. In the Civil Survey the lands of Stacumny are included in the parish of Donaghcumper. Stacumny was part of the St Wolstan inheritance of the Alens and is last mentioned as a separate entity in 1552 (*Fiants, Edward VI*, no. 1052). All of this suggests that Stacumny did not function as a parochial entity during the latter half of the sixteenth century. It is, however, a civil parish now.

[45] Donaghmore does not appear in the 1615 and 1630 visitations, nor does it appear in the Civil Survey. It was last mentioned as a separate entity in 1552 (*Fiants, Edward VI*, no. 1052). Like Stacumny, it may not have functioned in the later sixteenth century.

SELECT BIBLIOGRAPHY

1 MANUSCRIPT SOURCES

BODLEIAN LIBRARY, OXFORD

Carte MSS
Talbot MSS
Perrot MS 1 Letter book of Lord Deputy Perrot

BRITISH LIBRARY

Additional Charters
Additional MSS
Cotton MSS
Harleian MSS
Lansdowne MSS
Royal MSS

DUBLIN CORPORATION ARCHIVES

All Hallows Deeds
Expired Leases
Fr/Roll/2 Franchise Roll, 1468–1512
MR/25 Book of City Charters
MR/35 Account book of the city treasurer, 1534–1613
MS C1/J3/1 Recognisance Book, 1589–90

GUILDHALL LIBRARY, LONDON

MS 9537/2 Call book of 1561 visitation of the diocese of London
MS 11588/1 Court Minute Book of the Grocers' Company, 1556–1591

LAMBETH PALACE LIBRARY, LONDON

Carew MSS
Muniment Book F1/B Faculty Office register, reign of Elizabeth

MARSH'S LIBRARY

MS Z3.2.7 Annals of Dudley Loftus
MS Z4.2.19 Act book of the Dublin consistory court 1596–99

NATIONAL ARCHIVES OF IRELAND

CH 1/1 Statute roll 28–9 Henry VIII
Ferguson MSS, i–ix
RC 6/1 Repertory of chancery decrees 28 Henry VIII to 1624
Salved Chancery Pleadings Series A – Series Z, Series AA – Series BB

THE NATIONAL ARCHIVES OF THE UNITED KINGDOM (FORMERLY PUBLIC RECORD OFFICE AND HISTORICAL MANUSCRIPTS COMMISSION)

PRO AO 1 Declared Accounts (In Rolls)
PRO C 66 Chancery Patent Rolls
PRO C 82 Warrants for the Great Seal Series II
PRO DEL 4 High Court of Delegates: Acts
PRO DEL 5 High Court of Delegates: Sentences
PRO E 101 King's Remembrancer: Accounts Various
PRO E 334 Office of First Fruits and Tenths and predecessors: Composition Books
PRO LR 6 Receivers' Accounts: Series I
PRO PROB 11 Registered Copy Wills
PRO SP 1 Letters and Papers Henry VIII, General Series
PRO SP 4 Signatures by Stamp Henry VIII
PRO SP 10 State Papers Domestic Edward VI
PRO SP 11 State Papers Domestic Mary
PRO SP 12 State Papers Domestic Elizabeth I
PRO SP 46 State Papers Domestic Supplementary
PRO SP 60 State Papers Ireland Henry VIII
PRO SP 61 State Papers Ireland Edward VI
PRO SP 62 State Papers Ireland Mary
PRO SP 63 State Papers Ireland Elizabeth I to George III
PRO SP 65 State Papers Ireland Folios
PRO SP 66 State Papers Ireland Cases

NATIONAL LIBRARY OF IRELAND

D 2891 Will of Laurence Casse 1575
D 9964 – D 9966 Ussher Papers
D 27622 Will of Thomas More, 1594
GO MS 290 Fisher Abstracts: Dublin Consistorial Wills
MS 474 Includes a copy of *Valor Beneficiorum Ecclesiasticorum in Hibernia* (Dublin, 1741) with ms amendments by John Lodge, deputy keeper of the rolls (1754–74), witnessed by Mervyn Archdall and William Betham.

PUBLIC RECORD OFFICE OF NORTHERN IRELAND, BELFAST

MS D 430 no. 59 Will and inventory of William Hoggison, late mayor of Dublin, 1519
MS DIO/4/2/11 Archbishop Cromer's Register
MS DIO/4/2/13 Archbishop Dowdall's Register

REPRESENTATIVE CHURCH BODY LIBRARY, DUBLIN

C2 St Patrick's Cathedral Muniments
C6 Christ Church Cathedral Muniments
D6 Dublin Diocesan Registry Collection
Papers of Canon Leslie (MS 61)
P326 Records of the parish of St Werburgh, Dublin

ROYAL IRISH ACADEMY, DUBLIN

12.S.22–31 Haliday Collection: Deeds of the Gild of St Anne

TRINITY COLLEGE, DUBLIN

MS 79 Antiphonal of the parish church of St John the Evangelist, Dublin (late fifteenth century)
MS 566 Prerogative court and ordinary visitations and returns *c.*1590–1610
MS 567 Valor of Irish ecclesiastical benefices from 29 Henry VIII to 1591 (*c.*1594 to 1596)
MS 575 The journal of Sir Peter Lewis, chantor and proctor of Christ Church Cathedral, 1564–5
MS 576 Book of obits and martyrology of Christ Church Cathedral
MS 578 Miscellaneous documents collected by Ussher including an act in favour of the archbishop of Dublin, 3 and 4 Philip and Mary
MS 592 The English Conquest of Ireland, early fifteenth century
MS 593 The English Conquest of Ireland, with supplementary material from the Book of Howth, late sixteenth/early seventeenth century
MS 663 Heraldic collections including the patent for Gilbert Purdon's arms in 1588
MS 782 Miscellaneous documents collected by Ussher including a copy of the resignation of Lawrence Bryan, vicar of Garristown, 1570
MS 788 Account of James Ussher, chancellor of St Patrick's Cathedral, for the year of his proctorship ending midsummer 1607
MS 1207 Miscellaneous charters, enfeoffments, wills and indentures of the Ashburn, Passavant and Stanihurst families, 1246–1691
MS 1745 Board of First Fruits: Abstracts from rolls of accounts, Henry VIII to Charles I

2 PRIMARY PRINTED SOURCES

Aibidil Gaoidheilge agus Caiticiosma: Seaán Ó Cearnaigh's Irish primer of religion published in 1571, ed. Brian Ó Cuiv (Dublin, 1994).

Account roll of the priory of Holy Trinity, Dublin, 1337–1346, ed. James Mills, with a new introduction by J. Lydon and A. J. Fletcher (Dublin, 1996).

'Accounts of sums realised by sales of chattels of some suppressed Irish monasteries', ed. C. MacNeill, *JRSAI* 52 (1922), pp. 11–37.

Acts of the Privy Council of England 1542–1604, ed. J. R. Dasent (32 vols., London, 1890–1907).

'*Acts of the Privy Council in Ireland, 1556–1571*', ed. J. T. Gilbert, *HMC 15th Report*, Appendix III (London, 1897).

Ambassades en Angletere de Jean Du Bellay. La Première Ambassade (Septembre 1527–Février 1529). Correspondance Diplomatique, ed. V. L. Bourilly and P. DeVaissière (Paris, 1905).

Annála Connacht . . . (A.D. 1224–1544), ed. A. Martin Freeman (Dublin Institute for Advanced Studies, 1944).

The annals of Ireland by Friar John Clyn and Thady Dowling, together with the annals of Ross, ed. R. Butler (Dublin, 1849).

'The Archbishop of Armachane's opinion touching Ireland', ed. T. Gogarty in *LASJ* 2, no. 2 (1909), pp. 149–64.

'Archbishop Bulkeley's visitation of Dublin', ed. M. V. Ronan in *AH* 8 (1941), pp. 56–98.

'Archbishop Cromer's register', ed. L. P. Murray (contd. by A. Gwynn), *LASJ* 7 (1929–32), pp. 516–24; 8 (1933–6), pp. 38–49, 169–88, 257–74, 322–51; 9 (1937–40), pp. 36–41, 124–30; 10 (1941–4), pp. 117–27, 165–79.

Bale, John, *The Vocacyon of Johan Bale*, ed. P. Happé and J. N. King (Binghamton, New York, 1990).

'The bills and statutes of the Irish parliaments of Henry VII and Henry VIII', ed. D. B. Quinn, *Analecta* 10 (1941), pp. 71–169.

The book of obits and martyrology of the Cathedral Church of Holy Trinity, ed. J. Crosthwaite (Dublin, 1844).

Calendar of ancient deeds and muniments preserved in the Pembroke Estate Office, Dublin (Dublin, 1891).

Calendar of ancient records of Dublin in the possession of the municipal corporation, ed. J. T. Gilbert and R. M. Gilbert (19 vols., Dublin, 1889–1944).

Calendar of Archbishop Alen's register, c. 1172–1534; prepared and edited from the original in the registry of the united dioceses of Dublin and Glendalough and Kildare, ed. C. McNeill (Dublin, 1950).

Calendar of the Carew Manuscripts preserved in the archiepiscopal library at Lambeth, 1515–1624, ed. J. S. Brewer and W. Bullen (6 vols., London, 1867–73).

'Calendar of deeds of the Gild of S. Anne in S. Audoen's Church', ed. H. F. Berry, *PRIA* 25 C (1904–5), pp. 21–106.

Calendar of Fiants, Henry VIII to Elizabeth, *Reports of the deputy keeper, PROI*, 7–22 (Dublin, 1875–90).

Calendar of inquisitions formerly in the office of the Chief Remembrancer of the Exchequer prepared from the MSS of the Irish Record Commission, ed. M. C. Griffith (Dublin, 1991).

'Calendar of the Irish council book, 1581–1586', ed. D. B. Quinn, *Analecta* 24 (1967), pp. 91–180.

Calendar of letters, despatches and state papers, relating to the negotiations between England and Spain, ed. G. A. Bergenroth, G. A. Mattingly, P. De Gayangos, M. A. S. Hume and R. Tyler (13 vols., London 1862–1954).

'A calendar of the Liber Niger and Liber Albus of Christ Church, Dublin', ed. H. J. Lawlor, *PRIA* 27 C (1908–9), pp. 1–93.

'Calendar of the Liber Ruber of the diocese of Ossory', ed. H. J. Lawlor, *PRIA* 27 C (1908–9), pp. 159–208.

Calendar of the manuscripts of the . . . marquess of Salisbury . . . (23 vols., London, 1883–1973).

Calendar of papal registers, papal letters, ed. W. H. Bliss, C. Johnson, J. A. Twemlow, M. J. Haren and A. P. Fuller (19 vols., London [vols. i–xiv] and Dublin [vols. xv–xix], 1893–1998).

Calendar of the patent and close rolls of chancery in Ireland of the reigns of Henry VIII, Edward VI, Mary and Elizabeth, ed. J. Morrin (2 vols., Dublin, 1861–2).

Calendar of the patent rolls preserved in the Public Record Office [reigns of Henry VII, Edward VI, Philip and Mary, Elizabeth (1558–82)] (21 vols., London, 1914–86).

Calendar of Ormond deeds, vols. iii–vi (1413–1603), ed. E. Curtis (Dublin, 1935–43).

'A calendar of the register of Primate George Dowdall', ed. L. P. Murray, *LASJ* 6 (1925–8), pp. 90–100, 147–58, 213–28; 7 (1929–32), pp. 78–95, 258–75.

Calendars of state papers, domestic series, of the reigns of Edward VI, Mary, Elizabeth, 1547–1603, ed. R. Lemon and M. A. E. Green (7 vols., London, 1856–71).

Calendar of state papers, domestic series, of the reign of Edward VI 1547–1553, ed. C. S. Knighton (London, revised edn, 1992).

Calendar of state papers, domestic series, Mary I, ed. C. S. Knighton (London, revised edn, 1998).

Calendar of state papers and manuscripts relating to English affairs, existing in the archives and collections of Venice, ed. R. Brown, G. C. Bentinck, H. F. Brown and A. B. Hinds (38 vols., London, 1864–1947).

Calendar of state papers relating to English affairs preserved principally at Rome, in the Vatican Archives and Library, ed. J. M. Rigg (2 vols., London, 1916–26).

Calendar of state papers relating to Ireland, 1509–1603, ed. H. C. Hamilton, E. G. Atkinson and R. P. Mahaffy (11 vols., London, 1860–1912).

Calendar of state papers Ireland: Tudor period 1575–1575, ed. M. O'Dowd (PRO, London, 2000).

Campion, Edmund, *Two bokes of the histories of Ireland*, ed. A. F. Vossen (Assen, 1963).

Christ Church deeds, ed. M. J. McEnery and R. Refaussé (Dublin, 2001).

The chronicle and political papers of Edward VI, ed. W. K. Jordan (London, 1966).

The Civil Survey, A. D. 1654–56, ed. R. C. Simington (10 vols., Dublin, 1931–61).

Concilia Magnae Britaniae et Hiberniae, ed. D. Wilkins (4 vols., London, 1737).

Correspondence of Robert Dudley, Earl of Leycester, during his government of the Low Countries, in the years 1585 and 1586, ed. J. Bruce (Camden Society, 27, 1844).

Correspondence of Matthew Parker D. D. Archbishop of Canterbury, ed. J. Bruce and T. Perowne (Cambridge, 1853).

The correspondence of Reginald Pole, ed. T. F. Mayer (3 vols., Aldershot, 2002–4).

Court book of the liberty of St Sepulchre within the jurisdiction of the archbishop of Dublin 1586–90, ed. H. Wood (Dublin, 1930).

Crede Mihi: the most ancient register book of the archbishop of Dublin before the Reformation, ed. J. T. Gilbert (Dublin, 1897).

Crown surveys of lands 1540–41 with the Kildare rental begun in 1518, ed. G. MacNiocaill (Dublin, 1992).

The description of Ireland . . . in anno 1598, ed. E. Hogan (London, 1878).

Desiderata curiosa Hibernica, or a select collection of state papers, ed. J. Lodge (2 vols., Dublin, 1732).

The 'dignitas decani' of St. Patrick's Cathedral Dublin, ed. N. B. White (Dublin, 1957).

Documents illustrative of English church history, ed. H. Gee and W. J. Hardy (London, 1896).

'Documents relating to the medieval diocese of Armagh', ed. A. Gwynn in *AH* 13 (1947), pp. 1–26

Dowdall deeds, ed. C. McNeill and A. J. Otway-Ruthven (Dublin, 1960).

Dyer, Sir James, *Les reports des divers select matters et resolutions . . . en le several reignes de . . . Hen. 8 et Edw. 6 et . . . Mar. et Eliz.* (London, 1688).

The Egerton papers, ed. J. P. Collier (London, 1840).

The English conquest of Ireland A.D. 1166–1185, mainly from the 'Expugnatio Hibernica' of Geraldus Cambrensis, ed. F. J. Furnivall (London, 1896).

The first chapter act book of Christ Church Cathedral, Dublin 1574–1634, ed. R. Gillespie (Dublin, 1997).

Extents of Irish monastic possessions, 1540–1, from manuscripts in the Public Record Office, London, ed. N. B. White (Dublin, 1941).

Faculty Office registers 1534–1549. A calendar of the first two registers of the Archbishop of Canterbury's Faculty Office, ed. D. S. Chambers (Oxford, 1966).

Fitzwilliam Accounts 1560–65 (Annesley Collection), ed. A. K. Longfield (Dublin, 1960).

Giraldus Cambrensis, *Expugnatio Hibernica: the conquest of Ireland*, ed. A. B. Scott and F. X. Martin (Dublin, 1978).

'Guide to English financial records for Irish History, 1461–1588, with illustrative extracts, 1461–1509', ed. D. B. Quinn, *Analecta* 10 (1934), pp. 1–69.

Harpsfield, N., *A Treatise of the Pretended Divorce between Henry VIII and Catharine of Aragon*, ed. N. Pocock (London, 1878).

Herbert, Sir William, *Croftus sive de Hibernia Liber*, ed. A. Keaveney and J. Madden (Dublin, 1992).

Holinshed R., and Hooker, J., *Holinshed's chronicles of England, Scotland, Ireland* (6 vols., London, 1807–8).

The Irish cartularies of Llanthony Prima and Secunda, ed. E. St John Brooks (Dublin, 1953).

'John Hooker's diary, or journal, January 17 to February 23, 1568–9', ed. C. L. Falkiner, *PRIA* 25 C (1905), pp. 563–6.

'Journal of the Irish house of lords in Sir John Perrots's parliament 3 May 1585 – 13 May 1586', ed. F. J. Routledge, *EHR* 29 (1914), pp. 104–17.

Leabhar Branach. The book of the O'Byrnes, ed. Seán Mac Airt (Dublin, 1944).

Letters and memorials of state – from the De Lisle and Dudley papers, ed. A. Collins (2 vols., London, 1746).

Letters and papers, foreign and domestic, of the reign of Henry VIII, ed. J. S. Brewer, J. Gairdner and R. H. Brodie (32 vols., London, 1862–1932).

'Miscellanea Vaticano-Hibernia, 1420–1631', ed. J. Hogan, *AH* 4 (1915), p. 217.

'Obligationes pro annatis diocesis Dublinensis, 1421–1520', ed. A. Coleman, *AH* 2 (1913), appendix, pp. 1–37.

Original letters and papers in illustration of the history of the Church of Ireland during the reigns of Edward VI, Mary and Elizabeth, ed. E. P. Shirley (London, 1851).

Original letters relative to the English Reformation written during the reigns of King Henry VIII, King Edward VI and Queen Mary: chiefly from the Archives of Zurich, ed. H. Robinson (2 vols., Cambridge, 1846–7).

'The Perrot Papers: the letter-book of Lord Deputy Perrot between 9 July, 1585 and 26 May, 1586', ed. C. McNeill, *Analecta* 12 (1943), pp. 3–65.

Perrot, Sir James, *The chronicle of Ireland 1584–1608*, ed. H. Wood (Dublin, 1933).

Pontificia Hibernica: medieval papal chancery documents concerning Ireland, 640–1261, ed. M. P. Sheehy (2 vols., Dublin, 1962–5).

Proceedings and ordinances of the Privy Council of England, 1540–2, ed. H. Nicolas (London, 1837).

The proctor's accounts of Peter Lewis 1564–1565, ed. R. Gillespie (Dublin, 1996).

'Provincial and diocesan decrees of the diocese of Dublin during the Anglo-Norman period', ed. A. Gwynn, *AH* 11 (1944), pp. 31–117.

Quattro Documenti D'Inghilterr ed uno di Spagna Dell' Archivio di Mantova, ed. A. Portioli (Mantova, 1868).

Register of wills and inventories of the diocese of Dublin in the time of Archbishops Tregury and Walton, ed. H. F. Berry (Dublin, 1898).

The Registers of Christ Church Cathedral, Dublin, ed. R. Refaussé with C. Lennon (Dublin, 1998).

Registrum Cancellarii 1498–1506, ed. W. T. Mitchell (Oxford, 1980).

'Registrum Diocesis Dublinensis'. A sixteenth century Dublin precedent book, ed. N. B. White (Dublin, 1959).

Registrum Matthei Parker Diocesis Cantuariensis AD 1559–1575, ed. W. H. Frere, transcribed by E. Margaret Thompson (3 vols., Oxford, 1928–32).

Registrum Octaviani alias Liber Niger. The Register of Octavian de Palatio, archbishop of Armagh, 1487–1513, ed. M. A. Sughi (2 vols., Dublin, 1999).

'The Reportorium Viride of John Alen, archbishop of Dublin, 1533', ed. N. B. White, *Analecta* 10 (1941), pp. 173–217.

Sarpi, Paolo, under the pseudonym Pietro Soave Polano, *The Historie of the Councel of Trent*, translated by Nathaniel Brent (London, 1629).

Sidney State Papers, 1565–70, ed. T. Ó Laidhin (Dublin, 1962).

Spenser, Edmund, *A view of the present state of Ireland*, ed. by W. L. Renwick (Oxford, 1970).

Spicilegium Ossoriense, being a collection of original letters and papers illustrative of the history of the Irish church from the Reformation to the year 1800, ed. P. F. Moran (3 vols., Dublin, 1874–84).

The social state of the southern and eastern counties of Ireland in the sixteenth century, ed. H. F. Hore and J. Graves (Annuary of the Royal Historical and Archaelogical Association of Ireland for 1868–9).

Stanyhurst, Richard, *Holinshed's Irish Chronicle*, ed. L. Miller and E. Power (Dublin, 1979).

State papers concerning the Irish Church in the time of Queen Elizabeth, ed. W. M. Brady (London, 1868).

State papers, Henry VIII (11 vols., London, 1830–52).

Statute rolls of the parliament of Ireland: . . . reign of King Edward the Fourth, ed. H. F. Berry (2 vols., Dublin, 1934–9).

Statute rolls of the parliament of Ireland: reign of King Henry the Sixth, ed. H. F. Berry (Dublin, 1910).

Statute rolls of the Irish parliament: Richard III – Henry VIII, ed. P. Connolly (Dublin, 2002).

Statutes and ordinances and acts of the parliament of Ireland: King John to Henry V, ed. H. F. Berry (Dublin, 1907).

The statutes at large passed in the parliaments held in Ireland [1310–1776] (13 vols., Dublin, 1786).

Talbot, Peter, *Primatus Dubliniensis, or the primacy of the see of Dublin*, ed. W. E. Kenny (Dublin, 1947).

'Two early tours in Ireland', ed. J. P. Mahaffy, *Hermathena*, 17, no. 40 (1914).

Valor beneficiorum ecclesiasticorum in Hibernia (Dublin, 1741).

Valor Ecclesiasticus, temp. Henrici VIII, aucoritate regia institutus, ed. J. Caley and J. Hunter (6 vols., London, 1810–34).

Vetera monumenta Hibernorum et Scotorum, ed. A. Theiner (Rome, 1864).

Visitation articles and injunctions of the period of the Reformation, ed. W. H. Frere and W. M. Kennedy (3 vols., London, 1910).

The Walsingham letter-book or register of Ireland, May 1578 to December 1579, ed. J. Hogan and N. McNeill O'Farrell (Dublin, 1959).

White, Roland, 'Rowland White's "Discors touching Ireland", c. 1569', ed. N. Canny, *IHS* 20 (1977), pp. 439–63.

The Zurich letters, comprising the correspondence of several English bishops and others, with some of the Helvetian Reformers, during the early part of the reign of Elizabeth, ed. H. Robinson (2 vols., Cambridge, 1842–5).

3 REFERENCE WORKS

Brady, W. M., *The episcopal succession in England, Scotland and Ireland, 1400–1875* (3 vols. Rome, 1876–7).

Emden, A. B., *A biographical register of the university of Oxford to A.D. 1500* (3 vols. Oxford, 1957–9).

A biographical register of the university of Oxford to A.D. 1501 to 1540 (Oxford, 1974).

Foster, J., *Alumni Oxonienses: the members of the University of Oxford 1500–1714* (4 vols., Oxford, 1891).

Lascelles, R. (ed.), *Liber munerum publicorum Hiberniac ab anno 1152 usque ad 1827* (2 vols., London, 1824–52).

Matthew, H. C. G., and Harrison, B., (ed.), *Oxford Dictionary of National Biography: from the earliest times to the year 2000* (60 vols., Oxford, 2004).

Venn, J. and Venn, J. A., *Alumni Cantabrigiensis*, Part I (4 vols., Cambridge, 1922–7).

INDEX

Titles in the series